Where To Stay
in the

AMERICAN
NORTHWEST

Alaska, Wyoming, Montana
Oregon, Washington, Idaho
North & South Dakota

Phil Philcox

HUNTER
PUBLISHING, INC

Hunter Publishing, Inc.
300 Raritan Center Parkway
Edison NJ 08818
(908) 225 1900
Fax (908) 417 0482

ISBN 1-55650-683-X

Cover photograph:
Teton Range at Sunrise, Wyoming: Robert E. Barber/Global Pictures

Contents

Introduction

If you're northwest bound for business or pleasure, this is the ultimate guide to finding a place to bed down for the night. Need a convenient downtown hotel within walking distance of the Convention Center or a motel along the tourist strip with lighted tennis courts and a heated swimming pool? Prefer a high-rise apartment or private home rental for an extended stay? For total seclusion, consider a dude ranch high atop a mountain, yet only a short ride into the nearest town. Whether your choice is an out-of-the-way bed and breakfast or a hotel suite in the center of the business district, you'll find something to your liking – and budget – in this guide.

Included are the names and telephone numbers of regional rental sources that handle an assortment of accommodation options – from private homes to condos and apartments. These agencies are excellent sources of information on what's available in each area in different price ranges. Most have toll-free numbers you can call for information.

The toll-free and fax numbers can be contacted to request literature, rate cards and reservations. Many properties will fax their literature directly to your machine.

As of press time, the rates were current, based on interviews with the property owners. Rates are constantly changing and vary considerably with location and season, so use the rates listed to determine the price range of the property and always check the latest rates prior to making your reservations. Use the toll-free number when available. Most toll-free numbers listed are valid from all states but some properties have outside-their-state numbers or in-state numbers. If you reach an invalid number, check with the toll-free operator at 800-555-1212.

Also included is a list of chain hotels and motels, their locations and descriptions of their special clubs and offerings. You can contact them for free accommodations directories.

Abbreviations Used In This Guide:

SGL: single room - rate for one person.
DBL: double room - rate for two people sharing one room.
EFF: efficiency - usually one room with kitchen or kitchenette.
STS: suites.
1BR, 2BR, 3BR: 1- , 2- , or 3-bedroom condo, apartment, villa or town-house, usually with full kitchen facilities, and washer-dryer.
a/c: air conditioning.
NS rooms: rooms available for non-smokers.
NS: smoking not permitted on the property.

Restaurant: indicates there is a restaurant on the property, adjacent to it, or across the street.
Airport courtesy car: free transportation to and from local airports.
Airport transportation: transportation is available to and from local airports for a fee.
Local transportation: free transportation is available to local attractions.
American plan: all meals included in room rate.
Modified American plan: some meals included in room rates, usually breakfast and dinner.
CC: accepts major credit cards.

Rates shown are for single and double occupancies. When modified American plan and European plan are available, call for rates.

$00-$000: daily rate span.
$000W-$000W: weekly rate span.
$00/$000W: daily rate followed by weekly rate.

To keep future editions of this guide up to date, we request you submit any new listing, changes in information and current rates to Where To Stay, 131B North Bay Drive, Lynn Haven FL 32444. Please include all telephone numbers (including fax and toll-free) along with number of rooms, facilities, rates and other information of interest to travelers.

Chain Hotels

Locations and Special Deals

($) indicates there is a cost for membership

AmericInn
18101 Minnetonka Blvd.
Deephaven MN 55391
Reservations: 800-634-3444

Locations: Fargo ND.

Best Western
Box 10203
Phoenix AZ 85064
Reservations: 800-528-1234

Locations: Anchorage AK, Homer AK, Juneau AK, Ketchikan AK, Seward AK, Soldotna; Boise ID, Bonners Ferry ID, Burley ID, Coeur D'Alene ID, Driggs ID, Idaho Falls ID, Ketchum ID, Montpelier ID, Moscow ID, Mountain Home ID, Pocatello ID, Rexburg ID, Saint Anthony ID, Sandpoint ID, Twin Falls ID, Wallace ID; Big Sky MT, Billings MT, Bozeman MT, Butte MT, Dillon MT, Forsyth MT, Gardiner MT, Glendive MT, Great Falls MT, Hamilton MT, Helena MT, Kalispell MT, Laurel MT, Miles City MT, Missoula MT, Polson MT, Red Lodge MT, West Yellowstone MT; Bismarck ND, Dickinson ND, Fargo ND, Grand Forks ND, Mandan ND, Minot ND; Albany OR, Ashland OR, Baker City OR, Bend OR, Biggs OR, Brookings OR, Burns OR, Cannon Beach OR, Clackamas OR, Coos Bay OR, Corvallis OR, Cottage Grove OR, Eugene OR, Florence OR, Gold Beach OR, Grants Pass OR, Gresham OR, Harbor OR, Hillsboro OR, Hood River OR, John Day OR, Klamath Falls OR, La Grande OR, Lake Oswego OR, Lakeview OR, Medford OR, Newport OR, Oakridge OR, Ontario OR, Pendleton OR, Portland OR, Prineville OR, Redmond OR, Reedsport OR, Rouge River OR, Roseburg OR, Salem OR, Seaside OR, Sisters OR, Springfield OR, The Dalles OR, Tualatin OR, Wilsonville OR; Aberdeen SD, Belle Fourchee SD, Brookings SD, Canistota SD, Chamberlain SD, Custer SD, Deadwood SD, Hill City SD, Hot Springs SD, Kadoka SD, Keystone SD, Lead SD, Mitchell SD, Murdo SD, Pierre SD, Rapid City SD, Sioux Falls SD, Spearfish SD, Sturgis SD, Wall SD, Watertown SD; Auburn WA, Bellingham WA, Bellevue WA, Bremerton WA, Clarkston WA, Ellensburg WA, Enumclaw WA, Federal Way WA, Kelso WA, Kent WA, Kirkland WA, Leavenworth WA, Lynnwood WA, Marysville WA, Moses Lake WA, Mount Vernon WA, Oak Harbor WA, Port Angeles WA, Redmond WA, Richland WA, Ritzville WA, Seattle WA, Sequim WA, Snoqualmie Pass WA, Spokane WA, Tacoma WA, Turnwater WA, Vancouver WA, Walla Walla WA, Winthrop WA, Yakima WA; Afton WY, Alpine WY,, Casper WY, Cheyenne WY, Cody WY, Evanston WY, Gillette WY, Jackson WY, Laramie WY, Lusk WY, Powell

WY, Rawlins WY, Rock Springs WY, Sheridan WY, Sundance WY, Teton Village WY, Thermopolis WY, Wheatland WY, Worland WY.

The Gold Crown Club International Card earns points redeemable for room nights and other awards. Many locations offer a 10% discount to senior travelers on a space available basis with advanced reservations. The Government-Military Travel Program provides discounts to federal employees and military personnel.

Budget Host Inns
2601 Jackboro Highway
Fort Worth TX 76114
Reservations: 800-BUD-HOST

Locations: Bowman ND; Badlands SD, Chamberlain SD, Kennebec SD, Mitchell SD, Oacoma SD, Rapid City SD, Sioux Falls SD, Vermillion SD; Port Angeles WA.

Clarion-Choice Hotels
10750 Columbia Pike
Silver Spring MD 20901
Reservations: 800-221-2222

Clarion and Choice Hotels consist of Sleep Inns, Comfort Inns, Friendship Inns, Econo Lodges, Rodeway Inns, Quality Inns and Clarion Hotels and Resorts.

Locations: Anchorage AK; Boise ID, Caldwell ID, Coeur d'Alene ID, Idaho Falls ID, Ketchum ID, Mountain Home ID, Pocatello ID, Sandpoint ID, Twin Falls ID; Billings MT, Bozeman MT, Great Falls MT, Helena MT, Kalispell MT, Livingston MT, Miles City MT, Missoula MT, Whitefish MT; Dickenson ND, Fargo ND, Grand Forks ND, Minot ND, Rugby ND; Albany OR, Ashland OR, Baker City OR, Bend OR, Coburg OR, Corvallis OR, Cottage Grove OR, Klamath Falls OR, Medford OR, Milwaukee OR, Pendleton OR, Portland OR, Salem OR, Springfield OR, The Dalles OR, Wilsonville OR, Winchester Bay OR, Woodburn OR; Aberdeen SD, Brookings SD, Chamberlain SD, Keystone SD, Mitchell SD, Rapid City SD, Sioux Falls SD, Vermillion SD, Watertown SD, Yankton SD; Bellingham WA, Fife WA, Kelso WA, Kennewick WA, Lacey WA, Olympia WA, Pullman WA, Richland WA, Seattle WA, Sequim WA, Spokane WA, Sevenson WA, Sunnyside WA, Tacoma WA, Walla Walla WA, Washougal WA, Wehantchee WA, Yakima WA; Buffalo WY, Gillette WY, Jackson WY, Rock Springs WY.

Special discounts of 10%-20% are available at participating locations for members of AAA. The Small Organizations Savings (SOS) Program is available to companies with over 10 employees and offers a 10% discount off the first 15 rooms used by company employees. The Weekender Rate Program offers special room rates of $20, $30 or $35 per night with an advanced reservation. All local, state and federal government employees and military personnel receive special per diem rates and upgrades when available at participating hotels. The Family Plan allows children to stay free when sharing a parent's room. PrimeTime and PrimeTime Senior Saver for people over age 60 offers a 10% discount at all hotels year-round and a 30% discount at limited locations when you call 800-221-2222 and ask for the PrimeTime Senior Saver rate.

Coast Hotels and Resort
900 West Georgia St.
Vancouver BC Canada V6E 3V7
Reservations: 800-663-1144

Locations: *Anchorage AK; Portland OR; Everett WA, Seattle WA, Silverdale WA, Spokane WA, Wenatchee WA.*

Days Inn
2751 Buford Highway
Atlanta GA 30324
Reservations: 800-325-2525

Locations: *Anchorage AK; Coeur D'Alene ID, Pocatello ID, Rexburg ID; Billings MT, Bozeman MT, Butte MT, Glendive MT, Great Falls MT, Helena MT, Kalispell MT, Missoula MT, Polson MT, West Yellowstone MT; Clackamas OR, Portland OR, Tigard OR; Chamberlain SD, Deadwood SD, Mitchell SD, Oacoma SD, Pierre SD, Rapid City SD, Sioux Falls SD, Spearfish SD, Sturgis SD, Wall SD, Yankton SD; Bellevue WA, Everett WA, Kent WA, Mt. Vernon WA, Seattle WA, Spokane WA, Tacoma WA, Yakima WA; Casper WY, Cheyenne WY, Gillette WY, Jackson Hole WY, Rawlins WY, Rock Springs WY, Sheridan WY.*

The September Days Club ($) offers travelers over the age of 50 up to 40% discounts on rooms, 10% discounts on food and gifts, a quarterly club magazine, seasonal room discounts and special tours and trips. The Inn Credible Card is designed for business travelers and provides up to 30% savings on room rates, free stays for spouses and other benefits. The Days GemClub is a travel club for military personnel and government employees that offers up to 30% savings on room rates. SchoolDays Club for academic staff and educators offers a minimum of 10% savings on room rates, special group rates and additional benefits. The Sport Plus Club is designed for coaches and team managers who organize team travel and offers 10% discounts on room rates, special team rates and late check-outs.

Doubletree-Compri Hotels
410 North 44th Street
Phoenix AZ 85008
Reservations: 800-528-0444

Locations: *Boise ID; Seattle WA.*

Doubletree operates 38 hotels in the United States, including Doubletree Club Hotels that provide oversized rooms, complimentary, cooked-to-order breakfasts, club rooms and hosted evening receptions. Family Plans allow up to two children under the age of 18 to stay free when they share the rooms with their parents. For the business traveler, most hotels offer secretarial services, photocopying, fax machines and computer hook-up capabilities. A special discounted rate is available to seniors. A Corporate Plus Program is available at all business center locations.

Business Class offers quick check-in and check-out, complimentary breakfast in a private lounge, complimentary newspaper and additional benefits. The Entree Gold floor provides concierge services, an exclusive lounge for use by guests, complimentary breakfast and cocktail hour and use of a private boardroom.

Embassy Suites
222 Las Colinas Boulevard
Irving TX 75039
Reservations: 800-528-1100

Locations: *Portland OR; Seattle WA.*

Embassy Suites offer two-room suites with living room, bedroom and kitchenettes. Complimentary breakfasts are served daily and a two hour complimentary beverage program is offered nightly.

Hampton Inns
6800 Poplar
Memphis TN 38138
Reservations 800-426-7866

Locations: *Bellingham WA, Seattle WA, Spokane WA.*

Hampton Inns offer free continental breakfasts, free local telephone calls. Children under 18 stay free in same room with parents. Most Hampton Inns offer a Hospitality Suite that can be used as a small meeting facility. The LifeStyle 50 Club provides discounts for guests over age 50 with no charge for a third person staying in the room.

Hilton Hotels and Resorts
9336 Civic Center Drive
Beverly Hills CA 90209
Reservations 800-HILTON

Locations: *Anchorage AK; Eugene OR, Portland OR; Rapid City SD; Bellevue WA, Seattle WA; Casper WY.*

Zip-Out-Quick Check-Out is available to travelers using major credit cards. An itemized statement of charges is provided the night before departure. Many Hilton locations have hotels-within-hotels, Tower and Executive accommodations offering room upgrades, use of a private lounge, access to business services, complimentary cocktails and continental breakfast and use of telex, fax machines and photocopying equipment. The HHonors Guest Reward Program is a free program that earns points toward free or discounted stays at participating properties and members-only privileges that include rapid check-ins, free daily newspaper, free stay with spouse and free use of health club facilities when available.

The Corporate Rate Program offers business travelers guaranteed rates annually, speed reservations, Tower and Executive accommodations and Quick Check-Out facilities.

Hilton's Senior HHonors offers special amenities to travelers over the age of 60. Included are room discounts up to 50%, a 20% dinner discount and money-back guarantee, a private toll-free reservation number and automatic enrollment in Hilton's Guest Reward Programs. BounceBack Weekend offers a free, daily continental breakfast, children free in parents' rooms and special rates for Thursday to Sunday with a Saturday stay. During the summer, these discounted rates apply Monday to Wednesday.

Hilton Leisure Breaks includes packages for honeymooners and special occasions with special rates. Hilton Meeting 2000 is a network of business meeting facilities available at some locations and includes special meeting room, audiovisual systems, refreshments and assistance in providing meeting rooms and programs.

Holiday Inn
1100 Ashwood Parkway
Atlanta GA 30338
Reservations 800-HOLIDAY

Locations: Anchorage AK; Boise ID, Coeur D'Alene ID; Billings MT, Bozeman MT, Missoula MT; Bismarck ND, Fargo ND, Grand Forks ND, Minot ND; Cottage Grove OR, Eugene OR, Florence OR, Grants Pass OR, Portland OR, Wilsonville OR, Woodburn OR; Aberdeen SD, Brookings SD, Mitchell SD, Rapid City SD, Sioux Falls SD, Spearfish SD; Everett WA, Federal Way WA, Issaquah WA, Lynnwood WA, Pullman WA, Seattle WA, Spokane WA, Yakima WA; Casper WY, Cheyenne WY, Cody WY, Douglas WY, Gillette WY, Laramie WY, Riverton WY, Rock Springs WY, Sheridan WY, Thermopolis WY.

Holiday Inn Preferred Senior Traveler offers a 20% savings on the single-person rate and a 10% discount at participating restaurants. Members of the American Association of Retired Persons receive a 10% discount at participating hotels.

Best Break Bed and Breakfast packages are offered at participating hotels and includes a guest room and a breakfast coupon good for $12. Great Rates are offered with advance reservations and include discounts of at least 10%. Most Holiday Inns offer Government-Military rates based on the per diem rate offered government employees and contractors. Many hotels participate in the Government-Military Amenities program which offers coupons redeemable for free local phone calls with a $5 limit, 10% dinner discounts and a free continental breakfast. The Priority Club is designed for frequent travelers and provides points that can be exchanged for travel and merchandise awards.

Homewood Suites
3742 Lamar Avenue
Memphis TN 38195
Reservations: 800-225-5466

Locations: *Seattle WA.*

Howard Johnson
3838 East Van Buren
Phoenix AZ 85038
Reservations: 800-654-2000

Locations: *Pocatello ID; Billings MT; Medford OR, Ontario OR, Portland OR, Roseburg OR; Rapid City SD, Sioux Falls SD; Seattle WA, Tacoma WA; Cheyenne WY.*

The Howard Johnson Road Rally Program offers discounts to senior travelers over the age of 60 and members of AARP and other national senior's organizations. With advanced reservations, a 30% discount is available at some locations. The Family Plan lets children under the age of 12 stay free at all locations, with some properties extending the age limit to 18.

Government Rate Programs offer special rates to federal employees, military personnel and government contractors. The Corporate Rate Program offers special rates to companies and business travelers. Howard Johnson Executive Section offers guests special rooms, complimentary wake-up coffee and newspapers and snacks. Kids Go Hojo provides children with free FunPacks filled with toys, puzzles, coloring books and games.

Marriott
Marriott Drive
Washington DC 20058
Reservations: Marriott Hotels 800-228-9290; Courtyard by Marriott 800-321-2211; Fairfield Inn 800-228-2800; Residence Inn 800-331-3131

Marriott consists of Marriott Hotels and Resorts, Marriott Suites, Courtyard by Marriott, Residence Inns and Fairfield Inns.

Fairfield Inns - Locations: Bozeman MT, Great Falls MT; Bismarck ND, Fargo ND, Grand Forks ND, Minor ND.

Courtyard by Marriott Hotels - Locations: Seattle WA.

Residence Inns - Locations: Boise ID.

SuperSaver rates offer discounts on weekday and weekend stays at participating hotels. Discounts range from 10% and up. The TFB program (Two For Breakfast) offers discounts for weekend stays for two adults that includes complimentary breakfasts.

Advance Purchase Rates are discounts of up to 50% for advance, prepaid, non-refundable reservations 7, 14, 21 and 30 days in advance. Senior Citizen discounts for members of AARP and other senior groups are available at all participating hotels.

The Marriott Honored Guest Award offers special upgrades to members at participating hotels. After a 15-night stay during a 12-month period, members receive express checkout services, complimentary newspaper, check cashing privileges, free luggage tags and discounts.

Motel 6
14651 Dallas Parkway
Dallas TX 75240
Reservations: 800-437-7486

Locations: Boise ID, Chubbuck ID, Coeur D'Alene ID, Idaho Falls ID, Moscow ID, Twin Falls ID; Billings MT, Helena MT, Kalispell MT, Miles City MT; Bismarck ND, Fargo ND, Grand Forks ND; Burns OR, Coos Bay OR, Eugene OR, Grants Pass OR, Klamath Falls OR, Medford OR, Ontario OR, Pendleton OR, Portland OR, Salem OR, Springfield OR, Tigard OR, Troutdale OR; Mitchell SD, Rapid City SD, Sioux Falls SD; Bellingham WA, Centralia WA, Everett WA, Fife WA, Issaquah WA, Kelso WA, Kirkland WA, Moses Lake WA, Olympia WA, Pasco WA, Seattle WA, Spokane WA, Tacoma WA, Tumwater WA, Yakima WA; Casper WY, Cheyenne WA, Gilletee WA, Jackson WA, Laramie WA, Rock Springs WA.

National 9 Inns
2285 South Main
Salt Lake City UT 84115
Reservations: 800-524-9999

Locations: Boise ID; Burns OR, Portland OR; Bellevue WA, Burlington WA, Pullman WA, Seattle WA, Vancouver WA; Cheyenne WY.

Nendals
520 Pike Street
Seattle WA 98101
Reservations: 800-547-0106

Locations: Boise ID, Pocatello ID; Albany OR, Medford OR; Auburn WA, Everett WA, Long Beach WA, Pullman WA, Renton WA, Richland WA, Spokane WA.

Park Inn International Hotels
4425 West Airport Freeway
Irving TX 75062
Reservations: 800-437-PARK

Locations: Seattle WA.

The Silver Citizens Club offers a 20% room discount and 10% food discount at participating hotels, free morning paper and coffee, special directory, all-night emergency pharmacy telephone number and personal check cashing.

Radisson Hotels International
Carlson Parkway
Minneapolis MN 55459
Reservations: 800-333-3333

Locations: Billings MT; Bismarck ND, Fargo ND; Seattle WA.

Radisson operates 270 hotels and affiliates worldwide. Plaza Hotels are usually located in the city center or suburban locations. Suite Hotels offer oversized rooms with living room, mini-bar and kitchenettes. Resort Hotels usually include locations near beaches, golf course and recreational facilities.

Ramada Inn
1850 Parkway Place
Marietta GA 30067
Reservations: 800-2-RAMADA

Locations: Anchorage AK; Boise ID, Lewiston ID; Billings MT; Bismarck ND, Grand Forks ND; Beaverton OR, Corvallis OR, Portland OR; Bellingham WA, Des Moines WA, Everett WA, Olympia WA, Seattle WA, Spokane WA; Cheyenne WA, Gillette WA.

Membership in the Ramada Business Card Program earns points for trips and merchandise based on dollars spent at Ramada properties. The card is available free. Membership includes favorable rates, automatic room upgrade when available, express check-in and check-out, free newspaper on business days, free same-room accommodations for your spouse when you travel together, extended check-out times, newsletter and points redeemable for hotel stays, air travel, car rentals and over 10,000 Service Merchandise catalog items.

Participating Ramada Inn properties offer Super Save Weekend discounts. These rates apply on Friday, Saturday and Sunday for one- , two- and three-night stays. Extra person rates may apply for a third or fourth person in the room. Because some hotels limit availability on some dates, reservations are recommended.

When traveling with family or friends, the Ramada 4-for-1 Program permits up to four people to share the same room and pay the single rate. At participating properties, the Best Years Seniors Program provides travelers over the age of 60 who are members of AARP, the Global Horizons Club, Catholic Golden Age, The Golden Buckeye Club, Humana Seniors Association, The Retired Enlisted Association, The Retired Officers Association and United Airlines Silver Wings Plus with a 25% discount off regular room rates.

The Ramada Per Diem Value Program is available at more than 350 locations. Properties honor the maximum lodging per diem rates set by the U.S. General Services Administration. Federal employees, military personnel and employees of cost-reimbursable contractors traveling on official government business are eligible. In addition to the per diem limits for lodging, the single person room rate at participating locations includes full American breakfast and all applicable taxes. All Ramada properties provide corporate customers favorable rates. Companies need a minimum of 10 travelers with a combined total of 100 room nights per year.

Red Lion Hotels and Inns
4001 Main Street
Vancouver WA 98666
Reservations: 800-547-8010

Locations: Boise ID; Kalispell MT, Missoula MT; Astoria OR, Bend OR, Coos Bay OR, Eugene OR, Medford OR, Pendleton OR, Portland OR, Springfield OR; Aberdeen WA, Bellevue WA, Kelso WA, Richland WA, Seattle WA, Spokane WA, Vancouver WA, Wenatchee WA, Yakima WA.

Sheraton Hotels, Inns and Resorts
60 State Street
Boston MA 02109
Reservations: 800-325-3535

Locations: Anchorage AK; Billings MT, Great Falls MT; Portland OR; Seattle WA, Spokane WA, Tacoma WA.

ITT Sheraton Hotels, Resorts and All-Suite hotels are located in major gateway cities and business centers. All-Suites feature two-room suites with living and dining areas, bedroom, bath and additional features like sofa beds, wet bars and microwave ovens.

ITT Sheraton Inns are Sheraton's budget hotels, generally smaller in size and more informal in design than ITT Sheraton Hotels. Inns average 125 to 250 guest rooms and are usually located in medium to large cities and in suburban areas. All inns offer a full restaurant and professional meeting planner services.

ITT Sheraton Club International ($) offers additional guest services at over 400 participating hotels worldwide. Benefits include: automatic room upgrade whenever available; guaranteed 4 p.m. late check-out; Double Club points and free nights in select hotels throughout the year; Express pass check-in and check-out service with key ready upon arrival.

Shilo Inns
11600 Southwest Barnes Rd.
Portland OR 97225
Reservations: 800-222-2244

Locations: *Coeur d'Alene ID, Boise ID, Nampa ID, Idaho Falls ID; Helena MT; Portland OR, Tigard OR, Grants Pass R, Gresham OR, Klamath Falls OR, Medford OR, Newberg OR, Newport OR, Salem OR, Seaside OR, Springfield OR, Tillamook OR; Hazel Dell WA, Moses Lake WA, Richland WA, Spokane WA, Tacoma WA, Vacouver WA; Casper WY.*

Super 8 Motels
1910 8th Avenue NE
Aberdeen SD 57402
Reservations: 800-800-8000

Locations: *Anchorage AK, Fairbanks AK, Juneau AK, Ketchikan AK, Sitka AK; Boise ID, Coeur d'Alene ID, Driggs ID, Idaho Falls ID, Kellogg ID, Lewiston ID, Moscow ID, Nampa ID, Pocatello ID, Rexburg ID, Sandpoint ID, Twin Falls ID; Belgrade MT, Big Sky MT, Big Timer MT, Billings MT, Bozeman MT, Butte MT, Columbus MT, Conrad MT, Deer Lodge MT, Dillon MT, Gardiner MT, Glendive MT, Great Falls MT, Hamilton MT, Hardin MT, Havre MT, Helena MT, Kalispell MT, Lewistown MT, Libby MT, Livingston MT, Miles City MT, Missoula MT, Polson MT, Red Lodge MT, St. Regis MT, Swan Valley MT, West Yellowstone MT, Whitefish MT, Whitehall MT; Beulah ND, Bismarck ND, Bowman ND, Carrington ND, Devils Lake ND, Dickinson ND, Edgeley ND, Fargo ND, Grafton ND, Grand Forks ND, Jamestown ND, Minot ND, Tioga ND, Valley City ND, Wahpeton ND, Williston ND; Ashland OR, Baker City OR, Bend OR, Grants Pass OR, Klamath Falls OR, LaGrande OR, Ontario OR, Pendleton OR, Portland OR, Salem OR, The Dalles OR; Aberdeen SD, Arlington SD, Belle Fourche SD, Brookings SD, Chamberlain SD, Custer SD, Deadwood SD, Eagle Butte SD, Faulkton SD, Hill City SD, Hot Springs SD, Huron SD,*

SD, Stugis SD, Vermillion SD, Wagner SD, Wall SD, Watertown SD, Webster SD, Winner SD, Yankton SD; Bremerton WA, Ellensburg WA, Federal Way WA, Kelso WA, Kennewick WA, Long Beach WA, Moses Lake WA, Olympia WA, Port Angeles WA, Seattle WA, Spokane WA, Walla Walla WA, Yakima WA; Buffalo WA, Casper WA, Cheyenne WA, Cody WA, Douglas WA, Dubois WA, Evanston WA, Gillette WA, Green River WA, Jackson Hole WA, Laramie WA, Lovell WA, Powell WA, Rawlins WA, Riverton WA, Rock Springs WA, Sheridan WA, Torrington WA, Worland WA.

Travelers Inns
1800 East Imperial Highway
Brea CA 92621
Reservations: 800-633-8300

Locations: Bellingham WA, Port Angeles WA, Seattle WA, Tacoma WA.

TraveLodge
1973 Friendship Drive
El Cajon CA 92020
Reservations: 800-255-3050

Locations: Boise ID, Coeur d'Alene ID; Billings MT, Missoula MT; Sioux Falls SD; Forest Grove OR, Grants Pass OR, Klamath Falls OR, Portland OR, Roseburg OR; Bellevue WA, Bellingham WA, Ephrata WA, Everett WA, Moses Lake WA, Mount Vernon WA, Omak WA, Seattle WA, Spokane WA, Tacoma WA, Vancouver WA, Walla Walla WA, Yakima WA.

The Business Break Club Program offers a 10% discount off the lowest published room rate, express check-in and check-out, free local telephone calls and morning coffee and a special 800-number for fast reservations.

The Classic Travel Club is available to travelers over the age of 50. It offers room discounts of 15%, a quarterly newsletter, check cashing privileges, free morning coffee, car rental discounts and express check-in, check-out services.

Coaches, Athletic Directors and Educators are eligible for Team TraveLodge which offers a free stay with groups of 10 or more, a minimum 10% discount, upgrades for group leaders, late check-out, free morning coffee, newsletter and car rental discounts.

All federal, state and local government employees and members of the armed forces and their families traveling on official government business or pleasure receive special rates equal to or less than the prevailing per diem rates. Information on these rates is available from 800-GOVT-RES.

Under the Family Plan, there is no charge for children under the age of 17 when sharing a room with their parents. The Government Traveler-Value America Plan offers rates equal to or less than the prevailing per diem rates paid and is available to federal employees, military personnel and contractors on government business.

Westin Hotels and Resorts
The Westin Building
Seattle WA 98121
Reservations: 800-228-3000

Locations: Seattle WA.

At Westin hotels or resorts there is no charge for children under the age of 18 when they share the same room with parents or guardians. If more than one room is required to accommodate a family, the single guest room rate will apply to each room, regardless of the number of people occupying the room.

Wyndham Hotels and Resort
2001 Bryan Street, Suite 2300Dallas TX 75210
Reservations: 800-822-4200

Locations: Bothell WA, Seattle WA.

Accommodations Directory

Alaska

Rental and Reservation Services:

Accommodations Alaska Style (3605 Arctic Blvd., Anchorage, 99503; 907-278-8800, Fax 907-272-8800) bed and breakfast reservations.

Accommodations in Alaska (Box 110624, Anchorage 99511; 907-345-0624) homestay reservations.

Alaska Private Lodgings (4631 Caravelle Dr., Anchorage 99502; 907-248-2292) bed and breakfast reservations.

Bed and Breakfast Reservations (Box 10-1464, Anchorage 99510; 800-474-2262) bed and breakfasts reservations.

Anchorage

Area Code 907

A Arctic Loon Bed and Breakfast (Anchorage 99511; 345-4935) free breakfast, TV, a/c, no pets, CC. SGL/DBL$60-$90.

Alaska Chalet Bed and Breakfast (11031 Gulkana Circle, 99577; 694-1528) 2 rooms, free breakfast, TV, private baths, a/c, no pets, CC. SGL/DBL$45-$85.

Alaska's Cozy Comforts (10661 Elies Dr., 99516; 346-1957) free breakfast, TV, NS, airport transportation, no pets, CC. SGL/DBL$65-$75.

Anchorage Bed and Breakfast (2200 Banbury Dr., 99504; 333-1425) free breakfast, TV, NS, private baths, jacuzzi, no pets, CC. SGL/DBL$65-$75.

Anchorage Hotel (330 E St., 99501; 272-4553) 31 rooms, lounge, TV, wheelchair access, NS rooms, in-room refrigerators and microwaves, meeting facilities, no pets, children free with parents, senior rates, CC. SGL/DBL$80-$150.

ARA Denali Park Hotel (825 West 8th Ave., 99501; 279-2653, Fax 258-3668) 330 rooms, restaurant, lounge, TV, no pets, wheelchair access, NS rooms, senior rates, CC. SGL/DBL$45-$65.

Best Western Barratt Inn (4616 Spenard Rd., 99517; 243-3131, Fax 243-5620, 800-528-1234) 216 rooms, restaurant, lounge, exercise facilities, children free with parents, NS rooms, kitchenettes, in-room refrigerators, airport transportation, TV, laundry facilities, airport transportation, wheelchair access, pets OK, meeting facilities, senior rates, CC. SGL/DBL$55-$145.

Best Western Golden Lion Inn (1000 East 38th Ave., 99508; 561-1522, 800-528-1234) 83 rooms, restaurant, pool, exercise facilities, children free with parents, NS rooms, TV, laundry facilities, wheelchair access, pets OK, meeting facilities, senior rates, CC. SGL/DBL$90-$130.

Bonanza Lodge (4455 Juneau St., 99503; 563-3590, 800-428-8299) 50 rooms, TV, wheelchair access, NS rooms, pets OK, CC. SGL/DBL$65-$75.

Chelsea Inn (3836 Spenard Rd., 99517; 276-5002, Fax 277-7642) free breakfast, wheelchair access, pets OK, NS rooms, a/c, TV, CC. SGL/DBL$65-$75.

Colonial Inn (1713 Northwestern Ave., 99508; 277-6978) 3 rooms, bed and breakfast, free breakfast, TV, NS, no pets, CC. SGL/DBL$55-$75.

Comfort Inn Heritage Suites (111 West Warehouse Ave., 99501; 277-6887, 800-228-5150) 100 rooms and suites, free breakfast, indoor heated pool, sauna, whirlpools, kitchenettes, gift shop, children free with parents, laundry facilities, airport transportation, in-room refrigerators and coffee makers, free local calls, TV, CC. SGL/DBL$65-$265.

Connie's Bed and Breakfast (4151 Lakeridge Circle, 99502; 243-1606) bed and breakfast, TV, NS, shared bath, no pets, CC. SGL/DBL$50-$75.

Days Inn Downtown (321 East 5th Ave., 99501; 276-7226, 800-325-2525) 118 rooms, restaurant, lounge, TV, wheelchair access, NS rooms, pets OK, airport transportation, laundry facilities, in-room computer hookups, in-room refrigerators, senior rates, meeting facilities, CC. SGL/DBL$60-$80.

Down Home Bed and Breakfast (4520 MacAlister Dr., 99515; 243-4443) bed and breakfast, free breakfast, NS, no children, TV, no pets, CC. SGL/DBL$55-$65.

Eight Avenue Hotel (630 8th Ave. West, 99520; 274-6213) 21 rooms and 2-bedroom suites, kitchenettes, in-room computer hookups, laundry facilities, in-room refrigerators, coffee makers, TV, wheelchair access, NS rooms, senior rates, CC. SGL/DBL$80-$145.

Executive Suite Hotel (4360 Spenard Rd., 99517; 243-6366, Fax 248-2161, 800-770-6366) 102 1- and 2-bedroom suites, free breakfast, TV, wheelchair access, NS rooms, kitchenettes, local transportation, complimentary newspaper, free local calls, in-room coffee makers, VCRs, children free with parents, in-room computer hookups, meeting facilities, senior rates, CC. SGL/DBL$65-$245.

Hillside Motel (2150 Gambell St., 99503; 258-6006, Fax 279-8972) rooms and efficiencies, TV, wheelchair access, kitchenettes, in-room coffee makers, laundry facilities, NS rooms, senior rates, CC. SGL/DBL$46-$76.

Hilton Hotel (500 West 3rd Ave., 99501; 272-7411, Fax 265-7175, 800-HIL-TONS) 600 rooms and suites, restaurant, lounge, entertainment, indoor heated pool, exercise facilities, jacuzzi, sauna, children free with parents, in-room computer hookups, NS rooms, wheelchair access, no pets, 24-hour room service, laundry facilities, TV, airport transportation, meeting facilities, senior rates, CC. SGL/DBL$125-$280.

Holiday Inn Downtown (239 West 4th Ave., 99501; 279-8671, 800-HOLI-DAY) 251 rooms, restaurant, lounge, indoor heated pool, whirlpools, exercise facilities, sauna, in-room coffee makers, airport transportation, children under 19 free with parents, wheelchair access, a/c, TV, NS rooms, fax service, room service, in-room computer hookups, no pets, laundry service, meeting facilities for 220, senior rates, CC. SGL/DBL$70-$140.

The Lilac House (950 P St., 99501; 272-3553) bed and breakfast, free breakfast, TV, NS, private baths, antique furnishings, no pets, CC. SGL/DBL$65-$75.

Merrill Field Motel (420 Sitka St., 99501; 276-4547, Fax 276-5064) 39 rooms and suites, TV, wheelchair access, NS rooms, in-room refrigerators, airport transportation, laundry facilities, children free with parents, pets OK, senior rates, CC. SGL/DBL$50-$85.

Mush Inn (333 Concrete St., 99501; 277-4554, Fax 277-5721) pets OK, TV, CC. SGL/DBL$45-$58.

Putnam's Bed and Breakfast (2903 West 29th, 99517; 248-4255) free breakfast, TV, no pets, NS, shared baths, CC. SGL/DBL$50-$75.

Quality Inn Tower Suites (1200 L St., 99501; 276-0110, 800-221-2222) 180 rooms and suites, restaurant, lounge, entertainment, pool, exercise facilities, sauna, children free with parents, TV, room service, no pets, laundry service, NS rooms, in-room refrigerators and microwaves, airport transportation, no pets, meeting facilities, senior rates, CC. SGL/DBL$60-$135.

Qupqugiaq Bed and Breakfast (3801 Spenard Rd., 99517; 562-5681) free breakfast, TV, no pets, CC. SGL/DBL$42-$54.

Regal Alaskan Hotel (4800 Spenard Rd., 99517; 243-2300) 248 rooms, restaurant, lounge, whirlpools, exercise center, water view, pets OK, TV, wheelchair access, NS rooms, children free with parents, 24-hour room service, airport transportation, in-room refrigerators, senior rates, CC. SGL/DBL$130-$255.

Sixth and Bed and Breakfast (145 West 6th Ave., 99501; 279-5293) free breakfast, TV, no pets, NS, private baths, CC. SGL/DBL$50-$60.

Voyager Hotel (501 K St., 99501; 277-9501, 800-247-9070) 38 rooms, restaurant, lounge, TV, wheelchair access, NS rooms, no pets, airport transportation, senior rates, CC. SGL/DBL$80-$135.

Wesleyan House (3412 Wesleyan Dr., 99508; 337-7383) 2 rooms, bed and breakfast, pets OK, children free with parents, CC. SGL/DBL$50-$85.

Westcoast International Inn (3333 International Airport Rd., 99502; 243-2233, 800-426-0670) 141 rooms, restaurant, lounge, airport transportation, children free with parents, no pets, laundry service, kitchenettes, in-room refrigerators, a/c, TV, wheelchair access, NS rooms, senior rates, CC. SGL/DBL$100-$150.

Westmark Anchorage Hotel (720 West 5th Ave., 99501; 276-7676) 200 rooms, restaurant, lounge, exercise center, TV, wheelchair access, NS rooms, children free with parents, no pets, laundry service, airport transportation, in-room refrigerators, senior rates, CC. SGL/DBL$120-$198.

Barrow
Area Code 907

Top of the World Motor Inn (Barrow 99723; 852-3900) 40 rooms, TV, children free with parents, wheelchair access, NS rooms, no pets, in-room refrigerators, meeting facilities, senior rates, CC. SGL/DBL$120-$150.

Central
Area Code 907

Circle Hot Springs Resort (Central 99730; 520-5113, Fax 488-9239) 40 rooms, restaurant, lounge, TV, no pets, wheelchair access, NS rooms, meeting facilities, senior rates, CC. SGL/DBL$65-$70.

Cooper Landing
Area Code 907

Kenai Princess Lodge (Cooper Landing 99572; 595-1425) 50 rooms, restaurant, lounge, whirlpools, exercise center, TV, wheelchair access, no pets, children free with parents, laundry facilities, in-room refrigerators and coffee makers, meeting facilities, NS rooms, senior rates, CC. SGL/DBL$100-$200.

Vinton's Alpine Motel (Cooper Landing 99572; 595-1212) 12 rooms and efficiencies, TV, no pets, CC. SGL/DBL$45-$80.

Denali National Park
Area Code 907

Denali National Park Hotel (Denali National Park 99755; 683-2215) 100 rooms, restaurant, lounge, children free with parents, wheelchair access, no pets, local transportation, NS rooms, senior rates, CC. SGL/DBL$120-$135.

McKinley Chalet Resort (Denali National Park 99755; 683-2215) 288 rooms, restaurant, lounge, indoor heated pool, sauna, exercise center, in-room refrigerators and coffee makers, NS rooms, local transportation, no pets, children free with parents, senior rates, CC. SGL/DBL$145-$155.

McKinley Village Lodge (Denali National Park 99755; 683-2265) 50 rooms, restaurant, lounge, local transportation, children free with parents, no pets, meeting facilities, senior rates, CC. SGL/DBL$105-$116.

Mount McKinley Motor Lodge (Denali National Park 99755; 683-1240) 23 rooms, TV, wheelchair access, NS rooms, children free with parents, no pets, CC. SGL/DBL$100.

Princess Lodge (Denali National Park 99755; 683-2282) 282 rooms, restaurant, lounge, whirlpools, TV, wheelchair access, NS rooms, no pets, local transportation, water view, meeting facilities, senior rates, CC. SGL/DBL$80-$156.

Riverview Inn (Denali National Park 99755; 683-2663) 12 rooms, local transportation, TV, wheelchair access, NS rooms, no pets, children free with parents, airport transportation, senior rates, CC. SGL/DBL$120.

Ester
Area Code 907

Ester Gold Camps (3600 Main St., 99725; 479-2500, Fax 474-1780, 800-676-6925) 20 rooms, restaurant, lounge, entertainment, gift shop, TV, CC. SGL/DBL$47-$58.

Fairbanks
Area Code 907

Rental and Reservation Services:

Bed and Breakfast Reservation Services (1971 Kingfisher Dr., 99709; 479-8165, Fax 474-8448, 800-770-8165).

□□□

AAAA Care Bed and Breakfast (557 Fairbanks St., 99709; 479-2447, 800-478-2705) 6 rooms, free breakfast, pets OK, laundry facilities, private baths, TV, CC. SGL/DBL$75-$85.

Ah, Rose Marie Bed and Breakfast (302 Cowles St., 99701; 456-2040) 8 rooms, free breakfast, TV, airport transportation, private baths, no pets, CC. SGL/DBL$55-$68.

Alaska Heritage Inn (Fairbanks 99707; 451-6587, Fax 488-7899) 15 rooms, free breakfast, TV, no pets, CC. SGL/DBL$44-$54.

Alaska Golden Heart Bed and Breakfast (1680 Kiana St., 99709; 474-9406) 4 rooms, free breakfast, TV, airport transportation, pets OK, private baths, laundry facilities, CC. SGL/DBL$65-$85.

Alaska Motel (1546 Cushman St., 99701; 456-6393, Fax 452-4833) 36 rooms, laundry facilities, TV, no pets, wheelchair access, NS rooms, senior rates, CC. SGL/DBL$36-$58.

Alaska Range View Bed and Breakfast (Fairbanks 99710; 457-1619) 1 room, free breakfast, private bath, pets OK, CC. SGL/DBL$45-$90.

Alaskan House Bed and Breakfast (302 Charles St., 99701; 451-0435, Fax 452-3984) 6 rooms, free breakfast, airport transportation, laundry facilities, TV, no pets, meeting facilities, CC. SGL/DBL$46-$66.

Alaskan Iris Bed and Breakfast (Fairbanks 99711; 488-2308) 2 rooms, free breakfast, TV, pets OK, laundry facilities, CC. SGL/DBL$45-$55.

Alaskan Motor Inn (419 4th Ave., 99701; 452-4800, Fax 451-0107) 32 rooms, TV, no pets, wheelchair access, NS rooms, senior rates, CC. SGL/DBL$36-$46.

Alaskan Viewpoint Bed and Breakfast (1244 Viewpoint Dr., 99709; 479-7251) 5 rooms, free breakfast, TV, laundry facilities, private baths, no pets, CC. SGL/DBL$60-$80.

An Old Alaskan Country Inn on the Rivers Edge (204 Front St., 99701; 452-3342, Fax 451-8522) free breakfast, antique furnishings, NS, shared baths, TV, no pets, CC. SGL/DBL$65-$80.

Applesauce Inn (119 Gruening Way, 99712; 457-3392, Fax 457-3392) 4 rooms, free breakfast, TV, airport transportation, private baths, no pets, CC. SGL/DBL$45-$90.

Arctic Rose Bed and Breakfast (3019 Riverview Dr., 99709; 474-4787, Fax 474-8368) 3 rooms, free breakfast, TV, no pets, laundry facilities, CC. SGL/DBL$45-$65.

B&R Bed and Breakfast (650 Gradelle Ave., 99709; 479-3335) 4 rooms, free breakfast, TV, airport transportation, laundry facilities, pets OK, CC. SGL/DBL$38-$58.

Beaver Bend Bed and Breakfast (231 Iditarod, 99701; 452-3240) free breakfast, TV, NS, private baths, water view, no pets, CC. SGL/DBL$59-$66.

Bridgewater Hotel (723 1st Ave., 99701; 452-6661, Fax 452-6126, 800-528-4916) 95 rooms, restaurant, lounge, TV, airport transportation, no pets, wheelchair access, NS rooms, senior rates, CC. SGL/DBL$130-$140.

The Captain Bartlett Inn (1411 Airport Way, 99701; 452-1888, Fax 452-7674, 800-544-7528, 800-478-7900 in Alaska) 197 rooms, restaurant, lounge, entertainment, pool, a/c, TV, gift shop, wheelchair access, NS rooms, laundry facilities, pets OK, senior rates, CC. SGL/DBL$130-$139.

Cedar Creek Inn (Fairbanks 99710; 457-3392) 3 rooms, free breakfast, TV, airport transportation, laundry facilities, pets OK, CC. SGL/DBL$55-$65.

Chatanika Gold Camp (2235 Cowles St., 99701; 389-2414) 20 rooms, restaurant, lounge, TV, no pets, wheelchair access, NS rooms, airport transportation, laundry facilities, gift shop, senior rates, CC. SGL/DBL$44-$56.

Chatanika Lodge (5760 North Old Steese Hwy., 99712; 389-2164) 24 rooms, restaurant, lounge, entertainment, TV, no pets, wheelchair access, NS rooms, senior rates, CC. SGL/DBL$33-$43.

Chena Hot Springs Resort (Fairbanks 99707; 452-7867, Fax 456-3122) 58 rooms, restaurant, lounge, entertainment, TV, no pets, wheelchair access, NS rooms, airport transportation, gift shop, senior rates, CC. SGL/DBL$65-$105.

Chena Pump Inn and Trident Apartments (Fairbanks 99708; 479-6313) 12 rooms, bed and breakfast, free breakfast, airport transportation, pets OK, TV, CC. SGL/DBL$60-$80.

Chena River Bed and Breakfast (1001 Dolly Varden Lane, 99709; 479-2532) free breakfast, TV, no pets, NS, private baths, CC. SGL/DBL$50-$55.

Chokecherry Inn (946 Coppet, 99709; 474-9381) 7 rooms, free breakfast, TV, no pets, airport transportation, private baths, CC. SGL/DBL$55-$85.

Eleanor's Northern Lights Bed and Breakfast (360 State St., 99701; 452-2598) 7 rooms, free breakfast, TV, airport transportation, private baths, no pets, CC. SGL/DBL$45-$55.

Fairbanks Princess Hotel (4477 Pikes Landing Rd., 99709; 455-4477, Fax 455-4476, 800-426-0500) 200 rooms, restaurant, lounge, laundry facilities, gift shop, TV, no pets, wheelchair access, in-room refrigerators, NS rooms, airport transportation, in-room computer hookups, senior rates, CC. SGL/DBL$110-$178.

Fireweed Hideaway Bed and Breakfast (Fairbanks 99708; 457-2579) 2 rooms, free breakfast, NS, TV, kitchenettes, private baths, no pets, CC. SGL/DBL$40-$50.

Fox Creek Bed and Breakfast (2498 Elliott Hwy, 99712; 457-5494) 4 rooms, free breakfast, TV, laundry facilities, no pets, CC. SGL/DBL$35-$45.

Golden North Motel (4888 Old Airport Way, 99701; 479-6201, Fax 479-5766, 800-447-1910, 800-478-1910 in Alaska) 60 rooms, TV, airport transportation, NS rooms, laundry facilities, CC. SGL/DBL$60-$100.

Hillside Bed and Breakfast (310 Rambling Rd., 99712; 457-2664) free breakfast, TV, no pets, laundry facilities, kitchenettes, NS. SGL/DBL$35-$56.

Hotel Captain Hook (427 1st Ave., 99701; 456-4456, Fax 456-2696) 130 rooms, restaurant, lounge, entertainment, gift shop, TV, pets OK, wheelchair access, NS rooms, laundry facilities, senior rates, CC. SGL/DBL$50-$125.

Jan's Bed and Breakfast (1605 Marika Rd., 99709; 456-5431) 2 rooms, free breakfast, TV, airport transportation, private baths, no pets, CC. SGL/DBL$44-$54.

Midnight Sun Traveler (604 2nd St., 99701; 451-8106) free breakfast, TV, private baths, no pets. SGL/DBL$55-$65.

1940s Age Old Bed and Breakfast (319 15th Ave., 99701; 451-7526) 4 rooms, free breakfast, TV, pets OK, private bath, laundry facilities, NS, kitchenettes, airport transportation, CC. SGL/DBL$53-$68.

Noah's Rainbow Inn (700 Fairbanks St., 99709; 474-3666, Fax 474-3668) 100 rooms, TV, no pets, laundry facilities, wheelchair access, NS rooms, senior rates, CC. SGL/DBL$55-$75.

Old Town Bed and Breakfast (212 7th Ave., 99701; 458-7412) 3 rooms, free breakfast, TV, pets OK, laundry facilities, airport transportation, private baths, CC. SGL/DBL$55-$85.

Pioneer Bed and Breakfast (1119 2nd Ave., 99701; 452-5393) 2 rooms, free breakfast, TV, shared baths, no pets, CC. SGL/DBL$44-$56.

Point of View Bed and Breakfast (Fairbanks 99708; 455-8246, Fax 479-8246) 3 rooms, free breakfast, TV, no pets, private baths, CC. SGL/DBL$55-$75.

Regency Fairbanks Hotel (95 10th Ave., 99701; 452-3200, Fax 452-6505, 800-348-1340) 128 rooms, restaurant, lounge, entertainment, a/c, TV, wheelchair access, NS rooms, kitchenettes, laundry facilities, airport transportation, pets OK, senior rates, CC. SGL/DBL$155-$165.

Rocking Horse Bed and Breakfast (118 Glacier 99701; 458-7758) 3 rooms, free breakfast, TV, no pets, CC. SGL/DBL$35-$45.

Seven Gables Bed and Breakfast (4312 Birch Lane, 99708; 479-0751, Fax 479-2229) 9 rooms and 2-bedroom apartments, free breakfast, TV, laundry facilities, NS, private baths, jacuzzi, no pets, VCRs, airport transportation, CC. SGL/DBL$44-$85.

Sophie Station Hotel (1717 South University Ave., 99709; 479-3650, Fax 479-7951, 800-528-4916) 147 rooms, restaurant, lounge, TV, laundry facilities, children free with parents, airport transportation, no pets, wheelchair access, NS rooms, senior rates, CC. SGL/DBL$95-$165.

Stone Frost Downtown Inn (851 6th Ave., 99701; 457-5337, Fax 474-0532) 7 rooms, free breakfast, airport transportation, laundry facilities, private baths, TV, no pets, CC. SGL/DBL$55-$85.

Super 8 Motel (1909 Airport Way, 99701; 451-8888, Fax 451-6690, 800-800-8000) 77 rooms and suites, pets OK, children under 12 free with parents, free local calls, TV, in-room refrigerators and microwaves, fax service, NS rooms, wheelchair access, airport transportation, meeting facilities, senior rates, CC. SGL/DBL$99-$102.

Tamarac Inn Motel (252 Minnie St., 99701; 456-6406) 18 rooms, laundry facilities, no pets, kitchenettes, TV, CC. SGL/DBL$44-$54.

Taste of Alaska Lodge (551 Eberhardt Rd., 99712; 488-7855, Fax 488-3772) 5 rooms, free breakfast, laundry facilities, private baths, TV, no pets, CC. SGL/DBL$66-$86.

The Village Suites (205 Palace Circle, 99701; 456-7612, Fax 456-8358) 27 rooms and suites, TV, laundry facilities, kitchenettes, pets OK, wheelchair access, NS rooms, senior rates, CC. SGL/DBL$65-$105.

Wedgewood Resort (212 Wedgewood Dr., 99701; 452-1442, Fax 451-8184, 800-528-4916) 190 rooms, restaurant, lounge, kitchenettes, laundry facilities, no pets, NS rooms, TV, room service, senior rates, CC. SGL/DBL$140-$150.

Westmark Hotel (813 Noble St., 99701; 456-7711, Fax 451-7478, 800-544-0970) 238 rooms, restaurant, lounge, TV, no pets, wheelchair access, NS rooms, laundry facilities, meeting facilities, senior rates, CC. SGL/DBL$152-$157.

Girdwood
Area Code 907

Rental and Reservation Services:

Alyeska Accommodations (Girdwood 99587; 783-2000) rental chalets and condominiums.

□□□

Alyeska Resort (Girdwood 99587; 783-2222, Fax 783-2814) restaurant, lounge, TV, wheelchair access, NS rooms, CC. SGL/DBL$65-$88.

Glennallen
Area Code 907

The Caribou Hotel (Glennallen 99588; 822-3302) 46 rooms and 3-bedroom suites, whirlpools, children free with parents, pets OK, airport transportation, kitchenettes, TV, wheelchair access, NS rooms, senior rates, CC. SGL/DBL$70-$100.

Gustavus
Area Code 907

Glacier Bay Country Inn (Tong Rd., 99826; 697-2288) free breakfast, TV, NS, private baths. SGL/DBL$75-$135.

Glacier Bay Lodge (Gustavus 99826; 697-2226) 55 rooms, restaurant, lounge, NS rooms, children free with parents, water view, no pets, laundry facilities, local transportation, senior rates, CC. SGL/DBL$140.

Good River Bed and Breakfast (Gustavus 99826; 697-2214) free breakfast, TV, private baths, no pets. SGL/DBL$45-$65.

Haines
Area Code 907

Captains Choice Motel (Haines 99827; 766-3111) 39 rooms, airport transportation, TV, wheelchair access, NS rooms, in-room refrigerators, pets OK, senior rates, CC. SGL/DBL$65-$95.

The Eagles Nest Motel (1183 Haines Hwy., 99827; 766-2891) 9 rooms, TV, wheelchair access, NS rooms, transportation to local attractions, pets OK, senior rates, CC. SGL/DBL$55-$70.

Healy
Area Code 907

Denali Suites (Healy 99743; 683-2848) 4 suites, kitchenettes, laundry facilities, TV, CC. SGL/DBL$55-$75.

Historic Healy Hotel (Healy 99743; 683-2242, Fax 683-2243) 62 rooms, restaurant, gift shop, TV, no pets, wheelchair access, NS rooms, senior rates, CC. SGL/DBL$65-$85.

Totem Inn (Healy 99743; 683-2420, Fax 683-2384) 40 rooms, restaurant, lounge, gift shop, laundry facilities, pets OK, kitchenettes, TV, wheelchair access, NS rooms, senior rates, CC. SGL/DBL$55-$85.

Homer
Area Code 907

Best Western Bidarka Inn (575 Sterling Hwy., 99603; 235-8148, Fax 235-8140, 800-528-1234) 74 rooms, restaurant, lounge, spa, exercise facilities, airport transportation, children free with parents, NS rooms, TV, laundry facilities, wheelchair access, pets OK, meeting facilities, senior rates, CC. SGL/DBL$80-$126.

Homer Bed and Breakfast (Homer 99603; 235-8996) free breakfast, TV, private baths, sauna, NS, no pets, CC. SGL/DBL$50-$75.

Juneau
Area Code 907

Baranof Hotel (127 Franklin St., 99801; 586-2660) 193 rooms, restaurant, lounge, airport transportation, kitchenettes, TV, VCRs, children free with parents, no pets, wheelchair access, NS rooms, senior rates, CC. SGL/DBL$100-$135.

Best Western Country Lane Inn (9300 Glacier Hwy., 99801; 789-2818, 800-528-1234) 50 rooms and efficiencies, restaurant, free breakfast, airport transportation, children free with parents, NS rooms, in-room refrigerators and microwaves, local transportation, TV, laundry service, wheelchair access, pets OK, meeting facilities, senior rates, CC. SGL/DBL$78-$146.

Blueberry Lodge (9436 North Douglas Hwy., 99801; 463-5886) 5 rooms and 2-bedroom suites, free breakfast, NS, private baths, local transportation, modified American plan available, children free with parents, no pets, laundry facilities, senior rates, CC. SGL/DBL$60-$75.

Pearsons Pond Bed and Breakfast (4541 Sawa Circle, 99801; 789-3772) 3 rooms, free breakfast, whirlpools, TV, kitchenettes, shared bath, water view, NS rooms, no pets, CC. SGL/DBL$70-$148.

Prospector Motor Inn (375 Whittier St., 99801; 586-3737) 58 rooms, restaurant, lounge, entertainment, water view, children free with parents, pets OK, in-room coffee makers, airport transportation, TV, wheelchair access, NS rooms, meeting facilities, senior rates, CC. SGL/DBL$60-$125.

Silverbow Inn (120 2nd St., 99801; 586-4146) 6 rooms, no pets, NS, laundry service, children free with parents, CC. SGL/DBL$70-$110.

TraveLodge Airport (9200 Glacier Hwy., 99801; 789-9700, 800-578-7878) 86 rooms, restaurant, lounge, free breakfast, indoor heated pool, whirlpools, wheelchair access, complimentary newspaper, laundry service, TV, in-room refrigerators and microwaves, free local calls, fax service, NS rooms, children under 18 free with parents, pets OK, meeting facilities, senior rates, CC. SGL/DBL$85-$118.

Westmark Juneau Hotel (51 Egan Dr., 99801; 586-6900, Fax 463-3567) 104 rooms, restaurant, lounge, exercise center, no pets, airport transportation, TV, wheelchair access, NS rooms, meeting facilities, senior rates, CC. SGL/DBL$110-$155.

Kantishna
Area Code 907

Kantishna Roadhouse (Kantishna 99755; 683-2710, 800-942-7420) 27 rooms, restaurant, lounge, TV, no pets, wheelchair access, NS rooms, senior rates, CC. SGL/DBL$55-$85.

Ketchikan
Area Code 907

Best Western Landing Inn (3434 Tongass Ave., 99901; 225-5166, Fax 225-6900, 800-528-1234) 48 rooms, restaurant, lounge, entertainment, exercise center, children free with parents, NS rooms, TV, laundry facilities, wheelchair access, laundry service, no pets, local transportation, in-room refrigerators, microwaves and coffee makers, meeting facilities, senior rates, CC. SGL/DBL$73-$110.

Ingersol Hotel (303 Mission St., 99901; 225-2124) 58 rooms, TV, wheelchair access, NS rooms, children free with parents, no pets, laundry service, meeting facilities, senior rates, CC. SGL/DBL$50-$90.

Westmark Cape Fox Lodge (800 Venetian Way, 99901; 225-8001, Fax 225-8286) 72 rooms, restaurant, lounge, whirlpools, laundry service, airport transportation, no pets, TV, wheelchair access, NS rooms, meeting facilities, senior rates, CC. SGL/DBL$110-$150.

Kodiak
Area Code 907

Buskin River Inn (1395 Airport Way, 99615; 487-2700, Fax 487-4447) 51 rooms, restaurant, lounge, whirlpools, TV, in-room refrigerators, laundry facilities, children free with parents, pets OK, airport transportation, wheelchair access, NS rooms, meeting facilities, senior rates, CC. SGL/DBL$100-$116.

Westmark Kodiak Motor Inn (236 West Rezanof Dr., 99615; 486-5712) 81 rooms, restaurant, lounge, TV, wheelchair access, NS rooms, water view, children free with parents, in-room refrigerators and coffee makers, VCRs, no pets, airport transportation, meeting facilities, senior rates, CC. SGL/DBL$95-$128.

Kotzebue
Area Code 907

Nul-Luk-Vik Hotel (Kotzebue 99752; 442-3331/3332) 75 rooms, restaurant, TV, wheelchair access, NS rooms, senior rates, CC. SGL/DBL$125-$135.

Manley
Area Code 907

Manley Hot Springs Resort (Manley 99756; 672-3611, Fax 672-3461) 28 rooms and suites, restaurant, lounge, gift shop, laundry facilities, pets OK, TV, wheelchair access, NS rooms, senior rates, CC. SGL/DBL$65-$90.

Nome
Area Code 907

Nugget Inn (Nome 99762; 443-2323) 47 rooms, TV, wheelchair access, no pets, NS rooms, senior rates, CC. SGL/DBL$85-$95.

Petersburg
Area Code 907

Tides Inn (307 Dolphin St. North, 99833; 772-4288) 47 rooms and efficiencies, TV, wheelchair access, NS rooms, in-room refrigerators and microwaves, no pets, children free with parents, meeting facilities, senior rates, CC. SGL/DBL$70-$80.

Seward
Area Code 907

Best Western Hotel Seward (221 5th Ave., 99664; 224-2378, Fax 224-3112, 800-528-1234) 38 rooms, restaurant, lounge, children free with parents, NS rooms, TV, laundry facilities, wheelchair access, no pets, VCRs, in-room refrigerators and coffee makers, water view, local transportation, meeting facilities, senior rates, CC. SGL/DBL$85-$175.

Marina Motel (1603 Seward Hwy., 99664; 224-5518, Fax 224-5553) 18 rooms, whirlpools, pets OK, local transportation, TV, wheelchair access, NS rooms, senior rates, CC. SGL/DBL$45-$95.

Mountain View (201 Cascade Creek Rd., 99835; 747-8966) 5 rooms, free breakfast, TV, no pets, water view, airport transportation, CC. SGL/DBL$50-$70.

Swiss Chalet Bed and Breakfast (Eagle Lane, 99664; 224-3939) free breakfast, TV, NS, no children, private baths, no pets. SGL/DBL$57-$77.

Westmark Shee Atika Motor Inn (330 Seward St., 99835; 747-6241) 100 rooms, restaurant, lounge, TV, wheelchair access, NS rooms, children free with parents, VCRs, no pets, water view, senior rates, CC. SGL/DBL$100-$128.

The White House (Seward 99664; 224-3614) 5 rooms, free breakfast, TV, private baths, NS, no pets, senior rates. SGL/DBL$65-$85.

Skagway
Area Code 907

Westmark Inn (Skagway 99840; 983-6000, Fax 983-6100) 220 rooms, restaurant, lounge, no pets, children free with parents, wheelchair access, NS rooms, local transportation, laundry facilities, meeting facilities, senior rates, CC. SGL/DBL$125-$135.

Wind Valley Lodge (Skagway 99840; 893-2236) 29 rooms, TV, wheelchair access, NS rooms, pets OK, children free with parents, local transportation, laundry facilities, senior rates, CC. SGL/DBL$65-$75.

Soldotna
Area Code 907

Best Western King Salmon Motel (35545 Kenai Spur Hwy., 99669; 262-5857, Fax 262-9441, 800-528-1234) 49 rooms, restaurant, airport transportation, beauty shop, kitchenettes, children free with parents, NS rooms, TV, laundry facilities, wheelchair access, pets OK, meeting facilities, senior rates, CC. SGL/DBL$75-$123.

Denise Lake Lodge (Soldotna 99669; 262-1789) free breakfast, NS, private baths, TV, no pets. SGL/DBL$54-$78.

Johnson Brothers Lodge (Soldotna 99669; 262-5357) 5 rooms and efficiencies, no pets, laundry facilities, TV, CC. SGL/DBL$75-$94.

Sportsman Condos and Bed and Breakfast (Soldotna 99669; 262-7888) 2-bedroom condominiums, free breakfast, no pets, wheelchair access, TV, laundry facilities, kitchenettes, CC. SGL/DBL$85.

Talkeetna

Area Code 907

Alaska Log Cabin Bed and Breakfast (1 Beaver Rd., 99676; 733-2584, Fax 733-2720) cabin, kitchenettes, pets OK, TV, laundry facilities, CC. SGL/DBL$55-$85.

Tok

Area Code 907

Cleft of the Rock (Tok 99780; 883-4219) 5 rooms, free breakfast, TV, pets OK, shared baths, kitchenettes, children free with parents, SGL/DBL$48-$65.

Westmark Hotel (Tok 99780; 883-5174, Fax 883-5178) 92 rooms, restaurant, lounge, airport transportation, no pets, TV, children free with parents, wheelchair access, NS rooms, senior rates, CC. SGL/DBL$120-$130.

Valdez

Area Code 907

Colonial Inn (333 Klutina St., 99686; 835-4929) free breakfast, TV, no pets, private baths, CC. SGL/DBL$70.

Alpine Mountain Inn (325 Jago, 99686; 835-2624) 2 rooms, free breakfast, TV, private baths, NS, no children, no pets, CC. SGL/DBL$75.

Wasilla

Area Code 907

Country Lakes Bed and Breakfast (2651 East Palmer Hwy., 99687; 376-5868) rooms and cabin, free breakfast, NS, TV, no pets, CC. SGL/DBL$65-$100.

Idaho

Alta

Grand Targhee (Alta 83422; 353-2304, Fax 353-8148, 800-443-8146) 96 rooms and suites, restaurant, lounge, entertainment, heated pool, tennis courts, exercise center, gift shop, children free with parents, pets OK, game room, airport transportation, modified American plan available, airport transportation, a/c, TV, wheelchair access, NS rooms, senior rates, CC. SGL/DBL$75-$390.

American Falls

Hillview Motel (East I-86, 83211; 226-1515) 34 rooms, pool, a/c, TV, pets OK, in-room refrigerators, meeting facilities for 50, laundry facilities, senior rates, CC. SGL/DBL$30-$45.

Ronnez Motel (411 Lincoln, 83211; 226-9658) 10 rooms, a/c, TV, no pets, CC. SGL/DBL$20-$35.

Arco

D.K. Motel (316 South Front, 83213; 527-8282, 800-421-3287) 20 rooms, a/c, TV, kitchenettes, pets OK, CC. SGL/DBL$25-$40.

Lazy A Motel (318 West Grand, 83213; 527-8263) 22 rooms, a/c, TV, kitchenettes, pets OK, CC. SGL/DBL$25-$38.

Lost River Motel (405 Hwy. Dr., 83213; 527-3600) 15 rooms, a/c, TV, kitchenettes, pets OK, CC. SGL/DBL$25-$45.

Riverside Motel (Arco 83213; 527-8954) 10 rooms, a/c, kitchenettes, TV, pets OK, CC. SGL/DBL$25-$45.

Ashton

Four Seasons Motel (Ashton 83420; 652-7769) 14 rooms, a/c, TV, pets OK, CC. SGL/DBL$25-$55.

Jensen's Bed and Breakfast (Ashton 83420; 652-3356) 3 rooms, free breakfast, NS, TV, no pets. SGL$25, DBL$35.

Log Cabin Motel (1001 East Main St., 83420; 652-3956) 10 rooms, a/c, TV, pets OK, CC. SGL/DBL$25-$58.

Rankin Motel (Ashton 83420; 652-3570) 9 rooms, a/c, TV, CC. SGL/DBL$20-$35.

Athol
Area Code 208

Kelso Lake Resort (Route 1, 83801; 683-2297) 3 cabins, kitchenettes, TV, CC. SGL/DBL$10-$30.

Bayview
Area Code 208

Mac Donald's Hudson Bay Resort (Bayview 83803; 683-2211) 9 rooms, a/c, pets OK, TV, CC. SGL/DBL$45-$60.

Scenic Motel (Bayview 83803; 683-2215) 8 rooms, a/c, TV, pets OK, CC. SGL/DBL$35-$50.

Bellevue
Area Code 208

High Country Motel (Bellevue 83313; 788-2050) 10 rooms, TV, pets OK, a/c, CC. SGL/DBL$30-$50.

Blackfoot
Area Code 208

The Alder Inn (384 Alder St., 83221; 785-6968) bed and breakfast, restaurant, free breakfast, a/c, no pets, TV, CC. SGL/DBL$45-$55.

Riverside Inn (1229 Parkway Dr., 83221; 785-1348) 80 rooms, restaurant, pool, TV, a/c, pets OK, meeting facilities for 100, CC. SGL/DBL$35-$53.

Y Motel (1375 South Broadway, 83221; 785-1550) 21 rooms, TV, a/c, kitchenettes, CC. SGL/DBL$20-$35.

Bliss
Area Code 208

Amber Inn (Bliss 83314; 352-4441) 30 rooms and 2-bedroom efficiencies, a/c, pets OK, TV, CC. SGL/DBL$20-$35.

Boise

Area Code 208

Allison Ranch (7259 Cascade Dr., 83704; 376-5270) 1 room, TV, meeting facilities for 10. SGL$395W, DBL$750W.

Best Western Airport Motor Inn (2660 Airport Way, 83705; 384-5000, Fax 342-3060, 800-528-1234) 50 rooms, restaurant, lounge, outdoor pool, exercise facilities, children free with parents, a/c, NS rooms, TV, airport transportation, in-room refrigerators and coffee makers, complimentary newspaper, laundry facilities, wheelchair access, pets OK, meeting facilities, senior rates, CC. SGL/DBL$45-$60.

Best Western Safari Motor Inn (1070 Grove St., 83702; 344-6556, Fax 344-7240, 800-528-1234) 104 rooms, restaurant, free breakfast, lounge, outdoor pool, exercise facilities, children under 18 free with parents, a/c, NS rooms, TV, laundry facilities, in-room refrigerators and microwaves, wheelchair access, pets OK, meeting facilities, senior rates, CC. SGL/DBL$45-$60.

Best Western Vista Inn (2645 Airport Way, 83705; 336-8100, Fax 342-3060, 800-528-1234) 86 rooms, restaurant, lounge, indoor heated pool, exercise center, spa, sauna, children free with parents, a/c, NS rooms, TV, laundry facilities, wheelchair access, no pets, airport transportation, meeting facilities, senior rates, CC. SGL/DBL$50-$65.

Boisean Motel (1300 South Capitol Blvd., 83706; 343-3645, 800-365-3645) 135 rooms, restaurant, lounge, pool, a/c, TV, laundry facilities, wheelchair access, pets OK, meeting facilities for 50, senior rates, CC. SGL/DBL$20-$50.

Boulevard Motel (1121 South Capitol Blvd., 83706; 342-4629) 20 rooms, a/c, TV, pets OK, CC. SGL/DBL$20-$40.

Cabana Inn (1600 Main St., 83702; 343-6000) 50 rooms, a/c, TV, pets OK, laundry facilities, CC. SGL/DBL$25-$48.

Capri Motel (2600 Fairview, 83702; 344-8617) 44 rooms, restaurant, lounge, a/c, TV, pets OK, laundry facilities, CC. SGL/DBL$20-$35.

Comfort Inn Airport (2526 Airport Way, 83705; 336-0077, 800-228-5150) 60 rooms, indoor heated pool, whirlpools, no pets, a/c, TV, in-room refrigerators, VCRs, children free with parents, airport transportation, CC. SGL/DBL$40-$57.

Doubletree Hotel (475 Park Center Blvd., 83706; 345-2002, Fax 345-8354, 800-828-7447) 158 rooms and suites, restaurant, lounge, outdoor pool, whirlpools, exercise center, airport courtesy car, a/c, in-room computer hookups, VCRs, NS rooms, wheelchair access, TV, no pets, 2 meeting rooms, meeting facilities for 75, senior rates, CC. SGL/DBL$50-$80.

Flying J Travel Plaza (8000 Overland Rd., 83709; 322-4404) 88 rooms, heated pool, a/c, TV, wheelchair access, NS rooms, laundry facilities, pets OK, children free with parents, CC. SGL/DBL$30-$45.

Grandview Motel (1315 Federal Way, 83705; 342-8676) 20 rooms, a/c, TV, NS rooms, wheelchair access, CC. SGL/DBL$20-$35.

Holiday Inn Airport (3300 Vista Ave., 83705; 344-8365, 800-HOLIDAY) 265 rooms, restaurant, lounge, indoor heated pool, sauna, exercise facilities, children under 19 free with parents, wheelchair access, a/c, TV, NS rooms, fax service, room service, pets OK, laundry service, meeting facilities for 300, senior rates, CC. SGL/DBL$75-$90.

Holiday Motel (5416 Fairview Ave., 83706; 376-4631) 17 rooms, restaurant, pool, a/c, TV, NS rooms, wheelchair access, senior rates, CC. SGL/DBL$20-$30.

Idaho Heritage Inn (109 West Idaho, 83702; 342-8066) 5 rooms, free breakfast, airport transportation, in-room coffee makers, a/c, TV, NS rooms, CC. SGL/DBL$60-$75.

Idanha Hotel (928 Main St., 83702; 342-3611) 55 rooms, restaurant, a/c, TV, wheelchair access, NS rooms, laundry facilities, senior rates, CC. SGL/DBL$35-$75.

Mackay Bar Ranch (3190 Airport Way, 83705; 344-1881, 800-635-5336) 24 rooms, restaurant, a/c, TV, wheelchair access, NS rooms, laundry facilities, senior rates, CC. SGL/DBL$50-$150.

Motel 6 (2323 Airport Way, 83705; 344-3506, 505-891-6161) 91 rooms, pool, free local calls, children under 17 free with parents, NS rooms, wheelchair access, pets OK, a/c, TV, CC. SGL/DBL$32-$38.

Nendels Inn (2155 North Garden, 83704; 344-4030, 800-547-0106) 52 rooms, a/c, TV, VCRs, pets OK, children under 17 free with parents, senior rates, CC. SGL/DBL$35-$46.

Owyhee Plaza Hotel (1109 Main St., 83702; 343-4611, 800-821-7500 in Idaho) 100 rooms, restaurant, outdoor heated pool, a/c, TV, wheelchair access, NS rooms, laundry facilities, in-room refrigerators and coffee makers, pets OK, children free with parents, in-room computer hookups, meeting facilities, senior rates, CC. SGL/DBL$55-$95.

Park Suite Hotel (424 East Park Center Blvd., 83706; 342-1044, Fax 342-2763) 130 rooms, pool, exercise center, whirlpools, in-room refrigerators and microwaves, no pets, laundry facilities, airport transportation, a/c, TV, wheelchair access, NS rooms, senior rates, CC. SGL/DBL$60-$105.

Pioneer Inn at Bogus Basin (2405 Bogus Basin Rd., 83702; 336-4500, 800-367-4397) 70 rooms, restaurant, a/c, TV, wheelchair access, NS rooms, laundry facilities, senior rates, CC. SGL/DBL$40-$155.

Plaza Suite Hotel (409 South Cole Rd., 83709; 375-7666) 27 rooms, restaurant, indoor heated pool, a/c, in-room refrigerators and microwaves, children free with parents, no pets, TV, senior rates, meeting facilities, CC. SGL/DBL$40-$115.

Quality Inn Airport Suites (2717 Vista Ave., 83705; 343-7505, 800-221-2222) 79 rooms and suites, indoor pool, exercise facilities, children free with parents, a/c, TV, room service, laundry service, NS rooms, in-room refrigerators and microwaves, pets OK, airport transportation, meeting facilities, senior rates, CC. SGL/DBL$43-$66.

Ramada Inn (1025 South Capitol Blvd., 83706; 344-7971, Fax 345-6846, 800-2-RAMADA) 127 rooms and suites, restaurant, lounge, entertainment, outdoor heated pool, sauna, whirlpools, wheelchair access, NS rooms, free parking, airport transportation, pets OK, a/c, TV, children under 18 free with parents, room service, laundry facilities, meeting facilities, senior rates, CC. SGL/DBL$50-$60.

Red Lion Inn Downtowner (1800 Fairview, 83702; 344-7691, 800-547-8010) 182 rooms, restaurant, lounge, entertainment, pool, a/c, TV, wheelchair access, NS rooms, complimentary newspaper, fax service, in-room refrigerators, in-room computer hookups, airport transportation, laundry facilities, meeting facilities, senior rates, CC. SGL/DBL$50-$125.

Red Lion Inn Riverside (2900 Chinden Blvd., 83714; 343-1870, 800-547-8010) 308 rooms, restaurant, lounge, entertainment, outdoor heated pool, exercise center, a/c, TV, wheelchair access, NS rooms, complimentary newspaper, airport transportation, in-room computer hookups, fax service, laundry facilities, meeting facilities, senior rates, CC. SGL/DBL$70-$350.

Residence Inn by Marriott (1401 Lusk, 83706; 344-1200, 800-331-3131) 104 suites, free breakfast, heated pool, exercise center, in-room refrigerators, coffee makers and microwaves, laundry facilities, TV, a/c, VCRs, pets OK, complimentary newspaper, fireplaces, children free with parents, NS rooms, wheelchair access, meeting facilities, CC. SGL/DBL$65-$115.

River Inn (1140 Colorado Ave., 83706; 344-9988) 88 rooms, outdoor heated pool, laundry facilities, in-room refrigerators, a/c, TV, wheelchair access, NS rooms, laundry facilities, kitchenettes, no pets, senior rates, CC. SGL/DBL$45-$55.

Rodeway Inn (1115 North Curtis Rd., 83706; 376-2700, 800-424-4777) 98 rooms, restaurant, free breakfast, lounge, entertainment, indoor and outdoor heated pool, whirlpools, sauna, wheelchair access, NS rooms, children free with parents, no pets, airport transportation, in-room refrigerators and coffee makers, a/c, TV, meeting facilities, senior rates, CC. SGL/DBL$56-$76.

Sands Motel (1111 West State St., 83702; 343-2533) 18 rooms, a/c, TV, CC. SGL/DBL$20-$30.

Shepp Ranch (Boise 83705; 343-7729) 6 rooms, restaurant, TV, meeting facilities for 16. SGL$145, DBL$290.

Shilo Inn Riverside (3031 Main St., 83702; 344-3521, Fax 344-0318, 800-222-2244) 112 rooms and suites, indoor heated pool, whirlpools, exercise center, airport courtesy car, in-room refrigerators, a/c, TV, NS rooms, wheelchair access, children under 12 free with parents, pets OK, VCRs, laundry, meeting facilities, senior rates, CC. SGL/DBL$60-$70.

Shilo Inn Airport (4111 Broadway Ave., 83705; 343-7662, 800-222-2244) 78 rooms and suites, heated pool, sauna, whirlpools, exercise center, a/c, in-room refrigerators and microwaves, VCRs, airport transportation, pets OK, TV, NS rooms, wheelchair access, children under 12 free with parents, meeting facilities, senior rates, CC. SGL/DBL$60-$70.

Sleep Inn (2799 Airport Way, 83705; 336-7377, 800-221-2222) 69 rooms, restaurant, free breakfast, wheelchair access, NS rooms, in-room refrigerators and coffee makers, VCRs, airport transportation, children under 18 free with parents, senior rates, a/c, TV, meeting facilities, no pets, CC. SGL/DBL$45-$57.

State Motel (1115 North 28th St., 83702; 344-7254) 11 rooms, a/c, TV, pets OK, CC. SGL/DBL$20-$35.

The Statehouse Inn (981 Grove St., 83702; 342-4622) 85 rooms, restaurant, free breakfast, lounge, whirlpools, sauna, in-room refrigerators, a/c, TV, laundry facilities, airport courtesy car, meeting facilities for 100, senior rates, CC. SGL/DBL$45-$55.

Sulphur Creek Ranch (7153 West Emerald, 83704; 377-1188) 7 rooms, TV, no pets, CC. SGL/DBL$55-$65.

Sunliner Motel (3433 Chinden Blvd., 83714; 344-7647) 25 rooms, a/c, pets OK, TV, CC. SGL/DBL$25-$40.

Sunrise Inn (2730 Sunrise Rim Rd., 83705; 344-0805) 2 rooms, free breakfast, TV, a/c, no pets, CC. SGL/DBL$30-$40.

Super 8 Motel (2773 Elder St., 83705; 344-8871, Fax 336-3237, 800-800-8000) 110 rooms and suites, indoor heated pool, pets OK, children under 12 free with parents, free local calls, a/c, TV, VCRs, airport transportation, in-room refrigerators and microwaves, fax service, NS rooms, wheelchair access, meeting facilities, senior rates, CC. SGL/DBL$40-$50.

Travellers Motel (5620 Fairview, 83706; 343-0571) 11 rooms, a/c, TV, CC. SGL/DBL$19-$23.

University Inn (2360 University Dr., 83706; 345-7170) 80 rooms and suites, restaurant, heated whirlpools, pool, a/c, TV, pets OK, children free with parents, airport transportation, wheelchair access, NS rooms, laundry facilities, senior rates, CC. SGL/DBL$30-$45.

Victoria's White House (10325 West Victory Rd., 83709; 362-0507) 2 rooms, TV. SGL/DBL$25-$65.

West River Inn (3525 Chinden Blvd., 83714; 342-3646) 21 rooms, a/c, pets OK, TV, CC. SGL/DBL$22-$44.

Bonners Ferry
Area Code 208

Best Western Kootenai River Inn (Kootenai River Plaza, 83805; 267-8511, Fax 267-8511, 800-528-1234) 47 rooms, restaurant, lounge, indoor heated pool, whirlpools, exercise center, in-room refrigerators and coffee makers, gift shop, children free with parents, a/c, NS rooms, TV, fireplaces, laundry facilities, wheelchair access, pets OK, meeting facilities, senior rates, CC. SGL/DBL$60-$89.

Bonners Ferry Log Inn (Bonners Ferry 83805; 267-3986) 22 rooms, whirlpools, TV, no pets, CC. SGL/DBL$40-$66.

Kootenai Valley Motel (Bonners Ferry 83805; 267-7567) 21 rooms and efficiencies, a/c, TV, wheelchair access, in-room refrigerators, pets OK, children free with parents, NS rooms, senior rates, CC. SGL/DBL$45-$70.

The Lantern Motel (Route 4, 83805; 267-2422) 24 rooms, restaurant, pool, a/c, TV, wheelchair access, NS rooms, laundry, pets OK, senior rates, meeting facilities for 75, CC. SGL/DBL$44-$64.

Sunnyside Motel (Bonners Ferry 83805; 267-3611) 9 rooms, a/c, TV, pets OK, CC. SGL/DBL$20-$50.

Town and Country Inn (Bonners Ferry 83805; 267-7915) 7 rooms, whirlpools, no pets, kitchenettes, CC. SGL/DBL$35-$60.

Valley Motel (South Hwy. 85, 83805; 267-7567) 21 rooms, restaurant, a/c, TV, CC. SGL/DBL$28-$45.

Buhl

Area Code 208

Oregon Trail Motel (510 South Broadway, 83316; 543-6974) 9 rooms, a/c, TV, CC. SGL/DBL$22-$39.

Burley

Area Code 208

Best Western Burley Inn and Convention Center (800 North Overland Ave., 83318; 678-3501, Fax 678-9532, 800-528-1234) 128 rooms, restaurant, lounge, outdoor heated pool, whirlpools, children free with parents, a/c, NS rooms, TV, laundry, wheelchair access, in-room refrigerators, no pets, meeting facilities, senior rates, CC. SGL/DBL$45-$63.

Budget Motel (900 North Overland Ave., 83318; 678-2200, 800-635-4952, 800-632-3569 in Idaho) 95 rooms, whirlpools, laundry facilities, a/c, TV, pets OK, CC. SGL/DBL$25-$40.

Evergreen Motel (635 West Main St., 83318; 678-0356) 13 rooms, a/c, pets OK, TV, CC. SGL/DBL$16-$25.

Greenwell Motel (904 East Main St., 83318; 678-5576) 30 rooms and 2-bedroom efficiencies, a/c, in-room refrigerators and coffee makers, pets OK, TV, CC. SGL/DBL$22-$44.

Lampliter Motel (304 East Main St., 83318; 678-0031) 15 rooms, a/c, pets OK, TV, CC. SGL/DBL$20-$40.

Parish Motel (721 East Main St., 83318; 678-5505) 15 rooms, a/c, TV, pets OK, CC. SGL/DBL$28-$36.

Powers Motel (703 East Main St., 83318; 678-5521) 15 rooms, a/c, TV, CC. SGL/DBL$18-$35.

Starlite Motel (510 Overland, 83318; 678-7766) 7 rooms, a/c, pets OK, TV, CC. SGL/DBL$20-$40.

Calder

Area Code 208

St. Joe Lodge and Resort (Route 3, 83808; 245-3462) 6 rooms, a/c, TV, wheelchair access, NS rooms, laundry facilities, senior rates, CC. SGL/DBL$25.

Caldwell
Area Code 208

Comfort Inn (901 Specht Ave., 83605; 765-5500, Fax 664-0433, 800-228-5150) 65 rooms, restaurant, lounge, indoor heated pool, exercise facilities, whirlpools, sauna, free local calls, in-room refrigerators and coffee makers, complimentary newspaper, kitchenettes, no pets, a/c, TV, CC. SGL/DBL$55-$82.

Holiday Motel (512 Frontage Rd., 83605; 454-3888) 24 rooms, restaurant, a/c, TV, pets OK, wheelchair access, NS rooms, laundry facilities, senior rates, CC. SGL/DBL$24-$31.

Sundowner Motel (1002 Arthur St., 83605; 459-1585, 800-459-1585) 69 rooms, pool, a/c, TV, in-room refrigerators and microwaves, no pets, CC. SGL/DBL$28-$48.

Cambridge
Area Code 208

Frontier Motel (Cambridge 83610; 257-3851) 9 rooms, a/c, pets OK, TV, CC. SGL/DBL$10-$35.

Cascade
Area Code 208

Aurora Motel (Cascade 83661; 382-4948) 10 rooms and efficiencies, kitchenettes, pets OK, children free with parents, laundry facilities, a/c, TV, pets OK, CC. SGL/DBL$30-$55.

Wapiti Meadow Ranch (Cascade 83611; 382-4336) free breakfast, TV, a/c, American plan available, private baths, no pets. SGL/DBL$85.

Challis
Area Code 208

Northgate Inn (Challis 83226; 879-2490) 56 rooms, a/c, in-room refrigerators and microwaves, airport transportation, pets OK, children free with parents, VCRs, TV, wheelchair access, NS rooms, senior rates, meeting facilities, CC. SGL/DBL$30-$40.

Village Inn (Challis 83226; 879-4426) 54 rooms and efficiencies, restaurant, a/c, TV, wheelchair access, NS rooms, in-room refrigerators, senior rates, meeting facilities, CC. SGL/DBL$30-$48.

Chubbuck
Area Code 208

Days Inn (133 West Burnside, 83202; 237-0020, Fax 237-3216, 800-325-2525) 115 rooms, restaurant, lounge, outdoor pool, a/c, TV, wheelchair access, NS rooms, no pets, laundry facilities, meeting facilities, senior rates, CC. SGL/DBL$43-$70.

Motel 6 (291 West Burnside Ave., 83202; 237-7880, 505-891-6161) 134 rooms, pool, free local calls, children under 17 free with parents, NS rooms, wheelchair access, pets OK, a/c, TV, CC. SGL/DBL$24-$32.

Nendels Inn (4333 Yellowstone Ave., 83202; 237-3100, Fax 238-0038) 101 rooms, restaurant, lounge, entertainment, pool, whirlpools, sauna, a/c, TV, children under 17 free with parents, pets OK, in-room refrigerators and microwaves, airport transportation, laundry facilities, senior rates, CC. SGL/DBL$35-$50.

Coeur d'Alene
Area Code 208

The Blackwell House (820 Sherman Ave., 83814; 664-0656) 8 rooms and suites, restaurant, free breakfast, a/c, TV, children free with parents, local transportation, wheelchair access, NS rooms, antique furnishings, 1904 home, modified American plan available, senior rates, CC. SGL/DBL$70-$120.

Comfort Inn (2808 West Appleway, 83814; 765-5500, Fax 664-0433, 800-228-5150) 51 rooms, restaurant, pool, whirlpools, exercise facilities, sauna, kitchenettes, free local calls, complimentary newspaper, fax service, a/c, TV, CC. SGL/DBL$65-$137.

Coeur d'Alene Resort (Coeur d'Alene 83814; 765-4000, 800-688-5253) 338 rooms and suites, restaurant, lounge, indoor and outdoor heated pool, exercise center, sauna, whirlpools, airport transportation, in-room refrigerators and coffee makers, children free with parents, no pets, boutiques, water view, a/c, TV, wheelchair access, NS rooms, senior rates, CC. SGL/DBL$85-$600.

Comfort Inn (280 West Appleway, 83814; 765-5500, 800-221-2222) 51 rooms and suites, heated pool, whirlpools, sauna, in-room refrigerators and microwaves, VCRs, children free with parents, pets OK, laundry facilities, a/c, TV, meeting facilities, senior rates, CC. SGL/DBL$50-$110.

Days Inn (2200 Northwest Blvd., 83814; 667-8668, Fax 765-0933, 800-325-2525) 61 rooms and suites, free breakfast, whirlpools, sauna, exercise center, pets OK, a/c, TV, wheelchair access, NS rooms, in-room refrigerators, VCRs, laundry facilities, meeting facilities, senior rates, CC. SGL/DBL$45-$60, STS$73.

El Ranch Motel (1915 East Sherman Ave., 83814; 664-8794) 14 rooms and 2-bedroom efficiencies, a/c, TV, in-room refrigerators, microwaves and coffee makers, pets OK, children free with parents, wheelchair access, NS rooms, senior rates, CC. SGL/DBL$26-$65.

Fairfield Inn by Marriott (2303 North 4th St., 83814; 664-1649, 800-228-2800) 69 rooms, indoor heated pool, children under 18 free with parents, NS rooms, free cable TV, free local calls, in-room computer hookups, no pets, laundry service, a/c, wheelchair access, meeting facilities, fax service, senior rates, CC. SGL/DBL$60-$99.

Flamingo Motel (718 Sherman Ave., 83814; 664-2159) 13 rooms and 2-bedroom efficiencies, heated pool, whirlpools, a/c, TV, wheelchair access, in-room coffee makers, pets OK, airport transportation, NS rooms, senior rates, CC. SGL/DBL$39-$96.

Garden Motel (1808 Northwest Blvd., 83814; 664-2743) 23 rooms and suites, indoor heated pool, whirlpools, a/c, TV, wheelchair access, NS rooms, senior rates, CC. SGL/DBL$50-$110.

Greenbriar Inn (315 Wallace, 83814; 667-9660) 8 rooms, free breakfast, TV, whirlpools, 1908 inn, modified American plan available, NS, no pets, CC. SGL/DBL$50-$90.

Holiday Inn (414 West Appleway, 83814; 765-3200, Fax 664-1962, 800-HOLIDAY) 122 rooms, restaurant, lounge, entertainment, outdoor pool, exercise facilities, children under 19 free with parents, wheelchair access, a/c, TV, NS rooms, fax service, room service, no pets, laundry service, limousine service, meeting facilities, senior rates, CC. SGL/DBL$55-$65.

Lake City Inn (330 West Appleway, 83814; 765-3011) 60 rooms and efficiencies, no pets, children free with parents, VCRs, a/c, TV, wheelchair access, NS rooms, senior rates, CC. SGL/DBL$30-$70.

Motel 6 (416 Appleway, 83814; 664-6600, 505-891-6161) outdoor pool, free local calls, children under 17 free with parents, NS rooms, wheelchair access, pets OK, a/c, TV, CC. SGL/DBL$28-$35.

Pines Resort Motel (1422 Northwest Blvd., 83814; 664-8244) 68 rooms and suites, indoor and outdoor heated pool, whirlpools, in-room computer hookups, a/c, TV, wheelchair access, children free with parents, pets OK, laundry facilities, in-room refrigerators, NS rooms, senior rates, CC. SGL/DBL$40-$95.

Shilo Inn (702 West Appleway, 83814; 664-2300, Fax 800-222-2244) 138 rooms and suites, restaurant, lounge, indoor heated pool, whirlpools, sauna, airport courtesy car, a/c, TV, NS rooms, wheelchair access, in-room refrigerators, children under 12 free with parents, pets OK, meeting facilities, senior rates, CC. SGL/DBL$75-$110.

Silver Lake Motel (6160 Sunshine St., 83814; 772-8595) 22 rooms and suites, outdoor heated pool, whirlpools, a/c, TV, wheelchair access, NS rooms, in-room refrigerators and microwaves, kitchenettes, senior rates, CC. SGL/DBL$44-$90.

Super 8 Motel (505 West Appleway, 83814; 765-8880, 800-800-8000) 95 rooms and suites, no pets, children under 12 free with parents, free local calls, a/c, VCRs, TV, in-room refrigerators and microwaves, fax service, NS rooms, wheelchair access, meeting facilities, senior rates, CC. SGL/DBL$35-$79.

Warwick Inn (303 Military Dr., 83814; 765-6565) 3 rooms, free breakfast, TV, no pets, water view, NS, CC. SGL/DBL$45-$55.

Driggs
Area Code 208

Best Western Teton West Inn (476 North Main St., 83422; 354-2363, Fax 354-2962, 800-528-1234) 42 rooms and efficiencies, free breakfast, indoor heated pool, whirlpools, children free with parents, a/c, NS rooms, TV, laundry facilities, wheelchair access, pets OK, meeting facilities, senior rates, CC. SGL/DBL$45-$100.

Emmett
Area Code 208

The Fly W (Emmett 83617; 365-4946) 4 rooms, restaurant, a/c, TV, pets OK. SGL/DBL$50-$225.

Gillihan's Lodge (850 Jackson Ave., 83617; 365-5384) 5 rooms, restaurant, TV, pets OK, meeting facilities for 20. SGL/DBL$35-$105.

Fish Haven
Area Code 208

Bear Lake Bed and Breakfast (550 Loveland Lane, 83287; 945-2688) free breakfast, a/c, no pets, TV, water view, CC. SGL/DBL$50-$60.

Garden City
Area Code 208

Seven K Motel (3633 Chinden Blvd., 83714; 343-7723) 23 rooms, a/c, TV, CC. SGL/DBL$20-$45.

Hailey

Area Code 208

Airport Inn (820 4th Ave. South, 83333; 788-2477) 29 rooms, whirlpools, pets OK, children free with parents, a/c, TV, wheelchair access, NS rooms, in-room refrigerators and microwaves, VCRs, kitchenettes, laundry facilities, airport transportation, senior rates, CC. SGL/DBL$50-$60.

Idaho Falls

Area Code 208

Best Western AmeriTel Inn (900 Lindsay Blvd., 83402; 523-6000, Fax 523-0000, 800-528-1234) 93 rooms, restaurant, lounge, free breakfast, indoor heated pool, exercise center, spa, children free with parents, a/c, NS rooms, TV, laundry facilities, free local calls, airport courtesy car, wheelchair access, pets OK, meeting facilities, senior rates, CC. SGL/DBL$60-$73.

Best Western Driftwood Motel (575 River Pkwy., 83405; 523-2242, 800-528-1234) 74 rooms, restaurant, lounge, outdoor pool, exercise room, children free with parents, a/c, NS rooms, TV, in-room refrigerators, microwaves and coffee makers, kitchenettes, laundry facilities, wheelchair access, pets OK, meeting rooms, senior rates, CC. SGL/DBL$48-$70.

Best Western Stardust Motor Lodge (700 Lindsay Blvd., 83402; 522-2910, Fax 529-8361, 800-528-1234) 249 rooms, restaurant, free breakfast, lounge, entertainment, exercise room, in-room coffee makers, children free with parents, a/c, NS rooms, TV, laundry facilities, wheelchair access, no pets, meeting facilities, senior rates, CC. SGL/DBL$49-$100.

Comfort Inn (195 South Colorado Ave., 83402; 528-2804, 800-228-5150) 56 rooms, pool, a/c, TV, CC. SGL/DBL$45-$65.

Holiday Inn Westbank (475 River Pkwy., 83402; 523-8000, 800-432-1005, 800-HOLIDAY) 198 rooms, restaurant, lounge, pool, exercise facilities, children under 19 free with parents, wheelchair access, a/c, TV, NS rooms, fax service, room service, pets OK, laundry service, meeting facilities, senior rates, CC. SGL/DBL$50-$85.

Little Tree Inn (888 North Holmes, 83401; 523-5993) 92 rooms, restaurant, lounge, entertainment, heated pool, exercise center, whirlpools, airport transportation, a/c, TV, pets OK, children free with parents, wheelchair access, NS rooms, laundry facilities, in-room refrigerators and microwaves, senior rates, CC. SGL/DBL$50-$66.

Motel 6 (1448 Broadway, 83402; 522-0112, 505-891-6161) 80 rooms, restaurant, pool, free local calls, children under 17 free with parents, NS rooms, wheelchair access, pets OK, a/c, TV, CC. SGL/DBL$28-$35.

Quality Inn (850 Lindsay Blvd., 83402; 523-6260, Fax 522-8840, 800-221-2222) 127 rooms and suites, restaurant, lounge, entertainment, pool, exercise facilities, children free with parents, a/c, TV, pets OK, fax service, room service, laundry service, NS rooms, meeting facilities, senior rates, CC. SGL/DBL$40-$65.

Shilo Inn (780 Lindsay Blvd., 83402; 523-0088, 800-222-2244) 161 rooms and suites, restaurant, lounge, indoor heated pool, sauna, whirlpools, exercise center, pets OK, laundry facilities, airport courtesy car, in-room refrigerators, a/c, TV, NS rooms, wheelchair access, children under 12 free with parents, meeting facilities, senior rates, CC. SGL/DBL$90-$105.

Super 8 Motel (705 Lindsay Blvd., 522-8880, 800-800-8000) 92 rooms and suites, children under 12 free with parents, free local calls, a/c, TV, in-room refrigerators and microwaves, fax service, NS rooms, pets OK, wheelchair access, meeting facilities, senior rates, CC. SGL/DBL$37-$42.

Towne Lodge (255 E St., 83402; 523-2960) 40 rooms, laundry facilities, no pets, a/c, TV, senior rates, CC. SGL/DBL$28-$50.

Indian Valley
Area Code 208

Indian Valley Inn (Indian Valley 83632; 256-4423) 7 rooms, TV, CC. SGL/DBL$25-$35.

Irwin
Area Code 208

Swan Valley Bed and Breakfast (Irwin 83428; 483-4663, 800-241-SWAN) 4 rooms, free breakfast, TV, a/c, no pets, fireplace, CC. SGL/DBL$85

Kellogg
Area Code 208

Silverhorn Motel (699 West Cameron, 83837; 783-1151, 800-437-6437) 40 rooms, restaurant, a/c, TV, pets OK, laundry facilities, room service, gift shop, wheelchair access, NS rooms, senior rates, CC. SGL/DBL$50-$60.

Ketchum
Area Code 208

Bald Mountain Lodge (151 South Main St., 83340; 726-9963) 20 rooms and 2-bedroom suites, kitchenettes, TV, wheelchair access, NS rooms, senior rates, CC. SGL/DBL$65-$85.

Best Western Christiania Lodge (651 Sun Valley Rd., 83340; 726-3351, Fax 726-3055, 800-528-1234) 38 rooms, free breakfast, pool, sauna, kitchenettes, fireplaces, children free with parents, a/c, NS rooms, TV, laundry facilities, wheelchair access, pets OK, meeting facilities, senior rates, CC. SGL/DBL$60-$85.

Best Western Tyrolean Lodge (Cottonwood and 3rd Ave., 83340; 726-5336, Fax 726-2081, 800-528-1234) 56 rooms, free breakfast, spa, children free with parents, a/c, NS rooms, TV, laundry facilities, wheelchair access, pets OK, meeting facilities, senior rates, CC. SGL/DBL$70-$115.

Christopher Condo Hotel (351 2nd Ave. South, 83340; 726-5601, Fax 726-5617) 40 rooms and 2-bedroom suites, pool, whirlpools, TV, wheelchair access, NS rooms, kitchenettes, airport transportation, no pets, laundry facilities, children free with parents, senior rates, CC. SGL/DBL$60-$110.

Heidelberg Inn (1908 Warm Springs Rd., 83340; 726-5361) 30 rooms and suites, heated pool, whirlpools, sauna, TV, wheelchair access, laundry facilities, in-room refrigerators, microwaves and coffee makers, NS rooms, senior rates, CC. SGL/DBL$55-$115.

The Idaho Country Inn (134 Latigo Lane, 83353; 726-1019) 10 rooms, whirlpools, a/c, TV, wheelchair access, NS, senior rates, CC. SGL/DBL$85-$185.

Pinnacle Club Inn (100 Lloyd Dr., 83352; 726-5700) 9 rooms, restaurant, TV, wheelchair access, NS rooms, kitchenettes, no pets, in-room refrigerators, kitchenettes, VCRs, senior rates, CC. SGL/DBL$80-$150.

Sun Valley's Elkhorn Resort (Eklhorn Rd., 83354; 622-4511) 132 rooms and suites, restaurant, lounge, pool, a/c, TV, pets OK, laundry facilities, wheelchair access, NS rooms, senior rates, CC. SGL/DBL$58-$328.

Tamarack Lodge (291 Walnut Ave., 83353; 726-3344) 26 rooms, indoor heated pool, whirlpools, children free with parents, a/c, TV, wheelchair access, no pets, fireplaces, NS rooms, senior rates, CC. SGL/DBL$70-$115.

Lava Hot Springs

Area Code 208

Aladdin Bed and Breakfast (68 West Main St., 83246; 776-5288) 5 suites, free breakfast, hot tubs, a/c, TV, no pets, CC. SGL/DBL$45-$55.

Berti's Apartments (Lava Hot Springs, 83246; 776-5288) 6 1- and 2-bedroom apartments, a/c, kitchenettes, TV, no pets, CC. SGL/DBL$45-$66.

Dempsey Creek Townhouses (Lava Hot Springs, 83246; 776-5000) 16 1- and 2-bedroom apartments, kitchenettes, a/c, TV, CC. SGL/DBL$50-$60.

E-Z Livin' Inn (189 East Main St., 83246; 776-5407, Fax 776-5477) 7 1- and 2-bedroom apartments, TV, CC. SGL/DBL$50-$70.

Home Hotel and Motel (306 East Main St., 83246; 776-5507) 16 rooms, a/c, TV, no pets, wheelchair access, NS rooms, senior rates, CC. SGL/DBL$36-$38.

Hot Springs Village Condominiums (Hwy. 30, 83246; 776-5445) 34 1- and 2-bedroom condominiums, a/c, kitchenettes, TV, no pets, CC. SGL/DBL$60-$80.

Idaho Apartments (63 South First St., 83246; 776-5627) 11 1- and 2-bedroom apartments, a/c, fireplaces, hot tubs, game room, laundry facilities, TV, kitchenettes, no pets, CC. SGL/DBL$45-$55.

Kivi Lodge (Lava Hot Springs 83246; 776-5219) 36 rooms, a/c, TV, no pets, CC. SGL/DBL$36-$66.

Lava Hot Springs Inn (5 Portneuf Ave., 83246; 776-5830) 5 rooms, free breakfast, TV, 1930s inn, kitchenettes, water view, meeting facilities, CC. SGL/DBL$60-$75.

Lava Ranch Inn Motel (9611 Hwy. 30, 83246; 776-9917) 11 rooms, TV, kitchenettes, CC. SGL/DBL$38-$44.

Lava Spa Motel (359 East Main St., 83246; 776-5589) 8 rooms, jacuzzi, a/c, TV, CC. SGL/DBL$28-$36.

Oregon Trail Lodge (Lava Hot Springs 83246; 776-5050, 800-433-8910) 6 rooms, jacuzzi, a/c, TV, no pets, CC. SGL/DBL$45-$70.

Ranch Inn Motel (Lava Hot Springs 83246; 776-9917) 15 rooms, a/c, kitchenettes, TV, no pets, CC. SGL/DBL$45-$55.

Riverside Inn and Hot Springs (225 Portneuf Ave., 83246; 776-5504, 800-733-5504) 16 rooms, free breakfast, hot tubs, no pets, laundry facilities, game room, CC. SGL/DBL$35-$86.

Royal Inn (Lava Hot Springs 83246; 776-5216) 6 rooms, free breakfast, TV, a/c, antique furnishings, CC. SGL/DBL$60-$80.

Lewiston

Area Code 208

Pony Soldier Motor Inn (1716 Main St., 83501; 743-9526) 66 rooms and 2-bedroom suites, heated pool, whirlpools, in-room computer hookups, a/c, TV, wheelchair access, in-room refrigerators, NS rooms, senior rates, CC. SGL/DBL$53-$66.

Ramada Inn (621 21st St., 83501; 799-1000, 800-2-RAMADA) 136 rooms and suites, restaurant, lounge, pool, wheelchair access, NS rooms, free parking, pets OK, a/c, TV, children under 18 free with parents, room service, laundry facilities, airport transportation, in-room refrigerators and microwaves, meeting facilities, senior rates, CC. SGL/DBL$75-$105.

Sacajawea Motor Inn (1824 Main St. South, 83501; 746-1393) 90 rooms and 2-bedroom suites, restaurant, lounge, heated pool, whirlpools, a/c, TV, wheelchair access, NS rooms, in-room refrigerators and microwaves, VCRs, pets OK, meeting facilities, senior rates, CC. SGL/DBL$40-$50.

Super 8 Motel (3120 North South Hwy., 83501; 743-8808, Fax 743-8808, 800-800-8000) 62 rooms and suites, no pets, children under 12 free with parents, free local calls, a/c, TV, laundry facilities, VCRs, in-room refrigerators and microwaves, fax service, NS rooms, wheelchair access, meeting facilities, senior rates, CC. SGL/DBL$40-$50.

Tapadera Motor Inn (1325 Main St., 83501; 746-3311) 78 rooms, lounge, in-room computer hookups, a/c, TV, wheelchair access, NS rooms, pets OK, in-room refrigerators, senior rates, CC. SGL/DBL$40-$60.

McCall

Area Code 208

McCall Hotel (1101 North 3rd St., 83638; 634-8105) 22 rooms, water view, TV, wheelchair access, NS rooms, airport transportation, VCRs, no pets, senior rates, CC. SGL/DBL$55-$115.

Riverside Motel and Condominiums (400 West Lake St., 83638; 634-5610, Fax 634-4084) 29 rooms and 2-bedroom condominiums, TV, wheelchair access, NS rooms, kitchenettes, airport transportation, senior rates, CC. SGL/DBL$40-$48.

Scandia Inn Motel (401 North 3rd St., 83838; 634-7394) 16 rooms, no pets, TV, wheelchair access, NS rooms, senior rates, CC. SGL/DBL$40-$50.

Shore Lodge (501 West Lake St., 83638; 634-2244, 800-657-6464) 116 rooms and suites, restaurant, lounge, pool, whirlpool tub, sauna, exercise center, a/c, TV, wheelchair access, NS rooms, children free with parents, room service, local transportation, water view, meeting facilities, senior rates, CC. SGL/DBL$55-$135, STS$135-$200.

Montpelier
Area Code 208

Best Western Crest Motel (243 North 4th St., 83254; 847-1782, Fax 847-3519, 800-528-1234) 65 rooms and suites, restaurant, lounge, exercise facilities, children free with parents, a/c, NS rooms, TV, in-room refrigerators and coffee makers, laundry facilities, wheelchair access, pets OK, meeting facilities, senior rates, CC. SGL/DBL$48-$66.

Budget Motel (240 North 4th St., 83254; 847-1273) a/c, TV, kitchenettes, CC. SGL/DBL$26-$32.

Michelle Motel (601 North 4th St., 847-1772) 10 rooms, outdoor heated pool, TV, wheelchair access, NS rooms, senior rates, pets OK, laundry facilities, CC. SGL/DBL$35-$45.

Park Motel (745 Washington, 83254; 847-1911) 25 rooms, in-room refrigerators and microwaves, pets OK, a/c, TV, wheelchair access, NS rooms, senior rates, CC. SGL/DBL$26-$50.

Moscow
Area Code 208

Best Western University Inn (1516 Pullman Rd., 83843; 882-0550, Fax 883-3056, 800-528-1234) 173 rooms, restaurant, lounge, indoor heated pool, exercise facilities, sauna, jacuzzi, children free with parents, a/c, NS rooms, TV, laundry facilities, wheelchair access, pets OK, meeting facilities for 600, senior rates, CC. SGL/DBL$70-$99.

Hillcrest Motel (706 North Main St., 83843; 882-7579) 50 rooms, outdoor heated pool, a/c, TV, wheelchair access, NS rooms, in-room refrigerators, senior rates, CC. SGL/DBL$31-$41.

Mark IV Motor Inn (414 North Main St., 83843; 882-7557) 86 rooms and 1- and 2-bedroom suites, restaurant, lounge, indoor heated pool, a/c, TV, wheelchair access, NS rooms, airport transportation, in-room refrigerators, pets OK, senior rates, CC. SGL/DBL$30-$55.

Motel 6 (101 Baker St., 83843; 882-5511, 505-891-6161) 110 rooms, pool, free local calls, children under 17 free with parents, NS rooms, wheelchair access, pets OK, a/c, TV, CC. SGL/DBL$26-$34.

Super 8 Motel (175 Peterson Dr., 83843; 883-1503, 800-800-8000) 61 rooms and suites, pets OK, children under 12 free with parents, free local calls, a/c, TV, in-room refrigerators and microwaves, fax service, NS rooms, wheelchair access, meeting facilities, senior rates, CC. SGL/DBL$33-$46.

Mountain Home

Area Code 509

Best Western Foothills Motor Inn (1080 Hwy. 20, 83647; 587-8477, 800-528-1234) 76 rooms, restaurant, lounge, hot tub, sauna, children free with parents, a/c, NS rooms, TV, laundry facilities, wheelchair access, pets OK, meeting facilities, senior rates, CC. SGL/DBL$40-$70.

Hilander Motel (615 South 3rd West, 83647; 587-3311) 34 rooms and efficiencies, restaurant, lounge, pets OK, a/c, TV, wheelchair access, NS rooms, senior rates, CC. SGL/DBL$25-$38.

Motel Thunderbird (910 Sunset Strip, 83647; 587-7927) 27 rooms and efficiencies, pets OK, a/c, TV, wheelchair access, NS rooms, senior rates, CC. SGL/DBL$20-$45.

Rosestone Inn (495 North 3rd East, 83647; 587-8866) 5 rooms, free breakfast, TV, a/c, pets OK, NS, CC. SGL/DBL$35-$65.

Sleep Inn (1180 Hwy. 20, 83647; 587-9743, 800-221-2222) 60 rooms, a/c, TV, wheelchair access, children free with parents, pets OK, NS rooms, complimentary newspaper, in-room refrigerators and coffee makers, VCRs, TV, a/c, senior rates, CC. SGL/DBL$40-$45.

Towne Center Motel (410 North 2nd East, 83647; 587-3373, 800-529-3373) 31 rooms, pool, pets OK, a/c, TV, wheelchair access, NS rooms, senior rates, CC. SGL/DBL$25-$38.

Nampa

Area Code 208

Desert Inn (115 9th Ave. South, 83651; 467-1161) 40 rooms, pool, children free with parents, pets OK, in-room refrigerators and microwaves, a/c, TV, wheelchair access, NS rooms, senior rates, CC. SGL/DBL$40-$44.

Shilo Inn (617 Nampa Blvd., 83687; 466-8993, 800-222-2244) 61 rooms and suites, outdoor pool, whirlpools, sauna, airport courtesy car, a/c, TV, NS rooms, wheelchair access, VCRs, pets OK, in-room refrigerators and microwaves, children under 12 free with parents, meeting facilities, senior rates, CC. SGL/DBL$50-$70.

Shilo Inn Suites (1401 Shilo Dr., 83687; 465-3250, Fax 465-5929, 800-222-2244) 83 suites, restaurant, lounge, indoor heated pool, exercise center, whirlpools, sauna, airport courtesy car, a/c, TV, NS rooms, wheelchair access, in-room refrigerators and microwaves, airport transportation, room service, children under 12 free with parents, meeting facilities, senior rates, CC. SGL/DBL$68-$75.

Nordman

Area Code 208

Grandview Resort (Nordman 83848; 443-2433) 1- to 5-bedroom condominiums, restaurant, lounge, heated pool, water view, kitchenettes, no pets, laundry facilities, fireplaces, TV, wheelchair access, NS rooms, senior rates, CC. SGL/DBL$470-$865.

Pocatello

Area Code 208

Best Western Cottontree Inn (1415 Bench Rd., 83201; 237-7650, 800-528-1234) 147 rooms, restaurant, lounge, kitchenettes, indoor heated pool, exercise facilities, jacuzzi, children free with parents, a/c, NS rooms, kitchenettes, TV, laundry facilities, wheelchair access, pets OK, meeting facilities, senior rates, CC. SGL/DBL$55-$75.

Best Western Weston Inn (745 South 5th Ave., 83201; 233-5530, 800-528-1234) 55 rooms, restaurant, free breakfast, indoor heated pool, exercise center, children free with parents, a/c, NS rooms, TV, laundry facilities, wheelchair access, pets OK, meeting facilities, senior rates, CC. SGL/DBL$36-$48.

Comfort Inn (1333 Bench Rd., 83201; 237-8155, 800-228-5150) 52 rooms and suites, free breakfast, indoor heated pool, whirlpools, children free with parents, pets OK, a/c, TV, CC. SGL/DBL$43-$65.

Howard Johnson Hotel (1399 Bench Rd., 83201; 237-1400, Fax 238-0225, 800-I-GO-HOJO) 203 rooms, restaurant, lounge, entertainment, indoor heated pool, sauna, exercise center, children free with parents, wheelchair access, NS rooms, TV, a/c, airport transportation, fax service, complimentary newspaper, no pets, laundry facilities, senior rates, meeting facilities, CC. SGL/DBL$52-$66.

Imperial 400 Motel (1055 South 5th Ave., 83201; 233-5120) 28 rooms and efficiencies, heated pool, in-room refrigerators and microwaves, a/c, TV, wheelchair access, NS rooms, senior rates, CC. SGL/DBL$25-$35.

Sundial Inn (835 South 5th St., 83201; 233-0451) 53 rooms, restaurant, children free with parents, a/c, TV, wheelchair access, NS rooms, no pets, senior rates, CC. SGL/DBL$30-$38.

Super 8 Motel (1330 Bench Rd., 83210; 234-0888, 800-800-8000) 51 rooms and suites, no pets, children under 12 free with parents, free local calls, a/c, TV, in-room refrigerators and microwaves, fax service, NS rooms, wheelchair access, fax service, meeting facilities, senior rates, CC. SGL/DBL$38-$44.

Thunderbird Motel (1415 South 5th Ave., 83210; 232-6330) 45 rooms, heated pool, pets OK, a/c, TV, beauty shop, laundry facilities, CC. SGL/DBL$25-$38.

Post Falls

Area Code 208

Riverbend Inn (4104 Riverbend Ave., 83854; 773-3583, Fax 773-1306) 71 rooms, free breakfast, heated pool, whirlpools, children free with parents, no pets, a/c, TV, wheelchair access, NS rooms, laundry facilities, senior rates, CC. SGL/DBL$60-$70.

Suntree Inn (3705 5th Ave., 83854; 773-4541) 100 rooms, indoor heated pool, whirlpools, a/c, TV, wheelchair access, NS rooms, laundry facilities, children free with parents, pets OK, senior rates, CC. SGL/DBL$50-$62.

Priest Lake

Area Code 208

Hills Resort (Priest Lake 83856; 443-2551, Fax 443-2363) 51 rooms, cottages and apartments, tennis courts, laundry facilities, kitchenettes, a/c, TV, wheelchair access, NS rooms, pets OK, water view, senior rates, CC. SGL/DBL$600W-$1,600W.

Rexburg

Area Code 208

Best Western Cottontree Inn (450 West 4th South, 83440; 356-4646, 800-528-1234) 101 rooms, indoor heated pool, exercise facilities, children free with parents, a/c, NS rooms, TV, VCRs, laundry facilities, wheelchair access, pets OK, meeting facilities, senior rates, CC. SGL/DBL$53-$72.

Days Inn (271 South 2nd St. West, 83440; 356-9222, 800-325-2525) 42 rooms, heated pool, a/c, TV, wheelchair access, NS rooms, children free with parents, pets OK, laundry facilities, senior rates, CC. SGL/DBL$38-$55.

Ririe

Area Code 208

Granite Creek Guest Ranch (Ririe 83443; 525-1104) a/c, TV, no pets, wheelchair access, American plan available, CC. SGL/DBL$975W-$1,800W.

Saint Anthony
Area Code 208

Best Western Weston Inn (115 South Bridge St., 83445; 624-3711, 800-528-1234) 31 rooms, restaurant, children free with parents, a/c, NS rooms, TV, laundry facilities, wheelchair access, pets OK, meeting facilities, senior rates, CC. SGL/DBL$36-$55.

Salmon
Area Code 208

Motel DeLuxe (112 South Church St., 83467; 756-2231) 25 rooms and 2-bedroom efficiencies, a/c, TV, wheelchair access, pets OK, children free with parents, in-room refrigerators and microwaves, airport transportation, in-room computer hookups, NS rooms, senior rates, CC. SGL/DBL$25-$38.

Stagecoach Inn (201 Hwy. 93 North, 83467; 756-4251) 100 rooms, outdoor heated pool, children free with parents, a/c, TV, wheelchair access, no pets, laundry facilities, airport transportation, in-room computer hookups, NS rooms, meeting facilities, senior rates, CC. SGL/DBL$41-$69.

Suncrest Motel (705 Challis St., 83467; 756-2294) 20 rooms and efficiencies, airport transportation, kitchenettes, a/c, TV, wheelchair access, NS rooms, senior rates, CC. SGL/DBL$28-$38.

Williams Lake Resort (Salmon 83467; 756-2007) 26 rooms and condominiums, restaurant, lounge, TV, wheelchair access, NS rooms, kitchenettes, pets OK, children free with parents, water view, airport transportation, senior rates, CC. SGL/DBL$26-$100.

Sandpoint
Area Code 208

Best Western Connie's Motor Inn (323 Cedar St., 83664; 263-9581, Fax 263-3395, 800-528-1234) 53 rooms, restaurant, lounge, outdoor pool, exercise facilities, jacuzzi, children free with parents, a/c, NS rooms, TV, laundry facilities, wheelchair access, pets OK, meeting facilities, senior rates, CC. SGL/DBL$57-$150.

Bottle Bay Resort (1360 Bottle Bay Rd., 83864; 263-5916) 6 rooms, wheelchair access, pets OK, laundry facilities, NS rooms, senior rates, CC. SGL/DBL$400W-$550W.

Edgewater Resort Inn (56 Bridge St., 83864; 263-3194) 55 rooms and 1- and 2-bedroom condominiums, restaurant, lounge, whirlpools, sauna, a/c, TV, wheelchair access, NS rooms, meeting facilities, senior rates, CC. SGL/DBL$45-$120.

Lakeside Inn (106 Bridge St., 83864; 263-3717, 800-543-8126) 60 rooms and efficiencies, laundry facilities, pets OK, children free with parents, water view, a/c, VCRs, TV, wheelchair access, NS rooms, senior rates, CC. SGL/DBL$35-$90.

Monarch West Inn (Sandpoint 83864; 263-1222) 49 rooms and efficiencies, sauna, whirlpool bus, a/c, TV, VCRs, in-room refrigerators and micro-waves, laundry facilities, water view, wheelchair access, NS rooms, senior rates, CC. SGL/DBL$36-$90.

Quality Inn (807 North 5th Ave., 83864; 263-2111, 800-221-2222) 57 rooms and suites, restaurant, lounge, indoor heated pool, exercise facilities, whirlpools, children free with parents, water view, pets OK, a/c, TV, room service, laundry service, NS rooms, meeting facilities, senior rates, CC. SGL/DBL$40-$88.

Super 8 Motel (3245 Hwy. 95 North, 83864; 263-2210, 800-800-8000) 61 rooms and suites, no pets, children under 12 free with parents, free local calls, a/c, TV, in-room refrigerators and microwaves, fax service, NS rooms, wheelchair access, meeting facilities, senior rates, CC. SGL/DBL$35-$60.

Williams Lake Resort (Salmon 83467; 756-2007) a/c, TV, wheelchair access, NS rooms, senior rates, CC. SGL/DBL$40-$60.

Shoup
Area Code 208

Smith House Bed and Breakfast (49 Salmon River Rd., 83469; 394-2121) 5 rooms, free breakfast, TV, a/c, hot tub, NS, private baths, gift shop, no pets, CC. SGL/DBL$35-$65.

Stanley
Area Code 208

Mountain Village Lodge (Stanley 83278; 774-3661, 800-843-5475) 60 rooms and suites, restaurant, lounge, entertainment, laundry facilities, no pets, a/c, TV, wheelchair access, NS rooms, senior rates, CC. SGL/DBL$45-$65, STS$85-$128.

Idaho Rocky Mountain Ranch (Stanley 83278; 774-3544) 13 rooms and cabins, free breakfast, restaurant, laundry facilities, a/c, TV, wheelchair access, NS rooms, senior rates, CC. SGL/DBL$70-$125.

Sun Valley
Area Code 208

Clarion Hotel (Sun Valley 83354; 726-5900, Fax 726-3761, 800-221-2222) 58 rooms and suites, restaurant, lounge, free breakfast, no pets, NS rooms, children under 18 free with parents, room service, airport transportation, fireplaces, senior rates, meeting facilities, a/c, TV, CC. SGL/DBL$90-$175.

Idaho Country Inn (Sun Valley 83353; 726-1019, Fax 726-5718) 10 rooms, free breakfast, whirlpools, fireplaces, a/c, TV, wheelchair access, NS, senior rates, CC. SGL/DBL$125-$155.

Radisson Resort (Elkhorn Rd., 83354; 622-4511, Fax 622-3261, 800-333-3333) 220 rooms and suites, restaurant, lounge, entertainment, indoor and outdoor heated pool, exercise center, whirlpools, sauna, in-room refrigerators, microwaves and coffee makers, children free with parents, VCRs, wheelchair access, airport transportation, free parking, NS rooms, TV, a/c, children free with parents, pets OK, senior rates, CC. SGL/DBL$60-$390.

River Street Inn (Sun Valley 83353; 726-3611) 9 rooms and suites, free breakfast, hot tubs, TV, a/c, NS, private baths, in-room refrigerators, NS, pets OK, CC. SGL/DBL$95-$165.

Sun Valley Inn (1 Sun Valley Rd., 83353; 622-4111) 110 rooms and suites, restaurant, entertainment, heated pool, exercise center, a/c, TV, no pets, kitchenettes, in-room refrigerators and microwaves, airport transportation, laundry facilities, wheelchair access, NS rooms, senior rates, meeting facilities, CC. SGL/DBL$65-$150.

Sun Valley Lodge and Apartments (Sun Valley 83353; 622-411) 272 rooms and apartments, restaurant, lounge, indoor and outdoor pool, sauna, whirlpools, tennis courts, in-room refrigerators, VCRs, a/c, TV, wheelchair access, NS rooms, meeting facilities, senior rates, CC. SGL/DBL$65-$125.

Sun Valley Resort (Sun Valley 83353; 622-4111, 800-786-8259) 353 rooms and condominiums, restaurant, lounge, entertainment, indoor and outdoor heated pool, tennis courts, sauna, barber and beauty shop, gift shop, a/c, TV, wheelchair access, laundry facilities, no pets, in-room refrigerators, fireplaces, airport transportation, children free with parents, NS rooms, meeting facilities, senior rates, CC. SGL/DBL$100-$345.

Tamarack Lodge (Sun Valley 83353; 726-3344, Fax 726-3347, 800-521-5279) 26 rooms and suites, indoor heated pool, whirlpools, a/c, TV, in-room refrigerators and coffee makers, no pets, children free with parents, wheelchair access, NS rooms, senior rates, CC. SGL/DBL$90, STS$115-$136.

Swan Valley

Area Code 208

Hansen-Silver Guest Ranch (Swan Valley 83449; 483-2305) free breakfast, TV, a/c, no pets, CC. SGL/DBL$48-$68.

Tetonia

Area Code 208

Teton Ridge Ranch (200 Valley View Rd., 83452; 456-2650) 7 rooms and cottages, a/c, TV, children free with parents, pets OK, game room, airport transportation, American plan available, wheelchair access, NS rooms, senior rates, CC. SGL/DBL$300-$400.

Twin Falls

Area Code 208

Ameritel Inn (1377 Blue Lakes Blvd., 83301; 736-8000, Fax 734-7777, 800-822-8946) 88 roms and suites, restaurant, free breakfast, indoor heated pool, exercise center, laundry facilities, airport courtesy car, children free with parents, a/c, TV, wheelchair access, NS rooms, no pets, meeting facilities, senior rates, CC. SGL/DBL$60-$90.

Best Western Apollo Motor Inn (296 Addison Ave. West, 83301; 733-2010, 800-528-1234) 50 rooms, free breakfast, children free with parents, a/c, NS rooms, TV, laundry facilities, wheelchair access, pets OK, meeting facilities, senior rates, CC. SGL/DBL$38-$50.

Best Western Canyon Springs Inn (1357 Blue Lakes Blvd. North, 83301; 734-5000, 800-528-1234) 112 rooms, restaurant, lounge, outdoor pool, children free with parents, a/c, NS rooms, TV, laundry facilities, wheelchair access, airport transportation, pets OK, meeting facilities, senior rates, CC. SGL/DBL$56-$72.

Capri Motel (1341 Kimberly Rd., 83301; 733-6452) 23 rooms and efficiencies, a/c, TV, wheelchair access, NS rooms, no pets, senior rates, CC. SGL/DBL$25-$35.

Comfort Inn (1893 Canyon Springs Rd., 83301; 734-7494, 800-228-5150) 52 rooms and suites, free breakfast, indoor heated pool, whirlpools, pets OK, in-room refrigerators and microwaves, children under 18 free with parents, a/c, TV, CC. SGL/DBL$44-$66.

Econo Lodge (320 Main Ave. South, 83301; 733-8770, 800-4-CHOICE) 39 rooms, pool, children under 12 free with parents, no pets, senior rates, NS rooms, wheelchair access, a/c, TV, senior rates, CC. SGL/DBL$38-$60.

Monterey Motor Inn (433 Addison Ave., West, 83301; 733-5151) 28 rooms and efficiencies, outdoor heated pool, whirlpools, in-room refrigerators and microwaves, laundry facilities, a/c, TV, wheelchair access, NS rooms, senior rates, CC. SGL/DBL$25-$38.

Motel 6 (1472 Blue Lake Blvd. North, 83301; 734-3993, 505-891-6161) 157 rooms, pool, free local calls, children under 17 free with parents, NS rooms, wheelchair access, pets OK, a/c, TV, CC. SGL/DBL$26-$34.

Super 8 Motel (1260 Blue Lake Blvd. North, 83301; 734-5801, Fax 734-7556, 800-800-8000) 94 rooms and suites, exercise center, no pets, children under 12 free with parents, free local calls, a/c, TV, in-room refrigerators and microwaves, fax service, NS rooms, wheelchair access, meeting facilities, senior rates, CC. SGL/DBL$38-$48.

Weston Inn (906 Blue Lakes Blvd., 83301; 733-0650, Fax 733-8272) 203 rooms and suites, restaurant, lounge, heated pool, whirlpools, exercise center, sauna, in-room refrigerators, airport transportation, children free with parents, a/c, TV, wheelchair access, NS rooms, no pets, senior rates, CC. SGL/DBL$45-$53.

Wallace

Area Code 208

Best Western Wallace Inn (100 Front St., 83873; 752-1252, Fax 753-0981, 800-528-1234) 63 rooms, restaurant, lounge, indoor heated sauna, pool, exercise facilities, children free with parents, a/c, NS rooms, TV, laundry facilities, wheelchair access, pets OK, meeting facilities, senior rates, CC. SGL/DBL$58-$106.

Stardust Motel (410 Pine St., 83873; 752-1213) 43 rooms and efficiencies, a/c, TV, wheelchair access, NS rooms, kitchenettes, senior rates, CC. SGL/DBL$70-$79.

Weiser

Area Code 208

Indianhead Motel (747 Hwy. 95, 83672; 549-0331) 9 rooms and efficiencies, a/c, TV, laundry facilities, NS rooms, CC. SGL/DBL$30-$44.

Montana

Rental and Reservation Services:

Bed and Breakfast Western Adventure (806 Pooly Dr., 59104; 406-259-7993) bed and breakfast reservations.

Alberton
Area Code 406

River Edge Motel (Alberton 59820; 722-4418) 10 rooms, a/c, TV, pets OK, senior rates, CC. SGL/DBL$25-$50.

Anaconda
Area Code 406

Fairmont Hot Springs Resort (1500 Fairmont Rd., 59711; 797-3241) 153 rooms and suites, restaurant, lounge, entertainment, indoor and outdoor heated pools, exercise center, whirlpools, tennis courts, room service, game room, a/c, TV, VCRs, no pets, airport transportation, laundry facilities, kitchenettes, wheelchair access, NS rooms, senior rates, CC. SGL/DBL$65-$85.

Apgar
Area Code 406

Apgar Village Lodge (Apgar 59936; 888-5484) 48 rooms and 1- to 3-bedroom suites, TV, pets OK, kitchenettes, wheelchair access, NS rooms, senior rates, CC. SGL/DBL$55-$200.

Belgrade
Area Code 406

DJ Bar Ranch (5155 Round Mountain Rd., 59714; 388-7483) 3-bedroom home, hot tub, TV, CC. SGL/DBL$125.

Big Fork
Area Code 406

Burggraf's Country Lane Bed and Breakfast (Big Fork 59911; 837-4608) 5 rooms, free breakfast, TV, a/c, no pets, CC. SGL/DBL$75-$85.

Flathead Lake Lodge (Big Fork 59911; 837-4391) 31 rooms and cottages, restaurant, American plan available, tennis courts, TV, wheelchair access, NS rooms, laundry facilities, no pets, local transportation, fireplaces, senior rates, CC. SGL/DBL$1,426W-$2,750W.

Marina Cay Resort (180 Vista Lane, 59911; 837-5861, Fax 837-1118, 800-433-6516) 108 rooms and suites, restaurant, lounge, entertainment, heated pool, a/c, TV, wheelchair access, NS rooms, in-room refrigerators, no pets, laundry facilities, meeting facilities, senior rates, CC. SGL/DBL$60-$96, STS$150-$270.

O'Dauchain Country Inn (675 Ferndale Dr., 59911; 837-6851) 5 rooms, free breakfast, no pets, shared baths, airport transportation, antique furnishings, CC. SGL/DBL$55-$95.

Timbers Motel (Big Fork 59911; 837-6200) 40 rooms, heated pool, whirlpools, sauna, in-room coffee makers, a/c, TV, wheelchair access, pets OK, NS rooms, senior rates, CC. SGL/DBL$30-$60.

Big Sky
Area Code 406

Rental and Reservation Services:

Golden Eagle Lodge and Condominium Rentals (Big Sky 59716; 995-4800, 800-548-4488) condominium rentals.

Mountain Lodge at Big Sky (Big Sky 59716; 995-4560, 800-831-3509) condominium rentals.

Triple Creek Management Company (47560 Gallatin Rd., 59716; 995-4848, 800-548-4632) condominium rentals.

□□□

Best Western Buck's T-4 Lodge (Big Sky 59716; 995-4111, Fax 995-2191, 800-528-1234) 51 rooms and suites, restaurant, lounge, children free with parents, a/c, NS rooms, TV, laundry facilities, game room, gift shop, in-room coffee makers, wheelchair access, local transportation, pets OK, meeting facilities, senior rates, CC. SGL/DBL$55-$84.

Big Sky of Montana Resort (Big Sky 59716; 995-4211, 800-548-4486) 204 rooms and suites, restaurant, lounge, pool, sauna, exercise center, a/c, TV, meeting facilities for 700, CC. SGL/DBL$60-$125.

The Huntley Lodge (Big Sky 59716; 995-4211, Fax 994-4860) 298 rooms and suites, restaurant, lounge, heated pool, whirlpools, tennis courts, in-room refrigerators and coffee makers, pool, a/c, TV, wheelchair access, laundry facilities, no pets, NS rooms, meeting facilities, senior rates, CC. SGL/DBL$100-$460.

Lone Mountain Guest Ranch (Big Sky 59716; 995-4644) 23 cabins, restaurant, lounge, entertainment, tennis courts, whirlpools, fireplaces, gift shop, airport transportation, American plan available, TV, no pets, laundry facilities, CC. SGL/DBL$1,300W-$2,105W.

Big Timber

Area Code 406

Russell Lodge (Big Timber 59011; 832-5244) 42 rooms, restaurant, lounge, a/c, TV, wheelchair access, NS, laundry facilities, gift shop, no pets, senior rates, CC. SGL/DBL$35-$48.

Super 8 Motel (Big Timber 59011; 932-8888, 800-800-8000) 39 rooms and suites, restaurant, NS, no pets, children under 12 free with parents, free local calls, a/c, TV, in-room refrigerators and microwaves, fax service, wheelchair access, meeting facilities, senior rates, CC. SGL/DBL$40-$55.

Billings

Area Code 406

Airport Metra Inn (403 Main St., 59105; 245-6611) 105 rooms, restaurant, lounge, heated pool, kitchenettes, a/c, TV, wheelchair access, airport transportation, in-room refrigerators, VCRs, NS rooms, senior rates, CC. SGL/DBL$31-$40.

Best Western Ponderosa Inn (2511 1st Ave. North 59101; 259-5511, Fax 245-8004, 800-528-1234, 800-628-9081) 130 rooms, restaurant, lounge, pool, entertainment, exercise facilities, whirlpools, children free with parents, a/c, NS rooms, in-room coffee makers, TV, laundry facilities, wheelchair access, pets OK, meeting facilities, senior rates, CC. SGL/DBL$50-$68.

Billings Inn (880 North 29th St., 59101; 252-6800, 800-231-7782) 60 rooms, free breakfast, a/c, TV, wheelchair access, airport transportation, laundry facilities, in-room refrigerators and microwaves, children free with parents, NS rooms, pets OK, senior rates, CC. SGL/DBL$38-$45.

Cherry Tree Inn (823 North Broadway, 59101; 252-5603) 64 rooms, a/c, TV, wheelchair access, NS rooms, laundry facilities, kitchenettes, CC. SGL/DBL$30-$40.

Comfort Inn (2030 Overland Ave., 59102; 652-5200, 800-228-5150) 60 rooms, free breakfast, indoor heated pool, whirlpools, in-room refrigerators and microwaves, pets OK, children free with parents, game room, a/c, TV, VCRs, senior rates, CC. SGL/DBL$44-$68.

Days Inn (843 Parkway Lane, 59101; 252-4007, 800-325-2525) 46 rooms, free breakfast, a/c, TV, wheelchair access, NS rooms, pets OK, laundry facilities, senior rates, CC. SGL/DBL$38-$45.

Dude Ranch Lodge (415 North 29th St., 59101; 259-5561, Fax 259-5561, 800-221-3302) 55 rooms, restaurant, whirlpools, a/c, TV, wheelchair access, NS rooms, airport transportation, CC. SGL/DBL$35-$60.

Econo Lodge Downtown (2601 4th Ave. North, 59101; 245-6646, 800-4-CHOICE) 35 rooms, pool, children under 12 free with parents, no pets, senior rates, NS rooms, wheelchair access, a/c, TV, senior rates, CC. SGL/DBL$35-$55.

Elliott Inn (1345 Mullowney Lane, 59101; 252-2584, 800-333-6311) 116 rooms, restaurant, free breakfast, exercise center, pets OK, a/c, TV, children free with parents, airport transportation, laundry facilities, wheelchair access, NS rooms, senior rates, CC. SGL/DBL$38-$56.

Fairfield Inn by Marriott (2026 Overland Ave., 59102; 652-5330, 800-228-2800) 63 rooms and suites, free breakfast, indoor heated pool, children under 18 free with parents, NS rooms, free cable TV, free local calls, in-room refrigerators and microwaves, laundry service, game room, a/c, wheelchair access, fax service, meeting facilities, senior rates, CC. SGL/DBL$40-$64.

HoJo Inn (27th St. South, 59101; 248-4656, 800-I-GO-HOJO) 173 rooms, free breakfast, airport transportation, children free with parents, wheelchair access, NS rooms, TV, a/c, pets OK, laundry facilities, senior rates, meeting facilities, CC. SGL/DBL$38-$55.

Holiday Inn West (5500 Midland Rd., 59101; 248-7701, 800-HOLIDAY) 317 rooms, restaurant, lounge, indoor heated pool, exercise center, whirlpools, gift shop, beauty shop, boutiques, children under 19 free with parents, game room, wheelchair access, a/c, TV, NS rooms, fax service, room service, no pets, airport transportation, laundry service, meeting facilities, senior rates, CC. SGL/DBL$60-$100.

Josephine Bed and Breakfast (514 North 29th St., 59101; 248-5898) 3 rooms, free breakfast, TV, a/c, no pets, antique furnishings, shared baths, NS, CC. SGL/DBL$48-$68.

Juniper Motel (1315 North 27th St., 59101; 245-4128, 800-826-7530) free breakfast, restaurant, a/c, TV, in-room refrigerators, pets OK, children free with parents, kitchenettes, wheelchair access, airport transportation, NS rooms, senior rates, CC. SGL/DBL$40-$45.

Kelly Inn (5425 Midland Rd., 59101; 252-2700, 800-635-3559) 87 rooms, restaurant, heated pool, sauna, whirlpools, airport transportation, children free with parents, a/c, TV, wheelchair access, NS rooms, pets OK, laundry facilities, senior rates, CC. SGL/DBL$30-$58.

Motel 6 (5353 Midland Rd., 59102; 248-7551, 505-891-6161) 118 rooms, indoor heated pool, free local calls, children under 17 free with parents, NS rooms, wheelchair access, pets OK, a/c, TV, CC. SGL/DBL$25-$31.

Motel 6 (5400 Midland Rd., 59101; 252-0093, 505-891-6161) 99 rooms, pool, free local calls, children under 17 free with parents, NS rooms, wheelchair access, pets OK, a/c, TV, CC. SGL/DBL$25-$31.

Quality Inn Homestead Park (2036 Overland Ave., 59102; 652-1320, 800-221-2222) 120 rooms and suites, free breakfast, pool, exercise facilities, whirlpools, airport courtesy car, children free with parents, a/c, TV, room service, laundry service, NS rooms, meeting facilities, senior rates, CC. SGL/DBL$46-$70.

Radisson Hotel (Billings 59101; 245-5121, Fax 259-9862, 800-333-3333) 160 rooms and suites, restaurant, lounge, entertainment, in-room refrigerators, microwaves and coffee makers, children free with parents, no pets, airport transportation, VCRs, wheelchair access, free parking, NS rooms, TV, a/c, children free with parents, senior rates, CC. SGL/DBL$85-$95.

Ramada Inn (1223 Mullowney Lane, 59101; 248-7151, 800-2-RAMADA) 240 rooms and suites, restaurant, lounge, indoor heated pool, sauna, whirlpools, wheelchair access, NS rooms, free parking, pets OK, a/c, TV, in-room refrigerators, children under 18 free with parents, room service, laundry facilities, meeting facilities, senior rates, CC. SGL/DBL$45-$63.

Rimview Inn (1025 North 27th St., 59101; 248-2622, 800-551-1318) 54 rooms and 2- and 3-bedroom efficiencies, free breakfast, pets OK, pool, laundry facilities, a/c, TV, wheelchair access, NS rooms, senior rates, CC. SGL/DBL$30-$42.

Sheraton Hotel (27 North 27th St., 59101; 252-7400, 800-325-3535) 289 rooms and suites, restaurant, lounge, entertainment, pool, exercise facilities, whirlpools, no pets, airport transportation, NS rooms, gift shop, a/c, room service, TV, children free with parents, wheelchair access, meeting facilities, senior rates, CC. SGL/DBL$55-$85.

Super 8 Motel (5400 Southgate Dr., 59102; 248-8842, Fax 248-3063, 800-800-8000) 115 rooms and suites, free breakfast, pets OK, children under 12 free with parents, free local calls, a/c, TV, in-room refrigerators and microwaves, fax service, NS rooms, wheelchair access, meeting facilities, senior rates, CC. SGL/DBL$40-$48.

TraveLodge (3311 2nd Ave. North, 59101; 245-6345, 800-578-7878) 37 rooms, pool, wheelchair access, complimentary newspaper, laundry service, TV, a/c, free local calls, fax service, NS rooms, in-room refrigerators and microwaves, children under 18 free with parents, no pets, meeting facilities, senior rates, CC. SGL/DBL$60-$73.

Bozeman
Area Code 406

Rental and Reservation Services:

Big Sky Chalet Rentals (Bozeman 59715; 995-2665, 800-845-4428) rental 1- to 5-bedroom condominiums and chalets.

Golden Eagle Management (Bozeman 58715; 995-4800, 800-548-4488) rental rooms and condominiums.

□□□

Bergfeld Bed and Breakfast (8151 Sypes Canyon Rd., 59715; 586-7778) 4 rooms, free breakfast, TV, private baths, kitchenettes, a/c, no pets, CC. SGL/DBL$60.

Best Western City Center Motor Inn (507 West Main 59715; 587-3158, Fax 587-7470, 800-528-1234) 64 rooms and suites, restaurant, lounge, entertainment, indoor heated pool, exercise facilities, children free with parents, a/c, NS rooms, TV, laundry facilities, wheelchair access, no pets, meeting facilities for 100, senior rates, CC. SGL/DBL$45-$80.

Best Western Grand Tree Inn (1325 North 7th Ave., 59715; 587-5261, Fax 587-9437, 800-528-1234) 103 rooms and suites, restaurant, lounge, indoor heated pool, exercise facilities, jacuzzi, children free with parents, a/c, NS rooms, TV, airport transportation, laundry facilities, wheelchair access, pets OK, meeting facilities for 250, senior rates, CC. SGL/DBL$58-$90.

Blue Sky Motel (1010 East Main St., 59715; 587-2311) 24 rooms and suites, restaurant, jacuzzi, a/c, TV, CC. SGL/DBL$35-$45.

Bobcat Lodge (2307 West Main St., 59715; 587-5241) 80 rooms and two 3-bedroom houses, restaurant, indoor heated pool, sauna, kitchenettes, a/c, TV, CC. SGL/DBL$40-$60.

Bozeman Inn (Bozeman 59715; 587-3176, 800-648-7517) 45 rooms and suites, restaurant, lounge, outdoor heated pool, sauna, hot tub, free local calls, in-room refrigerators and microwaves, laundry facilities, pets OK, children free with parents, a/c, TV, CC. SGL/DBL$35-$60.

Cobb Hill Cottage (1499 Cobb Hill, 59715; 586-9788) rooms and efficiencies, TV, CC. SGL/DBL$55-$65.

Comfort Inn (1370 North 7th Ave., 59715; 587-2322, 800-228-5150) 60 rooms and suites, free breakfast, indoor heated pool, sauna, whirlpools, exercise facilities, no pets, airport courtesy car, a/c, TV, meeting facilities for 25, senior rates, CC. SGL/DBL$44-$75.

Continental Motor Inn (1324 East Main St., 59715; 587-9231) 60 rooms, a/c, TV, CC. SGL/DBL$25-$40.

Days Inn (1321 North 7th Ave., 58715; 587-5251, 800-325-2525) 79 rooms, free breakfast, jacuzzi, airport transportation, a/c, TV, wheelchair access, NS rooms, no pets, laundry facilities, senior rates, CC. SGL/DBL$38-$72.

Econo Lodge Downtown (122 West Main St., 59715; 587-4481, 800-4-CHOICE) 36 rooms, children under 12 free with parents, no pets, senior rates, NS rooms, wheelchair access, a/c, TV, senior rates, CC. SGL/DBL$36-$52.

Fairfield Inn by Marriott (828 Wheat Dr., 59715; 587-2222, 800-228-2800) 69 rooms and suites, indoor heated pool, spa, children under 18 free with parents, NS rooms, free cable TV, free local calls, laundry service, a/c, wheelchair access, fax service, kitchenettes, meeting facilities for 12, fax service, senior rates, CC. SGL/DBL$50-$90.

Hillard's Bed and Breakfast and Guest House (11521 Axtell County Rd., 59715; 763-4696) free breakfast, TV, NS, no children, private baths, a/c, no pets. SGL/DBL$40-$65.

Holiday Inn (5 Baxter Lane, 59715; 587-4561, 800-HOLIDAY) 178 rooms and suites, restaurant, lounge, indoor heated pool, exercise facilities, sauna, whirlpools, game room, airport transportation, children under 19 free with parents, wheelchair access, a/c, TV, NS rooms, fax service, room service, no pets, laundry service, meeting facilities for 400, senior rates, CC. SGL/DBL$60-$78.

Lumber Jack Log Cabins (70 Williams Ave, 59715; 763-4421) cabins, TV, kitchenettes, CC. SGL/DBL$55-$75.

Millers of Montana (1002 Zacharia Lane, 59715; 763-4102) 4 rooms, free breakfast, TV, a/c, no pets, CC. SGL/DBL$40-$60.

Mountain Sky Guest Ranch (Bozeman 59715; 587-1244, 800-548-3392) 27 rooms and cabins, heated pool, sauna, hot tub, TV, American plan available, CC. SGL/DBL$1,645W-$3,600W.

Our Neck of the Woods (603 West Babcok, 59715; 587-2621) free breakfast, TV, private baths, no pets, CC. SGL/DBL$40-$66.

Prime Rate Motel (805 Wheat Dr., 59715; 587-2100, 800-356-3004) 42 rooms and suites, free breakfast, jacuzzi, sauna, wheelchair access, children free with parents, no pets, a/c, TV, senior rates, CC. SGL/DBL$35-$46.

Rainbow Motel (510 North 7th Ave., 59715; 587-4200) 43 rooms, outdoor heated pool, kitchenettes, a/c, TV, pets OK, in-room coffee makers, kitchenettes, CC. SGL/DBL$25-$38.

Ranch House Motel (1201 East Main St., 59715; 587-4278) 15 rooms, free local calls, a/c, TV, CC. SGL/DBL$20-$35.

Royal 7 Motel (310 North 7th Ave., 59715; 587-3103) 47 rooms and suites, restaurant, whirlpools, a/c, TV, kitchenettes, pets OK, in-room refrigerators, CC. SGL/DBL$40-$55.

Sacajawea International Backpackers Hostel (405 West Olive St., 58715; 586-4659) beds, laundry facilities, TV. SGL$10.

Silver Forest Inn (15234 Bridger Canyon Rd., 59715; 586-1882) free breakfast, TV, a/c, no pets, CC. SGL/DBL$40-$60.

Sun House Bed and Breakfast (9986 Happy Acres West, 59715; 587-3651) free breakfast, TV, children under 5 free with parents, NS, jacuzzi, a/c, no pets, CC. SGL/DBL$55-$75.

Sunset Motel (810 North 7th Ave., 59715; 587-5536) 10 rooms, a/c, TV, CC. SGL/DBL$18-$28.

Super 8 Motel (800 Wheat Dr., 59715; 586-1521, 800-800-8000) 108 rooms and suites, restaurant, game room, no pets, children under 12 free with parents, free local calls, a/c, TV, in-room refrigerators and microwaves, fax service, NS rooms, wheelchair access, meeting facilities, senior rates, CC. SGL/DBL$45-$65.

Torch and Toes Bed and Breakfast (309 South 3rd Ave., 59715; 586-7285) 4 rooms, free breakfast, in-room refrigerators, NS, antique furnishings, TV, no pets, airport transportation, senior rates, CC. SGL/DBL$55-$70.

University Village Apartments (1711 South 11th Ave., 59715; 587-8046) 1- and 2-bedroom apartments, a/c, TV, CC. 1BR$45, 2BR$55-$85.

Voss Inn (310 South Wilson Ave., 59715; 587-0982) 6 rooms, free breakfast, TV, private bath, 1890s home, a/c, no pets, CC. SGL/DBL$60-$80.

Western Heritage Inn (1200 East Main St., 59715; 586-8534) 38 rooms, restaurant, free breakfast, whirlpools, exercise center, pets OK, a/c, TV, children free with parents, in-room refrigerators, laundry facilities, wheelchair access, NS rooms, senior rates, CC. SGL/DBL$40-$58.

Butte

Area Code 406

Best Western Plaza Inn (2900 Harrison Ave., 59701; 494-3500, Fax 494-7611, 800-528-1234) 134 rooms, restaurant, free breakfast, lounge, indoor heated pool, sauna, children free with parents, a/c, NS rooms, TV, laundry facilities, wheelchair access, pets OK, meeting facilities, senior rates, CC. SGL/DBL$50-$130.

Best Western Copper King Inn (4655 Harrison Ave. South, 59701; 494-6666, Fax 494-3274, 800-528-1234) 146 rooms, restaurant, lounge, indoor heated pool, jacuzzi, tennis courts, children free with parents, a/c, NS rooms, TV, laundry facilities, gift shop, wheelchair access, pets OK, meeting facilities, senior rates, CC. SGL/DBL$50-$78.

Best Western War Bonnet Inn (2100 Cornell Ave., 59701; 494-7800, Fax 494-2875, 800-528-1234) 134 rooms, restaurant, lounge, indoor heated pool, exercise facilities, children free with parents, a/c, NS rooms, TV, laundry facilities, wheelchair access, no pets, meeting facilities, senior rates, CC. SGL/DBL$55-$85.

Capri Motel (220 North Wyoming St., 59701; 723-4391, 800-342-2774) 68 rooms and efficiencies, laundry facilities, a/c, TV, wheelchair access, NS rooms, no pets, CC. SGL/DBL$30-$45.

Days Inn (2700 Harrison Ave., 59701; 494-7000, Fax 494-7701, 800-325-2525) 74 rooms, free breakfast, exercise center, jacuzzi, airport transportation, a/c, TV, wheelchair access, NS rooms, no pets, laundry facilities, senior rates, CC. SGL/DBL$48-$130.

Rocker Inn (12201 West Brown's Gulch Rd., 59701; 723-5464) 50 rooms, lounge, a/c, TV, children free with parents, pets OK, wheelchair access, NS rooms, in-room refrigerators, senior rates, CC. SGL/DBL$30-$44.

Super 8 Motel (2929 Harrison Ave., 59701; 494-6000, 800-800-8000) 104 rooms and suites, restaurant, free breakfast, no pets, children under 12 free with parents, free local calls, a/c, TV, in-room refrigerators and microwaves, fax service, NS rooms, wheelchair access, meeting facilities, senior rates, CC. SGL/DBL$36-$54.

Townhouse Inn (2777 Harrison Ave., 59701; 494-8850, 800-442-INNS) 150 rooms and suites, exercise center, sauna, whirlpools, laundry facilities, a/c, TV, wheelchair access, NS rooms, pets OK, children free with parents, airport transportation, meeting facilities, senior rates, CC. SGL/DBL$50-$60.

War Bonnet Inn (210 Cornell Ave., 59701; 494-7800) 134 rooms and suites, restaurant, lounge, entertainment, indoor heated pool, whirlpools, sauna, pets OK, a/c, TV, wheelchair access, NS rooms, children free with parents, airport transportation, senior rates, CC. SGL/DBL$55-$80.

Chinook
Area Code 406

Bear Paw Court (Chinook 59523; 357-2221) 16 rooms, TV, CC. SGL/DBL$38-$46.

Chinook Motor Inn (100 Indiana St., 59523; 357-2248) 38 rooms, restaurant, lounge, a/c, TV, children free with parents, pets OK, NS rooms, senior rates, CC. SGL/DBL$26-$40.

Columbia Falls
Area Code 406

Bad Rock Country Inn (480 Bad Rock Dr., 59912; 892-2829) 3 rooms, free breakfast, airport transportation, no pets, CC. SGL/DBL$75-$95.

Glacier Mountain Shadow Resort (7285 Hwy. 2 East, 59912; 892-7686) 22 rooms and apartments, laundry facilities, a/c, TV, wheelchair access, in-room refrigerators, microwaves and coffee makers, NS rooms, senior rates, CC. SGL/DBL$40-$52.

Meadow Lake Golf and Ski Resort (100 St. Andrews Dr., 59912; 892-7601, Fax 892-0330, 800-321-4653) 72 rooms and condominiums, restaurant, lounge, heated pool, tennis courts, a/c, TV, wheelchair access, NS rooms, children free with parents, no pets, laundry facilities, airport courtesy car, fireplaces, meeting facilities, senior rates, CC. SGL/DBL$85-$195.

Mountain Timbers Lodge (5385 Rabe Rd., 59912; 387-5830) 7 rooms, free breakfast, whirlpools, shared baths, wheelchair access, children free with parents, NS, game room, no pets, meeting facilities, senior rates, CC. SGL/DBL$50-$110.

Ol'River Bridge Inn (Columbia Falls 59912; 892-2181) 31 rooms, restaurant, lounge, entertainment, indoor heated pool, no pets, a/c, TV, wheelchair access, NS rooms, senior rates, CC. SGL/DBL$43-$49.

Plum Creek House (985 Vans Ave., 59912; 892-1816) 5 rooms, free breakfast, TV, a/c, no pets, CC. SGL/DBL$65-$85.

Turn in the River Inn (51 Penney Lane, 59912; 257-0724) 3 rooms, free breakfast, TV, a/c, no pets, senior rates, CC. SGL/DBL$75-$95.

Cut Bank
Area Code 406

Glacier Gateway Inn (1121 East Railroad St., 59427; 873-5544) 15 rooms and suites, a/c, TV, wheelchair access, in-room refrigerators and microwaves, children free with parents, NS rooms, pets OK, VCRs, senior rates, CC. SGL/DBL$39-$49.

Northern Motor Inn (609 West Main St., 59427; 873-5662) 61 rooms and efficiencies, indoor heated pool, whirlpools, a/c, TV, wheelchair access, NS rooms, in-room refrigerators, senior rates, CC. SGL/DBL$34-$50.

Deer Lodge
Area Code 406

Scharfs Motor Inn (819 Main St., 59722; 846-2810) 33 rooms, restaurant, a/c, TV, wheelchair access, NS rooms, children free with parents, in-room refrigerators and microwaves, pets OK, senior rates, CC. SGL/DBL$20-$40.

Super 8 Motel (1150 North Main St., 59722; 846-2370, 800-800-8000) 54 rooms, indoor heated pool, VCRs, children under 12 free with parents, free local calls, a/c, TV, in-room refrigerators and microwaves, fax service, NS rooms, wheelchair access, pets OK, meeting facilities, senior rates, CC. SGL/DBL$35-$50.

Dillon
Area Code 406

Best Western Paradise Inn (650 North Montana St., 59725; 683-4214, Fax 683-4216, 800-528-1234) 66 rooms, restaurant, lounge, indoor pool, exercise facilities, whirlpools, children free with parents, a/c, NS rooms, TV, laundry facilities, wheelchair access, pets OK, meeting facilities, senior rates, CC. SGL/DBL$39-$55.

Creston Motel (335 South Atlantic, 59725; 683-2341) 22 rooms, a/c, TV, wheelchair access, pets OK, NS rooms, children free with parents, in-room refrigerators and microwaves, senior rates, CC. SGL/DBL$25-$40.

Sundowner Motel (500 North Montana St., 59725; 683-2375) 32 rooms, restaurant, pets OK, a/c, TV, wheelchair access, children free with parents, NS rooms, airport transportation, in-room refrigerators, meeting facilities, CC. SGL/DBL$26-$38.

Super 8 Motel (550 North Montana St., 59725; 683-4288, Fax 683-6251, 800-800-8000) 46 rooms, no pets, children under 12 free with parents, free local calls, a/c, TV, in-room refrigerators and microwaves, fax service, NS rooms, wheelchair access, meeting facilities, senior rates, CC. SGL/DBL$30-$42.

Townhouse Inns (450 North Interchange, 59725; 683-6831) 46 rooms, lounge, indoor heated pool, laundry facilities, a/c, TV, wheelchair access, VCRs, in-room refrigerators, microwaves and coffee makers, pets OK, children free with parents, laundry facilities, NS rooms, senior rates, CC. SGL/DBL$35-$46.

East Glacier Park

Area Code 406

Glacier Park Lodge (East Glacier Park 59434; 226-5551, 800-332-9351 in Montana) 155 rooms and suites, restaurant, lounge, heated pool, gift shop, no pets, children under 12 free with parents, meeting facilities, CC. SGL/DBL$80-$160.

Jacobson's Cottages (East Glacier Park 59434; 226-4411) 12 cottages, kitchenettes, pets OK, children free with parents, TV, CC. SGL/DBL$45-$50.

Many Glacier Hotel (East Glacier Park 59434; 732-4411, 800-332-9351 in Montana) 210 rooms and 2-bedroom suites, restaurant, lounge, entertainment, no pets, water view, gift shop, children free with parents, CC. SGL/DBL$70-$90, STS$150.

Mountain Pine Motel (East Glacier Park 59434; 226-4403) 25 rooms, TV, pets OK, children free with parents, local transportation, CC. SGL/DBL$39-$55.

Rising Sun Motor Inn (East Glacier Park 59434; 732-5523, Fax 732-4481) 72 rooms and cabins, restaurant, children free with parents, no pets, CC. SGL/DBL$50-$67.

Swiftcurrent Motor Inn (East Glacier Park 59434; 226-5551, Fax 732-5595, 800-332-9351 in Montana) 88 rooms and 2-bedroom cottages, restaurant, laundry facilities, children under 12 free with parents, CC. SGL/DBL$20-$60.

Ennis

Area Code 406

El Western (Ennis 59729; 682-4217) 28 cabins, TV, wheelchair access, NS rooms, kitchenettes, fireplaces, CC. SGL/DBL$50-$80.

Fan Mountain Inn (Ennis 59729; no phone) a/c, TV, wheelchair access, NS rooms, senior rates, CC. SGL/DBL$55-$65.

Rainbow Valley Motel (Ennis 59729; 682-4264, 800-452-8254) 18 rooms and efficiencies, heated pool, a/c, TV, in-room refrigerators, no pets, wheelchair access, NS rooms, senior rates, CC. SGL/DBL$42-$50.

Emigrant
Area Code 406

Mountain Sky Guest Ranch (Emigrant 59027; 333-4911) 28 1- to 3-bedrooms and cabins, TV, wheelchair access, NS rooms, pets OK, fireplaces, kitchenettes, senior rates, CC. SGL/DBL$50-$80.

Ennis
Area Code 406

Fan Mountain Inn (207 North Main St., 59729; 682-5200) 28 rooms, and efficiencies, a/c, TV, in-room refrigerators and microwaves, CC. SGL/DBL$35-$50.

Rainbow Valley Motel (Ennis 59729; 682-4264, 800-452-8254) 18 rooms and 2-bedroom efficiencies, heated pool, in-room refrigerators and microwaves, no pets, water view, TV, wheelchair access, NS rooms, senior rates, CC. SGL/DBL$35-$60.

Forsyth
Area Code 406

Best Western Sundowner Inn (1018 Front St., 59327; 356-2115, Fax 356-2216, 800-528-1234) 40 rooms, restaurant, indoor heated pool, exercise facilities, children free with parents, a/c, NS rooms, TV, in-room refrigerators and coffee makers, laundry facilities, wheelchair access, pets OK, meeting facilities, senior rates, CC. SGL/DBL$45-$66.

Restwell Motel (810 Front St., 59327; 356-2771) 18 rooms and 2-bedroom efficiencies, a/c, TV, wheelchair access, NS rooms, children free with parents, in-room refrigerators, pets OK, senior rates, CC. SGL/DBL$22-$34.

Westwind Motor Inn (Forsyth 59237; 356-2038) 33 rooms and 1-bedroom efficiencies, a/c, TV, in-room refrigerators, pets OK, children free with parents, airport transportation, NS rooms, senior rates, CC. SGL/DBL$35-$40.

Gallatin Gateway
Area Code 406

Castle Rock Inn (65840 Gallatin Rd., 59730; 763-4243) 8 cabins, TV, CC. SGL/DBL$65-$85.

Cinnamon Lodge (37090 Gallatin Rd., 59730; 995-4253) cabins, TV, kitchenettes, CC. SGL/DBL$38-$46.

Gallatin Gateway Inn (Gallatin Gateway 59730; 763-4672) restaurant, lounge, pool, hot tub, a/c, TV, meeting facilities, CC. SGL/DBL$55-$65.

Gallatin West Guesthouse (12640 Axtell Gateway, 59730; 763-4513) TV, NS rooms, senior rates, CC. SGL/DBL$60-$80.

Nine Quarter Circle Ranch (5000 Taylor Fork Rd., 59730; 995-4132) 23 1- and 2-bedroom cabins, restaurant, lounge, spa, fireplace, TV, no pets, CC. SGL/DBL$40-$60.

Silver Creek Cabin (Gallatin Gateway 59730; 763-4887) cabin, TV, CC. SGL/DBL$60.

The 320 Guest Ranch (205 Buffalo Horn Creek, 59730; 995-4283, 800-243-0320) cabins and 3-bedroom homes, TV, CC. SGL/DBL$55-$85.

The Trout Club (Gallatin Gateway 59730; 586-1940) 3 cabins, TV, CC. SGL/DBL$80-$105.

Willowtree House (Gallatin Gateway 59730; 763-4769) 4 rooms, free breakfast, TV, shared bath, a/c, no pets, CC. SGL/DBL$65-$80.

Gardiner
Area Code 406

Absaroka Lodge (Gardiner 59030; 848-7414, 800-755-7414) 41 rooms and efficiencies, a/c, TV, children free with parents, pets OK, water view, kitchenettes, CC. SGL/DBL$75-$80.

Best Western by Mammoth Hot Springs Inn (Hwy. 89, 59030; 848-7311, Fax 848-7120, 800-528-1234) 85 rooms, restaurant, lounge, indoor heated pool, exercise facilities, jacuzzi, sauna, children free with parents, a/c, NS rooms, TV, laundry facilities, wheelchair access, pets OK, gift shop, meeting facilities, senior rates, CC. SGL/DBL$42-$95.

Flamingo Motor Lodge (Gardiner 59030; 848-7536) 8 rooms, a/c, TV, wheelchair access, NS rooms, children under 8 free with parents, no pets, senior rates, CC. SGL/DBL$30-$60.

Super 8 Motel (Gardiner 59030; 848-7401, 800-800-8000) 65 rooms and suites, indoor heated pool, pets OK, children under 12 free with parents, free local calls, a/c, TV, in-room refrigerators and microwaves, fax service, NS rooms, wheelchair access, water view, meeting facilities, senior rates, CC. SGL/DBL$85-$95.

Westernaire Motel (Gardiner 59030; 848-7397) 11 rooms, NS rooms, TV, CC. SGL/DBL$60-$70.

Wilson's Yellowstone River Motel (Gardiner 59030; 848-7303) 24 rooms and 2- and 3-bedroom efficiencies, TV, wheelchair access, kitchenettes pets OK, NS rooms, senior rates, CC. SGL/DBL$35-$55.

Yellowstone Village North (Gardiner 59030; 848-7417, 800-228-8158) 45 rooms and condominiums, indoor heated pool, sauna, no pets, in-room refrigerators, laundry facilities, a/c, TV, CC. SGL/DBL$30-$70.

Glasgow
Area Code 406

Campbell Lodge (534 3rd Ave. South, 59230; 228-9328) 31 rooms, a/c, TV, wheelchair access, children free with parents, airport transportation, NS rooms, senior rates, CC. SGL/DBL$31-$40.

Cottonwood Inn (Glasgow 59230; 228-8213, Fax 228-8248, 800-321-8213) 92 rooms and suites, restaurant, lounge, indoor pool, whirlpools, sauna, laundry facilities, local transportation, in-room refrigerators, pets OK, a/c, TV, wheelchair access, NS rooms, senior rates, CC. SGL/DBL$42-$75.

Glendive
Area Code 406

Best Western Holiday Lodge (222 North Kendrick, 59330; 365-5655, Fax 365-6233, 800-528-1234) 44 rooms, restaurant, lounge, indoor heated pool, sauna, gift shop, airport transportation, children free with parents, a/c, NS rooms, TV, laundry facilities, wheelchair access, pets OK, meeting facilities, senior rates, CC. SGL/DBL$48-$60.

Days Inn (2000 North Merrill Ave., 59330; 365-6011, 800-325-2525) 59 rooms, complimentary Days Inn breakfast, pets OK, a/c, TV, wheelchair access, NS rooms, laundry facilities, senior rates, CC. SGL/DBL$35-$48.

Budget Host Riverside Inn (Glendive 59330; 365-2349, 800-283-4678) 36 rooms, laundry facilities, NS rooms, wheelchair access, a/c, no pets, TV, children free with parents, senior rates, CC. SGL/DBL$28-$38.

El Centro Motel (112 South Kendrick Ave., 59330; 365-5211) 25 rooms and efficiencies, a/c, TV, wheelchair access, NS rooms, children free with parents, in-room refrigerators and microwaves, pets OK, kitchenettes, senior rates, CC. SGL/DBL$25-$33.

Jordan Motor Inn (223 North Merrill Ave., 59330; 365-3371) 69 rooms, restaurant, lounge, indoor heated pool, sauna, a/c, TV, wheelchair access, airport transportation, children under 12 free with parents, pets OK, NS rooms, senior rates, CC. SGL/DBL$40-$50.

Rustic Inn (1903 North Merrill Ave., 59330; 365-5636) 35 rooms, restaurant, lounge, indoor heated pool, a/c, TV, wheelchair access, NS rooms, modified American plan available, pets OK, VCRs, senior rates, CC. SGL/DBL$15-$40.

Super 8 Motel (1904 North Merrill Ave., 59330; 365-5671, 800-800-8000) 52 rooms and suites, pets OK, children under 12 free with parents, free local calls, a/c, TV, in-room refrigerators and microwaves, fax service, NS rooms, wheelchair access, meeting facilities, senior rates, CC. SGL/DBL$38-$52.

Great Falls

Area Code 406

Best Western Heritage Inn (1700 Fox Farm Rd., 59405; 761-1900, Fax 761-0136, 800-528-1234) 240 rooms, restaurant, lounge, entertainment, indoor heated whirlpools, pool, exercise facilities, children free with parents, a/c, NS rooms, TV, laundry facilities, wheelchair access, pets OK, fax service, game room, meeting facilities, senior rates, CC. SGL/DBL$65-$72.

Best Western Ponderosa Inn (220 Central Ave., 59401; 761-3410, 800-528-1234) 105 rooms, restaurant, lounge, sauna, children free with parents, a/c, NS rooms, TV, laundry facilities, wheelchair access, pets OK, meeting facilities, senior rates, CC. SGL/DBL$48-$66.

Budget Inn (2 Treasure State Dr., 59404; 453-1602, 800-527-0700) 60 rooms, restaurant, NS rooms, children free with parents, pets OK, a/c, airport transportation, TV, meeting facilities, senior rates, CC. SGL/DBL$41-$50.

Central Motel (715 Central Ave. West, 59404; 453-0161) 28 rooms and 2-bedroom efficiencies, whirlpools, a/c, pets OK, in-room refrigerators, TV, wheelchair access, NS rooms, senior rates, CC. SGL/DBL$30-$55.

The Chalet Inn (1204 4th Ave. North, 59401; 452-9001) free breakfast, TV, private baths, a/c, no pets, senior rates, CC. SGL/DBL$48-$56.

Comfort Inn (1120 9th St., 59403; 454-2727, 800-228-5150) 64 rooms and suites, free breakfast, indoor heated pool, whirlpools, children under 17 free with parents, in-room refrigerators and microwaves, pets OK, a/c, TV, CC. SGL/DBL$45-$70.

Days Inn (101 14th Ave. Northwest, 59404; 727-6565, 800-325-2525) 62 rooms, free breakfast, a/c, TV, wheelchair access, NS rooms, no pets, laundry facilities, senior rates, CC. SGL/DBL$40-$59.

Edelweiss Motor Inn (626 Central Ave. West, 59404; 452-9503) 20 rooms, a/c, TV, wheelchair access, gift shop, pets OK, NS rooms, senior rates, CC. SGL/DBL$28-$49.

Fairfield Inn by Marriott (1000 9th Ave. South, 59405; 454-3000, 800-228-2800) 63 rooms and suites, restaurant, free breakfast, indoor heated pool, spa, whirlpools, children under 18 free with parents, NS rooms, free cable TV, free local calls, laundry service, pets OK, game room, in-room refrigerators, a/c, wheelchair access, meeting facilities, fax service, senior rates, CC. SGL/DBL$49-$70.

Great Falls Inn (1400 South 29th St., 59405; 800-454-6010) 45 rooms and efficiencies, free breakfast, a/c, TV, wheelchair access, NS rooms, in-room refrigerators and microwaves, laundry facilities, children free with parents, senior rates, CC. SGL/DBL$38-$45.

Holiday Inn (400 10th Ave. South, 59405; 727-7200, 800-HOLIDAY) 170 rooms and suites, restaurant, lounge, entertainment, indoor heated pool, exercise facilities, whirlpools, sauna, children under 19 free with parents, wheelchair access, a/c, TV, NS rooms, fax service, room service, pets OK, airport courtesy car, in-room refrigerators and microwaves, laundry service, meeting facilities, senior rates, CC. SGL/DBL$60-$85.

O'Haire Motor Inn (Great Falls 59403; 454-2141, Fax 454-0211, 800-332-9819) 68 rooms and 2-bedroom suites, restaurant, indoor heated pool, a/c, TV, wheelchair access, NS rooms, children free with parents, no pets, airport transportation, senior rates, CC. SGL/DBL$45-$65.

Plaza Inn (1224 10th Ave. South, 59405; 452-9594) 20 rooms, a/c, TV, wheelchair access, NS rooms, pets OK, senior rates, CC. SGL/DBL$32-$55.

Rainbow Hotel (20 3rd St. North, 59401; 727-8200) 89 rooms, restaurant, lounge, entertainment, a/c, TV, children under 17 free with parents, no pets, airport transportation, NS rooms, senior rates, CC. SGL/DBL$50-$65.

Ski's Western Motel (2420 10th Ave. South, 59405; 453-3281) 25 rooms and 2-bedroom efficiencies, a/c, TV, wheelchair access, pets OK, senior rates, CC. SGL/DBL$32-$60.

Sovekammer Bed and Breakfast (1109 3rd Ave. North, 59401; 453-6620) 4 rooms, free breakfast, TV, airport transportation, antique furnishings, a/c, no pets, CC. SGL/DBL$50-$55.

Townhouse Inn (1411 10th Ave. South, 59405; 761-4600, Fax 761-7603) 108 rooms, restaurant, lounge, indoor heated pool, whirlpools, sauna, pets OK, airport transportation, room service, game room, a/c, TV, wheelchair access, NS rooms, senior rates, CC. SGL/DBL$60-$65.

Triple Crown Inn (621 Central Ave., 59401; 727-8300) 49 rooms, a/c, TV, wheelchair access, children under 12 free with parents, pets OK, NS rooms, senior rates, CC. SGL/DBL$35-$43.

Hamilton

Area Code 406

Best Western Hamilton Inn (409 South 1st St., 59840; 363-2142, 800-528-1234) 36 rooms, children free with parents, in-room refrigerators and microwaves, a/c, NS rooms, TV, laundry facilities, wheelchair access, no pets, meeting facilities, senior rates, CC. SGL/DBL$42-$57.

Town House Inn (1115 North 1st St., 59840; 363-6600, Fax 363-5644, 800-442-4667) 64 rooms, restaurant, exercise center, whirlpools, sauna, pets OK, children free with parents, in-room refrigerators, microwaves and coffee makers, a/c, TV, wheelchair access, NS rooms, senior rates, CC. SGL/DBL$42-$50.

Helena
Area Code 406

Alladin Motor Inn (2101 11th Ave., 59623; 443-2300, 800-541-2743 in Montana) 74 rooms, restaurant, lounge, indoor pool, sauna, whirlpools, pets OK, fireplaces, local transportation, a/c, TV, wheelchair access, NS rooms, meeting facilities, senior rates, CC. SGL/DBL$45-$54.

Best Western Colonial Inn (2301 Colonial Dr., 59623; 443-2100, 800-528-1234) 149 rooms and suites, restaurant, lounge, indoor and outdoor heated pool, exercise center, whirlpools, in-room refrigerators, barber and beauty shop, airport courtesy car, children free with parents, a/c, NS rooms, TV, laundry facilities, wheelchair access, pets OK, meeting facilities, senior rates, CC. SGL/DBL$60-$83.

Comfort Inn (750 Fee St., 59623; 443-1000, 800-228-5150) 56 rooms, restaurant, free breakfast, indoor heated pool, whirlpools, children free with parents, pets OK, a/c, in-room refrigerators, VCRs, TV, meeting facilities, senior rates, CC. SGL/DBL$45-$56.

Days Inn (2001 Prospect Ave., 59601; 442-3280, 800-325-2525) 96 rooms, free breakfast, pets OK, a/c, TV, wheelchair access, NS rooms, laundry facilities, senior rates, meeting facilities, CC. SGL/DBL$39-$80.

Econo Lodge Downtown (524 Last Chance Gulch, 59601; 442-0600, 800-4-CHOICE) 46 rooms, pool, children under 12 free with parents, no pets, senior rates, NS rooms, wheelchair access, a/c, TV, senior rates, CC. SGL/DBL$35-$55.

Jorgenson's Motel (1714 11th Ave., 59601; 442-1770, 800-272-1770 in Montana) 117 rooms and 2-bedroom efficiencies, restaurant, lounge, indoor heated pool, a/c, TV, wheelchair access, NS rooms, in-room refrigerators and coffee makers, pets OK, airport courtesy car, children free with parents, senior rates, meeting facilities, CC. SGL/DBL$35-$84.

Knights Rest Motel (1831 Eucilo, 59601; 442-6384) 10 rooms and 2-bedroom efficiencies, a/c, TV, wheelchair access, NS rooms, in-room refrigerators and microwaves, pets OK, senior rates, CC. SGL/DBL$30-$38.

Lamplighter Motel (1006 Madison, 59601; 442-9200) 14 rooms and 2- and 3-bedroom efficiencies, a/c, TV, in-room refrigerators, pets OK, NS rooms, senior rates, CC. SGL/DBL$26-$38.

Motel 6 (800 North Oregon, 59601; 442-9990, 505-891-6161) 80 rooms, pool, free local calls, children under 17 free with parents, NS rooms, wheelchair access, pets OK, a/c, TV, CC. SGL/DBL$27-$34.

Park Plaza Hotel (22 North Last Chance Gulch, 59601; 443-2200, Fax 442-4030, 800-332-2290 in Montana) 71 rooms, restaurant, lounge, a/c, TV, children free with parents, pets OK, airport transportation, meeting facilities, CC. SGL/DBL$55-$65.

Sanders Inn (328 North Ewing, 59601; 442-3309) 7 rooms, free breakfast, NS, no pets, 1875 inn, TV, airport transportation, antique furnishings, CC. SGL/DBL$55-$95.

Shilo Inn (2020 Prospect Ave., 59601; 442-0320, Fax 449-4426, 800-222-2244) 47 rooms, indoor heated pool, sauna, whirlpools, airport courtesy car, in-room refrigerators and microwaves, VCRs, laundry facilities, a/c, TV, NS rooms, wheelchair access, children under 12 free with parents, meeting facilities, senior rates, CC. SGL/DBL$47-$60.

Super 8 Motel (2201 11th Ave., 59601; 443-2450, 800-800-8000) 111 rooms and suites, restaurant, no pets, children under 12 free with parents, free local calls, a/c, TV, in-room refrigerators and microwaves, fax service, NS rooms, wheelchair access, meeting facilities, senior rates, CC. SGL/DBL$38-$55.

Jordan

Area Code 406

Hill Creek Guest Ranch (Hill Creek Route, 59337; 557-2224) free breakfast, American plan available, private baths, TV, a/c, no pets, CC. SGL/DBL$50-$65.

Kalispell

Area Code 406

Aero Inn (1830 Hwy. 93 South, 59901; 755-3798) 61 rooms, indoor heated pool, whirlpools, sauna, a/c, children free with parents, no pets, VCRs, kitchenettes, TV, wheelchair access, NS rooms, senior rates, CC. SGL/DBL$25-$80.

Best Western Outlaw Inn (1701 Hwy. 93 South, 59901; 755-6100, 800-528-1234) 224 rooms, restaurant, lounge, entertainment, indoor heated pool, whirlpools, tennis courts, exercise center, sauna, barber and beauty shop, children free with parents, a/c, NS rooms, TV, laundry facilities, wheelchair access, pets OK, meeting facilities, senior rates, CC. SGL/DBL$70-$128.

Cavanaugh's (20 North Main St., 59901; 752-6660, Fax 752-6628, 800-843-4667) 132 rooms and suites, restaurant, lounge, entertainment, indoor heated pool, sauna, whirlpools, barber and beauty shop, boutiques, gift shop, a/c, TV, wheelchair access, NS rooms, children free with parents, pets OK, senior rates, meeting facilities, CC. SGL/DBL$60-$110.

Days Inn (1550 Hwy. 93 North, 59901; 756-3222, Fax 756-3277, 800-325-2525) 53 rooms and suites, free breakfast, children free with parents, airport transportation, a/c, TV, wheelchair access, NS rooms, no pets, laundry facilities, senior rates, CC. SGL/DBL$40-$85.

Diamond Lil's (1680 Hwy. 93 South, 59901; 752-3467, 800-843-7301) 62 rooms and suites, outdoor heated pool, whirlpools, pets OK, children free with parents, a/c, TV, senior rates, CC. SGL/DBL$65-$70.

Four Seasons Motor Inn (350 North Main St., 59901; 755-6123) 101 rooms, heated pool, whirlpools, pets OK, laundry facilities, a/c, in-room coffee makers, TV, CC. SGL/DBL$45-$58.

Friendship Inn (1009 Hwy. 2 East, 59901; 257-7155, 800-424-4777) 30 rooms, exercise facilities, whirlpools, a/c, TV, no pets, NS rooms, children free with parents, wheelchair access, senior rates, CC. SGL/DBL$37-$83.

Glacier Gateway Motel (264 North Main St., 59901; 755-3330) 14 rooms and efficiencies, a/c, TV, wheelchair access, NS rooms, senior rates, CC. SGL/DBL$28-$75.

Kalispell (100 Main St., 59901; 752-8012, 800-858-7422) 40 rooms and 2-bedroom suites, restaurant, free breakfast, lounge, whirlpools, children under 12 free with parents, pets OK, entertainment, barber shop, children free with parents, a/c, TV, CC. SGL/DBL$45-$80.

Motel 6 (1540 Hwy. 93 South, 59901; 752-6355, 505-891-6161) 114 rooms, pool, free local calls, children under 17 free with parents, NS rooms, wheelchair access, pets OK, a/c, TV, CC. SGL/DBL$26-$39.

Red Lion Inn (1330 Hwy. 2 West, 59901; 755-6700, Fax 755-6717, 800-547-8010) 64 rooms and suites, restaurant, lounge, heated pool, pets OK, a/c, TV, wheelchair access, NS rooms, complimentary newspaper, fax service, laundry facilities, meeting facilities, senior rates, CC. SGL/DBL$50-$95.

Super 8 Motel (1341 1st Ave. West, 59901; 755-1888, Fax 755-1887, 800-800-8000) 74 rooms and suites, pets OK, laundry facilities, children under 12 free with parents, free local calls, a/c, TV, in-room refrigerators and microwaves, fax service, NS rooms, wheelchair access, senior rates, CC. SGL/DBL$45-$58.

White Birch Motel (17 Shady Lane, 59901; 752-4008) 8 rooms and 2-bedroom efficiencies, a/c, in-room coffee makers, pets OK, TV, wheelchair access, NS rooms, senior rates, CC. SGL/DBL$25-$70.

Lakeside

Area Code 406

Bayshore Motel (616 Lakeside, 59922; 857-3303) 12 rooms, TV, wheelchair access, NS rooms, water view, no pets, senior rates, CC. SGL/DBL$45-$80.

Lakeshore Motel (Lakeside 59922; 844-3304) 7 rooms and cottages, TV, no pets, water view, CC. SGL/DBL$40-$55.

Northernaire Motel (Lakeside 59922; 844-3864) 9 rooms and 2-bedroom efficiencies, a/c, TV, no pets, in-room coffee makers, wheelchair access, NS rooms, senior rates, CC. SGL/DBL$55-$70.

Lewiston

Area Code 406

B&B Motel (520 East Main St., 59457; 538-5496) 36 rooms and 2-bedroom efficiencies, a/c, TV, children under 12 free with parents, pets OK, kitchenettes, wheelchair access, NS rooms, senior rates, CC. SGL/DBL$32-$40.

Park Inn International (Lewiston, 59457; 538-8721, 800-437-PARK) 124 rooms and suites, restaurant, lounge, indoor and outdoor heated pool, whirlpools, pets OK, room service, gift shop, airport courtesy car, a/c, TV, children free with parents, complimentary newspaper, wheelchair access, NS rooms, senior rates, CC. SGL/DBL$47-$60.

Libby

Area Code 406

Budget Host Caboose Motel (714 West 9th, 59923; 293-6201, 800-283-4678) 29 rooms, laundry facilities, NS rooms, wheelchair access, a/c, in-room refrigerators, children under 12 free with parents, pets OK, TV, senior rates, CC. SGL/DBL$32-$45.

Super 8 Motel (448 Hwy. 2 West, 59923; 293-2771, 800-800-8000) 41 rooms and suites, outdoor heated pool, no pets, children under 12 free with parents, free local calls, a/c, TV, in-room refrigerators and microwaves, fax service, NS rooms, wheelchair access, pets OK, meeting facilities, senior rates, CC. SGL/DBL$36-$55.

Venture Motor Inn (443 Hwy. 2 West, 59923; 293-7711) 72 rooms, restaurant, indoor heated pool, whirlpools, a/c, TV, wheelchair access, NS rooms, pets OK, senior rates, CC. SGL/DBL$36-$60.

Livingston
Area Code 406

Budget Host Parkway Motel (1124 West Park, 59047; 222-3840, 800-283-4678) 28 rooms and efficiencies, outdoor heated pool, laundry facilities, NS rooms, wheelchair access, a/c, TV, pets OK, children free with parents, CC. SGL/DBL$26-$60.

Comfort Inn (I-90 and Hwy. 89, 59047; 800-228-5150) 49 rooms, indoor pool, whirlpools, a/c, TV, meeting facilities, CC. SGL/DBL$45-$65.

Del Mar Motel (Livingston 59047; 222-3120, Fax 222-3120) 32 rooms and 2-bedroom efficiencies, outdoor heated pool, a/c, TV, wheelchair access, in-room coffee makers, children free with parents, pets OK, NS rooms, senior rates, CC. SGL/DBL$28-$58.

Paradise Inn (Livingston 59047; 222-6320, 800-437-6291) 43 rooms, restaurant, lounge, indoor heated pool, whirlpools, a/c, TV, wheelchair access, pets OK, NS rooms, senior rates, CC. SGL/DBL$35-$50.

Super 8 Motel (105 Centennial Dr., 59047; 222-7711, 800-800-8000) 36 rooms and suites, restaurant, no pets, children free with parents, free local calls, a/c, TV, in-room refrigerators and microwaves, fax service, NS rooms, wheelchair access, meeting facilities, senior rates, CC. SGL/DBL$41-$48.

The Talcott House (405 West Lewis, 59047; 222-7699) free breakfast, private baths, exercise center, pets OK, children free with parents, airport transportation, CC. SGL/DBL$40-$65.

Yellowstone Motor Inn (1515 West Park, 59047; 222-6110) 99 rooms and 2-bedroom cabins, restaurant, lounge, indoor heated pool, children under 12 free with parents, pets OK, VCRs, kitchenettes, airport transportation, TV, CC. SGL/DBL$40-$65.

Loma
Area Code 406

Virgelle Mercantile (Loma 59460; 800-426-2926) 4 rooms, free breakfast, TV, NS, antique furnishings, 1912 home, a/c, no pets, CC. SGL/DBL$40.

Miles City
Area Code 406

Best Western War Bonnet Inn (1015 South Haynes Ave., 59301; 232-4560, Fax 232-0363, 800-528-1234) 54 rooms and suites, restaurant, free breakfast, lounge, indoor heated pool, exercise room, sauna, jacuzzi, children free with parents, a/c, NS rooms, TV, laundry facilities, wheelchair access, pets OK, meeting facilities, senior rates, CC. SGL/DBL$45-$62, STS$80-$90.

The Buckboard Inn (1006 Haynes Ave. Southeast 59301; 232-3550, 800-525-6303) 58 rooms, outdoor heated pool, hot tubs, airport transportation, children under 12 free with parents, pets OK, a/c, TV, senior rates, CC. SGL/DBL$28-$40.

Budget Host Inn (1209 South Haynes Ave., 59301; 232-5170, 800-283-4678) 56 rooms, indoor heated pool, sauna, laundry facilities, NS rooms, wheelchair access, a/c, TV, children under 12 free with parents, pets OK, senior rates, CC. SGL/DBL$31-$40.

Friendship Inn Olive Hotel (501 Main St., 59301; 232-2450, 800-424-4777) 34 rooms, restaurant, lounge, entertainment, pool, a/c, TV, no pets, NS rooms, children free with parents, wheelchair access, local transportation, fax service, senior rates, CC. SGL/DBL$35-$73.

Motel 6 (1314 Haynes Ave., 59301; 232-7040, 505-891-6161) 114 rooms, pool, free local calls, children under 17 free with parents, NS rooms, wheelchair access, pets OK, a/c, TV, CC. SGL/DBL$25-$31.

Super 8 Motel (Miles City 59301; 232-5261, 800-800-8000) 58 rooms and suites, free breakfast, pets OK, children under 12 free with parents, free local calls, VCRs, a/c, TV, fax service, NS rooms, wheelchair access, meeting facilities, senior rates, CC. SGL/DBL$26-$40.

Missoula
Area Code 406

Bel Aire Motel (300 East Broadway, 59802; 543-3183, 800-543-3184) 52 rooms and 2-bedroom efficiencies, indoor heated pool, a/c, TV, wheelchair access, NS rooms, pets OK, senior rates, CC. SGL/DBL$25-$55.

Best Western Executive Motor Inn (210 East Main St., 59802; 543-7221, 800-528-1234) 51 rooms, restaurant, outdoor heated pool, children free with parents, a/c, NS rooms, TV, laundry facilities, wheelchair access, pets OK, meeting facilities, senior rates, CC. SGL/DBL$40-$66.

Campus Inn (744 East Broadway, 59802; 549-5134, 800-232-8013) 89 rooms, outdoor heated pool, a/c, TV, wheelchair access, NS rooms, children under 16 free with parents, pets OK, VCRs, senior rates, CC. SGL/DBL$35-$55.

City Center Motel (338 East Broadway, 59802; 543-3193) 15 rooms, a/c, TV, wheelchair access, NS rooms, antique furnishings, senior rates, CC. SGL/DBL$35-$38.

Days Inn (Route 2, Missoula 59802; 721-9776, Fax 721-9781, 800-325-2525) 69 rooms, free breakfast, jacuzzi, airport transportation, a/c, TV, wheelchair access, in-room refrigerators, children under 12 free with parents, NS rooms, pets OK, laundry facilities, senior rates, CC. SGL/DBL$35-$80.

Downtowner Motel (502 East Broadway, 59802; 549-5191) a/c, TV, NS rooms, children under 12 free with parents, pets OK, in-room coffee makers, CC. SGL/DBL$26-$36.

Econo Lodge (1609 West Broadway, 59802; 543-7231, 800-4-CHOICE) 72 rooms, restaurant, lounge, entertainment, outdoor heated pool, whirlpools, children under 12 free with parents, no pets, NS rooms, wheelchair access, airport transportation, in-room refrigerators, VCRs, laundry facilities, a/c, TV, senior rates, CC. SGL/DBL$28-$75.

Family Inn (1031 East Broadway, 59807; 543-7371) 30 rooms, outdoor heated pool, children under 11 free with parents, a/c, TV, wheelchair access, no pets, kitchenettes, NS rooms, senior rates, CC. SGL/DBL$29-$38.

Four B's Inn North (4953 North Reserve St., 59802; 542-7550, Fax 721-5931, 800-272-9500) 67 rooms and suites, restaurant, whirlpools, a/c, TV, wheelchair access, NS rooms, children free with parents, laundry facilities, local transportation, in-room refrigerators and microwaves, pets OK, senior rates, CC. SGL/DBL$45-$60.

Four B's Inn South (3803 Brooks St., 59801; 251-2665) 79 rooms, whirlpools, a/c, TV, wheelchair access, laundry facilities, VCRs, airport transportation, pets OK, NS rooms, senior rates, CC. SGL/DBL$39-$55.

Goldsmith's (809 East Front St., 59801; 721-6732) 7 rooms, free breakfast, TV, no pets, NS, antique furnishings, water view, 1911 home, children free with parents, CC. SGL/DBL$55-$95.

Holiday Inn (200 South Pattee, 59802; 721-8550, 800-HOLIDAY) 200 rooms and suites, restaurant, lounge, entertainment, indoor heated pool, exercise facilities, gift shop, children under 19 free with parents, wheelchair access, in-room refrigerators, a/c, TV, NS rooms, fax service, room service, pets OK, laundry service, meeting facilities, senior rates, CC. SGL/DBL$57-$75.

Orange Street Budget Motor Inn (801 North Orange St., 59802; 721-3610) 81 ROOMS, a/c, TV, children under 12 free with parents, pets OK, in-room refrigerators, VCRs, airport transportation, NS rooms, senior rates, CC. SGL/DBL$40-$46.

Red Lion Inn (700 West Broadway, 59802;728-3300, Fax 728-4441, 800-547-8010) 76 rooms, restaurant, lounge, heated pool, exercise center, whirlpools, sauna, pets OK, a/c, TV, children free with parents, in-room refrigerators, airport transportation, wheelchair access, NS rooms, complimentary newspaper, fax service, laundry facilities, pets OK, meeting facilities, senior rates, CC. SGL/DBL$55-$70.

Red Lion Village Motor Inn (100 Madison St., 59801; 728-3100, Fax 728-2530, 800-547-8010) 172 rooms and suites, restaurant, lounge, entertainment, heated pool, whirlpools, a/c, TV, wheelchair access, NS rooms, complimentary newspaper, beauty shop, airport courtesy car, pets OK, fax service, laundry facilities, meeting facilities, senior rates, CC. SGL/DBL$65-$150.

Redwood Lodge (8060 Hwy. 93, 59802; 721-2110) 40 rooms, a/c, TV, children, heated pool, whirlpools, sauna, airport transportation, laundry facilities, in-room refrigerators, pets OK, a/c, TV, wheelchair access, NS rooms, senior rates, CC. SGL/DBL$50-$75.

Royal Motel (338 Washington St., 59802; 542-2184) 12 rooms and efficiencies, pets OK, a/c, TV, wheelchair access, NS rooms, senior rates, CC. SGL/DBL$38-$53.

Southgate Inn (3530 Brooks St., 59801; 251-2250, 800-247-2616) 81 rooms, heated pool, sauna, whirlpools, exercise center, a/c, no pets, TV, children under 12 free with parents, senior rates, no pets, airport transportation, CC. SGL/DBL$38-$62.

Super 8 Motel (3901 South Brooks, 59801; 251-2255, 800-800-8000) 104 rooms and suites, free breakfast, no pets, children under 12 free with parents, free local calls, a/c, TV, in-room refrigerators and microwaves, fax service, NS rooms, wheelchair access, meeting facilities, senior rates, CC. SGL/DBL$38-$48.

Thunderbird Motel (1009 East Broadway, 59802; 543-7251) 27 rooms and 2-bedroom efficiencies, indoor heated pool, whirlpools, sauna, in-room refrigerators, laundry facilities, a/c, TV, wheelchair access, NS rooms, senior rates, CC. SGL/DBL$35-$55.

Travelers Inn Motel (4850 North Reserve St., 59802; 728-8330) 27 rooms, a/c, TV, airport transportation, in-room refrigerators, NS rooms, senior rates, CC. SGL/DBL$27-$47.

TraveLodge (420 West Broadway, 59802; 728-4500, Fax 543-8118, 800-578-7878) 60 rooms, restaurant, lounge, pool, wheelchair access, complimentary newspaper, laundry service, TV, a/c, free local calls, fax service, NS rooms, in-room refrigerators and microwaves, children under 18 free with parents, no pets, meeting facilities, senior rates, CC. SGL/DBL$36-$55.

Val-U Inn (3001 Brooks St., 59801; 721-9600, 800-443-7777 in Montana) 84 rooms and suites, free breakfast, whirlpools, sauna, airport transportation, a/c, TV, wheelchair access, NS rooms, children free with parents, senior rates, CC. SGL/DBL$38-$58.

Ovando
Area Code 406

Lake Upsata Guest Ranch (Ovando 59834; 793-5890) rooms and cabins, restaurant, TV, CC. SGL/DBL$65-$85.

Polson
Area Code 406

Best Western Kwa Taq Nuk Resort (303 Hwy. 93 East, 59860; 883-3636, 800-528-1234) 112 rooms, restaurant, lounge, indoor and outdoor pool, exercise facilities, children free with parents, a/c, NS rooms, TV, laundry facilities, wheelchair access, pets OK, meeting facilities, senior rates, CC. SGL/DBL$50-$105.

Days Inn (914 Hwy. 93, 59860; 883-3120, 800-325-2525) 25 rooms, free breakfast, a/c, TV, wheelchair access, NS rooms, pets OK, laundry facilities, senior rates, CC. SGL/DBL$35-$60.

Port Polson Inn (Polson 59860; 883-5385, Fax 883-3998) 43 rooms, sauna, whirlpools, in-room refrigerators, laundry facilities, a/c, TV, wheelchair access, NS rooms, senior rates, CC. SGL/DBL$35-$70.

Ruth's Bed and Breakfast (802 7th Ave., West, 59860) 1 room, free breakfast, TV, a/c, no pets, NS, shared baths. SGL/DBL$18-$35.

Pray
Area Code 406

Chico Hot Springs (Pray 59065; 333-4933) restaurant, lounge, a/c, TV, CC. SGL/DBL$55-$68.

Red Lodge
Area Code 406

Best Western LuPine Inn (Red Lodge 59068; 446-1321, Fax 446-1465, 800-528-1234) 46 rooms, indoor heated pool, sauna, children free with parents, kitchenettes, game room, a/c, NS rooms, TV, laundry facilities, wheelchair access, pets OK, meeting rooms, senior rates, CC. SGL/DBL$50-$60.

Rock Creek Resort (Red Lodge 59068; 446-1111) 75 rooms and efficiencies, restaurant, indoor heated pool, whirlpools, exercise center, tennis courts, kitchenettes, children free with parents, game room, no pets, laundry facilities, a/c, TV, meeting rooms, CC. SGL/DBL$36-$60.

Super 8 Motel (1223 South Broadway, 59068; 446-2288, Fax 446-3162, 800-800-8000) 50 rooms and suites, indoor heated pool, whirlpools, pets OK, children under 12 free with parents, free local calls, a/c, TV, in-room refrigerators and microwaves, fax service, NS rooms, wheelchair access, meeting facilities, senior rates, CC. SGL/DBL$50-$56.

The Willows Inn (224 South Platt Ave., 59068; 446-3913) rooms and 2-bedroom cottage, free breakfast, NS, no children, private baths, antique furnishings, TV, a/c, no pets, CC. SGL/DBL$50-$70.

Yodeler Motel (601 South Broadway, 59068; 446-1435, Fax 446-1020) 23 rooms and 2-bedroom efficiencies, whirlpools, children under 12 free with parents, pets OK, a/c, TV, wheelchair access, in-room coffee makers, airport transportation, NS rooms, senior rates, CC. SGL/DBL$30-$48.

Cell Lake
Area Code 406

The Emily A (Cell Lake 59868; 677-3474, Fax 677-3333) 5 rooms, free breakfast, TV, fax service, shared baths, water view, a/c, no pets, CC. SGL/DBL$85.

Wilderness Gateway Inn (Cell Lake 59868; 677-2095) 19 rooms, pets OK, TV, CC. SGL/DBL$32-$45.

Shelby
Area Code 406

Crossroads Inn (Shelby 59474; 434-5134) 52 rooms, indoor heated pool, whirlpools, in-room refrigerators and microwaves, NS rooms, children under 16 free with parents, pets OK, laundry facilities, CC. SGL/DBL$40-$52.

O'Haire Manor Motel (204 2nd St., 59474; 434-5555) 40 rooms and 2-bedroom efficiencies, whirlpools, laundry facilities, pets OK, airport transportation, a/c, TV, NS rooms, senior rates, CC. SGL/DBL$26-$40.

Williams Court (525 1st St., 59474; 434-2254) 11 rooms and 2-bedroom efficiencies, no pets, TV, CC. SGL/DBL$32-$40.

Three Forks
Area Code 406

Broken Spur Motel (124 West Elm St., 58752; 285-3237, Fax 285-6514) 21 rooms, NS rooms, TV, children free with parents, pets OK, CC. SGL/DBL$30-$42.

Fort Three Forks Motel (10766 Hwy. 287, 59752; 285-3233) 24 rooms, TV, a/c, laundry facilities, pets OK, children under 11 free with parents, CC. SGL/DBL$30-$45.

Sacajewea Inn (5 North Main St., 59752; 285-6934, Fax 285-6515, 800-821-7326) 33 rooms, restaurant, TV, VCRs, modified American plan available, NS, a/c, children free with parents, pets OK, CC. SGL/DBL$40-$100.

Troy
Area Code 406

Bull Lake Guest Ranch (15303 Bull Lake Rd., 59935; 295-4228) 6 rooms, free breakfast, TV, a/c, no pets, shared baths, CC. SGL/DBL$35-$50.

Virginia City
Area Code 406

Fairweather Inn (Virginia City 59775; 843-5377, 800-648-7588) 53 rooms and cabins, restaurant, TV, no pets, CC. SGL/DBL$37-$45.

Nevada City Hotel and Cabins (Virginia City 59775; 843-5377) 31 rooms and cabins, pets OK, CC. SGL/DBL$40-$50.

West Yellowstone
Area Code 406

Rental and Reservation Services:

West Yellowstone Lodging (800-221-1151)

❑❑❑

Alpine Motel (120 Madison, 59758; 646-7544) 12 rooms and suites, no pets, TV, airport transportation, CC. SGL/DBL$35-$55.

Ambassador Motor Inn (315 Yellowstone Ave., 59758; 646-7365, Fax 646-9490) 52 rooms and 2-bedroom efficiencies, heated pool, whirlpools, laundry facilities, a/c, TV, wheelchair access, NS rooms, senior rates, CC. SGL/DBL$32-$70.

Best Western Crosswinds Motor Inn (201 Firehole, 59758; 646-9557, Fax 646-9592, 800-528-1234) 70 rooms, restaurant, lounge, indoor heated pool, exercise facilities, children free with parents, a/c, NS rooms, TV, airport transportation, laundry facilities, wheelchair access, pets OK, meeting facilities, senior rates, CC. SGL/DBL$35-$90.

Best Western Desert Inn (133 Canyon Ave., 59758; 646-7376, 800-528-1234) 57 rooms and 2-bedroom efficiencies, outdoor pool, children free with parents, a/c, NS rooms, TV, laundry facilities, airport transportation, wheelchair access, pets OK, meeting facilities, senior rates, CC. SGL/DBL$32-$90.

Best Western Executive Inn (West Yellowstone 59758; 646-7681, Fax 646-9549, 800-528-1234) 82 rooms, restaurant, pool, children free with parents, a/c, NS rooms, TV, laundry facilities, wheelchair access, in-room refrigerators and microwaves, pets OK, meeting facilities, senior rates, CC. SGL/DBL$45-$75.

Branding Iron Motel (201 Canyon Ave., 59758; 646-9411, Fax 646-9575, 800-217-4613) 75 rooms, a/c, TV, no pets, in-room refrigerators, laundry facilities, children under 12 free with parents, wheelchair access, NS rooms, senior rates, CC. SGL/DBL$35-$75.

Buckboard Motel (119 Electric St., 59758; 646-9020) 23 rooms and efficiencies, hot tub, in-room refrigerators, TV, pets OK, CC. SGL/DBL$35-$70.

City Center Motel (214 Madison Ave., 59758; 646-7337, Fax 646-7337, 800-742-0665) 25 rooms and 2- and 3-bedroom efficiencies, whirlpools, gift shop, local transportation, no pets, TV, meeting facilities, CC. SGL/DBL$25-$75.

Days Inn (118 Electric, 59758; 646-7656, Fax 646-7965, 800-325-2525) 45 rooms, restaurant, indoor heated pool, whirlpools, sauna, a/c, TV, wheelchair access, children free with parents, NS rooms, airport transportation, in-room refrigerators, pets OK, laundry facilities, senior rates, CC. SGL/DBL$42-$90.

Evergreen Motel (229 Firehole, 59758; 646-7655) 16 rooms, TV, laundry facilities, kitchenettes, no pets, NS rooms, CC. SGL/DBL$28-$60.

Lazy G Motel (West Yellowstone 59758; 646-7586) 15 rooms and efficiencies, TV, airport transportation, in-room refrigerators, no pets, CC. SGL/DBL$38-$68.

Midtown Motel (West Yellowstone 59758; 646-9490) 15 rooms, a/c, TV, pets OK, NS rooms, airport transportation, senior rates, CC. SGL/DBL$30-$65.

Pony Express Motel (West Yellowstone 59758; 646-7644, 800-323-9708) 16 rooms, TV, no pets, airport transportation, NS rooms, CC. SGL/DBL$40-$70.

Roundup Motel (3 Madison Ave., 59758; 646-7301) 26 rooms and efficiencies, outdoor heated pool, whirlpools, kitchenettes, airport transportation, no pets, TV, CC. SGL/DBL$40-$65.

Stage Coach Inn (West Yellowstone 59758; 646-7381, 800-842-2882) 80 rooms, restaurant, lounge, entertainment, a/c, TV, wheelchair access, NS rooms, airport courtesy car, no pets, in-room refrigerators, gift shop, laundry facilities, children free with parents, meeting facilities, senior rates, CC. SGL/DBL$45-$105.

Super 8 Motel (West Yellowstone 59758; 646-9584, 800-800-8000) 44 rooms and suites, restaurant, whirlpools, sauna, no pets, children under 12 free with parents, free local calls, a/c, TV, in-room refrigerators and micro-waves, fax service, NS rooms, wheelchair access, meeting facilities, senior rates, CC. SGL/DBL$35-$80.

Tepee Motor Lodge (105 Dunraven, 59758; 646-7391, Fax 646-9490) 18 rooms, whirlpools, pets OK, a/c, airport transportation, TV, senior rates, CC. SGL/DBL$30-$63.

Three Bears Motor Lodge (217 Yellowstone Ave., 59758; 646-7353) 44 rooms and 2-bedroom efficiencies, restaurant, lounge, heated pool, whirl-pools, in-room refrigerators and microwaves, pets OK, airport transporta-tion, a/c, TV, wheelchair access, NS rooms, senior rates, CC. SGL/DBL$30-$80.

Travelers Lodge (225 Yellowstone Ave., 59758; 646-9561, Fax 646-7965) 43 rooms, outdoor heated pool, whirlpools, in-room refrigerators, pets OK, a/c, TV, wheelchair access, NS rooms, airport transportation, senior rates, CC. SGL/DBL$40-$70.

Westward Ho Motel (16 Boundary St., 59758; 646-7331) 33 rooms, no pets, kitchenettes, airport transportation, NS rooms, TV, CC. SGL/DBL$30-$48.

Whitefish
Area Code 406

Chalet Motel (6430 Hwy. 93 south, 59937; 862-5581, Fax 862-3103, 800-462-3266) 33 rooms, indoor heated pool, whirlpools, sauna, TV, wheel-chair access, NS rooms, in-room refrigerators and microwaves, pets OK, children free with parents, senior rates, CC. SGL/DBL$30-$70.

Comfort Inn (6390 South Hwy. 93, 59937; 800-228-5150) 65 rooms, restau-rant, free breakfast, indoor heated pool, spa, whirlpools, free local calls, kitchenettes, children under 18 free with parents, pets OK, a/c, TV, CC. SGL/DBL$70-$200.

The Duck Inn (1305 Columbia Ave., 59937; 862-3925) 10 rooms, free breakfast, local transportation, whirlpools, NS, TV, no pets, CC. SGL/DBL$60-$90.

Good Medicine Lodge (537 Wisconsin Ave., 59937; 862-5488, Fax 862-5489) 9 rooms, free breakfast, laundry facilities, airport transportation, no pets, CC. SGL/DBL$45-$110.

Grouse Mountain Lodge (Whitefish 59937; 862-3999, Fax 862-0326, 800-321-8822) 144 rooms and suites, restaurant, lounge, entertainment, indoor heated pool, whirlpools, sauna, tennis courts, in-room refrigerators, game room, a/c, TV, wheelchair access, NS rooms, no pets, children free with parents, room service, local transportation, meeting facilities, senior rates, CC. SGL/DBL$60-$110.

Kandahar (Whitefish 59937; 862-6098, Fax 862-6095) 50 rooms and efficiencies, restaurant, sauna, whirlpools, TV, laundry facilities, children free with parents, no pets, kitchenettes, CC. SGL/DBL$75-$120.

Mountain Holiday (Whitefish 59937; 862-2548, 800-543-8064) 34 rooms, restaurant, indoor heated pool, sauna, whirlpools, a/c, children free with parents, laundry facilities, pets OK, in-room refrigerators, meeting facilities, senior rates, TV, CC. SGL/DBL$50-$60.

Quality Pine Inn (920 Spokane Ave., 59937; 862-7600, Fax 862-7616) 76 rooms and suites, free breakfast, exercise center, whirlpools, airport courtesy car, in-room refrigerators and microwaves, children free with parents, game room, a/c, pets OK, laundry facilities, TV, CC. SGL/DBL$80-$175.

Rocky Mountain Lodge (6510 Hwy. 93 South, 59937; 862-2569) 21 rooms, indoor heated pool, sauna, kitchenettes, children free with parents, a/c, TV, wheelchair access, NS rooms, no pets, senior rates, CC. SGL/DBL$45-$82.

Super 8 Motel (800 Spokane Ave., 59937; 862-8255, 800-800-8000) 40 rooms, pets OK, children under 12 free with parents, free local calls, a/c, TV, in-room refrigerators and microwaves, fax service, NS rooms, wheelchair access, meeting facilities, senior rates, CC. SGL/DBL$60-$80.

Wolf Point

Area Code 406

Homestead Inn (Wolf Point 59201; 653-1300, 800-231-0986) 47 rooms, free breakfast, TV, NS rooms, no pets, senior rates, CC. SGL/DBL$30-$38.

Sherman Motor Inn (200 East Main St., 59201; 653-1100, Fax 653-3456) 46 rooms, restaurant, pets OK, NS rooms, children free with parents, TV, a/c, CC. SGL/DBL$27-$35.

North Dakota

Ashley

Ashley Motel (201 West Main St., 58413; 288-3441) 15 rooms, a/c, TV, CC. SGL/DBL$35-$44.

Beach

Buckboard Inn (Beach 58621; 872-4794) 36 rooms, a/c, TV, wheelchair access, NS rooms, senior rates, VCRs, children free with parents, pets OK, CC. SGL/DBL$28-$35.

Westgate Motel (Hwy. 16, 58621; 872-4521) 10 rooms, a/c, TV, wheelchair access, CC. SGL/DBL$26-$32.

Belcourt

Anishinaubag (Belcourt 58316; 477-6542) cabins, TV. SGL/DBL$28-$36.

Belfield

Bel-Vu Motel (Belfield 58622; 575-4245) 21 rooms, a/c, TV, wheelchair access, senior rates, CC. SGL/DBL$35-$40.

Trappers Inn Motel (Belfield 58622; 575-4261, 800-284-1855) 69 rooms and suites, restaurant, lounge, a/c, TV, wheelchair access, NS rooms, senior rates, CC. SGL/DBL$40-$56.

Beulah

Dakota Waters Resort (Beulah 58523; 873-5800) 6 cabins, TV, CC. SGL/DBL$45-$55.

Lake Shore Cottages (Beulah 58523; 873-5882) kitchenettes, water view, laundry facilities, CC. SGL/DBL$56.

Super 8 Motel (720 Hwy. 49 North, 58523; 873-2850, 800-800-8000) 39 rooms and suites, no pets, children under 12 free with parents, free local calls, a/c, TV, in-room refrigerators and microwaves, fax service, NS rooms, wheelchair access, meeting facilities, senior rates, CC. SGL/DBL$55-$63.

Bismarck

Area Code 701

Best Western Doublewood Inn (1400 East Interchange, 58501; 258-7000, Fax 258-2001, 800-528-1234) 144 rooms, restaurant, lounge, whirlpools, sauna, children free with parents, a/c, NS rooms, in-room computer hookups, TV, laundry facilities, wheelchair access, airport transportation, pets OK, meeting facilities, senior rates, CC. SGL/DBL$55-$78.

Best Western Fleck House (122 East Thayer, 58501; 255-1450, Fax 258-3816, 800-528-1234) 58 rooms and suites, restaurant, free breakfast, heated pool, exercise facilities, children free with parents, a/c, NS rooms, TV, in-room coffee makers, pets OK, airport transportation, kitchenettes, laundry facilities, wheelchair access, meeting facilities, senior rates, CC. SGL/DBL$35-$50.

Bismarck Motor Hotel (2301 East Main Ave., 58501; 223-2474) 34 rooms and 2-bedroom efficiencies, children free with parents, a/c, TV, wheelchair access, NS rooms, senior rates, pets OK, CC. SGL/DBL$20-$33.

Comfort Inn (1030 Interstate Ave., 58501; 223-1911, Fax 223-1911, 800-228-5150) 148 rooms and 2-bedroom suites, indoor heated pool, whirlpools, exercise center, airport transportation, VCRs, in-room refrigerators, children free with parents, pets OK, a/c, TV, CC. SGL/DBL$35-$55.

Days Inn (1300 Capitol Ave., 58501; 223-9151, Fax 223-9423, 800-325-2525) 110 rooms, free breakfast, indoor heated pool, jacuzzi, a/c, TV, wheelchair access, NS rooms, no pets, laundry facilities, senior rates, CC. SGL/DBL$40-$65.

Expressway Inn (200 Bismarck Expressway, 58504; 222-2900, 800-456-6388) 162 rooms, free breakfast, outdoor heated pool, whirlpools, laundry facilities, pets OK, children free with paarents, a/c, TV, wheelchair access, NS rooms, senior rates, CC. SGL/DBL$28-$40.

Fairfield Inn by Marriott North (1120 Century Ave., 58501; 223-9077, 800-228-2800) 63 rooms, indoor heated pool, spa, children under 18 free with parents, NS rooms, remote control TV, free cable TV, pets OK, free local calls, laundry service, a/c, wheelchair access, meeting facilities, fax service, senior rates, CC. SGL/DBL$40-$67.

Fairfield Inn by Marriott South (135 Ivy Ave., 58504; 223-9293, 800-228-2800) 63 rooms, free breakfast, indoor heated pool, spa, children under 18 free with parents, NS rooms, free cable TV, free local calls, laundry service, a/c, wheelchair access, meeting facilities, fax service, senior rates, CC. SGL/DBL$36-$59.

Hillside Motel (Divide Ave., 58502; 223-7986) 16 rooms, a/c, TV, wheelchair access, NS rooms, senior rates, CC. SGL/DBL$33-$46.

Holiday Inn (605 East Broadway, 58502; 255-6000, Fax 223-0400, 800-HOLIDAY) 215 rooms, restaurant, lounge, indoor heated pool, exercise facilities, sauna, whirlpools, children under 19 free with parents, wheelchair access, a/c, TV, NS rooms, fax service, room service, no pets, laundry service, meeting facilities, senior rates, CC. SGL/DBL$55-$75.

Kelly Inn (1800 North 12th St., 58501; 223-8001) 101 rooms, restaurant, lounge, indoor heated pool, sauna, whirlpools, kitchenettes, VCRs, children free with parents, pets OK, airport transportation, a/c, TV, wheelchair access, NS rooms, senior rates, CC. SGL/DBL$42-$55.

Motel 6 (2433 State St., 58501; 255-6878, 505-891-6161) 101 rooms, pool, free local calls, children under 17 free with parents, NS rooms, wheelchair access, no pets, a/c, TV, CC. SGL/DBL$25-$28.

Radisson Hotel (800 South 3rd St., 58504; 258-7700, Fax 224-8212, 800-333-3333) 306 rooms and suites, restaurant, lounge, entertainment, pool, exercise center, in-room refrigerators, microwaves and coffee makers, children free with parents, VCRs, wheelchair access, free parking, NS rooms, TV, a/c, children free with parents, pets OK, senior rates, CC. SGL/DBL$60-$90.

Ramada Hotel (1152 Memorial Hwy., 58502; 223-9600, 800-2-RAMADA) 256 rooms and suites, restaurant, lounge, indoor heated pool, sauna, wheelchair access, NS rooms, free parking, pets OK, a/c, TV, children under 18 free with parents, room service, laundry facilities, in-room refrigerators and microwaves, airport transportation, meeting facilities, senior rates, CC. SGL/DBL$48-$55.

Redwood Motel (1702 East Broadway, 58502; 223-4138) 8 rooms, TV. SGL/DBL$28-$38.

Select Inn (1505 Interchange Ave., 58501; 223-8060, 800-641-1000) 102 rooms, free breakfast, a/c, TV, NS rooms, free local calls, pets OK, senior rates, laundry facilities, children under age 13 stay fee with parents, VCRs, fax service, meeting facilities, senior rates, CC. SGL/DBL$26-$36.

Super 8 Motel (1124 East Capitol Ave., 58501; 255-1314, 800-800-8000) 61 rooms and suites, pets OK, children under 12 free with parents, free local calls, a/c, TV, in-room refrigerators and microwaves, VCRs, fax service, NS rooms, wheelchair access, meeting facilities, senior rates, CC. SGL/DBL$35-$49.

Bottineau
Area Code 701

Norway House (Bottineau 58318; 228-3737) 46 rooms, restaurant, lounge, a/c, TV, wheelchair access, NS rooms, no pets, room service, airport courtesy car, senior rates, CC. SGL/DBL$27-$35.

Turtle Mountain Lodge (Bottineau 58318; 263-4206, 800-998-2375) 24 rooms, restaurant, lounge, entertainment, indoor pool, whirlpools, a/c, TV, wheelchair access, NS rooms, water view, pets OK, in-room refrigerators, senior rates, CC. SGL/DBL$30-$60.

Bowman
Area Code 701

Budget Host (704 Hwy. 12 West, 58623; 523-3243, Fax 523-3357, 800-283-4678) 40 rooms, restaurant, laundry facilities, pets OK, in-room coffee makers, sauna, NS rooms, wheelchair access, a/c, TV, in-room refrigerators and coffee makers, senior rates, children free with parents, CC. SGL/DBL$22-$40.

Downtown Motel (101 North Main St., 58523; 523-5621) 10 rooms and efficiencies, a/c, TV, wheelchair access, NS rooms, senior rates, CC. SGL/DBL$45-$65.

El-Vue Motel (Bowman 58523; 523-5224, 800-521-0379) 16 a/c rooms, TV, wheelchair access, NS rooms, senior rates, CC. SGL/DBL$33-$45.

North Winds Lodge (Bowman 58523; 523-5641) 16 rooms, outdooor heated pool, in-room coffee makers, pets OK, a/c, TV, wheelchair access, NS rooms, airport transportation, senior rates, CC. SGL/DBL$25-$38.

Super 8 Motel (614 3rd Ave. Southwest, 58523; 523-5613, 800-800-8000) 30 rooms and suites, sauna, whirlpools, pets OK, children under 12 free with parents, free local calls, a/c, TV, in-room refrigerators and microwaves, fax service, NS rooms, wheelchair access, meeting facilities, senior rates, CC. SGL/DBL$29-$45.

Trail Motel (208 Hwy. 12, 58523; 523-3291) 13 rooms, a/c, TV, CC. SGL/DBL$26-$35.

Cando
Area Code 701

Sportmans Motel (Hwy. 281, 58324; 968-4451) 17 rooms, a/c, TV, CC. SGL/DBL$45.

Carrington
Area Code 701

Blue Swan Inn Bed and Breakfast (629 2nd St. North, 58421; 652-3978) rooms, free breakfast, TV, a/c, no pets, CC. SGL/DBL$46-$66.

Chieftan Lodge (Hwy. 281, 58421; 652-3131) 51 rooms, restaurant, lounge, children free with parents, pets OK, a/c, TV, wheelchair access, NS rooms, senior rates, meeting facilities, CC. SGL/DBL$29-$40.

Del Claire Motel (355 South 2nd St., 58421; 652-3161) 28 rooms, a/c, TV, wheelchair access, NS rooms, senior rates, CC. SGL/DBL$23-$33.

Super 8 Motel (Hwy. 281, 58421; 652-3894, 800-800-8000) 30 rooms, whirlpools, pets OK, children under 12 free with parents, free local calls, a/c, TV, in-room refrigerators and microwaves, fax service, NS rooms, wheelchair access, in-room computer hookups, laundry facilities, meeting facilities, senior rates, CC. SGL/DBL$29-$39.

Devils Lake
Area Code 701

Artlare Motel (Hwy. 2 East, 58302; 662-4001, 800-280-4001) 80 rooms, restaurant, lounge, indoor heated a/c, TV, wheelchair access, NS rooms, senior rates, CC. SGL/DBL$$25-$32.

Comfort Inn (215 Hwy. 2 East, 58302; 662-6760, 800-228-5150) 60 rooms, indoor pool, whirlpools, game room, children free with parents, pets OK, in-room refrigerators and microwaves, fax service, a/c, TV, meeting facilities for 30, CC. SGL/DBL$34-$50.

Dakotah Friend Bed and Breakfast (Devils Lake 58301; 662-6327) free breakfast, TV, a/c, no pets, CC. SGL/DBL$66-$86.

Davis Motel (Hwy. 2 West, 58302; 662-4927) 23 rooms, TV, a/c. SGL/DBL$33-$38.

Days Inn (Hwy. 20 South, 58301; 662-5381, Fax 662-3578, 800-325-2525) 45 rooms, free breakfast, pets OK, a/c, TV, wheelchair access, NS rooms, in-room refrigerators and microwaves, children free with parents, pets OK, laundry facilities, senior rates, CC. SGL/DBL$33-$78.

Super 8 Motel (Devils Lake 58301; 662-8656, 800-800-8000) 39 rooms, free breakfast, restaurant, pets OK, children under 12 free with parents, free local calls, a/c, TV, in-room refrigerators and microwaves, fax service, NS rooms, wheelchair access, meeting facilities, senior rates, CC. SGL/DBL$28-$36.

Trails West Motel (Devils Lake 58301; 662-5011) 74 rooms, a/c, TV, wheelchair access, NS rooms, senior rates, CC. SGL/DBL$25-$32.

Woodland Resort (Devils Lake 58301; 662-5996) cabins, kitchenettees, water view, TV, CC. SGL/DBL$60.

Dickinson

Area Code 701

Best Western Red Coach Inn (71 12th St. West, 58601; 227-4310, Fax 227-4715, 800-528-1234) 136 rooms, restaurant, lounge, indoor heated pool, whirlpools, children free with parents, a/c, NS rooms, TV, laundry facilities, wheelchair access, pets OK, meeting facilities, senior rates, CC. SGL/DBL$38-$55.

Budget Inn (529 12th St., West, 58601; 225-9123, Fax 225-4077, 800-527-0700) 54 rooms, outdoor heated pool, NS rooms, children free with parents, pets OK, VCRs, a/c, TV, meeting facilities, CC. SGL/DBL$22-$40.

City Motel (1520 West Villard, 58601; 225-9909) 12 rooms, a/c, TV, CC. SGL/DBL$44-$54.

Comfort Inn (493 Elk Dr., 58601; 264-7300, 800-228-5150) 113 rooms and suites, free breakfast, indoor heated pool, whirlpool tubs, airport courtesy car, laundry facilities, children free with parents, pets OK, whirlpools, a/c, TV, CC. SGL/DBL$27-$49.

Friendship Inn (1000 West Villard, 58601; 225-6703, 800-424-4777) 35 rooms, pool, exercise facilities, a/c, TV, no pets, NS rooms, children free with parents, wheelchair access, senior rates, CC. SGL/DBL$29-$45.

Hospitality Inn and Convention Center (532 15th St., West, 58602; 227-1853, Fax 225-0090, 800-422-0949) 149 rooms and suites, restaurant, lounge, entertainment, indoor heated pool, whirlpools, sauna, a/c, pets OK, local transportation, TV, laundry facilities, wheelchair access, NS rooms, meeting facilities, senior rates, CC. SGL/DBL$38-$56.

Ivanhoe Inn (22 East Villard, 58602; 225-5119, 800-341-8000) 26 rooms, outdoor pool, a/c, TV, wheelchair access, NS rooms, senior rates, CC. SGL/DBL$23-$32.

Joyce's Home Away From Home (1561 1st Ave., East, 58602; 227-1524) rooms, free breakfast, TV, a/c, no pets, CC. SGL/DBL$35-$55.

Nodak Motel (600 East Villard St., 58601; 225-5119) 26 rooms and efficiencies, outdoor heated pool, kitchenettes, a/c, TV, in-room refrigerators and microwaves, pets OK, wheelchair access, NS rooms, senior rates, CC. SGL/DBL$23-$32.

Queen City Motel (1108 West Villard, 58601; 225-5121) 33 rooms, outdoor pool, a/c, TV, wheelchair access, NS rooms, senior rates, CC. SGL/DBL$26-$38.

Select Inn (642 12th St., West 58601; 227-1891, 800-641-1000) 59 rooms, free breakfast, a/c, TV, wheelchair access, NS rooms, laundry facilities, children free with parents, pets OK, fax service, meeting facilities, senior rates, CC. SGL/DBL$$20-$32.

Super 8 Motel (637 12th St., West, 58601; 227-1215, Fax 227-1807, 800-800-8000) 59 rooms and suites, children under 12 free with parents, free local calls, a/c, TV, in-room refrigerators and microwaves, fax service, VCRs, pets OK, NS rooms, wheelchair access, meeting facilities, senior rates, CC. SGL/DBL$28-$44.

Drayton
Area Code 701

Motel 66 (Drayton 58225; 454-6464) 25 rooms, pets OK, a/c, TV, wheelchair access, NS rooms, senior rates, CC. SGL/DBL$28-$38.

Fargo
Area Code 701

AmericInn (Fargo 58103; 800-634-3444) 43 rooms, restaurant, lounge, indoor heated pool, sauna, whirlpools, pets OK, laundry facilities, children under 12 free with parents, a/c, TV, wheelchair access, NS rooms, in-room refrigerators and microwaves, meeting facilities, CC. SGL/DBL$40-$58.

Best Western Doublewood Inn (3333 13th Ave. South, 58103; 235-3333, 280-9482, 800-528-1234) 173 rooms and suites, restaurant, lounge, entertainment, indoor heated pool, exercise facilities, jacuzzi, children free with parents, a/c, NS rooms, TV, laundry facilities, airport transportation, in-room refrigerators and microwaves, wheelchair access, pets OK, meeting facilities, senior rates, CC. SGL/DBL$63-$90.

Best Western Kelly Inn (3800 Main Ave., 58103; 282-2143, 800-528-1234) 133 rooms, outdoor heated pool, sauna, whirlpools, children free with parents, a/c, NS rooms, TV, laundry facilities, in-room refrigerators, wheelchair access, pets OK, meeting facilities, senior rates, CC. SGL/DBL$46-$64.

Bohligs Bed and Breakfast (1418 3rd Ave. South, 58102; 235-7867) free breakfast, TV, a/c, no pets, CC. SGL/DBL$44-$64.

Comfort Suites (1415 35th St. South, 58103; 237-5911, 800-228-5150) 66 rooms, indoor heated pool, whirlpools, pets OK, children free with parents, in-room refrigerators and microwaves, a/c, TV, meeting facilities, CC. SGL/DBL$50-$72.

Comfort Inn East (1407 35th St. South, 58103; 280-9666, 800-228-5150) 66 rooms, indoor heated pool, whirlpools, in-room refrigerators and microwaves, airport courtesy car, a/c, pets OK, TV, senior rates, CC. SGL/DBL$40-$61.

Comfort Inn West (3825 9th Ave. South, 58103; 282-9596, 800-228-5150) 56 rooms, indoor heated pool, airport courtesy car, pets OK, in-room refrigerators and microwaves, children free with parents, a/c, TV, CC. SGL/DBL$44-$63.

Country Suites (3316 13th Ave. South, 58103; 234-0565, 800-456-4000) 100 rooms, lounge, indoor heated pool, exercise center, children free with parents, pets OK, in-room refrigerators, microwaves and coffee makers, airport transportation, a/c, TV, wheelchair access, NS rooms, senior rates, meeting facilities, CC. SGL/DBL$62-$135.

Days Inn West (525 East Main Ave., 58078; 281-0000, Fax 281-0023, 800-325-2525) 61 rooms, free breakfast, indoor heated pool, jacuzzis, a/c, TV, wheelchair access, NS rooms, no pets, laundry facilities, senior rates, meeting facilities, CC. SGL/DBL$40-$85.

Days Inn West Acres (901 38th St. Southwest, 58103; 282-9100, 800-325-2525) 99 rooms, free breakfast, a/c, TV, wheelchair access, NS rooms, no pets, laundry facilities, senior rates, CC. SGL/DBL$40-$53.

Econo Lodge (1401 35th St. South, 58103; 232-3412, 800-4-CHOICE) 67 rooms, children under 12 free with parents, no pets, NS rooms, wheelchair access, local transportation, a/c, TV, senior rates, CC. SGL/DBL$29-$50.

Expressway Inn (1340 21st Ave. South, 58103; 235-3141, Fax 234-0474, 800-437-0044) 115 rooms, restaurant, lounge, entertainment, a/c, TV, wheelchair access, NS rooms, pets OK, meeting facilities, senior rates, CC. SGL/DBL$37-$45.

Fairfield Inn by Marriott (3902 9th Ave., 58103; 281-0494, Fax 281-0494, 800-228-2800) 63 rooms, indoor heated pool, spa, children under 18 free with parents, NS rooms, free cable TV, free local calls, laundry service, in-room refrigerators and microwaves, pets OK, airport transportation, a/c, wheelchair access, meeting facilities, fax service, senior rates, CC. SGL/DBL$38-$65.

Hampton Inn (3431 14th Ave. Southwest, 58103; 235-5566, 800-HAMP-TON) 75 rooms, restaurant, free breakfast, indoor heated pool, exercise facilities, children under 18 free with parents, NS rooms, wheelchair access, in-room computer hookups, fax service, TV, a/c, free local calls, pets OK, meeting facilities, senior rates, CC. SGL/DBL$45-$58.

Holiday Inn (3902 13th Ave. South, 58106; 282-2700, 800-HOLIDAY) 308 rooms, restaurant, lounge, heated pool, exercise facilities, sauna, whirlpools, pets OK, children under 19 free with parents, wheelchair access, a/c, TV, NS rooms, fax service, room service, laundry service, meeting facilities, senior rates, CC. SGL/DBL$65-$90.

Motel 6 (1202 36th St. South, 58103; 232-9251, 505-891-6161) 99 rooms, indoor heated pool, free local calls, children under 17 free with parents, NS rooms, wheelchair access, pets OK, a/c, TV, CC. SGL/DBL$24-$30.

Motel 6 (2202 South University Dr., 58103; 235-0570, 505-891-6161) 99 rooms, pool, free local calls, children under 17 free with parents, NS rooms, wheelchair access, pets OK, a/c, TV, CC. SGL/DBL$23-$39.

Motel 75 (3402 14th Ave. South, 58103; 232-1321) 102 roooms and 2-bedroom efficiencies, a/c, TV, wheelchair access, NS rooms, senior rates, CC. SGL/DBL$30-$40.

Radisson Hotel (201 5th St., North, 58102; 232-7363, 800-333-3333) 151 rooms and suites, restaurant, lounge, entertainment, whirlpools, sauna, exercise center, in-room refrigerators, microwaves and coffee makers, VCRs, airport transportation, wheelchair access, free parking, NS rooms, TV, a/c, children free with parents, pets OK, senior rates, CC. SGL/DBL$85-$95.

Scandia Hotel (717 4th St. North, 58102; 232-2661, 800-223-2913 in the Northwest) 58 rooms, a/c, TV, wheelchair access, NS rooms, CC. SGL/DBL$65-$85.

Select Inn (1025 38th St. Southwest, 58103; 282-6300, Fax 282-6308, 800-641-1000) 178 rooms and efficiencies, free breakfast, a/c, TV, NS rooms, free local calls, pets OK, senior rates, laundry facilities, children under age 13 stay free with parents, VCRs, fax service, meeting facilities, senior rates, CC. SGL/DBL$28-$66.

Sleep Inn (1921 44th St., 58103; 281-8240, 800-221-2222) 60 rooms, free breakfast, wheelchair access, exercise facilities, NS rooms, no pets, children under 18 free with parents, in-room computer hookups, senior rates, a/c, TV, meeting facilities, CC. SGL/DBL$38-$66.

Sunset Motel (Hwy. 10, 58103; 282-3266, 800-252-2207) 66 rooms, exercise center, spa, game room, a/c, TV, wheelchair access, NS rooms, senior rates, CC. SGL/DBL$58-$88.

Super 8 Motel (3518 Interstate Blvd., 58103; 232-9202, Fax 232-4543, 800-800-8000) 85 rooms and suites, no pets, children under 12 free with parents, free local calls, a/c, TV, in-room refrigerators and microwaves, fax service, NS rooms, wheelchair access, meeting facilities, senior rates, CC. SGL/DBL$30-$45.

Super 8 Motel (825 East Main Ave., 58103; 282-7121, Fax 277-9237, 800-800-8000) 42 rooms and suites, no pets, children under 12 free with parents, free local calls, a/c, TV, in-room refrigerators and microwaves, fax service, NS rooms, wheelchair access, meeting facilities, senior rates, CC. SGL/DBL$30-$44.

Townhouse Inn (301 3rd Ave. North, 58103; 232-8851, 800-437-4682) 109 rooms, restaurant, lounge, indoor heated pool, whirlpools, sauna, a/c, TV, wheelchair access, NS rooms, senior rates, CC. SGL/DBL$55-$75.

Garrison
Area Code 701

Garrison Motel (Hwy. 37, 58540; 463-2858) 30 rooms, pets OK, a/c, TV, wheelchair access, NS rooms, children free with parents, senior rates, CC. SGL/DBL$25-$35.

Indian Hills Resort (Garrison 58540; 743-4122) 4 2-bedroom condominiums and cabins, kitchenettes, water view, a/c, TV, CC. SGL/DBL$73.

Grand Forks
Area Code 701

Ambassador Motel (2021 South Washington; 772-3463) 30 rooms, a/c, TV, wheelchair access, NS rooms, senior rates, CC. SGL/DBL$36-$58.

Best Western Fabulous Westward Ho Motel (Hwy. 2 West, , 775-5341, Fax 775-3703, 800-528-1234) 107 rooms, restaurant, lounge, entertainment, outdoor pool, saunas, children free with parents, a/c, NS rooms, TV, laundry facilities, wheelchair access, pets OK, meeting facilities, senior rates, CC. SGL/DBL$45-$68.

Best Western Town House (710 1st Ave. North, 58230; 746-5411, Fax 746-1407, 800-528-1234) 103 rooms, restaurant, lounge, indoor heated pool, exercise facilities, sauna, whirlpools, children free with parents, a/c, in-room refrigerators, NS rooms, TV, laundry facilities, wheelchair access, pets OK, meeting facilities, senior rates, CC. SGL/DBL$55-$75.

C'Mon Inn (3051 32nd Ave. South, 58201; 775-3320, 800-255-2323) 80 rooms and suites, indoor pool, hot tubs, exercise center, a/c, TV, wheelchair access, NS rooms, senior rates, CC. SGL/DBL$55-$70, STS$80-$120.

Comfort Inn (3251 30th Ave. South, 58201; 775-7503, 800-228-5150) 67 rooms, indoor heated pool, whirlpools, a/c, TV, CC. SGL/DBL$44-$69.

Country Inn Suites (3350 32nd Ave. South, 58201; 775-5000) 89 rooms, indoor heated pool, whirlpools, sauna, in-room refrigerators and microwaves, pets OK, children free with parents, a/c, TV, wheelchair access, NS rooms, senior rates, CC. SGL/DBL$58-$70.

Days Inn (3101 34th St. South, 58201; 775-0060, 800-325-2525) 52 rooms, free breakfast, indoor heated pool, whirlpools, pets OK, in-room refrigerators, VCRs, a/c, TV, wheelchair access, NS rooms, laundry facilities, senior rates, CC. SGL/DBL$40-$80.

Econo Lodge (900 North 43rd St., 58201; 746-6666, 800-4-CHOICE) 44 rooms and suites, children under 12 free with parents, pets OK, senior rates, NS rooms, wheelchair access, free local telephone calls, in-room refrigerators, a/c, TV, senior rates, CC. SGL/DBL$34-$60.

Fairfield Inn by Marriott (3051 South 34th St., 58201; 775-7910, 800-228-2800) 62 rooms, indoor heated pool, spa, children under 18 free with parents, NS rooms, free cable TV, free local calls, laundry service, a/c, wheelchair access, meeting facilities, fax service, senior rates, CC. SGL/DBL$40-$63.

511 Reeves Bed and Breakfast (511 Reeves Dr., 58203; 775-3332) free breakfast, TV, a/c, no pets, CC. SGL/DBL$40-$60.

Holiday Inn (1210 North 43rd St., 58203; 772-7131, Fax 780-9112, 800-HOLIDAY) 150 rooms, restaurant, lounge, indoor and outdoor heated pool, exercise facilities, sauna, whirlpools, children under 19 free with parents, wheelchair access, a/c, in-room refrigerators, in-room computer hookups, airport transportation, TV, NS rooms, fax service, room service, no pets, laundry service, meeting facilities, senior rates, CC. SGL/DBL$55-$65.

Merrifield House (Route 1, 58201; 775-4250) free breakfast, TV, a/c, no pets, CC. SGL/DBL$35-$45.

Motel 6 (1211 47th St. North, 58203; 775-0511, 505-891-6161) 99 rooms, indoor heated pool, free local calls, children under 17 free with parents, NS rooms, wheelchair access, pets OK, a/c, TV, CC. SGL/DBL$24-$32.

North Star Inn (2100 South Washington St., 58201; 772-8151, 800-233-8151) 63 rooms and 2-bedroom efficiencies, restaurant, lounge, indoor heated pool, whirlpools, sauna, a/c, TV, wheelchair access, NS rooms, pets OK, children free with parents, senior rates, CC. SGL/DBL$35-$49.

Ramada Inn (1205 North 43rd St., 58203; 775-3951, Fax 775-9774, 800-2-RAMADA) 100 rooms and suites, restaurant, lounge, indoor and outdoor heated pool, wheelchair access, sauna, whirlpools, airport transportation, NS rooms, free parking, pets OK, a/c, TV, children under 18 free with parents, room service, laundry facilities, meeting facilities, senior rates, CC. SGL/DBL$54-$78.

Roadking Inn (1015 North 43rd St., 58203; 775-0691, 800-950-0691) 100 rooms, free breakfast, children free with parents, no pets, tennis courts, a/c, TV, wheelchair access, NS rooms, laundry facilities, senior rates, CC. SGL/DBL$33-$45.

Roadking Inn (3300 30th Ave. South, 58201; 746-1391) 80 rooms, free breakfast, children free with parents, a/c, TV, wheelchair access, laundry facilities, no pets, NS rooms, meeting facilities, senior rates, CC. SGL/DBL$36-$55.

Select Inn (1000 North 42nd St., 58203; 775-0555, Fax 775-9967, 800-641-1000) 120 rooms, free breakfast, a/c, TV, NS rooms, free local calls, pets OK, senior rates, laundry facilities, children under age 13 stay free with parents, VCRs, fax service, meeting facilities, senior rates, CC. SGL/DBL$26-$40.

Super 8 Motel (1122 North 43rd St., 58203; 775-8138, 800-800-8000) 33 rooms and suites, no pets, children under 12 free with parents, free local calls, a/c, TV, in-room refrigerators and microwaves, fax service, NS rooms, wheelchair access, meeting facilities, senior rates, CC. SGL/DBL$45-$53.

Harvey
Area Code 701

Americana Motel (575 Brewster East, 58341; 324-2293) 16 rooms, a/c, TV, wheelchair access, NS rooms, senior rates, CC. SGL/DBL$44-$48.

Amigo Motel (Harvey, 58341; 324-2510) 10 rooms, a/c, TV, CC. SGL/DBL$36-$50.

Artos Motel (Harvey 58341; 324-4602) 45 rooms, restaurant, lounge, a/c, TV, wheelchair access, NS rooms, senior rates, CC. SGL/DBL$38-$42.

Hazen
Area Code 701

Roughrider Motor Inn (Hwy. 200, 58545; 748-2209) 62 rooms, a/c, TV, game room, wheelchair access, NS rooms, senior rates, CC. SGL/DBL$48-$58.

Jamestown
Area Code 701

Buffalo Motel (1530 6th Ave. Southwest, 58401; 252-0180) 22 rooms, a/c, TV. SGL/DBL$44-$48.

Comfort Inn (811 20th St. Southwest, 58401; 252-7125, 800-228-5150) 52 rooms, restaurant, lounge, indoor heated pool, in-room refrigerators and microwaves, laundry facilities, VCRs, children free with parents, pets OK, a/c, TV, meeting facilities, CC. SGL/DBL$39-$60.

Country Charm Bed and Breakfast (Route 3, 58401; 251-1372, 800-331-1372) 3 rooms, free breakfast, TV, children over 12 welcome, airport courtesy car, antique furnishings, NS, 1890s inn, a/c, no pets. SGL/DBL$40-$50.

Dakota Inn (Jamestown 58401; 252-3611, Fax 251-1212) 123 rooms, restaurant, lounge, indoor heated pool, whirlpools, airport transportation, pets OK, children free with parents, a/c, TV, wheelchair access, NS rooms, senior rates, CC. SGL/DBL$39-$50.

Gladstone Select Hotel (111 2nd St. Northeast, 58401; 252-0700, 800-641-1000) 117 rooms, restaurant, lounge, indoor heated pool, whirlpools, pets OK, a/c, TV, wheelchair access, children free with parents, VCRs, airport transportation, NS rooms, senior rates, CC. SGL/DBL$36-$55.

Ranch House Motel (408 Business Loop West, 58401; 252-0222) 38 rooms, heated pool, a/c, TV, wheelchair access, NS rooms, kitchenettes, children free with parents, pets OK, laundry facilities, senior rates, CC. SGL/DBL$26-$36.

Select Inn (Jamestown 58401; 800-641-1000) 117 rooms, free breakfast, a/c, TV, NS rooms, free local calls, pets OK, senior rates, laundry facilities, children under age 13 stay free with parents, VCRs, fax service, meeting facilities, senior rates, CC. SGL/DBL$55-$59.

Sundowner Motel (119 Business Loop West, 58401; 252-2480) 24 rooms and efficiencies, a/c, TV, kitchenettes, senior rates, CC. SGL/DBL$55-$85.

Lake Metigoshe
Area Code 701

Crookstons Resort (Lake Metigoshe 58318; 263-4572) cabins, kitchenettes, CC. SGL/DBL$35-$60.

Turtle Mountain Lodge Resort (Lake Metigoshe 58318; 263-4206) 24 rooms, restaurant, lounge, indoor heated pool, hot tubs, a/c, TV, wheelchair access, NS rooms, senior rates, CC. SGL/DBL$65-$80.

Mandan
Area Code 701

Best Western Seven Seas Inn and Conference Center (2611 Old Red Trail, 58554; 633-74-1, Fax 663-0025, 800-528-1234) 102 rooms, restaurant, lounge, indoor heated pool, exercise facilities, jacuzzi, airport courtesy car, children

free with parents, a/c, NS rooms, TV, laundry facilities, wheelchair access, pets OK, meeting facilities, senior rates, CC. SGL/DBL$50-$60.

Colonial Motel (4631 Memorial Hwy., 58554; 663-9824) 35 rooms, lounge, outdoor pool, a/c, TV, wheelchair access, NS rooms, senior rates, CC. SGL/DBL$40-$60.

Elite Motel (1200 East Main St., 58554; 663-6497) 19 rooms, a/c, TV, wheelchair access, NS rooms, senior rates, CC. SGL/DBL$44-$48.

Modern Frontier Motel (4524 Memorial Hwy., 58554; 663-9856, 800-927-5661) 50 rooms, restaurant, a/c, TV, wheelchair access, NS rooms, senior rates, CC. SGL/DBL$31-$41.

River Ridge Inn (2630 Old Red Trail, 58554; 663-0001) 81 rooms, restaurant, lounge, a/c, TV, fax service, wheelchair access, NS rooms, senior rates, CC. SGL/DBL$35-$44.

McClusky

Area Code 701

McClusky Motor Motel (Hwy. 200, 58463; 363-2507) 11 rooms, a/c, TV, CC. SGL/DBL$28-$36.

Midstate Bed and Breakfast (Route 3, 58463; 363-2520) free breakfast, TV, a/c, no pets, CC. SGL/DBL$36-$60.

Medora

Area Code 701

Bad Lands Motel (Medora 58645; 623-4422) 116 rooms, outdoor heated pool, a/c, TV, wheelchair access, NS rooms, no pets, children free with parents, meeting facilities, CC. SGL/DBL$45-$60.

Medora Motel (East River Rd, 58645; 623-4422) 204 rooms, outdoor heated pool, tennis courts, a/c, TV, children free with parents, no pets, CC. SGL/DBL$44-$48.

Rough Riders Hotel (Medora 58645; 623-4433) 10 rooms and cabins, restaurant, TV, CC. SGL/DBL$47-$57.

Sully Inn (4th St. and Broadway, 58645; 623-4455) 19 rooms, restaurant, a/c, TV, CC. SGL/DBL$38-$42.

Minot

Area Code 701

Best Western International Inn (1505 North Broadway, 58701; 852-3161, Fax 838-5538, 800-528-1234) 270 rooms, restaurant, lounge, entertainment, indoor heated pool, exercise facilities, tennis courts, airport transportation, children free with parents, a/c, NS rooms, TV, laundry facilities, wheelchair access, pets OK, meeting facilities, senior rates, CC. SGL/DBL$50-$75.

Best Western Safari Inn (1510 26th Ave. Southwest, 58701; 852-4300, Fax 838-1234, 800-735-5868, 800-528-1234) 100 rooms and suites, restaurant, free breakfast, lounge, indoor heated pool, exercise facilities, children free with parents, a/c, NS rooms, TV, laundry facilities, wheelchair access, pets OK, meeting facilities, senior rates, CC. SGL/DBL$45-$90.

Broadway Inn (433 North Broadway, 58701; 838-6075) 5 rooms, free breakfast, TV, a/c, no pets, CC. SGL/DBL$50-$75.

Broadway Motel (1524 South Broadway, 58701; 838-5866) 13 rooms and efficiencies, a/c, TV, no pets, CC. SGL/DBL$33-$36.

Casa Motel (1900 Hwys. 2 and 52, 58701; 852-2352) 14 a/c rooms, TV, wheelchair access, NS rooms, laundry facilities, senior rates, CC. SGL/DBL$22-$32.

Comfort Inn (1515 22nd Ave. Southwest, 58701; 852-2201, 800-228-5150) 142 rooms, free breakfast, restaurant, indoor pool, whirlpools, a/c, TV, pets OK, meeting facilities for 220, CC. SGL/DBL$44-$69.

D over L Bed and Breakfast (Minot 58701; 722-3326) free breakfast, TV, a/c, no pets, CC. SGL/DBL$35-$70.

Dakota Inn (2401 West Bypass, 58701; 838-2700) 129 rooms, lounge, indoor heated pool, jacuzzi, a/c, TV, wheelchair access, laundry facilities, no pets, children free with parents, NS rooms, senior rates, CC. SGL/DBL$29-$45.

Dakota Rose Bed and Breakfast (510 4th Ave. Northwest, 58701; 838-3548) free breakfast, TV, a/c, no pets, CC. SGL/DBL$35-$65.

Days Inn (2100 4th St. Southwest, 58701; 852-3464, Fax 852-0501, 800-325-2525) 82 rooms, free breakfast, a/c, TV, wheelchair access, NS rooms, pets OK, laundry facilities, meeting facilities, senior rates, CC. SGL/DBL$35-$60.

Econo Lodge (1937 North Broadway, 58701; 852-5600, 800-4-CHOICE) 101 rooms, free breakfast, airport courtesy car, children under 12 free with parents, no pets, senior rates, NS rooms, wheelchair access, a/c, TV, senior rates, meeting facilities, CC. SGL/DBL$30-$55.

Fairfield Inn by Marriott (900 24th Ave. Southwest, 58701; 838-2424, 800-228-2800) 62 rooms, indoor heated pool, hot tubs, children under 18 free with parents, NS rooms, free cable TV, free local calls, laundry service, a/c, wheelchair access, fax service, meeting facilities, fax service, senior rates, CC. SGL/DBL$38-$70.

Friendship Inn (1900 East Burdick Expressway, 58701; 852-4488, 800-424-4777) 30 rooms, exercise facilities, a/c, TV, no pets, NS rooms, children free with parents, wheelchair access, senior rates, CC. SGL/DBL$32-$38.

Gordons Holiday Sport (1901 South Broadway, 58701; 852-4054) 40 rooms, restaurant, lounge, a/c, TV, wheelchair access, NS rooms, senior rates, CC. SGL/DBL$50-$66.

Hillcrest Motel (1416 South Broadway, 58702; 852-1214) 19 rooms and apartments, a/c, TV, CC. SGL/DBL$45-$55.

Holiday Inn (2305 North Broadway, 58701; 852-4161, 800-HOLIDAY) 172 rooms, restaurant, lounge, pool, exercise facilities, whirlpools, sauna, children under 19 free with parents, wheelchair access, a/c, TV, NS rooms, fax service, room service, no pets, laundry service, meeting facilities, senior rates, CC. SGL/DBL$60-$73.

Kenway Motel (1808 Burdick Expressway East, 58701; 852-2580) 20 rooms, a/c, TV, wheelchair access, NS rooms, senior rates, CC. SGL/DBL$28-$70.

Lois and Stan's Bed and Breakfast (1007 11th Ave. Northwest, 58701; 838-2244) free breakfast, TV, a/c, no pets, CC. SGL/DBL$40-$60.

The Muffin House (112 University Ave., East, 58701; 852-1488) free breakfast, TV, a/c, no pets, CC. SGL/DBL$60-$80.

Select Inn (225 22nd Ave. Northwest, 58701; 852-3411, 800-641-1000) 100 rooms, free breakfast, a/c, TV, NS rooms, free local calls, pets OK, senior rates, laundry facilities, children under age 13 stay free with parents, VCRs, fax service, meeting facilities, senior rates, CC. SGL/DBL$29-$37.

Sheraton Riverside Inn (2200 Burdick Expressway East, 58702; 852-2504, Fax 852-2630, 800-468-9969, 800-325-3535) 175 rooms and suites, restaurant, lounge, entertainment, indoor heated pool, exercise facilities, whirlpools, sauna, NS rooms, a/c, room service, TV, local transportation, barber and beauty shop, game room, children free with parents, wheelchair access, meeting facilities, senior rates, CC. SGL/DBL$45-$73.

Super 8 Motel (1315 North Broadway, 58701; 852-1817, 800-800-8000) 60 rooms and suites, restaurant, lounge, no pets, children under 12 free with parents, free local calls, a/c, TV, in-room refrigerators and microwaves, fax service, NS rooms, wheelchair access, laundry facilities, meeting facilities, senior rates, CC. SGL/DBL$30-$40.

Napoleon
Area Code 701

Downtowner Hotel (310 Main St., 58561; 754-2260) 6 rooms, TV. SGL/DBL35-$45.

Fettig Motel (Napoleon 58561; 754-2520) 4 rooms, a/c, TV, CC. SGL/DBL$47-$58.

New Town
Area Code 701

Cottage Inn (Main St., 58763; 627-4217) 17 rooms, a/c, TV, CC. SGL/DBL$40-$44.

Four Bears Casino and Lodge (New Town 58763; 627-4018, 800-294-5454) restaurant, lounge, entertainment, a/c, TV, wheelchair access, NS rooms, senior rates, CC. SGL/DBL$55.

Sunset Motel (Hwy. 23 East, 58763; 626-3317) 15 rooms, a/c, TV. SGL/DBL$36-$44.

West Dakota Inn (Hwy. 23 East, 58763; 627-3721) 15 rooms, air conditioning, TV. SGL/DBL$40-$50.

Park River
Area Code 701

Alexander House (Hwy. 17 West, 58270; 284-7141) 21 rooms, restaurant, lounge, a/c, TV, wheelchair access, NS rooms, senior rates, CC. SGL/DBL$35-$45.

Regent
Area Code 701

Pleasant View Bed and Breakfast (Regent 58650; 563-4543) free breakfast, TV, a/c, no pets, CC. SGL/DBL$56-$68.

Fin & Feathers Farmstead (Regent 58650; 563-4499) free breakfast, TV, a/c, no pets, CC. SGL/DBL$50-$65.

Dancin' Dakota Bed and Breakfast (Regent 58650; 563-4631) free breakfast, TV, a/c, no pets, CC. SGL/DBL$35-$55.

Rolla

Area Code 701

Bilmar Motel (Rolla 58367; 477-3157, 800-521-0443) 36 rooms, restaurant, lounge, sauna, whirlpools, a/c, TV, wheelchair access, NS rooms, senior rates, CC. SGL/DBL$40-$50.

Northern Lights Motel (Rolla 58367; 477-6164, 800-535-6145) 17 rooms, a/c, TV, CC. SGL/DBL$45-$56.

Rugby

Area Code 701

C&R Motel (Rugby 58368; 776-5241) a/c, TV. SGL/DBL$26-$40.

Center Motel (Hwy. 2 West, 58368; 776-5272) 20 rooms, a/c, TV, laundry facilities, CC. SGL/DBL$38-$44.

Econo Lodge (Hwy. 2 East, 58368; 776-5776, 800-4-CHOICE) 61 rooms and suites, restaurant, free breakfast, lounge, indoor heated pool, whirlpools, complimentary newspapers, children under 12 free with parents, no pets, NS rooms, wheelchair access, a/c, TV, senior rates, meeting facilities, CC. SGL/DBL$38-$60.

Hub Motel (Rugby 58368; 776-5833) 17 rooms, restaurant, lounge, a/c, TV, CC. SGL/DBL$28-$36.

St. John

Area Code 701

Cross Roads Range (St. John 58369; 244-5225) 17 rooms and cabins, restaurant, TV, CC. SGL/DBL$45-$70.

Steele

Area Code 701

Lone Steer Motel (Steele 54842; 475-2221) 60 rooms, restaurant, lounge, pool, sauna, jacuzzis, a/c, TV, wheelchair access, NS rooms, senior rates, CC. SGL/DBL$38-$55.

The OK Motel (3rd Ave. Northeast 54842; 475-2440) 10 rooms, TV. SGL/DBL$30-$40.

Tioga
Area Code 701

Super 8 Motel (Tioga 58852; 664-3395, 800-800-8000) 30 rooms and suites, sauna, no pets, children under 12 free with parents, free local calls, a/c, TV, in-room refrigerators and microwaves, fax service, NS rooms, wheelchair access, meeting facilities, senior rates, CC. SGL/DBL$60-$68.

Valley City
Area Code 701

Bel-Air Motel (Valley City 58072; 845-3620) 30 rooms, a/c, TV, CC. SGL/DBL$30.

The Bonhus House on Third (341 3rd Ave. Northwest, 58072; 845-2229) 4 rooms, free breakfast, TV, a/c, no pets, CC. SGL/DBL$44-$64.

Flickertail Inn (Valley City 58072; 845-5278) 38 rooms, a/c, TV, CC. SGL/DBL$45-$55.

Midtown Motel (906 East Main St., 58072; 845-2830) 13 rooms, a/c, TV, pets OK, wheelchair access, local transportation, NS rooms, senior rates, CC. SGL/DBL$20-$30.

The Prairie Inn (140 3rd Ave. Southeast, 58072; 845-1560) 38 rooms and efficiencies, restaurant, kitchenettes, a/c, TV, wheelchair access, NS rooms, senior rates, CC. SGL/DBL$36-$46.

Super 8 Motel (Valley City 58072; 845-1140, 800-800-8000) 30 rooms, no pets, children under 12 free with parents, free local calls, a/c, TV, in-room refrigerators and microwaves, fax service, NS rooms, wheelchair access, meeting facilities, senior rates, CC. SGL/DBL$29-$44.

Valley City Motel (1139 West Main St., 58072; 845-2208) 8 rooms, a/c, NS, no pets, CC. SGL/DBL$29-$36.

The Wagon Wheel Inn (Valley City 58072; 845-5333) 58 rooms, indoor heated pool, whirlpool tubs, jacuzzis, a/c, TV, pets OK, wheelchair access, in-room refrigerators and microwaves, NS rooms, meeting facilities, senior rates, CC. SGL/DBL$30-$40.

Wahpeton
Area Code 701

Adams Fairview Bonanza Bed and Breakfast (17170 82nd St. Southeast, 58075; 274-8262) free breakfast, TV, a/c, no pets, CC. SGL/DBL$40-$80.

Comfort Inn (209 13th St. South, 58075; 642-1115, 800-228-5150) 46 rooms, free breakfast, indoor pool, whirlpools, game room, in-room refrigerators, no pets, a/c, TV, CC. SGL/DBL$38-$55.

Starlite Motel (167 South 11th St., 58075; 642-6627) 22 rooms, a/c, TV, wheelchair access, CC. SGL/DBL$40-$56.

Super 8 Motel (210 Bypass, 58075; 642-8731, 800-800-8000) 59 rooms and suites, restaurant, lounge, no pets, children under 12 free with parents, free local calls, a/c, TV, in-room refrigerators and microwaves, fax service, NS rooms, wheelchair access, meeting facilities, senior rates, CC. SGL/DBL$32-$44.

Walhalla
Area Code 701

Forestwood Inn (Walhalla 58282; 549-2651) 29 rooms, whirlpools, sauna, a/c, TV, wheelchair access, NS rooms, senior rates, CC. SGL/DBL$36-$46.

Hill View Motel (120 Hwy. 32 South 58282; 549-3300) 12 rooms, hot tub, a/c, TV, CC. SGL/DBL$28-$38.

Watford City
Area Code 701

Four Eyes Motel (122 South Main St, 58854; 842-4126) 14 rooms, a/c, TV, wheelchair access, NS rooms, senior rates, CC. SGL/DBL$30-$38.

McKenzie Inn (Hwy. 85 West, 58854; 842-3980) 14 rooms, hot tubs, a/c, TV, wheelchair access, NS rooms, senior rates, CC. SGL/DBL$46.

Waterford City Inn (Hwy. 85 West, 58854; 842-3686, 800-201-3686 in North Dakota) 50 rooms, restaurant, lounge, hot tub, a/c, TV, wheelchair access, NS rooms, senior rates, CC. SGL/DBL$38-$48.

Williston
Area Code 701

Airport International Inn (Williston 58801; 774-0241) 150 rooms, restaurant, lounge, indoor heated pool, whirlpools, pets OK, local transportation, room service, a/c, TV, wheelchair access, NS rooms, senior rates, meeting facilities, CC. SGL/DBL$38-$74.

El Ranch Motor Hotel (1623 2nd Ave. West, 58801; 572-6321) 92 rooms, restaurant, lounge. SGL/DBL$48-$56.

Select Inn (Williston 58801; 572-4242, 800-641-1000) 60 rooms, indoor pool, whirlpools, free breakfast, a/c, TV, NS rooms, free local calls, pets

OK, senior rates, laundry facilities, children under age 13 stay free with parents, VCRs, fax service, meeting facilities, senior rates, CC. SGL/DBL$30-$39.

Super 8 Motel (2324 2nd Ave., West, 58801; 572-8371, 800-800-8000) 82 rooms and suites, indoor pool, whirlpools, no pets, children under 12 free with parents, free local calls, a/c, TV, in-room refrigerators and microwaves, fax service, NS rooms, wheelchair access, meeting facilities, senior rates, CC. SGL/DBL$25-$39.

Oregon

Reservation and Rental Services:

Bed and Breakfast Reservations (800-841-5448).

Bed and Breakfast Reservations (800-944-6196).

Agness
Area Code 503

Lucas Pioneer Ranch and Lodge (3904 Couger Lane, 97406; 247-7443) 20 rooms, restaurant, free breakfast, TV, a/c, pets OK, CC. SGL/DBL$36-$60.

Albany
Area Code 503

Best Western Pony Soldier Motor Inn (315 Airport Rd. Southeast, 97321; 928-6322, Fax 928-8124, 800-528-1234) 72 rooms, restaurant, free breakfast, lounge, whirlpools, children free with parents, a/c, NS rooms, TV, laundry facilities, wheelchair access, in-room refrigerators, pets OK, meeting facilities, senior rates, CC. SGL/DBL$65-$88.

Brier Rose Inn (206 7th Ave. Southwest, 97321; 926-0345) 4 rooms, free breakfast, TV, a/c, pets OK, NS, CC. SGL/DBL$49-$69.

Budget Inn (2727 East Pacific Blvd., 97321; 926-4246, 800-527-0700) 47 rooms, pool, NS rooms, children free with parents, pets OK, a/c, laundry facilities, TV, meeting facilities, CC. SGL/DBL$33-$40.

Comfort Inn (251 Airport Rd. Southeast, 97321; 928-0921, 800-228-5150) 50 rooms, restaurant, free breakfast, indoor pool, whirlpools, sauna, wheelchair access, free local calls, complimentary newspaper, pets OK, a/c, TV, wheelchair access, CC. SGL/DBL$60-$125.

Marco Polo Motel (2410 East Pacific Blvd., 97321; 926-4401) 18 rooms, TV, CC. SGL/DBL$25-$30.

Motel Orleans (1212 Southeast Price Rd., 97321; 926-0170) 83 rooms and 2-bedroom efficiencies, restaurant, lounge, entertainment, indoor heated pool, a/c, laundry facilities, TV, pets OK, wheelchair access, NS rooms, in-room refrigerators and microwaves, senior rates, meeting facilities, CC. SGL/DBL$35-$54.

Nendels Valu-Inn (3125 Santiam Hwy. Southeast, 97321; 926-1538, 800-547-0106) 59 rooms, restaurant, outdoor pool, NS rooms, pets OK, a/c, TV, children under 17 free with parents, senior rates, CC. SGL/DBL$39-$44.

Stardust Motel (2735 East Pacific Blvd., 97321; 926-4233) 30 rooms, a/c, TV, pets OK, kitchenettes, NS rooms, water view, CC. SGL/DBL$22-$45.

Aloha
Area Code 503

American Motor Inn (3333 Southwest 198th St., 97006; 642-4531) 50 rooms, a/c, TV, CC. SGL/DBL$35-$45.

Arlington
Area Code 503

Village Inn Motel (131 Beech St., 97812; 454-2646) 34 rooms, restaurant, lounge, a/c, TV, pets OK, wheelchair access, laundry facilities, NS rooms, senior rates, CC. SGL/DBL$42-$48.

Ashland
Area Code 503

Ashland Motel (1145 Siskiyou Blvd., 97520; 482-2561) 27 rooms, restaurant, outdoor heated pool, kitchenettes, a/c, TV, no pets, wheelchair access, laundry facilities, NS rooms, senior rates, CC. SGL/DBL$49-$69.

Ashland Valley Inn (1193 Siskiyou Blvd., 97520; 482-2641) 64 rooms, restaurant, lounge, outdoor heated pool, a/c, TV, pets OK, wheelchair access, NS rooms, senior rates, meeting facilities, CC. SGL/DBL$32-$78.

Best Western Bard's Inn (132 North Main St., 97520; 482-0049, Fax 488-3259, 800-528-1234) 79 rooms, restaurant, lounge, outdoor pool, sauna, whirlpools, children free with parents, a/c, NS rooms, TV, laundry facilities, wheelchair access, pets OK, meeting facilities, senior rates, CC. SGL/DBL$65-$115.

Best Western Heritage Inn (434 Valley View Rd., 482-6932, 800-528-1234) 53 rooms, restaurant, free breakfast, indoor and outdoor heated pool, exercise facilities, whirlpools, free local calls, complimentary newspaper, kitchenettes, children free with parents, a/c, NS rooms, TV, laundry facilities, wheelchair access, pets OK, meeting facilities, senior rates, CC. SGL/DBL$40-$135.

Buckhorn Springs Country Inn (2200 Buckhorn Springs Rd., 97520; 488-2200) 14 rooms, restaurant, free breakfast, kitchenettes, a/c, TV, no pets, wheelchair access, NS rooms, senior rates, CC. SGL/DBL$65-$100.

Chanticleer Inn (120 Gresham St., 97520; 482-1919) 6 rooms, free breakfast, airport transportation, antique furnishings, fireplace, no pets, a/c, wheelchair access, NS rooms, senior rates, CC. SGL/DBL$115-$155.

Country Willows (1313 Clay St., 97520; 488-1590) 7 rooms, free breakfast, fireplace, in-room refrigerators and microwaves, NS rooms, senior rates, CC. SGL/DBL$65-$155.

Cowslip's Belle Bed and Breakfast (159 North Main St., 97520; 488-2901) 4 rooms, free breakfast, TV, NS, private baths, antique furnishings, a/c, no pets, CC. SGL/DBL$59-$105.

Edinburgh Lodge (586 East Main St., 97520; 488-1050) 6 rooms, TV, NS rooms. SGL/DBL$35-$44.

Hillside Inn (1520 Siskiyou Blvd., 98520; 482-2626) 31 rooms, outdoor pool, a/c, TV, kitchenettes, CC. SGL/DBL$65.

The Iris Bed and Breakfast (59 Manzanita St., 97520; 488-2286) 5 rooms, free breakfast, TV, a/c, no pets, CC. SGL/DBL$92.

Knights Inn (2359 Ashland St., 97520; 482-5111, 800-843-5644) 40 rooms, restaurant, lounge, outdoor heated pool, wheelchair access, NS rooms, TV, a/c, in-room refrigerators and microwaves, pets OK, fax service, VCRs, senior rates, CC. SGL/DBL$36-$58.

Lithia Rose on the Park (163 Granite St., 97520; 482-1882) 5 rooms, TV. SGL/DBL$50.

Lithia Springs Country Inn (2165 West Jackson Rd., 97520; 482-7128) 7 rooms, free breakfast, TV, a/c, local transportation, fireplaces, no meeting facilities, pets, CC. SGL/DBL$85-$125.

Manor Motel (476 North Main St., 97520; 482-2246) 11 rooms, TV, CC. SGL/DBL$28-$32.

Mark Antony Hotel (212 East Main St., 97520; 482-1721) 65 rooms, restaurant, lounge, outdoor a/c, TV, no pets, wheelchair access, NS rooms, meeting facilities, senior rates, CC. SGL/DBL$26-$110.

The McCall House (153 Oak St., 97520; 482-9296) 9 rooms, free breakfast, NS, 1880s home, no pets, children over 11 welcome, a/c, TV, wheelchair access, NS rooms, senior rates, CC. SGL/DBL$100-$115.

The Morical House (668 North Main St., 97520; 482-2254) 5 rooms, free breakfast, TV, a/c, no pets, NS, CC. SGL/DBL$95-$115.

Mount Ashland Inn (550 Mount Ashland Rd., 97520; 482-8707) 5 rooms, free breakfast, restaurant, whirlpools, TV, in-room refrigerators, children over 12 welcome, no pets, NS, fireplaces, meeting facilities, CC. SGL/DBL$65-$125.

Oak Hill Country Bed and Breakfast (2190 Siskiyou Blvd., 97520; 482-1554) 5 rooms, free breakfast, TV, fireplaces, a/c, no pets, CC. SGL/DBL$90.

Palm Motel (1065 Siskiyou Blvd., 97520; 482-2626) 13 rooms, outdoor pool, kitchenettes, a/c, TV, CC. SGL/DBL$30-$140.

Quality Inn (2520 Ashland St., 97520; 488-2330, 800-221-2222) 60 rooms and suites, restaurant, free breakfast, outdoor heated pool, exercise facilities, children free with parents, a/c, TV, wheelchair access, room service, laundry service, limousine service, no pets, airport transportation, kitchenettes, NS rooms, meeting facilities, senior rates, CC. SGL/DBL$45-$80.

Regency Inn (50 Lowe Rd., 97520; 482-4700, 800-482-4701) 40 rooms and 2-room suites, restaurant, outdoor pool, free local calls, NS, a/c, TV, no pets, in-room refrigerators and microwaves, wheelchair access, senior rates, CC. SGL/DBL$35-$51.

Romeo Inn (295 Idaho St., 97520; 488-0884) 6 rooms and suites, free breakfast, outdoor heated pool, NS rooms, in-room refrigerators, microwaves and coffee makers, wheelchair access, antique furnishings, TV, a/c, no pets, fireplaces, CC. SGL/DBL$95-$175.

Shrew's House (570 Siskiyou Blvd., 97520; 482-9214) 3 rooms, free breakfast, outdoor pool, TV, a/c, no pets, CC. SGL/DBL$88-$98.

Stratford Inn (11470 Hwy. 66, 97520; 482-0614, 800-547-4741) 53 rooms, indoor heated pool, whirlpools, kitchenettes, TV, in-room refrigerators, kitchenettes, NS, a/c, no pets, CC. SGL/DBL$90-$130.

Super 8 Motel (2350 Ashland St., 97520; 482-8887, 800-800-8000) 67 rooms and suites, restaurant, indoor and outdoor pool, pets OK, children under 12 free with parents, free local calls, a/c, laundry facilities, TV, in-room refrigerators and microwaves, fax service, NS rooms, wheelchair access, meeting facilities, senior rates, CC. SGL/DBL$50-$68.

Timbers Motel (1450 Ashland St., 97520; 482-4242) 28 rooms and 2-bedroom efficiencies, restaurant, outdoor heated pool, a/c, TV, no pets, wheelchair access, in-room refrigerators, NS rooms, kitchenettes, senior rates, CC. SGL/DBL$30-$52.

Treon's Country Homestay (1819 Colestin Rd., 97520; 482-0746) free breakfast, TV, a/c, no pets, fireplaces, NS, game room, CC. SGL/DBL$65-$80.

Winchester Inn (35 South 2nd St., 97520; 488-1115) 7 rooms, free breakfast, antique furnishings, no pets, children free with parents, 1880s inn, a/c, TV, wheelchair access, NS rooms, senior rates, CC. SGL/DBL$75-$110.

Windmill's Ashland Hills Inn (2525 Ashland St., 97520; 482-8310) 159 rooms and suites, restaurant, lounge, entertainment, outdoor heated pool, whirlpools, beauty shop, room service, in-room refrigerators, children free with parents, in-room computer hookups, a/c, TV, airport transportation, wheelchair access, pets OK, NS rooms, meeting facilities, senior rates, CC. SGL/DBL$45-$135.

Woods House Bed and Breakfast (333 North Main St., 97520; 488-1598) 6 rooms, free breakfast, NS, airport transportation, antique furnishings, a/c, no pets, fireplaces, CC. SGL/DBL$65-$110.

Astoria

Area Code 503

Astoria Dunes Motel (288 West Marine Dr., 97130; 325-7111) 58 rooms, indoor heated pool, whirlpools, a/c, TV, no pets, wheelchair access, NS rooms, in-room refrigerators, water view, senior rates, airport transportation, CC. SGL/DBL$45-$75.

Astoria Inn (3391 Irving Ave., 97103; 325-8153) 3 rooms, free breakfast, TV, 1890 home, NS, private baths, water view, airport transportation, antique furnishings, a/c, no pets. SGL/DBL$70-$80.

Bayshore Motor Inn (555 Hamburg St., 97103; 325-2205) 36 rooms, a/c, in-room refrigerators, children free with parents, pets OK, laundry facilities, water view, in-room coffee makers, TV, senior rates, CC. SGL/DBL$50-$70.

City Center Motel (495 Marine Dr., 97103; 325-4211) a/c, TV, CC. SGL/DBL$30-$40.

Columbia River Inn (1681 Franklin Ave., 97103; 325-5044) 5 rooms, free breakfast, TV, gift shop, airport transportation, 1870s inn, a/c, no pets, fireplaces, water view, laundry facilities, CC. SGL/DBL$65-$85.

Crest Motel (Route 30, 97103; 325-3141) 40 rooms and 2-bedroom efficiencies, free breakfast, whirlpools, water view, laundry facilities, TV, wheelchair access, in-room refrigerators, pets OK, children free with parents, NS rooms, senior rates, CC. SGL/DBL$45-$80.

Franklin Street Station Bed and Breakfast (1140 Franklin Ave., 97130; 325-4314) 6 rooms, free breakfast, airport transportation, water view, TV, a/c, no pets, CC. SGL/DBL$63-$115.

Grandview Bed and Breakfast (1574 Grand Ave., 97130; 325-5555) 9 rooms, free breakfast, TV, a/c, no pets, airport transportation, water view, CC. SGL/DBL$40-$120.

Inn-Chanted Bed and Breakfast (707 8th St., 97130; 325-5223) 3 rooms, free breakfast, TV, a/c, no pets, fireplaces, NS, airport transportation, water view, CC. SGL/DBL$65-$110.

Red Lion Inn (400 Industry St., 97130; 325-7373, 800-547-8010) 124 rooms, restaurant, lounge, entertainment, a/c, TV, wheelchair access, NS rooms, complimentary newspaper, children under 16 free with parents, fax service, room service, airport transportation, water view, pets OK, laundry facilities, meeting facilities, senior rates, CC. SGL/DBL$60-$94.

Rivershore Motel (59 West Marine Dr., 97130; 325-2921) 43 rooms, TV, CC. SGL/DBL$28-$38.

Rosebriar Hotel (636 14th St., 97130; 325-7427, 800-487-0224) 11 rooms, free breakfast, TV, NS, water view, pets OK, fireplaces, kitchenettes, water view, meeting facilities, CC. SGL/DBL$50-$110.

Baker City
Area Code 503

A Demain Bed and Breakfast (1790 4th St., 97814; 523-2509) 2 rooms, free breakfast, TV, a/c, kitchenettes, no pets, CC. SGL/DBL$55-$65.

Best Western Sunridge Inn (1 Sunridge Lane, 97814; 523-6444, Fax 523-6446, 800-528-1234) 124 rooms, restaurant, lounge, outdoor heated sauna, children free with parents, a/c, NS rooms, in-room refrigerators, airport transportation, TV, laundry facilities, wheelchair access, pets OK, meeting facilities, senior rates, CC. SGL/DBL$55-$70.

Eldorado Inn (695 Campbell St., 97814; 523-6494) 56 rooms, indoor heated pool, whirlpools, a/c, TV, pets OK, wheelchair access, NS rooms, senior rates, CC. SGL/DBL$36-$49.

Friendship Inn (134 Bridge St., 97814; 523-6571, 800-424-4777) 40 rooms, a/c, TV, no pets, NS rooms, kitchenettes, children free with parents, wheelchair access, senior rates, CC. SGL/DBL$25-$43.

Green Gables Motel (2533 10th St., 97814; 523-5588) 12 rooms, a/c, TV, pets OK, kitchenettes, laundry facilities, CC. SGL/DBL$33-$36.

Lariet Motel (880 Elm St., 97814; 523-6381) 15 rooms, a/c, laundry facilities, TV, CC. SGL/DBL$23-$30.

Oregon Trail Bed and Breakfast (Baker City 97814; 523-2014) 1 room, free breakfast, TV, a/c, pets OK, NS, CC. SGL/DBL$60.

Oregon Trail Motel (211 Bridge St., 97814; 523-5844) 54 rooms, restaurant, outdoor pool, a/c, TV, pets OK, wheelchair access, NS rooms, senior rates, CC. SGL/DBL$32-$38.

Powder River Bed and Breakfast (Baker City 97814; 523-7143) 2 rooms, free breakfast, TV, a/c, pets OK, meeting facilities, CC. SGL/DBL$60.

Quality Inn (810 Campbell St., 97814; 523-2242, 800-221-2222) 54 rooms and suites, free breakfast, children free with parents, a/c, TV, wheelchair access, room service, laundry service, in-room refrigerators, NS rooms, pets OK, meeting facilities, senior rates, CC. SGL/DBL$39-$49.

Royal Motor Inn (2205 Broadway, 97814; 523-6324) 36 rooms, outdoor heated pool, a/c, children free with parents, TV, pets OK, CC. SGL/DBL$33-$39.

Super 8 Motel (250 Campbell St., 97814; 523-8282, 800-800-8000) 48 rooms and suites, indoor heated pool, exercise center, no pets, children under 12 free with parents, free local calls, a/c, TV, laundry facilities, in-room refrigerators and microwaves, fax service, NS rooms, wheelchair access, meeting facilities, senior rates, CC. SGL/DBL$44-$58.

Trail Motel (2815 10th St., 97814; 523-4646) 4 rooms, TV, CC. SGL/DBL$36-$42.

The Western Motel (3055 10th St., 97814; 523-3700) 14 rooms, a/c, TV, pets OK, CC. SGL/DBL$27-$34.

Bandon

Area Code 503

Rental and Reservation Services:

Sunset Oceanfront Accommodations (1755 Beach Loop Dr., 97411; 347-2453, Fax 347-3636) rental rooms, cabins and condominiums.

□□□

Brandon Beach Motel (1110 11th St. Southwest, 97411; 347-4430) 28 rooms, restaurant, a/c, TV, pets OK, kitchenettes, water view, wheelchair access, NS rooms, senior rates, CC. SGL/DBL$45-$65.

Brandon Wayside Motel (Hwy. 42 South, 97411; 347-3421) 10 rooms, a/c, TV, CC. SGL/DBL$28-$40.

Caprice Motel (Bandon 97411; 347-4494) 15 rooms, a/c, TV, pets OK, kitchenettes, in-room coffee makers, CC. SGL/DBL$25-$48.

Harbor View Motel (355 Hwy. 101, 97411; 347-4417, 800-526-0209) 59 rooms and cottages, free breakfast, kitchenettes, TV, pets OK, airport transportation, wheelchair access, NS rooms, in-room refrigerators and coffee makers, water view, meeting facilities, senior rates, CC. SGL/DBL$46-$85.

The Inn at Face Rock (3225 Beach Loop Rd., 97411; 800-638-3092) 55 rooms, restaurant, lounge, kitchenettes, water view, pets OK, a/c, TV, wheelchair access, NS rooms, meeting facilities, senior rates, CC. SGL/DBL$49-$89.

La Kris Motel (Hwy. 101 South, 97411; 347-3610) 12 rooms, restaurant, lounge, kitchenettes, a/c, TV, pets OK, wheelchair access, NS rooms, senior rates, CC. SGL/DBL$32-$65.

Lamplighter Motel (40 North Ave., 97411; 347-4477) 16 rooms, kitchenettes, pets OK, a/c, TV, CC. SGL/DBL$25-$45.

Lighthouse Bed and Breakfast (650 Jetty Rd., 97411; 347-9316) 4 rooms, free breakfast, TV, a/c, no pets, water view, fireplaces, CC. SGL/DBL$75-$100.

Sea Star Guesthouse (370 2nd St., 97411; 347-9632) 4 rooms, restaurant, free breakfast, TV, a/c, no pets, water view, kitchenettes, CC. SGL/DBL$60-$100.

Sunset Ocean Resort (1755 Beach Loop Rd., 97411; 347-2453) 58 rooms and suites, restaurant, lounge, whirlpools, water view, kitchenettes, fireplaces, laundry facilities, a/c, TV, pets OK, wheelchair access, NS rooms, senior rates, CC. SGL/DBL$35-$175.

Table Rock Motel (840 Beach Loop Rd., 97411; 347-2700) 15 rooms, a/c, TV, pets OK, kitchenettes, CC. SGL/DBL$30-$75.

Windermere Motel (3250 Beach Loop Rd., 97411; 347-3710) 17 rooms, a/c, TV, CC. SGL/DBL$28-$30.

Beaverton
Area Code 503

Courtyard by Marriott (8500 Southwest Nimbus Dr., 97005; 641-3200, Fax 641-1287, 800-331-3131) 149 rooms and suites, restaurant, lounge, free breakfast, indoor heated pool, whirlpools, exercise center, in-room refrigerators, microwaves and coffee makers, a/c, no pets, complimentary newspaper, children free with parents, kitchenettes, TVs and VCRs, NS rooms, wheelchair access, meeting facilities, senior rates, CC. SGL/DBL$65-$100.

Greenwood Inn (10700 Southwest Allen Blvd., 97005; 643-7444) 253 rooms, restaurant, lounge, entertainment, pool, whirlpools, exercise center, sauna, room service, local transportation, pets OK, a/c, TV, wheelchair access, NS rooms, senior rates, CC. SGL/DBL$75-$150.

Peppertree Motor Inn (10720 Southwest Allen Blvd., 97005; 641-7477) 73 rooms, restaurant, indoor heated pool, exercise center, laundry facilities, a/c, TV, no pets, wheelchair access, airport transportation, NS rooms, senior rates, CC. SGL/DBL$45-$53.

Ramada Inn (13455 Southwest Canyon Rd., 97005; 643-9100, 800-2-RAMADA) 143 rooms and suites, restaurant, free breakfast, lounge, heated pool, exercise center, wheelchair access, NS rooms, free parking, pets OK, a/c, TV, children under 18 free with parents, room service, kitchenettes, laundry facilities, meeting facilities, senior rates, CC. SGL/DBL$80-$90.

Satellite Motel (13295 Southwest Canyon Rd., 97005; 646-2155) 48 rooms, outdoor pool, laundry facilities, a/c, TV, no pets, wheelchair access, NS rooms, senior rates, CC. SGL/DBL$38.

Shilo Inn (9900 Southwest Canyon Rd., 97005; 297-2551, 800-222-2244) 141 rooms and suites, restaurant, lounge, entertainment, outdoor pool, exercise facilities, room service, pets OK, airport courtesy car, in-room refrigerators, a/c, TV, NS rooms, wheelchair access, children under 12 free with parents, meeting facilities, senior rates, CC. SGL/DBL$67-$88.

Valu-Inn (12255 Southwest Canyon Rd., 97005; 646-4131) 60 rooms, free breakfast, heated pool, a/c, TV, in-room refrigerators, pets OK, CC. SGL/DBL$36-$55.

Bend

Area Code 503

Bend Alpine Hostel (19 Southwest Century Dr., 97702; 389-3813) 7 rooms, a/c, fireplaces, laundry facilities, TV, meeting facilities, CC. SGL/DBL$21-$35.

Best Western Entrada Lodge (19221 Century Dr., 97702; 382-4080, 800-528-1234) 79 rooms, restaurant, indoor heated pool, sauna, whirlpools, children free with parents, a/c, NS rooms, TV, laundry facilities, wheelchair access, pets OK, meeting facilities, senior rates, CC. SGL/DBL$55-$65.

Best Western Woodstone Inn (721 Northeast 3rd St., 97701; 382-1515, 800-528-1234) 102 rooms, restaurant, lounge, indoor heated pool, exercise facilities, whirlpools, free local calls, children free with parents, a/c, NS rooms, TV, laundry facilities, wheelchair access, pets OK, meeting facilities, senior rates, CC. SGL/DBL$55-$93.

Cascade Motel Lodge (420 Southeast 3rd St., 97702; 382-2612) 30 rooms, outdoor pool, laundry facilities, pets OK, local transportation, kitchenettes, a/c, TV, CC. SGL/DBL$35-$55.

Cimarron Motel (201 Northeast 3rd St., 97710; 382-8282) 119 rooms, free breakfast, heated outdoor pool, whirlpools, pets OK, children free with parents, kitchenettes, a/c, TV, senior rates, CC. SGL/DBL$38-$65.

Cold Springs Resort (Bend 97702; 595-6271) 22 rooms, restaurant, outdoor pool, pets OK, a/c, TV, laundry facilities, water view, fireplaces, wheelchair access, NS rooms, senior rates, CC. SGL/DBL$48-$89.

Comfort Inn (61200 South Hwy. 97, 97702; 388-2227, Fax 388-8820, 800-221-2222) 65 rooms, indoor heated pool, TV, NS rooms, wheelchair access, in-room refrigerators, microwaves and coffee makers, children under 16 free with parents, pets OK, senior rates, CC. SGL/DBL$40-$84.

Dunes Motel (1515 Northeast 3rd St., 97701; 382-6811) 30 rooms, whirlpools, TV, CC. SGL/DBL$35-$45.

Farewell Bend Bed and Breakfast (29 North West Greeley, 382-4374) 2 rooms, free breakfast, TV, a/c, no pets, NS, 1920s home, private baths, laundry facilities, no children, CC. SGL/DBL$65-$90.

Hampton Inn (15 Northeast Butler Rd., 97710; 388-4114, 800-HAMPTON) 99 rooms, free breakfast, outdoor heated pool, exercise facilities, whirlpools, children under 18 free with parents, NS rooms, wheelchair access, in-room computer hookups, fax service, TV, a/c, free local calls, pets OK, in-room refrigerators, meeting facilities, senior rates, CC. SGL/DBL$55-$65.

Holiday Motel (880 Southeast 3rd St., 97710; 382-4620) 25 rooms, kitchenettes, fireplaces, pets OK, a/c, TV, wheelchair access, NS rooms, senior rates, CC. SGL/DBL$30-$34.

The Inn of the Seventh Mountain (Bend 97709; 382-8711, 800-452-6810) 300 rooms and condominiums, restaurant, lounge, entertainment, outdoor heated pool, whirlpools, sauna, tennis courts, water view, fireplaces, kitchenettes, airport transportation, in-room refrigerators and coffee makers, laundry facilities, game room, fireplaces, senior rates, meeting facilities, CC. SGL/DBL$52-$275.

Lara House Bed and Breakfast (640 Northwest Congress, 97710; 388-4064) 5 rooms, free breakfast, TV, a/c, no pets, CC. SGL/DBL$65-$85.

Mill Inn (642 Northwest Colorado Ave., 97710; 389-9198) 10 rooms, free breakfast, TV, a/c, no pets, laundry facilities, fireplaces, CC. SGL/DBL$37-$63.

Mirror Pond House (1054 Northwest Harmon Blvd., 97710; 389-1680) free breakfast, TV, a/c, no pets, private baths. SGL/DBL$60-$90.

Mount Bachelor Village (19717 Mount Bachelor Dr., 97702; 389-5900) 85 rooms and 1- and 2-bedroom condominiums, restaurant, lounge, outdoor heated pool, exercise center, in-room refrigerators and microwaves, laundry facilities, water view, a/c, VCRs, TV, no pets, wheelchair access, NS rooms, senior rates, CC. SGL/DBL$65-$260.

Rainbow Motel (154 Northeast Franklin Ave., 97701; 382-1821) 24 rooms, kitchenettes, laundry facilities, a/c, TV, CC. SGL/DBL$30-$46.

Red Lion Inn North (1415 Northeast 3rd St., 97703; 382-7011, 800-547-8010) 75 rooms, restaurant, lounge, entertainment, heated pool, whirlpools, sauna, a/c, TV, wheelchair access, NS rooms, complimentary newspaper, fax service, laundry facilities, meeting facilities, senior rates, CC. SGL/DBL$45-$64.

Red Lion Inn South (849 Northeast 3rd St., 97701; 382-8382, 800-547-8010) 74 rooms, outdoor heated pool, whirlpools, a/c, TV, pets OK, wheelchair access, NS rooms, complimentary newspaper, fax service, laundry facilities, meeting rooms, senior rates, CC. SGL/DBL$50-$65.

Red Lion Motel (64201 Tyler Rd., 97701; 382-1957, 800-547-8010) 11 rooms, restaurant, outdoor pool, a/c, TV, wheelchair access, NS rooms, complimentary newspaper, fax service, laundry facilities, local transportation, meeting rooms, senior rates, CC. SGL/DBL$65-$85.

The Riverhouse Motor Inn (3075 North Hwy. 97, 97701; 389-3111, 800-547-3928, 800-452-6878) 220 rooms and suites, restaurant, lounge, entertainment, indoor and outdoor heated pools, exercise center, spa, a/c, TV, room service, free local calls, local transportation, fireplaces, water view, pets OK, wheelchair access, NS rooms, in-room refrigerators, microwaves and coffee makers, senior rates, meeting facilities, CC. SGL/DBL$60-$90, STS$100-$150.

Riverside Motel and Condominiums (1565 Northwest Hill St., 97702; 389-2363, 800-284-BEND) 100 rooms, indoor heated pool, water view, kitchenettes, wheelchair access, NS rooms, pets OK, meeting facilities, senior rates, CC. SGL/DBL$49-$69.

Sanoma Lodge (450 Southeast 3rd St., 97702; 382-4891) 17 rooms, kitchenettes, airport transportation, a/c, TV, no pets, wheelchair access, NS rooms, senior rates, CC. SGL/DBL$30-$45.

Shilo Inn Suites Hotel (3105 Riley Rd., 97701; 389-9600, Fax 382-4130, 800-222-2244) 121 rooms and suites, restaurant, lounge, entertainment, indoor and outdoor pool, whirlpools, sauna, exercise center, airport courtesy car, in-room refrigerators and coffee makers, a/c, TV, NS rooms, wheelchair access, water view, pets OK, children under 12 free with parents, meeting facilities, senior rates, CC. SGL/DBL$55-$125.

Twin Lakes Resort (11200 South Century Dr., 97706; 593-6526) 14 rooms, restaurant, outdoor pool, water view, kitchenettes, pets OK, laundry facilities, a/c, TV, CC. SGL/DBL$60-$90.

Super 8 Motel (1275 South Hwy. 97; 97702; 388-6888, 800-800-8000) 79 rooms and suites, indoor and outdoor heated pool, pets OK, children under 12 free with parents, free local calls, a/c, TV, in-room refrigerators and microwaves, fax service, NS rooms, wheelchair access, laundry facilities, meeting rooms, senior rates, CC. SGL/DBL$54.

Biggs
Area Code 503

Best Western Riviera (Biggs Rufus Hwy., 97065; 739-2501, Fax 739-2091, 800-528-1234) 40 rooms, restaurant, lounge, free breakfast, indoor heated pool, children free with parents, a/c, NS rooms, TV, laundry facilities, wheelchair access, pets OK, meeting rooms, senior rates, CC. SGL/DBL$45-$68.

Nu Vu Motel (91495 Biggs-Rufus Hwy., 97065; 739-2525) 17 rooms, a/c, water view, CC. SGL/DBL$33-$35.

Black Butte
Area Code 503

Black Butte Ranch (Hwy. 10, 97759; 595-6211, 800-452-7455) 100 rooms and condominiums, restaurant, lounge, indoor and outdoor heated pool, exercise center, lighted tennis courts, game room, fireplaces, a/c, TV, no pets, wheelchair access, NS rooms, senior rates, meeting facilities, CC. SGL/DBL$70-$250.

Blue River
Area Code 503

Sleepy Hollow Motel (54791 McKenzie Hwy., 97413; 822-3805) 19 rooms, TV, no pets, in-room refrigerators, CC. SGL/DBL$32-$44.

Boardman
Area Code 503

Dodge City Inn (1st and Front Sts., 97818; 481-2451) 40 rooms, restaurant, lounge, outdoor pool, room service, pets OK, a/c, TV, wheelchair access, NS rooms, meeting facilities, senior rates, CC. SGL/DBL$37-$44.

Nugget Inn (105 Front St. Southwest, 97818; 481-2775) 20 rooms, outdoor heated pool, whirlpools, in-room refrigerators and microwaves, a/c, TV, pets OK, children under 12 free with parents, kitchenettes, senior rates, CC. SGL/DBL$38-$48.

Brookings

Area Code 503

Best Western Brookings Inn (1143 Cheto Ave., 97415; 469-2173, Fax 469-2996, 800-528-1234) 68 rooms, restaurant, lounge, sauna, whirlpools, children free with parents, a/c, NS rooms, TV, laundry facilities, wheelchair access, pets OK, meeting rooms, senior rates, CC. SGL/DBL$40-$68.

Cheto River Inn (21202 High Prairie Rd., 97415; 469-2114, 800-327-2688) 3 rooms, free breakfast, TV, a/c, no pets, NS, no children, private baths, CC. SGL/DBL$85.

Gold Beach Resort and Condominiums (1330 South Ellensburg Ave., 97415; 247-7066) 39 rooms and condominiums, restaurant, lounge, indoor and outdoor pool, a/c, TV, no pets, wheelchair access, NS rooms, meeting facilities, senior rates, CC. SGL/DBL$89-$99.

Harbor Inn Motel (15991 Hwy. 101 South, 97415; 469-3194, Fax 469-0479) 30 rooms, pets OK, TV, senior rates, CC. SGL/DBL$35-$65.

Holmes Sea Cove Bed and Breakfast (17350 Holmes Dr., 97415 469-3025) 3 rooms, free breakfast, TV, a/c, no pets, wheelchair access, CC. SGL/DBL$80-$95.

Pacific Sunset Inn (1144 Chetco Ave., 97415; 469-2141) 40 rooms, restaurant, lounge, kitchenettes, a/c, TV, pets OK, in-room refrigerators, children free with parents, airport transportation, wheelchair access, NS rooms, senior rates, CC. SGL/DBL$69-$79.

Spindrift Motor Inn (1215 Chetco Ave., 97425; 469-5345, 800-292-1171) 35 rooms, restaurant, in-room refrigerators, TV, wheelchair access, no pets, NS rooms, senior rates, CC. SGL/DBL$30-$58.

Burns

Area Code 503

Best Western Ponderosa Motel (577 West Monroe, 97720; 573-2047, 800-528-1234) 52 rooms, restaurant, lounge, outdoor pool, children free with parents, a/c, NS rooms, TV, laundry facilities, wheelchair access, pets OK, meeting facilities, senior rates, CC. SGL/DBL$35-$50.

Motel 6 (997 Oregon Ave., 97720; 573-3013, 505-891-6161) 122 rooms, pool, free local calls, children under 17 free with parents, NS rooms, wheelchair access, pets OK, a/c, TV, CC. SGL/DBL$25-$32.

Orbit Motel (Burns 97720; 573-2046, 800-235-6155) 31 rooms, heated pool, pets OK, a/c, TV, wheelchair access, NS rooms, senior rates, CC. SGL/DBL$26-$40.

Royal Inn (999 Oregon Ave., 97720; 573-5295) 38 rooms, restaurant, indoor heated pool, whirlpools, children under 12 free with parents, laundry facilities, a/c, TV, pets OK, wheelchair access, NS rooms, senior rates, CC. SGL/DBL$38-$47.

Silver Spur Motel (789 Broadway, 97720; 573-2077, 800-400-2077 in Oregon) 26 rooms, free breakfast, exercise center, airport transportation, pets OK, a/c, TV, wheelchair access, NS rooms, senior rates, CC. SGL/DBL$33-$37.

Cannon Beach
Area Code 503

Rental and Reservation Services:

Ecola Creek Management (800-873-2749) rental suites, houses and cottages.

□□□

Best Western Surfs and Resort (Oceanfront and Gower St., 97110; 436-2274, 800-528-1234) 75 rooms, restaurant, lounge, indoor heated pool, children free with parents, a/c, NS rooms, TV, laundry facilities, wheelchair access, fireplaces, kitchenettes, pets OK, meeting rooms, senior rates, CC. SGL/DBL$125-$155.

Cannon Beach Hotel (1116 South Hemlock St., 97110; 436-1392) 9 rooms, free breakfast, restaurant, TV, a/c, no pets, fireplaces, wheelchair access, room service, CC. SGL/DBL$49-$120.

Grey Whale Inn (164 Kenai, 97110; 436-2848) 5 rooms, TV, no pets, NS, no children, CC. SGL/DBL$70-$125.

Hallmark Resort (1400 South Hemlock, 97110; 436-1566, Fax 436-0324, 800-345-5676 in Oregon) 131 rooms and cottages, restaurant, indoor heated pool, whirlpools, exercise center, sauna, in-room refrigerators, pets OK, gift shop, local transportation, a/c, TV, wheelchair access, NS rooms, senior rates, CC. SGL/DBL$80-$210.

The Hearthstone Inn (Cannon Beach 97110; 436-2266) 4 rooms, fireplaces, kitchenettes, TV, CC. SGL/DBL$75-$85.

Lands End Motel (263 West 2nd St., 97110; 436-2264) 14 rooms, laundry facilities, a/c, TV, no pets, wheelchair access, NS rooms, meeting facilities, senior rates, CC. SGL/DBL$60-$160.

Major Motel (2863 Pacific St., 97110; 436-2241) 24 rooms and 2-bedroom efficiencies, water view, in-room refrigerators, fireplaces, TV, no pets, CC. SGL/DBL$60-$100.

Schooner's Cove Oceanfront Motel (188 North Larch St., 97110; 436-2300) 30 rooms, kitchenettes, fireplaces, laundry facilities, a/c, TV, wheelchair access, NS rooms, senior rates, meeting rooms, CC. SGL/DBL$89-$149.

Stephanie Inn (2740 South Pacific, 97110; 436-2221, Fax 436-9711) 46 rooms and suites, whirlpools, restaurant, lounge, water view, local transportation, in-room refrigerators, TV, CC. SGL/DBL$110-$170.

Tern Inn Bed and Breakfast (2 rooms, free breakfast, TV, a/c, kitchenettes, fireplaces, no pets, CC. SGL/DBL$85-$105.

The Viking Motel (Cannon Beach 97110; 436-2274) 6 rooms, indoor heated pool, pets OK, fireplaces, a/c, TV, wheelchair access, NS rooms, senior rates, CC. SGL/DBL$129-$149.

Camp Sherman
Area Code 503

Lake Creek Lodge (Camp Sherman Rd., 97730; 595-6331) 16 rooms, restaurant, outdoor pool, kitchenettes, a/c, TV, wheelchair access, fireplaces, pets OK, laundry facilities, airport transportation, NS rooms, meeting rooms, senior rates, CC. SGL/DBL$65-$75.

Metoliuw River Lodges (Camp Sherman 97730; 595-6290) 12 rooms, kitchenettes, water view, a/c, TV, fireplaces, airport transportation, CC. SGL/DBL$54-$97.

Cascade Locks
Area Code 503

Scandian Motor Lodge (Columbia Gorge Center 97014; 374-8417) 30 rooms, restaurant, laundry facilities, water view, no pets, a/c, TV, wheelchair access, NS rooms, senior rates, CC. SGL/DBL$43-$48.

Shahala at the Locks (1280 Northeast Forest Lane, 97014; 374-8222) 7 rooms, free breakfast, TV, a/c, no pets, wheelchair access, laundry facilities, water view, meeting facilities, CC. SGL/DBL$55-$90.

Charleston
Area Code 503

Captain John's Motel on Small Boat Basin (8061 Kingfisher Dr., 97420; 888-4041) 44 rooms and efficiencies, restaurant, lounge, a/c, TV, wheelchair access, NS rooms, senior rates, meeting facilities, CC. SGL/DBL$35-$70.

Clackamas
Area Code 503

Best Western Inn (12855 Southeast 97th, 97015; 652-1500, Fax 786-4191, 800-528-1234) 137 rooms, restaurant, lounge, free breakfast, outdoor pool, exercise facilities, children free with parents, a/c, NS rooms, TV, airport transportation, laundry facilities, wheelchair access, pets OK, meeting facilities, senior rates, CC. SGL/DBL$65-$100.

Clackamas Inn (16010 Southeast 82nd, 97015; 650-5340, Fax 657-2826) 43 rooms and efficiencies, outdoor heated pool, whirlpools, a/c, TV, children free with parents, pets OK, in-room refrigerators and microwaves, wheelchair access, NS rooms, senior rates, CC. SGL/DBL$55-$60.

Cypress Inn (9040 Southeast Adams, 97015; 655-0062, Fax 655-1861) 105 rooms, whirlpools, airport transportation, a/c, TV, in-room refrigerators, wheelchair access, NS rooms, senior rates, CC. SGL/DBL$60-$72.

Days Inn (9717 Southeast Sunnyside Rd., 97015; 654-1600, Fax 659-2702, 800-325-2525) 110 rooms, free breakfast, whirlpools, sauna, a/c, TV, wheelchair access, NS rooms, no pets, laundry facilities, airport transportation, in-room refrigerators, senior rates, CC. SGL/DBL$50-$120.

Coburg
Area Code 503

Econo Lodge (33100 Van Duyn Rd., 97401; 484-2000, 800-4-CHOICE) 105 rooms, restaurant, lounge, children under 12 free with parents, no pets, senior rates, NS rooms, wheelchair access, a/c, TV, meeting rooms, senior rates, CC. SGL/DBL$34-$58.

Coos Bay
Area Code 503

Best Western Holiday Motel (411 North Bayshore Dr., 97420; 269-5111, 800-528-1234) 76 rooms, restaurant, indoor heated pool, exercise facilities, sauna, kitchenettes, children free with parents, a/c, NS rooms, TV, laundry facilities, wheelchair access, pets OK, meeting rooms, senior rates, CC. SGL/DBL$45-$66.

Blackberry Inn Bed and Breakfast (843 Central, 97420; 267-6951) 4 rooms, free breakfast, TV, a/c, no pets, CC. SGL/DBL$35-$65.

Edgewater Inn (275 East Johnson St., 97420; 267-0423, Fax 267-4343) 82 rooms, indoor heated pool, whirlpools, kitchenettes, a/c, TV, in-room refrigerators, microwaves and coffee makers, airport transportation, water view, wheelchair access, NS rooms, senior rates, CC. SGL/DBL$67-$75.

Motel 6 (1445 Bayshore Dr., 97420; 267-7171, 505-891-6161) 94 rooms, pool, sauna, free local calls, children under 17 free with parents, NS rooms, wheelchair access, pets OK, a/c, TV, CC. SGL/DBL$30-$36.

Red Lion Inn (1313 North Bayshore Dr., 97420; 267-4141, Fax 267-2884, 800-547-8010) 145 rooms and 2-bedroom efficiencies, restaurant, lounge, pool, a/c, TV, wheelchair access, NS rooms, complimentary newspaper, children free with parents, fax service, laundry facilities, airport courtesy car, pets OK, meeting facilities, senior rates, CC. SGL/DBL$55-$80.

Sea Psalm Motel (1250 Cape Arago Hwy., 97420; 888-9053) 8 rooms, TV, CC. SGL/DBL$25-$35.

The Upper Room Chalet (308 North 8th St., 97420; 269-5385) 4 rooms, free breakfast, entertainment, pool, TV, a/c, no pets, meeting facilities, NS rooms, CC. SGL/DBL$38-$70.

Corvallis

Area Code 503

A Bed and Breakfast (2515 Southwest 45th St., 97330; 757-7321) 2 rooms, free breakfast, TV, laundry facilities, fireplaces, a/c, no pets, CC. SGL/DBL$60-$75.

Best Western Grand Manor Inn (925 Northwest Garfield, 97330; 758-8571, 800-528-1234) 55 rooms, restaurant, free breakfast, outdoor pool, exercise facilities, children free with parents, a/c, NS rooms, TV, in-room refrigerators and microwaves, laundry facilities, wheelchair access, pets OK, meeting facilities, senior rates, CC. SGL/DBL$65-$100.

Corvallis Budget Inn (1480 Southwest 3rd St., 97330; 752-8756) 24 rooms, a/c, TV, kitchenettes, NS rooms, CC. SGL/DBL$27-$50.

Econo Lodge (101 Northwest Van Buren, 97330; 752-9601, 800-4-CHOICE) 61 rooms, restaurant, lounge, whirlpools, children under 12 free with parents, no pets, NS rooms, wheelchair access, a/c, TV, meeting facilities, senior rates, CC. SGL/DBL$35-$85.

Harrison House (2310 Northwest Harrison, 97330; 752-6248) 3 rooms, free breakfast, TV, in-room refrigerators, NS, antique furnishings, 1930s home, pets OK, CC. SGL/DBL$45-$60.

The Jason Inn (800 Northwest 9th St., 97330; 753-7326) 51 rooms, restaurant, pool, a/c, TV, wheelchair access, pets OK, NS rooms, senior rates, CC. SGL/DBL$36-$48.

Madison Inn (660 Southwest Madison Ave., 97333; 757-1274) 8 rooms, free breakfast, antique furnishings, no pets, local transportation, CC. SGL/DBL$50-$110.

Orleans Motel (935 Northwest Garfield, 97330; 758-9125, 800-626-1900) 61 rooms and suites, whirlpools, children free with parents, a/c, TV, wheelchair access, NS rooms, senior rates, CC. SGL/DBL$35-$54.

Ramada Inn (1550 Northwest 9th St., 97330; 753-9151, Fax 758-7089) 120 rooms and 2-bedroom efficiencies, restaurant, heated pool, lounge, entertainment, a/c, TV, wheelchair access, NS rooms, in-room refrigerators and coffee makers, senior rates, CC. SGL/DBL$60-$85.

Shady Maple Farm (27183 Bundy Rd., 97330; 847-5992) 3 rooms, free breakfast, TV, a/c, no pets, CC. SGL/DBL$55-$85.

Shanico Inn (1113 Northwest 9th, 97330; 754-7474, 800-432-1233) 76 rooms, restaurant, outdoor heated pool, children free with parents, a/c, TV, wheelchair access, NS rooms, in-room refrigerators, pets OK, senior rates, CC. SGL/DBL$42-$65.

Cottage Grove
Area Code 503

Best Western The Village Green (725 Row River Rd., 97424; 942-2491, Fax 942-2386, 800-528-1234) 96 rooms, restaurant, lounge, entertainment, indoor heated pool, whirlpools, children free with parents, a/c, NS rooms, TV, laundry facilities, wheelchair access, gift shop, airport transportation, pets OK, meeting facilities, senior rates, CC. SGL/DBL$59-$90.

City Center Motel (737 Hwy. 99 South, 97424; 942-8322) 12 rooms and efficiencies, pets OK, a/c, TV, wheelchair access, NS rooms, water view, senior rates, CC. SGL/DBL$25-$33.

Comfort Inn (845 Gateway Blvd., 97424; 942-9747, 800-228-5150) 58 rooms, outdoor heated pool, whirlpools, a/c, in-room refrigerators and microwaves, children under 17 free with parents, pets OK, TV, wheelchair access, CC. SGL/DBL$45-$63.

Econo Lodge (1601 Gateway Blvd., 97424; 942-1000, 800-4-CHOICE) 41 rooms, restaurant, children under 12 free with parents, no pets, senior rates, NS rooms, wheelchair access, in-room microwaves, laundry facilities, a/c, TV, senior rates, CC. SGL/DBL$40-$55.

Rainbow Motel (1030 Pacific Hwy. 99 North, 97424; 942-5132) 24 rooms, kitchenettes, pets OK, a/c, TV, wheelchair access, NS rooms, senior rates, CC. SGL/DBL$36-$44.

Stardust Motel (455 Bear Creek Rd., 97424; 942-5706) 18 rooms and efficiencies, kitchenettes, pets OK, laundry facilities, a/c, TV, wheelchair access, NS rooms, CC. SGL/DBL$25-$35.

Depoe Bay
Area Code 503

The Channel House Inn (35 Ellingson St., 97341; 765-2140, Fax 765-2191, 800-447-2140) 12 rooms, free breakfast, children free with parents, kitchenettes, water view, a/c, TV, wheelchair access, NS, senior rates, CC. SGL/DBL$165-$200.

Gracie's Landing Bed and Breakfast (235 Southeast Bay View Ave., 97342; 765-2322) 13 rooms, free breakfast, restaurant, whirlpools, TV, no pets, CC. SGL/DBL$65-$100.

Holiday Surf Lodge (Hwy. 101, 97341; 765-2135) 87 rooms and house, indoor pool, kitchenettes, laundry facilities, TV, NS rooms, fireplaces, meeting facilities, CC. SGL/DBL$39-$335 (rental house).

The Inn at Arch Rock (70 Northwest Sunset St., 97341; 765-2560) 12 rooms and efficiencies, TV, wheelchair access, pets OK, NS rooms, CC. SGL/DBL$45-$90.

Pirates Cove (Hwy. 101, 97341; 765-2477) 2 rooms, free breakfast, TV, a/c, no pets, NS rooms, wheelchair access, CC. SGL/DBL$95.

Surfsider Resort (Depoe Bay 97341; 764-2311, 800-662-2378) 40 rooms and efficiencies, restaurant, lounge, indoor and outdoor heated pool, whirlpools, sauna, a/c, TV, wheelchair access, NS rooms, gift shop, fireplaces, children free with parents, pets OK, senior rates, CC. SGL/DBL$70-$95.

Trollers Lodge (355 Southwest Hwy. 101, 97341; 765-2287) 12 rooms and efficiencies, NS rooms, TV, water view, CC. SGL/DBL$49-$69.

The Whale Inn (416 Hwy. 101; 97341; 765-2789) 11 rooms, TV, water view, pets OK, NS rooms, fireplaces, CC. SGL/DBL$45-$90.

Elmira
Area Code 503

The Dome Bed and Breakfast (24454 Warthen Rd., 97437; 935-3138) 2 rooms, free breakfast, TV, no pets, CC. SGL/DBL$45.

McGillivray's Log Home Bed and Breakfast (88680 Evers Rd., 97437; 935-3564) free breakfast, TV, a/c, no pets, NS, private baths, antique furnishings, CC. SGL/DBL$50-$70.

Enterprise
Area Code 503

Melody Ranch Motel (402 West North St., 97828; 426-4986) 14 rooms, TV, kitchenettes, NS rooms, local transportation, no pets, CC. SGL/DBL$38-$42.

Ponderosa Motel (102 East Greenwood St., 97828; 426-3186) 25 rooms, a/c, TV, wheelchair access, pets OK, NS rooms, senior rates, CC. SGL/DBL$42-$44.

Eugene
Area Code 503

Argus Inn Motel (2121 Franklin Blvd., 97403; 342-1243) 104 rooms and suites, restaurant, lounge, outdoor pool, exercise center, a/c, TV, wheelchair access, NS rooms, free local calls, senior rates, meeting facilities, CC. SGL/DBL$40-$52.

Barrons Motor Inn (1859 Franklin Blvd., 97403; 342-6383, 800-444-6383) 60 rooms and suites, restaurant, free breakfast, whirlpools, a/c, TV, children free with parents, free local calls, complimentary newspaper, in-room refrigerators, pets OK, wheelchair access, NS rooms, senior rates, CC. SGL/DBL$35-$69.

Best Western New Oregon Motel (1655 Franklin Blvd., 97403; 683-3669, Fax 484-5556, 800-528-1234) 128 rooms, restaurant, indoor heated pool, whirlpools, sauna, exercise facilities, children free with parents, in-room refrigerators, a/c, NS rooms, TV, laundry facilities, wheelchair access, pets OK, meeting facilities, senior rates, CC. SGL/DBL$45-$68.

Campbell House (252 Pearl St., 97401; 343-1119) 14 rooms, free breakfast, TV, a/c, no pets, fireplaces, wheelchair access, meeting facilities, CC. SGL/DBL$70-$175.

Campus Inn (390 East Broadway, 97401; 343-3376, 800-888-6313) 60 rooms, a/c, TV, wheelchair access, NS rooms, pets OK, senior rates, CC. SGL/DBL$38-$65.

Eugene Motor Lodge (476 East Broadway, 97401; 344-5233) 49 rooms, pool, pets OK, kitchenettes, a/c, TV, wheelchair access, NS rooms, CC. SGL/DBL$34-$40.

Getty's Emerald Garden Bed and Breakfast (640 Audel, 97404; 688-6344) free breakfast, TV, a/c, NS, private baths, sauna, hot tubs, no pets, CC. SGL/DBL$60-$68.

Hilton Hotel (66 East 6th Ave., 97401; 342-2000, Fax 342-6661, 800-HIL-TONS) 270 rooms and suites, restaurant, lounge, entertainment, indoor pool, whirlpools, exercise facilities, children free with parents, NS rooms, wheelchair access, in-room refrigerators, pets OK, local transportation, gift shop, room service, laundry facilities, a/c, TV, business services, meeting facilities, senior rates, CC. SGL/DBL$100-$135, STS$225-$298.

Holiday Inn (225 Coburg Rd., 97401; 342-5181, 800-HOLIDAY) 148 rooms, restaurant, lounge, entertainment, indoor heated pool, exercise facilities, children under 19 free with parents, wheelchair access, a/c, TV, NS rooms, fax service, room service, pets OK, laundry service, game room, airport transportation, meeting facilities for 350, senior rates, CC. SGL/DBL$48-$65.

The Lyon and the Lambe (988 Lawrence at 10th St., 97401; 683-3160) free breakfast, whirlpools, private bath, TV, a/c, no pets, CC. SGL/DBL$65-$85.

Manor Motel (599 East Broadway, 97401; 345-2331) 25 rooms, outdoor pool, a/c, TV, wheelchair access, NS rooms, senior rates, CC. SGL/DBL$26-$38.

Motel 6 (3690 Glenwood Dr., 97403; 687-2395, 505-891-6161) 59 rooms, pool, free local calls, children under 17 free with parents, NS rooms, wheelchair access, pets OK, a/c, TV, CC. SGL/DBL$28-$34.

Red Lion Inn (205 Coburg Rd., 97401; 342-5201, 800-547-8010) 138 rooms, restaurant, lounge, entertainment, heated pool, a/c, TV, wheelchair access, NS rooms, complimentary newspaper, local transportation, fax service, pets OK, laundry facilities, meeting rooms, senior rates, CC. SGL/DBL$65-$88.

Sixty-Six Motel (755 East Broadway, 97401; 342-5041) 66 rooms, pets OK, a/c, TV, wheelchair access, NS rooms, senior rates, CC. SGL/DBL$28-$32.

Timbers Motel (540 East Broadway, 97401; 342-3345) 34 rooms, outdoor pool, room service, a/c, TV, wheelchair access, NS rooms, senior rates, CC. SGL/DBL$32-$49.

Valley River Inn (1000 Valley River Way, 97401; 687-0123, Fax 683-5121, 800-543-8266) 257 rooms and suites, restaurant, lounge, entertainment, heated pool, sauna, whirlpools, a/c, TV, pets OK, local transportation, water view, room service, wheelchair access, in-room refrigerators and coffee makers, NS rooms, meeting facilities, senior rates, CC. SGL/DBL$100-$300.

Florence

Area Code 503

Americana Motel (3829 Hwy. 101, 97439; 997-7115) 29 rooms, indoor pool, laundry facilities, NS rooms, TV, kitchenettes, CC. SGL/DBL$45-$50.

Best Western Pier Point Inn (85626 Hwy. 101, 97439; 997-7191, 800-528-1234) 56 rooms, restaurant, lounge, whirlpools, sauna, water view, game room, children free with parents, a/c, NS rooms, TV, laundry facilities, wheelchair access, pets OK, meeting facilities, senior rates, CC. SGL/DBL$55-$105.

Blue Heron Inn (6563 Hwy. 126, 97439; 997-4091) 4 rooms, free breakfast, TV, fireplaces, water view, NS rooms, no pets, CC. SGL/DBL$65-$85.

Driftwood Shores Resort (88416 First Ave., 97439; 997-8263, 800-824-8774) 136 rooms and apartments, restaurant, lounge, indoor heated pool, whirlpools, sauna, in-room refrigerators and coffee makers, no pets, water view, TV, meeting facilities, senior rates, CC. SGL/DBL$55-$110.

Fish Mill Lodge (4844 Fish Mill Way, 97439; 997-2511) 10 rooms, pool, kitchenettes, water view, TV, CC. SGL/DBL$45-$65.

Holiday Inn (Hwy. 101, 97439; 997-7797, Fax 997-7895, 800-HOLIDAY) 50 rooms, restaurant, lounge, whirlpools, exercise center, children under 19 free with parents, wheelchair access, a/c, TV, NS rooms, fax service, room service, no pets, in-room computer hookups, kitchenettes, laundry service, meeting facilities, senior rates, CC. SGL/DBL$50-$90.

Le Chateau Motel (1084 Hwy. 101, 97439; 997-3481) 48 rooms, outdoor heated pool, sauna, whirlpools, laundry facilities, no pets, in-room refrigerators, CC. SGL/DBL$30-$60.

Lighthouse Inn (155 Hwy. 101, 97439; 997-3221, Fax 997-8256) 28 rooms and 2-bedroom efficiencies, TV, no pets, NS rooms, CC. SGL/DBL$35-$85.

Money Saver Motel (170 Hwy. 101, 97439; 997-7131) 40 rooms, NS rooms, pets OK, CC. SGL/DBL$32-$60.

Park Motel (Hwy. 101 South, 97439; 997-2643) 15 rooms, restaurant, TV, NS rooms, pets OK, fireplaces, CC. SGL/DBL$43-$54.

Villa West Motel (901 Hwy. 101, 97439; 997-3457) 22 rooms, restaurant, lounge, NS rooms, wheelchair access, TV, pets OK, CC. SGL/DBL$35-$55.

Garibaldi
Area Code 503

Gracy Manor (119 East Driftwood St., 97138; 322-3369) 3 rooms, free breakfast, TV, a/c, no pets, CC. SGL/DBL$50-$60.

Harbor View Inn (302 Mooring Basin Rd., 97138; 322-3251) 20 rooms, fireplaces, TV, wheelchair access, water view, NS rooms, CC. SGL/DBL$40-$50.

Hill Top House (617 Holly Ave., 97138; 322-3221) 3 rooms, free breakfast, TV, a/c, no pets, CC. SGL/DBL$75-$95.

Tilla-Bay Motel (Garibaldi 97138; 322-3405) 11 rooms, kitchenettes, pets OK, laundry facilities, TV, CC. SGL/DBL$31-$39.

Gleneden Beach

Area Code 503

Beachcombers Haven (7045 Northwest Glen Ave., 97388; 764-2252) 4 rooms and efficiencies, TV, water view, laundry facilities, CC. SGL/DBL$100-$125.

Salishan Lodge (Gleneden Beach 97388; 764-2371, 800-452-2300) 205 rooms and suites, restaurant, lounge, entertainment, indoor heated pool, sauna, whirlpools, exercise facilities, lighted tennis courts, barber and beauty shop, in-room refrigerators, a/c, TV, wheelchair access, NS rooms, pets OK, boutiques, meeting facilities, senior rates, CC. SGL/DBL$160-$235, STS$290-$575.

Gold Beach

Area Code 503

Azalea Lodge (775 South Hwy. 101, 97444; 247-6635) 16 rooms and suites, restaurant, TV, NS rooms, laundry facilities, CC. SGL/DBL$36-$48.

Best Western Inn of the Beachcomber (1250 South Hwy. 101, 97444; 247-6691, Fax 247-7981, 800-528-1234) 49 rooms, restaurant, lounge, indoor heated whirlpools, pool, exercise facilities, children free with parents, water view, a/c, NS rooms, TV, laundry facilities, wheelchair access, pets OK, meeting facilities, senior rates, CC. SGL/DBL$50-$100.

Clear Sky Lodging (268 10th St., 97444; 247-6456) 7 rooms, a/c, TV, kitchenettes, laundry facilities, water view, wheelchair access, NS rooms, senior rates, CC. SGL/DBL$100-$180.

Endicott Gardens (95768 Jerry's Flat Rd., 97444; 247-6513) 4 rooms, free breakfast, no pets, CC. SGL/DBL$55-$75.

The Inn at Golden Beach (1435 South Ellensburg Ave., 97444; 247-6606) 41 rooms and efficiencies, TV, water view, pets OK, local transportation, CC. SGL/DBL$45-$59.

Ireland's Rustic Lodge (1120 South Ellensburg Ave., 97444; 247-7718) 40 rooms and efficiencies, laundry facilities, NS rooms, TV, fireplaces, pets OK, CC. SGL/DBL$40-$61.

Jot's Resort (94360 Wedderburn Loop, 97444; 247-6676) 100 rooms and 1- to 3-bedroom suites, restaurant, lounge, entertainment, indoor heated pool, whirlpools, sauna, TV, kitchenettes, water view, children free with parents, pets OK, CC. SGL/DBL$50-$115.

River Bridge Inn (1010 Jerry's Flat Rd., 97444; 247-4533) 50 rooms and efficiencies, whirlpools, water view, pets OK, laundry facilities, children free with parents, TV, wheelchair access, CC. SGL/DBL$45-$85.

Shore Cliff Inn (1100 Hwy. 101, 97444; 247-7091) 38 rooms, restaurant, lounge, wheelchair access, NS rooms, a/c, TV, no pets, CC. SGL/DBL$42-$72.

Tu Tu Tun Lodge (96550 North Bank Rogue, 97444; 247-6664) 18 rooms and suites, restaurant, lounge, pool, pets OK, water view, a/c, TV, wheelchair access, NS rooms, senior rates, CC. SGL/DBL$100-$189.

Grants Pass
Area Code 503

Ahlf House Bed and Breakfast (762 Northwest 6th St., 97526; 474-1374) free breakfast, TV, a/c, no pets, 1902 home, antique furnishings, NS. SGL/DBL$65-$75.

Best Western Grants Pass Inn (111 North Agness Ave., 97526; 476-1117, Fax 479-4315, 800-528-1234) 84 rooms, restaurant, lounge, indoor heated pool, exercise facilities, children free with parents, a/c, NS rooms, TV, laundry facilities, wheelchair access, pets OK, meeting facilities, senior rates, CC. SGL/DBL$65-$125.

Chriswood Inn (220 Northwest A St., 97526; 474-9733) 4 rooms, free breakfast, TV, a/c, NS rooms, no pets, meeting facilities, CC. SGL/DBL$55-$65.

Country Paradise (330 Humberd Lane, 97527; 429-3650) free breakfast, private baths, NS, pool, TV, a/c, no pets, CC. SGL/DBL$110-$125.

Del Rogue Motel (2600 Rogue River Hwy., 97527; 479-2111) 14 rooms and efficiencies, a/c, TV, wheelchair access, NS rooms, laundry facilities, no pets, senior rates, CC. SGL/DBL$40-$65.

Holiday Inn (111 Northeast Agness Ave., 97526; 800-HOLIDAY) 80 rooms, restaurant, lounge, indoor heated pool, exercise facilities, sauna, airport transportation, children under 19 free with parents, wheelchair access, a/c, TV, NS rooms, fax service, room service, no pets, laundry service, meeting facilities for 150, senior rates, CC. SGL/DBL$55-$68.

Motel 6 (1800 Northeast 7th St., 97526; 474-1331, 505-891-6161) 122 rooms, pool, free local calls, children under 17 free with parents, NS rooms, wheelchair access, pets OK, a/c, TV, CC. SGL/DBL$28-$34.

Orleans Motel (1889 Northeast 6th St., 97526; 479-8301) 61 rooms, restaurant, pool, NS rooms, a/c, TV, no pets, senior rates, CC. SGL/DBL$25-$50.

Paradise Ranch Inn (7000 Monument Dr., 97526; 479-4333) 18 rooms, free breakfast, heated pool, whirlpools, lighted tennis courts, no pets, airport transportation, game room, water view, children free with parents, a/c, TV, wheelchair access, NS rooms, senior rates, CC. SGL/DBL$75-$125.

Pine Meadow Inn (1000 Crow Rd., 97527; 471-6277) 3 rooms, free breakfast, TV, fireplaces, no pets, CC. SGL/DBL$95-$110.

Redwood Motel (815 Northeast 6th St., 97526; 476-0878) 24 rooms and efficiencies, restaurant, outdoor heated pool, pets OK, in-room coffee makers, kitchenettes, a/c, TV, wheelchair access, NS rooms, senior rates, CC. SGL/DBL$38-$55.

River Shore Resort Motel (2520 Rouge River Hwy., 97526; 476-6203) 6 rooms, kitchenettes, a/c, TV, water view, CC. SGL/DBL$45-$60.

Riverside Inn (971 Southeast 6th St., 97526; 476-6873, 800-334-4567) 174 rooms and suites, restaurant, lounge, entertainment, outdoor heated pool, sauna, kitchenettes, no pets, in-room coffee makers, children free with parents, gift shop, beauty shop, a/c, TV, wheelchair access, NS rooms, senior rates, CC. SGL/DBL$65-$250.

Rogue River Inn (6285 Rogue River Hwy., 97527; 582-1120, Fax 582-9752, 800-822-2895) 21 rooms, free breakfast, outdoor pool, pets OK, kitchenettes, laundry facilities, water view, a/c, TV, wheelchair access, NS rooms, senior rates, CC. SGL/DBL$33-$82.

Royal Vue (110 Northeast Morgan Lane, 97526; 470-5381, 800-547-7555) 60 rooms, restaurant, lounge, entertainment, outdoor heated pool, whirlpools, sauna, room service, in-room refrigerators, laundry facilities, pets OK, a/c, TV, wheelchair access, NS rooms, senior rates, CC. SGL/DBL$40-$65.

Shilo Inn (1880 Northwest 6th St., 97526; 479-8391, Fax 474-7344, 800-222-2244) 70 rooms and suites, restaurant, free breakfast, outdoor pool, sauna, whirlpools, airport courtesy car, in-room refrigerators, a/c, TV, NS rooms, wheelchair access, children under 12 free with parents, meeting facilities, senior rates, CC. SGL/DBL$46-$70.

Weasku Inn (5560 Rouge River Hwy., 97527; 955-1077) 8 rooms, free breakfast, TV, wheelchair access, water view, local transportation, a/c, pets OK, fireplaces, CC. SGL/DBL$95-$250.

Wilson House Inn (746 Northwest 6th St., 97526; 479-4754) 4 rooms, free breakfast, private baths, antique furnishings, NS, TV, a/c, no pets, CC. SGL/DBL$75-$85.

Gresham
Area Code 503

Best Western Inn (1060 Northeast Cleveland Ave., 97030; 665-1591, Fax 669-7265, 800-528-1234) 75 rooms, restaurant, lounge, free breakfast, heated pool, children free with parents, a/c, NS rooms, TV, laundry facilities, in-room refrigerators, wheelchair access, no pets allowed, meeting facilities, senior rates, CC. SGL/DBL$70-$85.

Kabuto Motel (18323 Southeast Stark St., 97030; 666-6464) 42 rooms, wheelchair access, a/c, TV, meeting facilities, no pets, CC. SGL/DBL$40-$45.

TraveLodge (23705 Northeast Sandy Blvd., 97030; 666-6623, 800-578-7878) 44 rooms, restaurant, lounge, free breakfast, pool, wheelchair access, complimentary newspaper, laundry service, TV, a/c, free local calls, fax service, NS rooms, in-room refrigerators and microwaves, children under 18 free with parents, no pets, meeting facilities, senior rates, CC. SGL/DBL$55-$68.

Halfway
Area Code 503

Birch Leaf Farm (Route 1, 97834; 742-2990) 5 rooms, free breakfast, TV, NS, private baths, a/c, no pets, CC. SGL/DBL$45-$75.

Halfway Motel (170 South Main St., 97834; 742-5722) 23 rooms, a/c, TV, wheelchair access, NS rooms, wheelchair access, senior rates, CC. SGL/DBL$35-$45.

Harbor
Area Code 503

Best Western Beachfront Inn (16008 Boat Basin Rd., 97415; 469-7779, Fax 469-0283, 800-528-1234) 78 rooms, outdoor heated pool, hot tubs, water view, in-room refrigerators and microwaves, kitchenettes, children free with parents, a/c, NS rooms, TV, laundry facilities, wheelchair access, pets OK, meeting facilities, senior rates, CC. SGL/DBL$55-$175.

Hermiston
Area Code 503

Posada Inn (655 North 1st St., 97838; 567-7777, Fax 567-3085) 90 rooms, restaurant, outdoor pool, kitchenettes, laundry facilities, no pets, local transportation, a/c, TV, wheelchair access, NS rooms, senior rates, CC. SGL/DBL$36-$45.

Sands Motel (835 North 1st St., 97838; 3500 Northeast Cornell Rd., 97838; 567-5516) 39 rooms and suites, restaurant, lounge, pets OK, a/c, TV, wheelchair access, NS rooms, senior rates, CC. SGL/DBL$35-$55.

The Way Inn (625 South Hwy. 395, 97838; 567-5561) 30 rooms and efficiencies, pool, pets OK, a/c, wheelchair access, TV, NS rooms, CC. SGL/DBL$28-$35.

Hillsboro

Area Code 503

Best Western Inn (3500 Northeast Cornell Rd., 97124; 648-3500, Fax 640-2789, 800-528-1234) 124 rooms, restaurant, lounge, entertainment, outdoor pool, exercise facilities, hot tubs, whirlpools, children free with parents, a/c, NS rooms, TV, laundry facilities, wheelchair access, pets OK, meeting facilities, senior rates, CC. SGL/DBL$65-$100.

Park Dunes (622 Southeast 10th St., 97123; 640-4791, 800-548-0163) 58 rooms, restaurant, a/c, TV, no pets, laundry facilities, wheelchair access, NS rooms, in-room refrigerators and coffee makers, senior rates, CC. SGL/DBL$35-$50.

Town House Motel (432 Southeast Baseline Rd., 97123; 648-3168) 32 rooms, a/c, TV, kitchenettes, no pets, NS rooms, CC. SGL/DBL$30-$40.

Hood River

Area Code 503

Best Western Hood River Inn (1108 East Marina Way, 97031; 386-2200, Fax 386-8905, 800-528-1234) rooms, pool, exercise facilities, children free with parents, a/c, NS rooms, TV, laundry facilities, wheelchair access, pets OK, meeting facilities, senior rates, CC. SGL/DBL$70-$145.

Brown's Bed and Breakfast (3000 Reed Rd., 97031; 386-1545) 2 rooms, free breakfast, TV, no pets, laundry facilities, NS rooms, CC. SGL/DBL$60.

Columbia Gorge Hotel (4000 Westcliff Dr., 97031; 386-5566, Fax 386-3359, 800-345-1921) 46 rooms and suites, restaurant, lounge, entertainment, water view, pets OK, a/c, TV, wheelchair access, local transportation, NS rooms, senior rates, CC. SGL/DBL$125-$295.

Hood River Hotel (102 Oak St., 97031; 386-1900) 41 rooms, restaurant, lounge, water view, kitchenettes, wheelchair access, NS rooms, TV, CC. SGL/DBL$60-$95.

Lakecliff Estate (3820 Westcliff Dr., 97031; 386-7000) 4 rooms, free breakfast, TV, fireplaces, water view, NS rooms, no pets, CC. SGL/DBL$80-$90.

Meredith Gorge Motel (4300 Westcliff Dr., 97031; 386-1515) 21 rooms, a/c, TV, water view, NS rooms, pets OK, CC. SGL/DBL$38-$45.

State Street Inn (1005 State St., 97031; 386-1899) 4 rooms, free breakfast, game room, water view, TV, local transportation, children free with parents, NS, no pets, CC. SGL/DBL$50-$80.

Vagabond Lodge (4070 Westcliff Dr., 97031; 386-2992) 40 rooms and suites, restaurant, pets OK, water view, a/c, TV, wheelchair access, NS rooms, senior rates, CC. SGL/DBL$35-$70.

Jacksonville
Area Code 503

McCully House Inn (240 East California St., 97530; 899-1942) 3 rooms, free breakfast, restaurant, private baths, NS, TV, a/c, no pets, CC. SGL/DBL$75-$86.

Jacksonville Inn (175 East California St., 97530; 899-1900) 8 rooms and cottage, restaurant, free breakfast, TV, a/c, no pets, private baths, antique furnishings, CC. SGL/DBL$80-$120.

Judge Tou Velle House (455 North Oregon, 97530; 899-8938) free breakfast, NS, private baths, antique furnishings, TV, a/c, no pets, CC. SGL/DBL$75-$120.

Reames House 1868 (540 East California St., 97530; 899-1868) 4 rooms, free breakfast, NS, private baths, antique furnishings, TV, a/c, no pets, CC. SGL/DBL$75-$100.

The Touvelle House (455 North Oregon St., 97530; 899-8938) 6 rooms, free breakfast, outdoor heated pool, TV, a/c, laundry facilities, no pets, meeting facilities, CC. SGL/DBL$90-$145.

John Day
Area Code 503

Best Western Inn (315 West Main St., 97845; 575-1700, 800-528-1234) 36 rooms, indoor heated pool, exercise center, children free with parents, a/c, NS rooms, TV, laundry facilities, wheelchair access, pets OK, meeting rooms, senior rates, CC. SGL/DBL$45-$85.

Dreamers Lodge (144 North Canyon Blvd., 97845; 575-0526, 800-654-2849) 25 rooms, a/c, TV, wheelchair access, airport transportation, in-room refrigerators, in-room coffee makers, pets OK, NS rooms, senior rates, CC. SGL/DBL$32-$60.

Gold Country Motel (250 East Main St., 97845; 575-2100) 14 rooms, restaurant, lounge, TV, no pets, local transportation, CC. SGL/DBL$39-$46.

Sunset Inn (390 West Main St., 97845; 575-1462, 800-452-4899 in Oregon) 43 rooms and suites, restaurant, lounge, indoor heated pool, whirlpools, a/c, TV, wheelchair access, NS rooms, no pets, room service, senior rates, CC. SGL/DBL$32-$40, STS$55-$60.

Joseph
Area Code 503

Bed, Bread and Trail (700 South Main St., 97846; 432-9765, 800-452-3781) 5 rooms, free breakfast, NS, TV, children over 12 welcome, CC. SGL/DBL$50-$60.

Flying Arrow Resort (59782 Wallowa Lake Hwy., 97846; 432-2951) 20 cottages, heated pool, fireplaces, water view, no pets, in-room refrigerators, kitchenettes, a/c, wheelchair access, NS rooms, TV, senior rates, CC. SGL/DBL$60-$125.

Indian Lodge (201 South Main St., 97846; 432-2651) 16 rooms, TV, a/c, laundry facilities, no pets, NS rooms, CC. SGL/DBL$43-$50.

Wallowa Lake Lodge (60060 Wallowa Lake Hwy., 97846; 432-9821) 30 rooms, suites and cottages, restaurant, entertainment, outdoor pool, fireplaces, water view, kitchenettes, gift shop, no pets, TV, NS, meeting facilities, CC. SGL/DBL$65-$115, STS$85-$108.

Junction City
Area Code 503

Black Bart Bed and Breakfast (94125 Love Lake Rd., 97448; 998-1904) free breakfast, TV, a/c, NS, no children, antique furnishings, private baths, no pets, CC. SGL/DBL$63-$75.

Guest House Motel (1335 Ivy St., 97448; 998-6524) 22 rooms, a/c, TV, wheelchair access, NS rooms, local transportation, pets OK, senior rates, CC. SGL/DBL$40-$50.

Klamath Falls
Area Code 503

Best Western Klamath Inn (4061 South 6th St., 97603; 882-1200, Fax 882-2729, 800-528-1234) 52 rooms, restaurant, free breakfast, indoor heated pool, whirlpools, pool, children free with parents, a/c, NS rooms,

TV, laundry facilities, in-room refrigerators, wheelchair access, no pets, meeting facilities, senior rates, CC. SGL/DBL$50-$65.

Cimmaron Motor Inn (3060 South 6th St., 97603; 882-4601, 800-742-2648) 163 rooms and efficiencies, restaurant, outdoor heated pool, pets OK, kitchenettes, a/c, TV, wheelchair access, NS rooms, senior rates, CC. SGL/DBL$40-$50.

Comfort Inn (2500 South 6th St., 97601; 884-9999, 800-228-5150) 57 rooms, free breakfast, indoor pool, whirlpools, exercise center, no pets, a/c, TV, wheelchair access, CC. SGL/DBL$55-$110.

Econo Lodge (75 Main St., 97601; 884-7735, 800-4-CHOICE) 51 rooms, pool, children under 12 free with parents, no pets, NS rooms, wheelchair access, a/c, TV, senior rates, CC. SGL/DBL$34-$51.

Hill View Motel (5543 South 6th St., 97601; 883-7771) 16 rooms, a/c, pets OK, TV, laundry facilities, NS rooms, CC. SGL/DBL$40-$50.

Klamath Manor (219 Pine St., 97601; 883-5459) 3 rooms, free breakfast, TV, fireplaces, NS, no pets, CC. SGL/DBL$55-$70.

Maverick Motel (1220 Main St., 97601; 882-6688) 49 rooms, free breakfast, outdoor heated pool, no pets, a/c, TV, wheelchair access, NS rooms, senior rates, CC. SGL/DBL$28-$50.

Molatores Motor Inn (100 Main St., 97601; 882-4666, Fax 883-8795, 800-732-2025) 105 rooms and suites, restaurant, outdoor heated pool, whirlpools, laundry facilities, no pets, a/c, TV, wheelchair access, NS rooms, senior rates, meeting facilities, CC. SGL/DBL$35-$80.

Motel 6 (5136 South 6th St., 97630; 884-2110, 505-891-6161) 61 rooms, pool, free local calls, children under 17 free with parents, NS rooms, wheelchair access, pets OK, a/c, TV, CC. SGL/DBL$28-$34.

Red Lion Inn (3612 South 6th St., 97630; 882-7938, 800-547-8010) 108 rooms, restaurant, lounge, entertainment, pool, a/c, TV, wheelchair access, NS rooms, complimentary newspaper, fax service, laundry facilities, meeting facilities, senior rates, CC. SGL/DBL$63-$75.

Super 8 Motel (3805 Hwy. 97 North, 97601; 884-8880, Fax 994-0235, 800-800-8000) 61 rooms, whirlpools, no pets, children under 12 free with parents, free local calls, a/c, TV, in-room refrigerators and microwaves, fax service, NS rooms, wheelchair access, meeting facilities, senior rates, CC. SGL/DBL$36-$60.

Thompson's Bed and Breakfast (1420 Wild Plum Court, 97601; 882-7938) 4 rooms, free breakfast, TV, a/c, no pets, water view, laundry facilities, NS rooms, CC. SGL/DBL$55-$70.

TraveLodge (11 Main St., 97601; 882-4494, 800-578-7878) 47 rooms, out-door pool, wheelchair access, complimentary newspaper, laundry service, TV, a/c, water view, free local calls, fax service, NS rooms, in-room refrigerators and microwaves, children under 18 free with parents, no pets, meeting facilities, senior rates, CC. SGL/DBL$55-$65.

Lafayette

Area Code 503

Kelty Estate Bed and Breakfast (675 Hwy. 99 West, 97127; 864-3740) free breakfast, TV, a/c, NS, 1872 home, antique furnishings, no pets, CC. SGL/DBL$66.

LaGrande

Area Code 503

Best Western Pony Soldier Inn (2612 Island Ave., 97850; 963-7195, 800-528-1234) 151 rooms, pool, whirlpools, sauna, children free with parents, a/c, NS rooms, TV, laundry facilities, wheelchair access, in-room refrigerators, pets OK, meeting facilities, senior rates, CC. SGL/DBL$58-$75.

Broken Arrow Lodge (2215 East Adams Ave., 97850; 963-7116) 34 rooms, restaurant, pets OK, laundry facilities, TV, a/c, meeting facilities, CC. SGL/DBL$28-$36.

Moon Motel (2116 Adams Ave., 97850; 963-2724) 9 rooms, a/c, TV, no pets, laundry facilities, CC. SGL/DBL$26-$28.

Pitcher Inn (608 N Ave., 97850; 963-9152) 4 rooms, free breakfast, TV, a/c, NS rooms, no pets, CC. SGL/DBL$65-$85.

Royal Motor Inn (1510 Adams Ave., 97850; 963-4154) 45 rooms, children free with parents, NS rooms, pets OK, local transportation, fireplaces, TV, meeting rooms. SGL/DBL$33-$40.

Stange Manor Inn (1612 Walnut St., 97850; 963-2400) 4 rooms, free break-fast, TV, NS, antique furnishings, CC. SGL/DBL$70-$95.

Super 8 Motel (2407 East R Ave., 97850; 963-8080, Fax 963-2825, 800-800-8000) 64 rooms and suites, no pets, children under 12 free with parents, free local calls, a/c, TV, in-room refrigerators and microwaves, fax service, NS rooms, wheelchair access, meeting facilities, senior rates, CC. SGL/DBL$40-$80.

Lake Oswego
Area Code 503

Best Western Sherwood Inn (15700 Southwest Upper Boones Ferry, 97034; 620-2980, Fax 639-9010, 800-528-1234) 57 rooms, restaurant, lounge, indoor heated pool, children free with parents, a/c, NS rooms, TV, laundry facilities, wheelchair access, pets OK, meeting facilities, senior rates, CC. SGL/DBL$45-$80.

Lakeshore Motor Hotel (210 North State St., 97034; 636-9679) 32 rooms, outdoor pool, a/c, TV, kitchenettes, wheelchair access, laundry facilities, NS rooms, water view, CC. SGL/DBL$55-$95.

Phoenix Inn (14905 Southwest Bangy Rd., 97034; 624-7400) 62 rooms, indoor heated pool, exercise center, pets OK, a/c, TV, wheelchair access, laundry facilities, room service, meeting facilities, CC. SGL/DBL$56-$70.

Lakeview
Area Code 503

Best Western Skyline Motor Inn (414 North G St., 97630; 947-2194, Fax 947-3100, 800-528-1234) 38 rooms, restaurant, free breakfast, indoor heated pool, exercise facilities, hot tubs, in-room refrigerators and coffee makers, children free with parents, a/c, NS rooms, TV, laundry facilities, wheelchair access, pets OK, meeting facilities, senior rates, CC. SGL/DBL$45-$66.

Interstate 8 Motel (354 North K St., 97630; 947-3341) 32 rooms, restaurant, kitchenettes, a/c, TV, pets OK, laundry facilities, CC. SGL/DBL$30-$38.

Lakeview Lodge (301 North G St., 97630; 947-2181, Fax 947-2572) 40 rooms and efficiencies, a/c, TV, wheelchair access, NS rooms, pets OK, senior rates, CC. SGL/DBL$32-$60.

Lincoln City
Area Code 503

Anchor Motel and Lodge (4417 Southwest Hwy. 101, 97367; 996-3810) 29 rooms and efficiencies, pets OK, NS rooms, laundry facilities, meeting rooms, CC. SGL/DBL$30-$65.

Best Western Lincoln Sands Inn (535 Northwest Inlet St., 97367; 800-528-1234) pool, exercise facilities, children free with parents, a/c, NS rooms, TV, laundry facilities, wheelchair access, pets OK, meeting rooms, senior rates, CC. SGL/DBL$75-$110.

Best Western Rama Inn (4430 Southwest Hwy. 101, 97367; 994-6060, 800-528-1234) 60 rooms, indoor heated pool, exercise center, children free with parents, a/c, NS rooms, TV, laundry facilities, wheelchair access, pets OK, meeting rooms, senior rates, CC. SGL/DBL$80-$130.

Brey House Oceanview (3725 Northwest Keel, 97367; 994-7123) 4 rooms, free breakfast, NS, TV, fireplaces, kitchenettes, no pets, CC. SGL/DBL$60-$80.

Coho Inn (1635 Northwest Harbor Ave., 97367; 994-3684, 800-848-7006) 50 rooms and suites, whirlpools, sauna, fireplaces, pets OK, a/c, TV, wheelchair access, NS rooms, senior rates, CC. SGL/DBL$48-$98.

Cozy Beachfront Resort (515 Northwest Inlet Ave., 97367; 994-2950, Fax 996-4332, 800-553-2683) 68 rooms and suites, heated pool, whirlpools, no pets, fireplaces, water view, children free with parents, a/c, TV, wheelchair access, NS rooms, senior rates, CC. SGL/DBL$45-$225.

D Sands Motel (171 Southwest Hwy. 101, 97367; 994-5244, 800-527-3925) 63 efficiencies, indoor heated pool, whirlpools, water view, a/c, TV, wheelchair access, children free with parents, no pets, NS rooms, senior rates, CC. SGL/DBL$90-$110.

Dock of the Bay (1116 Southwest 51st St., 97367; 996-3549, 800-362-5229) 24 1- and 2-bedroom efficiencies, whirlpools, sauna, pets OK, kitchenettes, a/c, TV, wheelchair access, NS rooms, senior rates, CC. SGL/DBL1BR$80-$100, 2BR$110-$150.

The Inn at Spanish Head (4009 Hwy. 101, 97367; 996-2161, 800-452-8127) 121 efficiencies, restaurant, outdoor heated pool, sauna, whirlpools, a/c, TV, wheelchair access, NS rooms, no pets, game room, room service, meeting facilities, senior rates, CC. SGL/DBL$95-$250.

Lincoln Shores (136 Northeast Hwy. 101, 97367; 994-8155, 800-423-6240) 30 rooms, water view, a/c, TV, wheelchair access, pets OK, kitchenettes, NS rooms, senior rates, CC. SGL/DBL$30-$90.

Nordic Motel (2133 Northwest Inlet Ave., 97367; 994-8145, 800-452-3558) 52 rooms and efficiencies, indoor pool, whirlpools, sauna, game room, in-room coffee makers, water view, pets OK, fireplaces, a/c, TV, wheelchair access, NS rooms, senior rates, meeting facilities, CC. SGL/DBL$63-$85.

Red Carpet Inn (2645 Northwest Inlet Ave., 97367; 994-2134, 800-251-1962) 34 rooms and suites, indoor pool, water view, in-room coffee makers, fireplaces, children free with parents, TV, a/c, NS rooms, pets OK, meeting facilities, senior rates, CC. SGL/DBL$45-$85.

Shilo Inn Resort (1501 Northwest 40th Place, 97367; 994-3655, 800-222-2244) 187 rooms and suites, restaurant, lounge, entertainment, indoor heated pool, whirlpools, sauna, airport courtesy car, in-room refrigerators, a/c, TV, NS rooms, wheelchair access, children under 12 free with parents, pets OK, in-room refrigerators, local transportation, gift shop, meeting facilities, senior rates, CC. SGL/DBL$50-$100.

Westshore Oceanfront Motel (3127 Southwest Anchor Ave., 97367; 996-2001, 800-621-3187) 10 rooms and efficiencies, water view, wheelchair access, pets OK, NS rooms, kitchenettes, CC. SGL/DBL$40-$60.

Madras
Area Code 503

Hoffy's Motel (600 North Hwy. 26, 97741; 475-4633) 81 rooms, restaurant, indoor heated pool, a/c, TV, wheelchair access, pets OK, laundry facilities, NS rooms, senior rates, meeting facilities, CC. SGL/DBL$35-$100.

Juniper Motel (414 North Hwy. 26, 97741; 475-6186) 22 rooms, kitchenettes, a/c, TV, pets OK, wheelchair access, NS rooms, senior rates, CC. SGL/DBL$55-$75.

Sonnys Motel (1539 Southwest Hwy. 97, 97741; 475-7217, 800-624-6137) 44 rooms and suites, restaurant, free breakfast, lounge, outdoor heated pool, whirlpools, laundry facilities, a/c, TV, in-room refrigerators, pets OK, wheelchair access, NS rooms, senior rates, CC. SGL/DBL$35-$45, STS$55-$65.

McKenzie Bridge
Area Code 503

Cedarwood Lodge (56535 McKenzie Hwy., 97423; 822-3351) 7 rooms and efficiencies, water view, kitchenettes, NS rooms, no pets, laundry facilities. SGL/DBL$50-$90.

Historic Log Cabin Inn (56483 McKenzie Hwy., 97413; 822-3432) 8 rooms, restaurant, lounge, water view, fireplaces, laundry facilities, meeting facilities, no pets, senior rates, CC. SGL/DBL$55-$65.

Horse Creek Lodge (56228 McKenzie Hwy., 97413; 822-3267) 8 rooms, kitchenettes, fireplaces, laundry facilities, water view, no pets, CC. SGL/DBL$75-$200.

McMinnville
Area Code 503

Baker Street Bed and Breakfast (129 South Bakers St., 97128; 472-5575) 3 rooms, free breakfast, TV, a/c, fireplaces, NS rooms, laundry facilities, kitchenettes, no pets, CC. SGL/DBL$65-$125.

Best Western Inn (2035 South Hwy. 99 West, 97128; 472-4900, 800-528-1234) 65 rooms, restaurant, indoor heated pool, exercise center, children

free with parents, a/c, NS rooms, TV, laundry facilities, wheelchair access, pets OK, meeting facilities, senior rates, CC. SGL/DBL$62-$80.

Orchard View Bed and Breakfast (16540 Northwest Orchard View Rd., 97128; 472-0165) 4 rooms, free breakfast, TV, no pets, CC. SGL/DBL$60-$80.

Paragon Motel (2065 South Hwy. 99 West, 97128; 472-9493, 800-525-5469) 55 rooms, free breakfast, outdoor heated pool, in-room refrigerators, a/c, TV, wheelchair access, NS rooms, pets OK, meeting facilities, senior rates, CC. SGL/DBL$35-$82.

Safari Motor Inn (345 North Hwy. 99 West, 97128; 472-5187, Fax 434-6380, 800-321-5543) 90 rooms, restaurant, lounge, whirlpools, a/c, TV, wheelchair access, NS rooms, senior rates, CC. SGL/DBL$38-$50.

Steiger Haus (360 Wilson St., 97128; 472-0821) 5 rooms, free breakfast, TV, a/c, no pets, local transportation, fire places, meeting facilities, CC. SGL/DBL$65-$90.

Youngberg Hill Farm Inn (10660 Youngberg Hill Rd., 97128; 472-2727) 5 rooms, free breakfast, TV, a/c, no pets, wheelchair access, fireplace, laundry facilities, NS rooms, meeting facilities, senior rates, CC. SGL/DBL$75-$100.

Medford

Area Code 503

Best Western Medford Inn (1015 South Riverside Ave., 97501; 773-8266, Fax 734-5447, 800-528-1234) 112 rooms, restaurant, lounge, outdoor pool, exercise facilities, children free with parents, a/c, NS rooms, TV, laundry facilities, wheelchair access, no pets, meeting rooms, senior rates, CC. SGL/DBL$45-$130.

Best Western Pony Soldier Motor Inn (2340 Crater Lake Hwy., 97504; 779-2001, Fax 779-7304, 800-528-1234) 72 rooms, restaurant, free breakfast, lounge, heated pool, in-room refrigerators, children free with parents, a/c, NS rooms, TV, laundry facilities, wheelchair access, pets OK, meeting rooms, senior rates, CC. SGL/DBL$65-$78.

Cedar Lodge (518 North Riverside Ave., 97501; 773-7361) 79 rooms and suites, restaurant, lounge, outdoor heated pool, pets OK, children free with parents, a/c, TV, wheelchair access, NS rooms, senior rates, CC. SGL/DBL$30-$55.

HoJo Inn (525 South River Side, 97501; 772-6133, Fax 776-6984, 800-I-GO-HOJO) 36 rooms and suites, free breakfast, a/c, TV, free local calls, kitchenettes, airport transportation, wheelchair access, NS rooms, no pets, laundry facilities, senior rates, CC. SGL/DBL$44-$66.

Holiday Inn (2300 Crater Lake Hwy., 97504; 779-3141, Fax 779-2623, 800-HOLIDAY) 164 rooms and suites, restaurant, lounge, indoor heated pool, exercise facilities, children under 19 free with parents, wheelchair access, a/c, airport transportation, TV, NS rooms, fax service, room service, no pets, laundry service, meeting facilities, senior rates, CC. SGL/DBL$55-$120.

Horizon Motor Inn (1154 East Barnett Rd., 97505; 779-5085, 800-452-2255) 129 rooms and suites, restaurant, heated pool, whirlpools, sauna, local transportation, a/c, TV, wheelchair access, NS rooms, senior rates, CC. SGL/DBL$50-$60, STS$100-$150.

Knights Inn (500 North Riverside Ave., 97501; 773-3676, 800-626-1900, 800-843-5644) 83 rooms, restaurant, pool, NS rooms, TV, a/c, no pets, senior rates, CC. SGL/DBL$25-$32.

Motel 6 North (2400 Biddle Rd., 97504; 779-0550, 505-891-6161) 116 rooms, pool, free local calls, children under 17 free with parents, NS rooms, wheelchair access, pets OK, a/c, TV, CC. SGL/DBL$32-$38.

Motel 6 South (950 Alba Dr., 97504; 773-4290, 505-891-6161) 167 rooms, pool, free local calls, children under 17 free with parents, NS rooms, wheelchair access, pets OK, a/c, TV, CC. SGL/DBL$28-$34.

Motel Orleans (850 Alba Dr., 97504; 779-6730) 50 rooms, restaurant, outdoor pool, NS rooms, TV, a/c, no pets, CC. SGL/DBL$30-$50.

Quality Inn (2345 Crater Lake Hwy., 97504; 770-1234, 800-221-2222) 124 rooms and suites, restaurant, lounge, pool, exercise facilities, hot tubs, whirlpools, fireplaces, no pets, children free with parents, a/c, in-room refrigerators, airport courtesy car, TV, wheelchair access, room service, laundry service, NS rooms, meeting facilities, senior rates, CC. SGL/DBL$70-$100, STS$165-$250.

Red Lion Inn (200 North Riverside Ave., 97501; 779-5811, 800-547-8010) 186 rooms and suites, restaurant, lounge, entertainment, heated pool, a/c, TV, wheelchair access, NS rooms, complimentary newspaper, fax service, airport transportation, laundry facilities, meeting facilities, senior rates, CC. SGL/DBL$80-$250.

Shilo Inn (2111 Biddle Rd., 97540; 770-5151, 800-222-2244) 48 rooms and suites, airport courtesy car, in-room refrigerators, a/c, TV, NS rooms, local transportation, pets OK, wheelchair access, children under 12 free with parents, meeting facilities, senior rates, CC. SGL/DBL$51-$60.

Windmill Inn (1950 Biddle Rd., 97540; 779-0050, 800-547-4747) 123 rooms and efficiencies, restaurant, lounge, heated pool, whirlpools, sauna, children under 18 free with parents, airport courtesy car, pets OK, a/c, TV, wheelchair access, complimentary newspaper, NS rooms, meeting facilities, senior rates, CC. SGL/DBL$50-$75.

Milton-Freewater

Area Code 503

Morgan Inn (104 North Columbia, 97862; 938-5547) 32 rooms, a/c, laundry facilities, wheelchair access, TV, NS rooms, no pets, CC. SGL/DBL$35-$70.

Out West Motel (Route 1, 97862; 938-6647) 10 rooms, a/c, kitchenettes, pets OK, TV, CC. SGL/DBL$32-$39.

Milwaukie

Area Code 503

Econo Lodge (17330 Southeast McLoughlin Blvd., 97222; 654-2222, 800-4-CHOICE) 22 rooms and suites, pool, spa, children under 12 free with parents, no pets, senior rates, NS rooms, wheelchair access, a/c, TV, senior rates, CC. SGL/DBL$45-$68.

Maynard's Motel (14015 Southeast McLoughlin Blvd., 97222; 659-2125) 40 rooms, kitchenettes, a/c, TV, wheelchair access, NS rooms, senior rates, CC. SGL/DBL$35-$45.

Monmouth

Area Code 503

Courtesy Inn (270 North Pacific Hwy., 97361; 838-4438) 35 rooms, restaurant, NS rooms, pets OK, wheelchair access, a/c, TV, CC. SGL/DBL$40-$50.

Mount Hood

Area Code 503

Falcon Crest Inn (87287 Government Camp Loop Hwy., 97028; 272-3403) 5 rooms, restaurant, lounge, free breakfast, pool, exercise center, NS rooms, TV, meeting facilities, CC. SGL/DBL$85-$140.

Mount Hood Inn (87450 Government Camp Loop Hwy., 97028; 273-3205, 800-443-7777) 56 rooms, TV, laundry facilities, pets OK, CC. SGL/DBL$90-$145.

Newburg

Area Code 503

Belangers Secluded Bed and Breakfast (19719 Northeast Williamson Rd., 97132; 538-2635) 2 rooms, free breakfast, TV, a/c, no pets, NS rooms, fireplaces, CC. SGL/DBL$40-$50.

Partridge Farm (4300 East Portland Rd., 97132; 538-2050) 4 rooms, free breakfast, TV, a/c, no pets, CC. SGL/DBL$60-$95.

Shilo Inn (501 Sitka Ave., 97132; 537-0303, 800-222-2244) 60 rooms and suites, outdoor pool, airport courtesy car, in-room refrigerators, a/c, TV, NS rooms, wheelchair access, children under 12 free with parents, laundry facilities, pets OK, meeting facilities, senior rates, CC. SGL/DBL$59-$71.

Springbrook Hazelnut Farm (30295 North Hwy. 99 West, 97132; 538-4606) 5 rooms, free breakfast, TV, a/c, NS, no pets, CC. SGL/DBL$75-$125.

Newport
Area Code 503

Best Western Inn (744 Southwest Elizabeth St., 97365; 265-8853, Fax 265-9449, 800-528-1234) 72 rooms, free breakfast, water view, airport courtesy car, complimentary newspaper, children free with parents, a/c, NS rooms, TV, laundry facilities, wheelchair access, pets OK, meeting facilities, senior rates, CC. SGL/DBL$80-$115.

Embarcadero Resort Motel (1000 Southeast Bay Blvd., 97365; 265-8521, Fax 265-7844, 800-547-4779) 100 rooms and suites, restaurant, lounge, indoor heated pool, sauna, whirlpools, laundry facilities, no pets, airport transportation, water view, a/c, TV, wheelchair access, NS rooms, senior rates, CC. SGL/DBL$85-$165.

Hotel Newport (3019 North Coast Hwy., 97365; 265-9411) 145 rooms, restaurant, lounge, outdoor heated pool, TV, wheelchair access, NS rooms, room service, water view, meeting facilities, senior rates, CC. SGL/DBL$84-$98.

Little Creek Cove (3641 Northwest Oceanview Dr., 97365; 265-8587, Fax 265-4567) 29 efficiencies, a/c, TV, wheelchair access, NS rooms, senior rates, CC. SGL/DBL$85-$125.

Newport Motor Inn (1311 North Coast Hwy., 97365; 265-8516) 39 rooms, restaurant, lounge, laundry facilities, NS rooms, pets OK, TV, senior rates, CC. SGL/DBL$39-$42.

Ocean House Bed and Breakfast (4920 Northwest Woody Way, 97365; 265-6158) 4 rooms, free breakfast, TV, a/c, water view, NS, no pets, CC. SGL/DBL$60-$100.

Puerto Nuevo Inn (544 Southwest Hwy. 101, 97365; 265-5767) 32 rooms and efficiencies, water view, NS rooms, no pets, wheelchair access, TV, CC. SGL/DBL$40-$100.

Shilo Inn Resort (536 Southwest Elizabeth St., 97365; 265-7701, Fax 265-5687, 800-222-2244) 179 rooms and suites, restaurant, lounge, entertainment, indoor pool, water view, pets OK, airport courtesy car, in-room refrigerators, a/c, TV, NS rooms, wheelchair access, children under 12 free with parents, meeting facilities, senior rates, CC. SGL/DBL$85-$380.

Sylvia Beach Hotel (267 Northwest Cliff St., 97365; 265-5428) 20 rooms, bed and breakfast, restaurant, free breakfast, outdoor pool, fireplaces, wheelchair access, NS rooms, no pets, meeting facilities. SGL/DBL$65-$130.

Tides Inn (715 Southwest Bay St., 97365; 265-7202) 10 rooms and efficiencies, water view, pets OK, TV, laundry facilities, CC. SGL/DBL$35-$79.

The Viking Condominiums (729 Northwest Coast St., 97365; 265-2477) 24 1- and 2-bedroom condominiums, outdoor heated pool, fireplaces, laundry facilities, water view, kitchenettes, no pets, CC. SGL/DBL$85-$150.

Val-U-Inn (531 Southwest Fall St., 97365; 265-6203, 800-443-7777) 71 rooms and efficiencies, water view, laundry facilities, pets OK, TV, wheelchair access, meeting facilities, CC. SGL/DBL$52-$125.

Whaler Motel (155 Southwest Elizabeth St., 97365; 265-9261, 800-433-9444) 61 rooms and efficiencies, a/c, TV, kitchenettes, pets OK, local transportation, in-room refrigerators, children free with parents, wheelchair access, NS rooms, senior rates, CC. SGL/DBL$75-$95.

Willeer's Motel (754 Southwest Coast Hwy., 97365; 265-2241, 800-945-5377) 33 rooms and efficiencies, NS rooms, laundry facilities, pets OK, TV, wheelchair access, kitchenettes, water view, senior rates. SGL/DBL$38-$75.

North Bend
Area Code 503

Bay Bridge Motel (33 Hwy. 101, 97459; 756-3151) 16 rooms and efficiencies, a/c, TV, wheelchair access, NS rooms, children free with parents, pets OK, in-room refrigerators, senior rates, CC. SGL/DBL$40-$65.

Pony Village Motor Inn (Virginia Ave., 97459; 756-3191) 119 rooms, restaurant, lounge, outdoor heated pool, exercise center, NS rooms, wheelchair access, pets OK, TV, CC. SGL/DBL$42-$55.

Oakridge
Area Code 503

Best Western Inn (47443 Hwy. 58, 97463; 782-2212, Fax 782-2811, 800-528-1234) 40 rooms, restaurant, free breakfast, heated pool, exercise facilities, children free with parents, a/c, NS rooms, TV, laundry facilities, wheelchair access, pets OK, meeting facilities, senior rates, CC. SGL/DBL$43-$58.

Oakridge Motel (48197 Hwy. 58 East, 97463; 782-2432) 10 rooms, restaurant, a/c, TV, NS rooms, pets OK, senior rates, CC. SGL/DBL$28-$32.

Ontario
Area Code 503

Best Western Inn (251 Goodfellow St., 97914; 889-2600, Fax 889-2259, 800-528-1234) 61 rooms, restaurant, lounge, free breakfast, indoor heated pool, exercise facilities, children free with parents, a/c, NS rooms, TV, laundry facilities, wheelchair access, pets OK, meeting facilities, senior rates, CC. SGL/DBL$45-$78.

Colonial Motor Inn (1395 Tapadera Ave., 97914; 889-9615, 800-727-5014) 84 rooms, restaurant, indoor pool, pets OK, a/c, NS rooms, TV, CC SGL/DBL$20-$38.

Fireside Motel (1737 North Oregon St., 97914; 889-3101) 26 rooms and efficiencies, restaurant, outdoor pool, a/c, TV, wheelchair access, NS rooms, pets OK, laundry facilities, senior rates, CC. SGL/DBL$28-$55.

Holiday Motel (615 East Idaho Ave., 97914; 889-9188) 72 rooms and suites, restaurant, outdoor heated pool, pets OK, local transportation, a/c, TV, wheelchair access, NS rooms, senior rates, CC. SGL/DBL$27-$37.

Howard Johnson (1249 Tapadera Ave., 97914; 889-8621, Fax 889-8023, 800-I-GO-HOJO) 97 rooms, restaurant, lounge, pool, children free with parents, wheelchair access, NS rooms, TV, a/c, no pets, laundry facilities, fax service, senior rates, meeting facilities for 200, CC. SGL/DBL$48-$60.

Motel 6 (275 Northeast 12th Ave., 97914; 889-6617, 505-891-6161) 126 rooms, outdoor heated pool, free local calls, children under 17 free with parents, NS rooms, wheelchair access, pets OK, a/c, TV, CC. SGL/DBL$24-$30.

The Plaza Motel (1144 Southwest 4th Ave., 97914; 889-9641) 21 rooms, outdoor pool, exercise center, a/c, wheelchair access, TV, senior rates, CC. SGL/DBL$45-$55.

Regency Crest Inn (88 North Oregon St., 97914; 889-6449) 34 rooms, outdoor pool, a/c, TV, pets OK, CC. SGL/DBL$29-$32.

Stockmans Motel (81 Southwest 1st St., 97914; 889-4446) 28 rooms, restaurant, lounge, a/c, TV, pets OK, laundry facilities, NS rooms, meeting facilities, senior rates, CC. SGL/DBL$28-$50.

Oregon City
Area Code 503

Hydrangea Bed and Breakfast (716 Center St., 97045; 650-4421) 2 rooms, free breakfast, TV, a/c, no pets, laundry facilities, kitchenettes, CC. SGL/DBL$60.

The Inn of the Oregon Trail (416 South McLoughlin Blvd., 97045; 656-2089) 4 rooms, free breakfast, restaurant, TV, a/c, water view, fireplaces, no pets, meeting facilities, CC. SGL/DBL$48-$85.

Jagger House (512 6th St., 97045; 657-7820) 3 rooms, free breakfast, TV, a/c, no pets, NS, CC. SGL/DBL$65-$70.

Val-U Inn (1900 Clackamette Dr., 97045; 655-7141, Fax 655-1927, 800-443-7777) 120 rooms and suites, restaurant, heated pool, whirlpools, sauna, water view, a/c, TV, wheelchair access, NS rooms, pets OK, room service, meeting facilities, senior rates, CC. SGL/DBL$55-$116.

Oswego
Area Code 503

Residence Inn by Marriott (115200 Southwest Bangy Rd., 97305; 684-2603, 800-331-3131) 112 1- and 2-bedroom suites, free breakfast, in-room refrigerators, coffee makers and microwaves, laundry facilities, TV, a/c, VCRs, pets OK, complimentary newspaper, fireplaces, children free with parents, NS rooms, wheelchair access, meeting facilities, CC. SGL/DBL$110-$145.

Otter Rock
Area Code 503

Alpine Chalets (Otter Crest Loop Rd., 97369; 765-2572) 12 rooms, TV, CC. SGL/DBL$50.

The Inn at Otter Crest (Otter Rock 97369; 765-2111, Fax 765-2047, 800-452-2101) 97 rooms, restaurant, lounge, entertainment, heated pool, sauna, whirlpools, in-room refrigerators, a/c, TV, wheelchair access, NS rooms, no pets, water view, laundry facilities, gift shop, senior rates, CC. SGL/DBL$100-$150.

Pendleton
Area Code 503

Best Western Inn (400 Southeast Nye Ave., 97801; 276-2135, Fax 278-2129, 800-528-1234) 50 rooms, restaurant, free breakfast, whirlpools, children

free with parents, a/c, NS rooms, TV, laundry facilities, wheelchair access, pets OK, meeting facilities, senior rates, CC. SGL/DBL$50-$68.

Chaparral Motel (620 Tutuilla Rd. Southwest, 97801; 276-8854) 51 rooms and efficiencies, restaurant, a/c, TV, wheelchair access, NS rooms, pets OK, kitchenettes, senior rates, CC. SGL/DBL$40-$60.

Econo Lodge Downtown (Pendleton 97801; 276-5252, 800-4-CHOICE) 51 rooms, pool, children under 12 free with parents, no pets, senior rates, NS rooms, wheelchair access, a/c, TV, senior rates, CC. SGL/DBL$30-$45.

Graham's Bed and Breakfast (704 South Main St., 97801; 278-1743) 4 rooms, free breakfast, TV, a/c, no pets, CC. SGL/DBL$36-$56.

Longhorn Motel (411 Southwest Dorion, 97801; 276-7531) 36 rooms, restaurant, a/c, pets OK, NS rooms, CC. SGL/DBL$33-$36.

Motel 6 (325 Southeast Nye Ave., 97801; 276-3160, 505-891-6161) 122 rooms, pool, free local calls, children under 17 free with parents, NS rooms, wheelchair access, pets OK, a/c, TV, CC. SGL/DBL$28-$34.

Red Lion Inn (304 Southeast Nye Ave., 97801; 276-6111, 800-547-8010) 168 rooms, restaurant, lounge, entertainment, outdoor heated pool, a/c, TV, wheelchair access, NS rooms, complimentary newspaper, fax service, laundry facilities, room service, pets OK, airport transportation, meeting facilities, senior rates, CC. SGL/DBL$75-$95.

Seven Inn (Pendleton, 97801; 276-4711) 50 rooms, restaurant, TV, pets OK, NS rooms, CC. SGL/DBL$35-$40.

Swift Station Inn (602 Southeast Byers Ave., 97801; 276-3739) 3 rooms, free breakfast, TV, a/c, no pets, NS rooms, CC. SGL/DBL$60-$100.

Portland

Area Code 503

Rental and Reservation Services:

Northwest Bed and Breakfast (610 Southwest Broadway, 97205; 243-7616) bed and breakfast reservations.

□ □ □

Alladin Motor Inn (8905 Southwest 30th St., 97205; 246-8241, 800-292-4466) 52 rooms, a/c, TV, kitchenettes, pets OK, laundry facilities, free local calls, senior rates, CC. SGL/DBL$65-$85.

Ben Stark Hotel and International Hostel (1022 Southwest Stark St., 97205; 274-1223) 96 rooms, laundry facilities, no pets, NS rooms, CC. SGL/DBL$39-$49.

The Benson Hotel (309 Southwest Broadway, 97205; 228-2000, Fax 226-4603, 800-426-0670) 290 rooms and suites, restaurant, lounge, entertainment, a/c, TV, wheelchair access, airport transportation, room service, pets OK, meeting facilities, CC. SGL/DBL$145-$600.

Best Western Inn (9727 Northeast Sandy Blvd., 97220; 255-1400, Fax 256-3842, 800-528-1234) 166 rooms, restaurant, lounge, free breakfast, outdoor heated pool, children free with parents, a/c, NS rooms, TV, laundry facilities, airport transportation, wheelchair access, pets OK, meeting facilities, senior rates, CC. SGL/DBL$46-$60.

Best Western Inn (4911 Northeast 82nd Ave., 97220; 255-9771, Fax 255-9774, 800-528-1234) 52 rooms, free breakfast, outdoor heated pool, airport transportation, in-room refrigerators, kitchenettes, children free with parents, a/c, NS rooms, TV, laundry facilities, wheelchair access, no pets, meeting rooms, senior rates, CC. SGL/DBL$50-$65.

Best Western Inn (4319 Northwest Yeon, 97210; 497-9044, Fax 497-1030, 800-528-1234) 65 rooms, free breakfast, indoor heated pool, whirlpools, sauna, complimentary newspaper, free local calls, children free with parents, a/c, NS rooms, TV, laundry facilities, wheelchair access, pets OK, meeting facilities, senior rates, CC. SGL/DBL$48-$125.

Best Western Inn at the Coliseum (10 North Weidler St., 97227; 239-9900, Fax 236-3306, 800-528-1234) 178 rooms, restaurant, lounge, indoor heated pool, exercise facilities, children free with parents, a/c, airport transportation, room service, NS rooms, TV, laundry facilities, wheelchair access, no pets, meeting rooms, senior rates, CC. SGL/DBL$60-$78.

Best Western Inn at the Convention Center (420 Northeast Holladay St., 97232; 233-6331, Fax 233-2677, 800-528-1234) 95 rooms, restaurant, children free with parents, a/c, NS rooms, TV, laundry facilities, wheelchair access, pets OK, meeting facilities, senior rates, CC. SGL/DBL$65-$90.

Best Western Pony Soldier Inn Airport (9901 Northeast Sandy Blvd., 97220; 256-1504, Fax 256-5928, 800-528-1234) 104 rooms and suites, restaurant, lounge, free breakfast, heated pool, exercise facilities, children free with parents, a/c, NS rooms, TV, laundry facilities, wheelchair access, no pets, airport transportation, in-room refrigerators, meeting facilities, senior rates, CC. SGL/DBL$70-$140.

Cabana Motel (1707 Northeast 82nd Ave., 97220; 252-0224) 41 rooms, a/c, NS rooms, no pets, TV, CC. SGL/DBL$32.

Cape Cod Bed and Breakfast (5733 Southwest Dickinson, 97220; 246-1839) 2 rooms, free breakfast, spa, NS, TV, a/c, no pets, CC. SGL/DBL$50-$66.

Caravan Motel (2401 Southwest 4th Ave., 97201; 226-1121, 800-248-0506) 40 rooms, restaurant, heated pool, a/c, TV, wheelchair access, NS rooms, senior rates, CC. SGL/DBL$45-$55.

Chestnut Tree Inn (9699 Southeast Stark St., 97216; 255-4444) 58 rooms, restaurant, a/c, TV, NS rooms, no pets, in-room refrigerators, CC. SGL/DBL$37-$52.

Comfort Inn (431 Northeast Multnomah, 97232; 233-7933, 800-228-5150) 79 rooms, indoor heated pool, a/c, no pets, complimentary newspaper, free local calls, TV, wheelchair access, meeting facilities, CC. SGL/DBL$64-$89.

Courtyard by Marriott (11550 Northeast Airport Way, 97220; 252-3200, 800-331-3131) 150 rooms and suites, free breakfast, restaurant, lounge, entertainment, indoor heated pool, in-room refrigerators, microwaves and coffee makers, a/c, VCRs, no pets, complimentary newspaper, airport courtesy car, children free with parents, kitchenettes, a/c, TV, NS rooms, wheelchair access, meeting facilities, senior rates, CC. SGL/DBL$70-$100.

Cypress Inn Downtown (809 Southwest King St., 97205; 226-6288, 800-225-4205) 82 rooms and efficiencies, free breakfast, in-room refrigerators, a/c, TV, pets OK, local transportation, laundry facilities, wheelchair access, NS rooms, senior rates, CC. SGL/DBL$45-$75.

Delta Inn (9930 North Whitaker Rd., 97217; 289-1800, 800-833-1800) 212 rooms and suites, restaurant, airport courtesy car, pets OK, children free with parents, a/c, TV, wheelchair access, NS rooms, laundry facilities, game room, meeting facilities, senior rates, CC. SGL/DBL$45-$60.

Econo Lodge (518 Northeast Holiday St., 97232; 234-4391, 800-4-CHOICE) 35 rooms, children under 12 free with parents, no pets, senior rates, NS rooms, wheelchair access, a/c, TV, senior rates, CC. SGL/DBL$42-$80.

Econo Lodge (9520 Northeast Sandy Blvd., 97220; 252-6666, 800-4-CHOICE) 36 rooms and suites, sauna, whirlpools, children under 12 free with parents, no pets, NS rooms, wheelchair access, laundry facilities, in-room refrigerators and microwaves, fax service, a/c, TV, senior rates, CC. SGL/DBL$52-$65.

Econo Lodge East Port (4512 Southeast 82nd Ave., 97266; 774-8876, 800-4-CHOICE) 38 rooms, children under 12 free with parents, no pets, senior rates, NS rooms, wheelchair access, a/c, TV, senior rates, CC. SGL/DBL$40-$65.

Friendship Inn Coliseum (305 North Broadway, 97227; 284-5181, 800-424-4777) 20 rooms, exercise facilities, a/c, TV, no pets, NS rooms, children free with parents, wheelchair access, senior rates, CC. SGL/DBL$35-$48.

General Hookers Bed and Breakfast (125 Southwest Hooker St., 97201; 222-4435) free breakfast, TV, antique furnishings, NS, private baths, no children, a/c, no pets, CC. SGL/DBL$75-$120.

Georgian House (1828 Northeast Siskiyou St., 97205; 281-2250) 4 rooms, free breakfast, TV, a/c, no pets, NS rooms, laundry facilities, fireplaces, CC. SGL/DBL$50-$85.

The Governor Hotel (611 Southwest 10th St., 97205; 224-3400, Fax 224-9426, 800-554-3465) 100 rooms and suites, restaurant, lounge, indoor heated pool, exercise center, whirlpools, sauna, a/c, TV, wheelchair access, NS rooms, in-room refrigerators, no pets, room service, meeting facilities, senior rates, CC. SGL/DBL$135-$500.

Heathman Hotel (1009 Southwest Broadway, 97205; 241-4100, 800-551-0011) 151 rooms and suites, restaurant, lounge, entertainment, a/c, TV, wheelchair access, gift shop, no pets, room service, NS rooms, senior rates, CC. SGL/DBL$135-$375.

Heartmans Heart Bed and Breakfast (2837 Northeast 20th Ave., 97212; 281-2182) free breakfast, TV, jacuzzi, 1911 home, private baths, a/c, no pets, CC. SGL/DBL$60-$82.

Heron House Inn (2545 Northwest Westover Rd., 97210; 274-1846) 5 rooms, free breakfast, pool, NS, no pets, CC. SGL/DBL$85-$175.

Hilton Hotel (921 Southwest 6th Ave., 97204; 226-1611, Fax 220-2565, 800-HILTONS) 455 rooms and suites, restaurant, lounge, entertainment, pool, exercise facilities, barber and beauty shop, airport transportation, room service, children free with parents, NS rooms, wheelchair access, no pets, laundry facilities, a/c, TV, business services, meeting rooms, senior rates, CC. SGL/DBL$145-$165, STS$400-$1,000.

HoJo Inn (3939 Northeast Hancock St., 97212; 288-6891, 800-I-GO-HOJO) 48 rooms, free breakfast, pool, children free with parents, wheelchair access, NS rooms, TV, a/c, no pets, laundry facilities, senior rates, meeting facilities, CC. SGL/DBL$48-$63.

Holiday Inn Airport (8439 Northeast Columbia Blvd., 97220; 256-5000, Fax 257-4742, 800-HOLIDAY) 286 rooms and suites, restaurant, lounge, indoor heated pool, exercise facilities, children under 19 free with parents, wheelchair access, a/c, airport courtesy car, pets OK, TV, NS rooms, fax service, room service, laundry service, meeting facilities, senior rates, CC. SGL/DBL$80-$225.

The Hostess House (5758 Northeast Emerson, 97218; 282-7892) free breakfast, NS, private baths, TV, a/c, no pets, CC. SGL/DBL$44-$58.

Howard Johnson (7101 Northeast 82nd Ave., 97220; 255-6711, Fax 254-3370, 800-I-GO-HOJO) 137 rooms, restaurant, lounge, outdoor pool, sauna, jacuzzi, room service, children free with parents, wheelchair access, NS rooms, TV, a/c, no pets, laundry facilities, senior rates, meeting facilities, CC. SGL/DBL$62-$75.

Imperial Hotel (400 Southwest Broadway, 97205; 228-7221) 168 rooms, restaurant, lounge, wheelchair access, NS rooms, children free with parents, airport transportation, CC. SGL/DBL$55-$70.

The John Palmer House (4314 North Mississippi Ave., 97217; 284-5893) 7 rooms and suites, free breakfast, whirlpools, restaurant, NS, private baths, local transportation, 1890 home, antique furnishings, TV, a/c, no pets, CC. SGL/DBL$40-$125.

Madison Motel and Apartments (3620 Northeast 82nd Ave., 97201; 257-4981) 12 rooms and apartments, exercise center, TV, no pets, laundry facilities, kitchenettes, local transportation, senior rates, CC. SGL/DBL$40-$50.

Mallory Hotel (729 Southwest 15th St., 97205; 224-6311, 800-228-8657) 143 rooms and suites, restaurant, lounge, a/c, TV, wheelchair access, NS rooms, in-room refrigerators, no pets, senior rates, CC. SGL/DBL$55-$90.

Mark Spencer Hotel (409 Southwest 11th Ave., 97201; 224-3293, 800-548-3934) 101 efficiencies, a/c, children free with parents, laundry facilities, in-room refrigerators, TV, wheelchair access, NS rooms, senior rates, CC. SGL/DBL$60-$85.

Marriott (1401 Southwest Front Ave., 97201; 226-7600, Fax 221-1789, 800-331-3131) 503 rooms and suites, restaurant, free breakfast, lounge, entertainment, indoor heated, exercise center, whirlpools, sauna, in-room refrigerators, microwaves and coffee makers, VCRs, no pets, complimentary newspaper, room service, barber and beauty shop, airport transportation, children free with parents, kitchenettes, a/c, TV, NS rooms, wheelchair access, meeting facilities, senior rates, CC. SGL/DBL$135-$500.

Motel 6 (3104 Southeast Powell Blvd., 97202; 238-0600, 505-891-6161) 69 rooms, pool, free local calls, children under 17 free with parents, NS rooms, wheelchair access, pets OK, a/c, TV, CC. SGL/DBL$32-$38.

Portland Inn (1414 Southwest 6th Ave., 97220; 221-1611) 173 rooms and suites, restaurant, lounge, entertainment, outdoor pool, a/c, TV, wheelchair access, NS rooms, room service, meeting facilities, senior rates, CC. SGL/DBL$49-$80.

Portland White House (1914 Northeast 22nd Ave., 97212; 287-7131) 6 rooms, free breakfast, TV, NS, game room, room service, a/c, no pets, CC. SGL/DBL$85-$115.

Quality Inn Airport (8247 Northeast Sandy Blvd., 97220; 256-4111, 800-221-2222) 120 rooms and suites, restaurant, lounge, entertainment, pool, exercise facilities, children free with parents, a/c, TV, airport courtesy car, pets OK, wheelchair access, room service, laundry service, NS rooms, meeting facilities, senior rates, CC. SGL/DBL$65-$80, STS$100-$125.

Ramada Inn Airport (6221 Northeast 82nd Ave., 97220; 255-6511, Fax 255-8417, 800-2-RAMADA) 202 rooms and suites, restaurant, lounge, heated pool, exercise center, whirlpools, sauna, wheelchair access, NS rooms, free parking, pets OK, a/c, TV, children under 18 free with parents, airport courtesy car, fireplaces, room service, laundry facilities, meeting facilities, senior rates, CC. SGL/DBL$75-$250.

Red Lion Inn (1401 North Hayden Island Dr., 97217; 283-2111, Fax 283-4718, 800-547-8010) 352 rooms and suites, restaurant, lounge, entertainment, heated pool, barber and beauty shop, airport courtesy car, gift shop, room service, a/c, TV, wheelchair access, NS rooms, complimentary newspaper, fax service, laundry facilities, in-room refrigerators, water view, meeting facilities, senior rates, CC. SGL/DBL$100-$140, STS$200-$400.

Red Lion Inn (909 North Hayden Island Dr., 97217; 283-4466, Fax 283-4843, 800-547-8010) 320 rooms and suites, restaurant, lounge, entertainment, outdoor heated pool, whirlpools, tennis courts, water view, pool, a/c, TV, wheelchair access, NS rooms, complimentary newspaper, pets OK, airport courtesy car, fax service, laundry facilities, meeting facilities, senior rates, CC. SGL/DBL$105-$450.

Red Lion Inn (1000 Northeast Multnomah St., 97323; 281-6111, Fax 284-8553, 800-547-8010) 476 rooms and suites, restaurant, lounge, entertainment, pool, whirlpools, exercise center, a/c, TV, wheelchair access, NS rooms, pets OK, airport courtesy car, in-room refrigerators, complimentary newspaper, fax service, laundry facilities, meeting facilities, senior rates, CC. SGL/DBL$110-$565.

Riverplace Hotel (1510 West Harborway, 97201; 228-3233, Fax 295-6161, 800-426-0670) 84 rooms and suites, restaurant, lounge, entertainment, whirlpools, sauna, fireplaces, 24-hour room service, a/c, TV, wheelchair access, in-room refrigerators, pets OK, boutiques, meeting facilities for 200, CC. SGL/DBL$145-$165, STS$180-$500.

Riverside Inn (50 Southwest Morrison St., 97204; 221-0711, 800-648-6440) 138 rooms, restaurant, lounge, room service, children free with parents, no pets, a/c, TV, wheelchair access, NS rooms, senior rates, meeting facilities, CC. SGL/DBL$72-$88.

Rose Manor Inn (4546 Southeast McLoughlin Blvd., 97202; Fax 232-5201, 800-252-8333) 76 rooms and 2-bedroom suites, restaurant, pool, kitchenettes, a/c, TV, CC. SGL/DBL$44, STS$49.

Sheraton Airport (8235 Northeast Airport Way, 97220; 281-2500, Fax 249-7602, 800-325-3535) 215 rooms and suites, restaurant, lounge, entertainment, indoor heated pool, exercise facilities, whirlpools, sauna, NS rooms, a/c, room service, TV, children free with parents, airport transportation, wheelchair access, meeting facilities, senior rates, CC. SGL/DBL$98-$395.

Shilo Inn Airport (11707 Northeast Airport Way, 97220; 252-7500, 800-222-2244) 200 rooms and suites, restaurant, free breakfast, lounge, indoor heated pool, whirlpools, exercise center, sauna, airport courtesy car, in-room refrigerators, a/c, TV, NS rooms, wheelchair access, children under 12 free with parents, meeting facilities, senior rates, CC. SGL/DBL$110-$130.

Super 8 Motel (11011 Northeast Holman, 97220; 257-8988) 79 rooms and suites, pets OK, children under 12 free with parents, free local calls, a/c, TV, in-room refrigerators and microwaves, fax service, NS rooms, wheelchair access, meeting facilities, senior rates, CC. SGL/DBL$61.

TraveLodge Suites (7740 Southeast Powell Blvd., 97206; 788-9394, Fax 788-9378, 800-578-7878) 39 suites, free breakfast, whirlpools, sauna, wheelchair access, complimentary newspaper, laundry service, TV, a/c, free local calls, fax service, NS rooms, in-room refrigerators and microwaves, pets OK, children under 18 free with parents, no pets, meeting facilities, senior rates, CC. SGL/DBL$55-$65.

Vintage Plaza (422 Southwest Broadway, 97205; 228-1212, Fax 228-3598, 800-243-0555) 110 rooms and suites, restaurant, lounge, exercise center, a/c, TV, wheelchair access, NS rooms, no pets, gift shop, airport transportation, room service, meeting facilities, senior rates, CC. SGL/DBL$140-$195.

Redmond
Area Code 503

The Inn at Eagle Crest (Redmond 97756; 923-2453, 800-682-4786) 75 rooms and suites, restaurant, outdoor heated pool, whirlpools, lighted tennis courts, a/c, TV, wheelchair access, NS rooms, airport courtesy car, no pets, laundry facilities, gift shop, senior rates, CC. SGL/DBL$65-$130.

Nendels Inn (521 South 6th St., 97756; 923-7378, 800-547-0106) 48 rooms and suites, restaurant, free breakfast, lounge, exercise center, fireplaces, a/c, TV, boutiques, airport courtesy car, no pets, children under 17 free with parents, in-room refrigerators, senior rates, CC. SGL/DBL$50-$70.

Redmond Inn (1545 Hwy. 97 South, 97756; 548-1091) 46 rooms and efficiencies, restaurant, outdoor heated pool, kitchenettes, no pets, a/c, TV,
wheelchair access, NS rooms, senior rates, CC. SGL/DBL$40-$57.

Village Squire Motel (629 South 5th St., 97756; 548-2105, 800-548-2102) 24
rooms, a/c, TV, wheelchair access, NS rooms, airport transportation, no
pets, senior rates, CC. SGL/DBL$40-$45.

Reedsport
Area Code 503

Best Western Salbasgeon Inn (1400 Highway Ave., 97467; 271-4831, Fax
271-4832, 800-528-1234) 42 rooms and suites, indoor heated pool, whirlpools, children free with parents, a/c, NS rooms, TV, laundry facilities,
wheelchair access, in-room refrigerators, pets OK, meeting facilities, senior rates, CC. SGL/DBL$50-$110.

Douglas Country Inn (1894 Winchester Ave., 97467; 271-3686) 23 rooms
and efficiencies, pets OK, NS rooms, CC. SGL/DBL$32-$34.

Salbasgeon Inn (45209 Hwy. 38, 97467; 271-2025) 12 rooms and suites,
a/c, TV, wheelchair access, water view, pets OK, kitchenettes, NS rooms,
senior rates, CC. SGL/DBL$50-$90.

Western Hills Motel (1821 Winchester Ave., 97467; 271-2149) 21 rooms
and efficiencies, pool, pets OK, in-room refrigerators, TV, NS rooms, a/c,
CC. SGL/DBL$29-$32.

Rice Hill
Area Code 503

Ranch Motel (581 John Long Rd., 97462; 849-2126) 25 rooms, restaurant,
lounge, a/c, TV, pets OK, laundry facilities, NS rooms, CC. SGL/DBL$27-$75.

Rockaway Beach
Area Code 503

Broadwater Vacation Rentals (105 Southwest 6th Ave., 97136; 355-2248)
10 rooms and efficiencies, NS rooms, laundry facilities, water view, TV,
fireplaces, no pets, kitchenettes, CC. SGL/DBL$50-$130.

Ocean Locomotion Motel (19130 Alder Ave., 97136; 355-2093) 8 rooms and
efficiencies, water view, pets OK, fireplaces, TV, CC. SGL/DBL$45-$75.

Sand Dollar Motel (105 Northwest 23rd St., 97136; 355-2301) 10 rooms,
TV, NS rooms, pets OK, CC. SGL/DBL$35-$75.

Silver Sands Motel (215 South Pacific, 97136; 355-2206, 800-457-8972) 64 rooms and efficiencies, indoor pool, whirlpools, sauna, water view, a/c, TV, wheelchair access, no pets, in-room refrigerators and coffee makers, fireplaces, NS rooms, senior rates, CC. SGL/DBL$70-$100.

Surfside Motel (101 Northwest 11th Ave., 97136; 355-2312) 65 rooms and efficiencies, indoor pool, water view, pets OK, fireplaces, a/c, TV, wheelchair access, NS rooms, senior rates, CC. SGL/DBL$35-$150.

Tradewinds Motel (523 North Pacific Ave., 97136; 355-2112) 19 rooms, TV, fireplaces, kitchenettes, wheelchair access, pets OK, CC. SGL/DBL$52-$140.

Roseburg
Area Code 503

Best Western Inn (511 Southeast Stephens St., 97470; 673-6625, 800-528-1234) 52 rooms, restaurant, children free with parents, a/c, NS rooms, TV, laundry facilities, wheelchair access, no pets, senior rates, CC. SGL/DBL$45-$58.

Casa Loma Motel (1107 Northeast Stephens St., 97479; 673-5569) 18 rooms, a/c, laundry facilities, pets OK, TV, NS rooms, CC. SGL/DBL$28-$35.

Diamond Lake Resort (Diamond Lake 97479; 793-3333) 93 rooms, restaurant, lounge, outdoor pool, laundry facilities, kitchenettes, wheelchair access, water view, pets OK, NS rooms, meeting facilities, senior rates, CC. SGL/DBL$55-$135.

The House of Hunter (813 Southeast Kane St., 97479; 672-2335) 5 rooms, free breakfast, TV, a/c, no pets, local transportation, NS rooms, laundry facilities, fireplaces, CC. SGL/DBL$40-$70.

Howard Johnson (978 Northeast Stephens St., 97470; 673-5082, 800-I-GO-HOJO) rooms and 2-room suites, restaurant, pool, jacuzzi, kitchenettes, children free with parents, wheelchair access, NS rooms, TV, a/c, no pets, laundry facilities, senior rates, meeting facilities, CC. SGL/DBL$45-$80.

Orleans Motel (427 Northwest Garden Valley Blvd., 97470; 673-5561, 800-626-1900) 72 rooms and efficiencies, restaurant, pool, a/c, TV, wheelchair access, NS rooms, no pets, children free with parents, kitchenettes, meeting facilities, senior rates, CC. SGL/DBL$35-$58.

Shady Oaks Motel (2945 Old Hwy. 99 South, 97470; 672-2608) 12 rooms, a/c, no pets, TV, NS rooms, CC. SGL/DBL$30-$37.

Umpqua House of Oregon (7338 Oak Hill Rd., 97470; 459-4700) 2 rooms, free breakfast, exercise center, TV, a/c, pets OK, laundry facilities, CC. SGL/DBL$50.

Windmill Inn (1450 Mulholland Dr., 97470; 673-0901, 800-547-4747) 128 rooms, restaurant, free breakfast, outdoor pool, whirlpools, sauna, a/c, TV, wheelchair access, NS rooms, pets OK, local transportation, meeting facilities, senior rates, CC. SGL/DBL$55-$88.

Saint Helens

Area Code 503

Hopkins House (105 South 1st, 97051; 397-4676) 3 rooms, free breakfast, NS, fireplace, antique furnishings, children under 3 free with parents, private baths, TV, a/c, no pets, CC. SGL/DBL$50-$70.

Salem

Area Code 503

Alcove Motel (3654 Portland Rd. Northeast, 97301; 362-4510) 22 rooms, restaurant, kitchenettes, laundry facilities, in-room refrigerators, a/c, TV, pets OK, room service, CC. SGL/DBL$27-$37.

Best Western Mill Creek Inn (3125 Ryan Drive, Southeast, 97301; 585-3332, Fax 375-9618, 800-346-9659, 800-528-1234) 109 rooms and suites, indoor heated pool, exercise center, tennis courts, children free with parents, a/c, NS rooms, TV, laundry facilities, in-room refrigerators, wheelchair access, pets OK, meeting facilities, senior rates, CC. SGL/DBL$60-$71.

Best Western New Kings Inn (3658 Market St. Northeast, 97301; 581-1559, 800-528-1234) 101 rooms, restaurant, indoor heated pool, exercise center, tennis court, children free with parents, a/c, NS rooms, in-room refrigerators, TV, laundry facilities, wheelchair access, pets OK, meeting facilities, senior rates, CC. SGL/DBL$55-$61.

Best Western Pacific Highway Inn (4646 Portland Rd. Northeast; 97301; 390-3200, Fax 393-7989, 800-528-1234) 52 rooms, restaurant, indoor heated pool, exercise center, in-room refrigerators, a/c, TV, children free with parents, a/c, NS rooms, TV, laundry facilities, wheelchair access, pets OK, meeting facilities, senior rates, CC. SGL/DBL$50-$61.

City Center Motel (510 Liberty St. Southeast, 97301; 364-0121, Fax 581-0554, 800-289-0121) 30 rooms, restaurant, laundry facilities, NS rooms, a/c, TV, pets OK, CC. SGL/DBL$38-$48.

Eagle Crest (4401 Northwest Eagle Crest, 97301; 364-3960) 2 rooms, free breakfast, TV, a/c, no pets, CC. SGL/DBL$50.

Execulodge (200 Commercial St. Southeast, 97301; 363-4123, Fax 363-8993, 800-452-7879) 114 rooms, restaurant, lounge, outdoor pool, room service, kitchenettes, in-room refrigerators, a/c, TV, meeting facilities, senior rates, CC. SGL/DBL$60-$75.

Grand Motel (1555 State St., 97301; 581-2466) 42 rooms, outdoor heated pool, pets OK, in-room coffee makers, children free with parents, a/c, TV, CC. SGL/DBL$31-$52.

Hampshire House (975 D Street, Northeast 97301; 370-7181) 2 rooms, free breakfast, TV, a/c, no pets, CC. SGL/DBL$45-$90.

Holiday Lodge Motel (1400 Hawthorne Ave. Northeast, 97301; 585-2323, 800-545-5071) 70 rooms, restaurant, lounge, entertainment, outdoor heated pool, a/c, TV, pets OK, NS rooms, CC. SGL/DBL$30-$37.

Homeport Inn (1875 Fisher Rd. Northeast, 97301; 588-5423) 70 rooms, restaurant, a/c, pets OK, in-room refrigerators, kitchenettes, TV, senior rates, CC. SGL/DBL$31-$37.

Lamplighter Inn (3195 Portland Rd. Northeast, 97301; 585-2900) 40 rooms, restaurant, outdoor pool, in-room refrigerators, laundry facilities, a/c, TV, CC. SGL/DBL$28-$40.

Mar Don Motel (3355 Portland Rd. Northeast, 97301; 585-2089) 12 rooms, restaurant, kitchenettes, in-room refrigerators, pets OK, a/c, TV, CC. SGL/DBL$25-$33.

Marquee House (333 Wyatt Center Northeast, 97301; 391-0837) 5 rooms, free breakfast, TV, a/c, no pets, CC. SGL/DBL$48-$75.

Motel 6 South Salem (2250 Mission St. Southeast, 97302; 588-7191, 505-891-6161) 78 rooms, outdoor pool, free local calls, children under 17 free with parents, NS rooms, wheelchair access, pets OK, a/c, TV, CC. SGL/DBL$30-$36.

Motel 6 North Salem (1401 Hawthorne Ave. Northeast, 97301; 371-8024, 505-891-6161) 115 rooms, restaurant, outdoor pool, free local calls, children under 17 free with parents, NS rooms, wheelchair access, pets OK, a/c, TV, CC. SGL/DBL$32-$38.

Oregon Capitol Inn (745 Commercial St. Southeast, 97301; 363-2451) 92 rooms, restaurant, a/c, pets OK, TV, CC. SGL/DBL$30-$45.

Phoenix Inn (4370 Commercial St. Southeast, 97301; 588-9220, Fax 585-3616, 800-445-4498) 89 rooms, indoor heated pool, exercise center, pets OK, in-room refrigerators, kitchenettes, a/c, TV, CC. SGL/DBL$52-$62.

Quality Inn Hotel and Conference Center (3301 Market St. Northeast, 97301; 370-7888, 800-221-2222) 150 rooms and suites, restaurant, lounge, entertainment, indoor heated whirlpools, sauna, pool, exercise facilities, children free with parents, a/c, TV, wheelchair access, room service, laundry service, pets OK, room service, NS rooms, meeting facilities, senior rates, CC. SGL/DBL$45-$150.

Shilo Inn Salem Suites Motel (3304 Market St. Northeast, 97301; 581-4001, Fax 399-9385, 800-222-2244) 89 rooms and suites, indoor heated pool, exercise center, airport courtesy car, in-room refrigerators, a/c, TV, NS rooms, wheelchair access, children under 12 free with parents, meeting facilities, laundry facilities, senior rates, CC. SGL/DBL$75-$79.

State House Inn (2146 State St., 97301; 588-1340, 800-800-6712) 6 rooms, free breakfast, TV, a/c, NS, no pets, in-room refrigerators, kitchenettes, CC. SGL/DBL$45-$70.

Super 8 Motel (1288 Hawthorne Ave. Northeast 97301; 370-8888, Fax 370-8927, 800-800-8000) 79 rooms and suites, restaurant, outdoor pool, no pets, children under 12 free with parents, free local calls, a/c, TV, in-room refrigerators and microwaves, fax service, NS rooms, laundry facilities, wheelchair access, meeting facilities, senior rates, CC. SGL/DBL$46-$55.

Travelers Inn Motel (3230 Portland Rd. Northeast, 97301; 581-21444) 27 rooms and suites, restaurant, laundry facilities, wheelchair access, no pets, in-room refrigerators, kitchenettes, a/c, TV, CC. SGL/DBL$25-$35.

Tiki Lodge (3705 Market St. Northeast 97301; 581-4441, Fax 581-4441) 50 rooms, restaurant, outdoor pool, pets OK, kitchenettes, in-room refrigerators, a/c, TV, CC. SGL/DBL$31-$56.

Sandlake

Area Code 503

Sandlake Country Inn (8505 Galloway Rd., 97112; 965-6745) 4 rooms and suites, whirlpools, free breakfast, NS, no pets, game room, antique furnishings, 1890s inn, CC. SGL/DBL$65-$115.

Sandy

Area Code 503

Big Foot Motel (47000 Southeast Hwy. 26, 97055; 668-9664) 5 rooms, restaurant, kitchenettes, no pets, CC. SGL/DBL$30-$45.

Brookside Bed and Breakfast (45232 Southeast Paha Loop, 97055; 668-4766) 5 rooms, free breakfast, TV, a/c, no pets, NS, laundry facilities, CC. SGL/DBL$35-$45.

Fernwood Inn at Alder Creek (54850 Hwy. 26 East, 97055; 622-3570) 2 rooms, free breakfast, water view, no pets, CC. SGL/DBL$75.

Seal Rock
Area Code 503

Blackberry Inn (6576 Northwest Pacific Coast Hwy. 101, 97376; 563-2259) free breakfast, TV, a/c, no pets, children free with parents, NS, no children, fireplaces, private baths, jacuzzi, CC. SGL/DBL$68-$85.

Seaside
Area Code 503

Beachwood Bed and Breakfast (671 Beach Dr., 97138; 738-9585) 3 rooms, free breakfast, TV, NS, fireplaces, no pets, CC. SGL/DBL$70-$105.

The Boarding House (208 North Holladay Dr., 97138; 738-9055) 7 rooms, free breakfast, TV, water view, fireplaces, NS, 1890s home, children free with parents, airport courtesy car, senior rates, CC. SGL/DBL$60-$100.

Coast River Inn (800 South Holladay Dr., 97138; 738-8474) 26 rooms and efficiencies, TV, wheelchair access, NS rooms, children free with parents, in-room refrigerators, senior rates, CC. SGL/DBL$45-$70.

Colonial Motor Inn (1120 North Holladay Dr., 97138; 738-6295, 800-221-3804) 9 rooms, TV, water view, laundry facilities, VCRs, NS rooms, fax service, CC. SGL/DBL$65-$89.

Ebb Tide Motel (300 North Promenade, 97138; 738-8371, 800-468-6232) 83 rooms and efficiencies, indoor heated pool, in-room refrigerators, pets OK, a/c, TV, wheelchair access, NS rooms, senior rates, CC. SGL/DBL$60-$120.

Gearhart by the Sea (Gearhart 97138; 738-8331, 800-547-0115) 76 1- and 2-bedroom condominiums, restaurant, lounge, indoor heated pool, water view, a/c, TV, wheelchair access, kitchenettes, no pets, laundry facilities, NS rooms, meeting facilities, senior rates, CC. 1BR$100-$125, 2BR$105-$135.

Gilbert Inn (341 Beach Dr., 97138; 738-9770) 10 rooms and suites, free breakfast, antique furnishings, TV, wheelchair access, NS rooms, senior rates, CC. SGL/DBL$69-$95.

Hi-Tide Motel (30 Ave. G, 97138; 738-8414, 800-621-9876) 64 rooms and efficiencies, indoor pool, whirlpools, TV, NS rooms, water view, CC. SGL/DBL$75-$125.

Hillcrest Inn (118 North Columbia, 97138; 738-6273) 26 rooms, TV, fireplaces, wheelchair access, kitchenettes, laundry facilities, no pets, NS rooms, senior rates, CC. SGL/DBL$42-$89.

Huntley Inn (441 2nd Ave., 97138; 738-9581, 800-448-5544) 48 rooms and suites, free breakfast, indoor pool, sauna, whirlpools, laundry facilities, pets OK, in-room refrigerators, a/c, TV, wheelchair access, NS rooms, senior rates, CC. SGL/DBL$60-$135.

The Inn on the Prom (361 South Prom, 97138; 738-6343) 25 rooms, outdoor pool, kitchenettes, NS rooms, no pets, CC. SGL/DBL$50-$125.

Mariner Motel (429 South Holladay Dr., 97138; 738-3690) 34 rooms, outdoor heated pool, kitchenettes, wheelchair access, NS rooms, TV, CC. SGL/DBL$42-$75.

Oceanfront Motel (50 1st Ave., 97138; 738-5661) 35 rooms, water view, kitchenettes, no pets, wheelchair access, NS rooms, TV, CC. SGL/DBL$50-$75.

Riverside Inn Bed and Breakfast (430 South Holladay Dr., 97138; 738-8254) 11 rooms, free breakfast, TV, a/c, no pets, wheelchair access, kitchenettes, water view, NS rooms, CC. SGL/DBL$50-$95.

Riverview Inn (555 Ave. G., 97138; 738-0670) 21 rooms, airport transportation, no pets, NS rooms, in-room refrigerators, CC. SGL/DBL$45-$60.

Roger's Inn (436 South Downing, 97138; 738-7367) 5 rooms, TV, kitchenettes, laundry facilities, no pets, CC. SGL/DBL$45-$185.

Royale Motel (531 Ave. A, 97138; 738-9541) 26 rooms, a/c, TV, wheelchair access, NS rooms, senior rates, CC. SGL/DBL$45-$58.

Seaside Beach Club (561 South Prom, 97138; 738-7113) 20 rooms, laundry facilities, NS rooms, wheelchair access, no pets, kitchenettes, TV, CC. SGL/DBL$45-$55.

Shilo Inn Seaside East (900 South Holladay Dr., 97138; 738-0549, Fax 738-0532, 800-222-2244) 58 rooms and suites, free breakfast, indoor heated pool, sauna, whirlpools, airport courtesy car, in-room refrigerators, a/c, TV, NS rooms, wheelchair access, children under 12 free with parents, meeting facilities, senior rates, CC. SGL/DBL$85-$105.

Shilo Inn Seaside Oceanfront (30 North Prom, 97138; 738-9571, 800-222-2244) 112 rooms and suites, restaurant, lounge, indoor heated pool, exercise center, airport courtesy car, in-room refrigerators, a/c, TV, NS rooms, wheelchair access, room service, children under 12 free with parents, meeting facilities, senior rates, CC. SGL/DBL$97-$187.

Tenth Avenue Bed and Breakfast (125 10th Ave., 97138; 738-0643) 4 rooms, free breakfast, TV, no pets, CC. SGL/DBL$55.

Tides Condominiums (2316 Beach Dr., 97138; 738-6317) 38 1- and 2-bedroom condominiums, outdoor heated pool, fireplace, water view, kitchenettes, no pets, TV, CC. SGL/DBL$54-$106.

Sisters

Area Code 503

Best Western Inn (505 Hwy. 20 West, 97759; 549-1234, Fax 549-0171, 800-528-1234) 49 rooms, outdoor heated pool, whirlpools, children free with parents, a/c, NS rooms, TV, laundry facilities, wheelchair access, pets OK, meeting facilities, senior rates, CC. SGL/DBL$55-$75.

Blue Lake Resort (Northwest Sisters Hwy., 97759; 595-6671) 12 rooms, restaurant, TV, water view, fireplaces, kitchenettes, no pets, CC. SGL/DBL$65-$105.

Conklin's Guest House (69013 Camp Polk Rd., 97759; 549-0123) 5 rooms, free breakfast, outdoor pool, NS rooms, water view, TV, no pets, CC. SGL/DBL$70-$100.

The Butte Properties (Black Butte Ranch, 97759; 549-3422) 25 rooms, restaurant, lounge, outdoor heated pool, laundry facilities, NS rooms, no pets, fireplaces, kitchenettes, CC. SGL/DBL$55-$350.

Springfield

Area Code 503

Best Western Grand Manor Inn (971 Kruse Way, 97477; 726-4769, 800-528-1234) 65 suites, restaurant, free breakfast, indoor pool, sauna, exercise center, children free with parents, a/c, NS rooms, TV, laundry facilities, in-room refrigerators, wheelchair access, no pets, meeting facilities, senior rates, CC. SGL/DBL$55-$69.

Gateway Inn (3540 Gateway Rd., 97477; 726-1212, Fax 746-9504) 91 rooms, restaurant, lounge, outdoor heated pool, in-room refrigerators, laundry facilities, children free with parents, pets OK, a/c, TV, wheelchair access, NS rooms, senior rates, CC. SGL/DBL$45-$60.

Motel 6 (3752 International Court, 97477; 741-1105, 505-891-6161) 131 rooms, pool, free local calls, children under 17 free with parents, NS rooms, wheelchair access, pets OK, a/c, TV, CC. SGL/DBL$26-$32.

Orleans Motel (3315 Gateway, 97447; 746-1314) 71 rooms, whirlpools, TV, a/c, children free with parents, pets OK, senior rates, CC. SGL/DBL$40-$48.

Pacific 9 Motel Inn (3550 Gateway, 97446; 726-9266, 800-722-9462) 119 rooms, restaurant, pool, no pets, children free with parents, a/c, TV, wheelchair access, NS rooms, senior rates, CC. SGL/DBL$25-$35.

Red Lion Inn (3280 Gateway Rd., 97477; 726-8181, Fax 747-1866, 800-547-8010) 234 rooms and 2-bedroom suites, restaurant, lounge, entertainment, heated pool, whirlpools, tennis courts, rooms, restaurant, lounge, a/c, TV, wheelchair access, NS rooms, in-room refrigerators, airport transportation, children free with parents, pets OK, complimentary newspaper, fax service, laundry facilities, meeting facilities, senior rates, CC. SGL/DBL$60-$88.

Rodeway Inn (3405 Baldy View Lane, 97477; 746-8471, 800-424-4777) 75 rooms and efficiencies, restaurant, lounge, entertainment, indoor heated pool, exercise facilities, wheelchair access, NS rooms, children free with parents, airport transportation, a/c, TV, pets OK, senior rates, CC. SGL/DBL$50-$66.

Shilo Inn (3350 Gateway St., 97447; 747-0332, Fax 726-0587, 800-222-2244) 143 rooms and suites, restaurant, free breakfast, pool, lounge, airport courtesy car, in-room refrigerators, a/c, TV, NS rooms, wheelchair access, children under 12 free with parents, pets OK, airport transportation, meeting facilities, senior rates, CC. SGL/DBL$45-$64.

Village Inn Motel (1875 Mohawk Blvd., 97447; 747-4546) 70 rooms, restaurant, lounge, outdoor pool, a/c, wheelchair access, TV, pets OK, laundry facilities, NS rooms, senior rates, CC. SGL/DBL$45-$50.

Sublimity
Area Code 503

Best Western Sunrise Inn (300 Sublimity Blvd., 97385; 769-9579, 800-528-1234) 25 rooms, children free with parents, a/c, NS rooms, TV, laundry facilities, wheelchair access, pets OK, meeting facilities, senior rates, CC. SGL/DBL$50-$60.

Sunriver
Area Code 503

Sunriver Lodge (Sunriver 97707; 593-1221, 800-547-3922) 250 1- to 3-bedroom rooms and homes, restaurant, lounge, entertainment, indoor and outdoor pool, hot tubs, whirlpools, sauna, exercise center, a/c, TV, wheelchair access, NS rooms, no pets, game room, water view, senior rates, CC. SGL/DBL$110-$355.

Sutherlin
Area Code 503

Ponderosa Inn (Sutherlin 97479; 459-2236) 60 rooms, restaurant, lounge, a/c, NS rooms, wheelchair access, TV, pets OK, meeting facilities, CC. SGL/DBL$43-$55.

Town and Country Motel (1386 West Central Ave., 97479; 459-9615) 17 rooms, a/c, TV, pets OK, NS rooms, CC. SGL/DBL$45-$55.

The Dalles
Area Code 503

Best Western Inn (2nd and Liberty, 97058; 296-9017, Fax 296-3002, 800-528-1234) 65 rooms, restaurant, lounge, outdoor heated pool, children free with parents, a/c, NS rooms, TV, laundry facilities, in-room refrigerators, wheelchair access, no pets, room service, meeting facilities, senior rates, CC. SGL/DBL$42-$66.

Captain Gray's Guest House (210 West 4th St., 97058; 298-8222) 3 rooms, free breakfast, outdoor pool, pets OK, TV, a/c, NS rooms, CC. SGL/DBL$50-$65.

Days Inn (2500 West 6th St., 97058; 296-1167, 800-325-2525) 71 rooms, free breakfast, a/c, TV, wheelchair access, NS rooms, no pets, laundry facilities, senior rates, CC. SGL/DBL$55-$68.

The Inn at the Dalles (3550 Southeast Frontage Rd., 97058; 296-1167, Fax 296-3920, 800-982-3496) 47 rooms and suites, indoor pool, no pets, water view, a/c, TV, wheelchair access, NS rooms, senior rates, CC. SGL/DBL$32-$65.

Oregon Motor Motel (200 West 2nd St., 97058; 296-9111) 54 rooms, outdoor pool, a/c, TV, wheelchair access, NS rooms, senior rates, CC. SGL/DBL$38-$44.

Quality Inn (2114 West 6th, 97058; 298-5161, 800-221-2222) 85 rooms and suites, restaurant, lounge, pool, exercise facilities, whirlpools, children free with parents, a/c, TV, room service, laundry service, NS rooms, wheelchair access, no pets, meeting facilities, senior rates, CC. SGL/DBL$48-$70.

Shamrock Motel (118 West 4th St., 97058; 296-5464) 25 rooms, a/c, TV, kitchenettes, pets OK, NS rooms, CC. SGL/DBL$33-$40.

Shilo Inn (Bret Clodfelter Way, 97058; 298-5502, 800-222-2244) 112 rooms and suites, restaurant, lounge, outdoor heated pool, exercise center, airport courtesy car, in-room refrigerators, a/c, TV, NS rooms, wheelchair access, children under 12 free with parents, room service, pets OK, water view, room service, meeting facilities, senior rates, CC. SGL/DBL$50-$95.

Williams House Inn (608 West 6th St., 97058; 296-2889) 3 rooms, free breakfast, TV, a/c, no pets, laundry facilities, CC. SGL/DBL$55-$75.

Tigard

Area Code 503

Best Western Inn (17993 LWR Boones Ferry Rd., 97224; 620-2030, 800-528-1234) 68 rooms, restaurant, free breakfast outdoor pool, exercise facilities, jacuzzi, fax service, children free with parents, a/c, NS rooms, TV, laundry facilities, wheelchair access, pets OK, meeting facilities, senior rates, CC. SGL/DBL$55-$115.

Days Inn (11455 Southwest Pacific Hwy., 97223; 246-8451, 800-325-2525) 51 rooms, restaurant, outdoor pool, a/c, TV, wheelchair access, NS rooms, no pets, laundry facilities, senior rates, CC. SGL/DBL$43-$78.

Embassy Suites Hotel (9000 Southwest Washington Square Rd., 97223; 644-4000) 354 rooms, restaurant, lounge, entertainment, indoor heated pool, whirlpools, sauna, room service, a/c, TV, room service, wheelchair access, NS rooms, meeting facilities, senior rates, CC. SGL/DBL$120-$145.

Motel 6 (17950 Southwest McEwan Rd., 97224; 620-2066, 505-891-6161) 118 rooms, pool, free local calls, children under 17 free with parents, NS rooms, wheelchair access, pets OK, a/c, TV, CC. SGL/DBL$28-$34.

Motel 6 (17959 Southwest McEwan Rd., 97224; 684-0760, 505-891-6161) 80 rooms, pool, free local calls, children under 17 free with parents, NS rooms, wheelchair access, pets OK, a/c, TV, CC. SGL/DBL$28-$34.

Shilo Inn (10830 Southwest Greenburg Rd., 97224; 620-4320, 800-222-2244) 77 rooms and suites, exercise center, pets OK, laundry facilities, local transportation, airport courtesy car, in-room refrigerators, a/c, TV, NS rooms, wheelchair access, children under 12 free with parents, meeting facilities, senior rates, CC. SGL/DBL$58-$68.

Tillamook

Area Code 503

Blue Haven Inn ((3025 Gienger Rd., 97141; 842-2265) free breakfast, NS, no children, antique furnishings, 1916 home, TV, a/c, no pets, CC. SGL/DBL$50-$68.

El Rey Sands (815 Main Ave., 97141; 842-7511, 800-257-1185) 22 rooms and suites, restaurant, a/c, TV, wheelchair access, NS rooms, in-room coffee makers, no pets, senior rates, CC. SGL/DBL$47-$65.

Mar-Clair Inn (11 Main Ave., 97141; 842-7571, 800-331-6857) 47 rooms and suites, restaurant, outdoor heated pool, sauna, kitchenettes, no pets, a/c, TV, wheelchair access, NS rooms, senior rates, CC. SGL/DBL$52-$95.

Shilo Inn (2515 North Main Ave., 97141; 842-7971, 800-222-2244) 100 rooms and suites, restaurant, lounge, indoor heated pool, whirlpools, exercise center, room service, airport courtesy car, in-room refrigerators, a/c, TV, NS rooms, wheelchair access, children under 12 free with parents, pets OK, meeting facilities, senior rates, CC. SGL/DBL$62-$77.

Tillamook Inn (1810 North Hwy. 101, 97141; 842-4413) 27 rooms, kitchenettes, TV, NS rooms, children free with parents, CC. SGL/DBL$30-$48.

Tolovana Park
Area Code 503

Tolovana Inn (Tolovana Park 97145; 436-2211, Fax 436-0134, 800-333-8890) 180 rooms and suites, indoor pool, whirlpools, fireplaces, pets OK, kitchenettes, in-room refrigerators, game room, a/c, TV, CC. SGL/DBL$65-$165.

Troutdale
Area Code 503

McMenamins Edgefield (2126 Southwest Halsey St., 97060; 669-8610) 59 rooms, bed and breakfast, restaurant, lounge, a/c, wheelchair access, TV, NS rooms, meeting facilities, senior rates, CC. SGL/DBL$35-$95.

Motel 6 (1610 Northwest Frontage Rd., 97060; 665-2254, 505-891-6161) 123 rooms, pool, free local calls, children under 17 free with parents, NS rooms, wheelchair access, pets OK, a/c, TV, CC. SGL/DBL$28-$34.

Phoenix Inn (477 Northwest Phoenix Dr., 97060; 669-6500) 73 rooms, indoor heated pool, whirlpools, exercise center, a/c, pets OK, laundry facilities, children free with parents, local transportation, wheelchair access, senior rates, meeting facilities, CC. SGL/DBL$43-$58.

Umatilla
Area Code 503

The Heather Inn (705 Williamette Ave., 97882; 922-4871) 68 rooms, restaurant, lounge, outdoor pool, room service, NS rooms, TV, wheelchair access, a/c, children free with parents, senior rates, CC. SGL/DBL$47-$60.

Rest-A-Bit Motel (1370 6th St., 97882; 922-3271) 36 rooms, a/c, kitchenettes, TV, NS rooms, local transportation, children free with parents, CC. SGL/DBL$45-$65.

Waldport

Area Code 503

Alsea Manor Motel (190 Southwest Arrow, 97394; 563-3249) 16 rooms, restaurant, water view, pets OK, water view, NS rooms, TV, CC. SGL/DBL$50-$55.

Cape Cod Cottages (4250 Southwest Pacific Coast Hwy., 97394; 563-2106) 11 cottages, TV, fireplaces, NS rooms, water view, kitchenettes, children free with parents, senior rates, CC. SGL/DBL$60-$68.

The Cliff House (1450 Adahi St., 97394; 563-2506) 5 rooms, free breakfast, TV, a/c, NS, fireplaces, water view, no pets, CC. SGL/DBL$95-$225.

Colleen's Country Bed and Breakfast (1806 Lucy Lane, 97394; 563-2301) 1 room, free breakfast, TV, a/c, pets OK, fireplace, CC. SGL/DBL$65.

Sea Stones Cottages (6317 Southwest Pacific Coast Hwy., 97394; 547-3118) 6 cottages, kitchenettes, pets OK, fireplaces, water view, children free with parents, CC. SGL/DBL$30-$65.

Sundown Motel (5050 Southwest Pacific Coast Hwy., 97394; 563-3018, 800-535-0192) 8 rooms and efficiencies, water view, pets OK, TV, children free with parents, CC. SGL/DBL$40-$75.

Waldport Motel (170 Southwest Arrow, 97394; 563-3050) 13 rooms, restaurant, lounge, kitchenettes, pets OK, laundry facilities, senior rates, CC. SGL/DBL$30-$45.

Warm Springs

Area Code 503

Kah-Nee-Ta Resort (Warm Springs 97761; 553-1112, Fax 553-1070, 800-831-1071) 139 rooms and 2-bedroom cottages, restaurant, lounge, entertainment, heated pool, tennis courts, sauna, exercise center, a/c, TV, wheelchair access, pets OK, gift shop, NS rooms, senior rates, CC. SGL/DBL$90-$250.

Warrentown

Area Code 503

Shilo Inn (1609 East Harbor Dr., 97146; 861-2181, 800-222-2244) 62 rooms and suites, restaurant, lounge, indoor heated pool, exercise center, room service, airport courtesy car, in-room refrigerators, a/c, TV, NS rooms, wheelchair access, pets OK, children under 12 free with parents, meeting facilities, senior rates, CC. SGL/DBL$63-$100.

West Linn
Area Code 503

Prospector's Bed and Breakfast (5035 Prospect Ave., 97068; 656-7451) 1 room, free breakfast, TV, water view, no pets, CC. SGL/DBL$55-$65.

Walden House Bed and Breakfast (1847 5th Ave., 97068; 655-4960) 2 rooms, free breakfast, NS rooms, no pets, CC. SGL/DBL$60.

Wilsonville
Area Code 503

Best Western Inn (30800 Southwest Parkway, 97070; 682-2288, Fax 682-1088, 800-528-1234) 61 rooms, free breakfast, outdoor pool, exercise facilities, children free with parents, a/c, NS rooms, TV, laundry facilities, free local calls, wheelchair access, pets OK, meeting facilities, senior rates, CC. SGL/DBL$65-$86.

Comfort Inn (8855 Southwest Citizen Dr., 97070; 682-9000, 800-228-5150) 64 rooms, indoor heated pool, whirlpools, exercise center, no pets, a/c, TV, wheelchair access, no pets, CC. SGL/DBL$50-$98.

Motel Orleans (8815 Sun Place, 9707; 682-3184) 76 rooms, outdoor pool, laundry facilities, NS rooms, wheelchair access, kitchenettes, children free with parents, meeting facilities, CC. SGL/DBL$35-$50.

Super 8 Motel (25438 Southwest Parkway Ave., 97070; 682-2088, 800-800-8000) 72 rooms and suites, pets OK, children under 12 free with parents, free local calls, a/c, TV, in-room refrigerators and microwaves, fax service, NS rooms, wheelchair access, meeting facilities, senior rates, CC. SGL/DBL$48.

Winchester Bay
Area Code 503

Friendship Inn (390 Broadway, 97467; 271-4871, 800-424-4777) 51 rooms and suites, exercise facilities, whirlpools, kitchenettes, water view, a/c, TV, no pets, NS rooms, children free with parents, wheelchair access, senior rates, CC. SGL/DBL$50-$88.

Woodburn
Area Code 503

Comfort Inn (120 Northeast Amey Rd., 97071; 982-1727, 800-228-5150) 49 rooms, outdoor heated pool, whirlpools, sauna, no pets, kitchenettes, complimentary newspaper, gift shop, a/c, laundry facilities, free local calls, TV, wheelchair access, no pets, CC. SGL/DBL$57-$88.

Fairway Inn Motel (2450 Country Club Court, 97071; 981-3211) 46 rooms, outdoor pool, a/c, wheelchair access, TV, children free with parents, pets OK, NS rooms, senior rates, CC. SGL/DBL$32-$50.

Yachats

Area Code 503

Adobe Resort Inn (1555 Hwy. 101, 97498; 547-3141, 800-522-3623) 93 rooms and suites, restaurant, whirlpools, sauna, exercise center, a/c, TV, in-room refrigerators and coffee makers, pets OK, fireplaces, water view, wheelchair access, NS rooms, senior rates, CC. SGL/DBL$55-$140.

Amaroo Inn (4455 Hwy. 101 North, 97498; 547-3639) 2 rooms, free breakfast, outdoor pool, NS rooms, water view, fireplaces, TV, a/c, no pets, CC. SGL/DBL$70-$100.

Burd's New Inn (664 Yachats River Rd., 97498; 547-3683) 2 rooms, free breakfast, TV, a/c, no pets, fireplaces, water view, CC. SGL/DBL$80-$85.

Fireside Motel (1881 Hwy. 101 North, 97498; 547-3636, 800-336-3573) 43 rooms and 1-bedroom cottages, a/c, TV, kitchenettes, pets OK, in-room refrigerators, water view, wheelchair access, NS rooms, senior rates, CC. SGL/DBL$40-$120.

Gull Haven Lodge (94770 Hwy. 101 North, 97498; 547-3583) 8 rooms and efficiencies, fireplaces, water view, pets OK, children free with parents, NS rooms, CC. SGL/DBL$35-$75.

Holiday Market and Motel (5933 Hwy. 101 North, 98498; 547-3120, 800-HOLIDAY) 7 rooms, children under 19 free with parents, wheelchair access, a/c, TV, NS rooms, fax service, room service, pets OK, laundry service, meeting facilities, senior rates, CC. SGL/DBL$36-$56.

Hovey Manor (1010 Hwy. 101, 97498; 547-4412) rooms, free breakfast, TV, a/c, no pets, fireplaces, CC. SGL/DBL$90-$110.

Oregon House (94288 Hwy. 101 South, 97498; 547-3329) 10 rooms, fireplaces, NS rooms, CC. SGL/DBL$40-$105.

Rock Park Cottages (431 West 2nd St., 97498; 547-3214) 6 rooms and efficiencies, water view, NS rooms, pets OK, children free with parents, CC. SGL/DBL$52-$60.

The Sanderling (7304 Southwest Pacific Coast Hwy., 97498; 563-4752) 4 rooms, free breakfast, TV, a/c, no pets, NS rooms, water view, meeting facilities, CC. SGL/DBL$95-$150.

Sea Quest Bed and Breakfast (95354 Hwy. 101, 97498; 547-3782) 5 rooms, free breakfast, outdoor pool, TV, a/c, NS, fireplaces, no pets, meeting facilities, CC. SGL/DBL$95-$250.

Serenity Bed and Breakfast (5985 Yachats River Rd., 97498; 547-3813) free breakfast, TV, jacuzzi, NS, private baths, a/c, no pets, CC. SGL/DBL$75-$100.

Shamrock Lodgettes (105 Hwy. 101 South, 97498; 547-3312, Fax 547-3943, 800-845-5028) 19 cottages, exercise center, water view, TV, in-room refrigerators and coffee makers, fireplaces, children free with parents, pets OK, CC. SGL/DBL$65-$90.

Silver Surf Motel (3767 North Hwy. 101, 97498; 547-3175) 24 rooms and efficiencies, TV, water view, laundry facilities, NS rooms, children free with parents, CC. SGL/DBL$57-$79.

Wayside Lodge (5773 North Hwy. 101, 97498; 547-3450) 7 rooms, kitchenettes, water view, TV, NS rooms, fireplaces, children free with parents, CC. SGL/DBL$40-$70.

Ziggurat Bed and Breakfast (95330 Hwy. 101 South, 98498; 547-3925) 2 rooms, free breakfast, TV, water view, NS rooms, a/c, no pets, CC. SGL/DBL$85-$110.

Yamhill

Area Code 503

Flying M Ranch (23029 Northwest Flying M Rd., 97148; 662-3222) 35 rooms, restaurant, lounge, fireplaces, wheelchair access, kitchenettes, laundry facilities, NS rooms, children free with parents, CC. SGL/DBL$45-$90.

South Dakota

Aberdeen
Area Code 605

Breeze Inn Motel (1216 6th Ave. Southwest, 57401; 225-4222) 19 rooms and efficiencies, restaurant, a/c, TV, wheelchair access, NS rooms, in-room refrigerators and microwaves, pets OK, senior rates, CC. SGL/DBL$24-$33.

Best Western Ramkota Inn (1400 8th Ave. Northwest, 57401; 229-4040, Fax 229-0480, 800-528-1234) 154 rooms, restaurant, lounge, indoor pool, exercise center, airport transportation, children free with parents, a/c, NS rooms, TV, laundry facilities, wheelchair access, pets OK, meeting facilities for 2,000, senior rates, CC. SGL/DBL$49-$60.

Comfort Inn (2923 6th Ave. Southeast, 57401; 226-0097, 800-221-2222) 40 rooms, whirlpools, exercise center, airport transportation, a/c, TV, children free with parents, NS rooms, wheelchair access, senior rates, CC. SGL/DBL$40-$45.

Holiday Inn (2727 6th Ave. Southeast, 57401; 225-3600, Fax 225-6704, 800-HOLIDAY) 153 rooms, restaurant, lounge, entertainment, indoor heated pool, exercise center, sauna, airport transportation, children under 19 free with parents, wheelchair access, a/c, TV, NS rooms, fax service, room service, pets OK, laundry service, meeting facilities, senior rates, CC. SGL/DBL$40-$70.

Super 8 Motel (2405 6th Ave. Southeast, 57401; 229-5005, 800-800-8000) 112 rooms, indoor heated pool, sauna, no pets, children under 12 free with parents, free local calls, a/c, TV, in-room refrigerators and microwaves, fax service, NS rooms, airport transportation, wheelchair access, meeting facilities, senior rates, CC. SGL/DBL$31-$39.

The White House Inn (500 6th Ave. Southwest, 57401; 225-5000, Fax 225-6730) 96 rooms, in-room refrigerators, airport transportation, children free with parents, pets OK, a/c, TV, wheelchair access, NS rooms, meeting facilities, senior rates, CC. SGL/DBL$30-$36.

Belle Fourche
Area Code 605

Ace Motel (109 6th Ave., 57717; 892-2612) 14 rooms and 2-bedroom efficiencies, a/c, TV, wheelchair access, NS rooms, in-room refrigerators, children free with parents, pets OK, senior rates, CC. SGL/DBL$18-$50.

Best Western Inn (518 National St., 57717; 892-2691, Fax 892-6405, 800-528-1234) 30 rooms, restaurant, lounge, outdoor pool, exercise center, children free with parents, a/c, NS rooms, TV, laundry facilities, wheelchair access, pets OK, meeting facilities, senior rates, CC. SGL/DBL$36-$80.

Lariet Motel (1022 Elkhorn, 57717; 892-2601) 11 rooms, a/c, TV, pets OK, NS rooms, senior rates, CC. SGL/DBL$25-$50.

Sunset Motel (Belle Fourche 57717; 892-2508) 14 rooms and efficiencies, pets OK, a/c, TV, wheelchair access, airport transportation, in-room coffee makers, NS rooms, senior rates, CC. SGL/DBL$22-$49.

Super 8 Motel (501 National St., 57717; 892-3361, 800-800-8000) 43 rooms, no pets, children under 12 free with parents, free local calls, a/c, TV, in-room refrigerators and microwaves, fax service, NS rooms, wheelchair access, meeting facilities, senior rates, CC. SGL/DBL$49-$56.

Beresford
Area Code 605

Crossroads Motel (1409 West Cedar, 57704; 763-2020) 20 rooms, children free with parents, pets OK, a/c, TV, CC. SGL/DBL$22-$32.

Brookings
Area Code 605

Best Western Inn (2515 East 6th St., 57006; 692-9421, Fax 692-9429, 800-528-1234) 82 rooms and suites, restaurant, lounge, indoor heated pool, exercise center, children free with parents, a/c, NS rooms, TV, laundry facilities, wheelchair access, pets OK, meeting facilities, senior rates, CC. SGL/DBL$50-$67, STS$80-$105.

Comfort Inn (514 Sunrise Ridge Rd., 57006; 692-9566, Fax 692-9511, 800-221-2222) 53 rooms and suites, whirlpools, in-room refrigerators, no pets, a/c, TV, senior rates, CC. SGL/DBL$37-$48.

Holiday Inn (2500 East 6th St., 57006; 692-9471, Fax 692-5807, 800-HOLIDAY) 125 rooms, restaurant, lounge, indoor heated pool, exercise center, airport transportation, children under 19 free with parents, wheelchair access, a/c, TV, NS rooms, fax service, room service, no pets, laundry service, meeting facilities, senior rates, CC. SGL/DBL$50-$55.

Malinda Motel (144 Main Ave. South, 57006; 692-6338) 14 rooms, a/c, TV, NS rooms, no pets, in-room coffee makers, CC. SGL/DBL$28-$35.

Canistota

Area Code 605

American Presidents Motel (Custer 57730; 673-3373) 10 rooms and efficiencies, outdoor heated pool, whirlpools, a/c, TV, wheelchair access, kitchenettes, NS rooms, senior rates, CC. SGL/DBL$20-$60.

Bavarian Inn (Custer 57730; 673-2902, 800-657-4312) 64 rooms, restaurant, indoor and outdoor heated pool, tennis courts, whirlpools, a/c, children free with parents, laundry facilities, TV, in-room refrigerators and coffee makers, pets OK, wheelchair access, NS rooms, senior rates, CC. SGL/DBL$25-$80.

Best Western Hi-Ho Inn (Custer 57730; 673-2275, 800-528-1234) 89 rooms, restaurant, lounge, indoor heated pool, exercise center, whirlpools, children free with parents, a/c, NS rooms, TV, laundry facilities, wheelchair access, no pets, meeting facilities, senior rates, CC. SGL/DBL$35-$93.

Black Hills Balloons Bed and Breakfast (Custer 57730; 673-2520) 4 rooms, free breakfast, no pets, CC. SGL/DBL$65-$75.

Blue Bell Lodge and Resort (Custer 57730; 255-4531, Fax 255-4563) 35 rooms and cabins, restaurant, laundry facilities, in-room refrigerators, TV, wheelchair access, NS rooms, senior rates, CC. SGL/DBL$75-$140.

Blue Roof Inn (515 Crook St., 57730; 673-2821) 21 rooms and efficiencies, heated pool, whirlpools, no pets, a/c, TV, wheelchair access, NS rooms, senior rates, CC. SGL/DBL$32-$70.

Chief Motel (120 Mt. Rushmore Rd., 57730; 673-2318) 33 rooms and 2-bedroom efficiencies, indoor heated pool, whirlpools, sauna, pets OK, a/c, TV, wheelchair access, NS rooms, senior rates, CC. SGL/DBL$27-$69.

Custer Mansion Bed and Breakfast (35 Centennial Dr., 57730; 673-3333) 6 rooms, free breakfast, TV, a/c, no pets, 1891 home, NS, CC. SGL/DBL$45-$58.

Custer Motel (109 Mt. Rushmore Rd., 57730; 673-2876) 31 rooms and efficiencies, pool, no pets, a/c, TV, wheelchair access, NS rooms, senior rates, CC. SGL/DBL$20-$65.

Dakota Cowboy Inn (208 West Mt. Rushmore Rd., 57730; 673-4659) 48 rooms and 2-bedroom efficiencies, restaurant, heated pool, a/c, TV, wheelchair access, NS rooms, senior rates, CC. SGL/DBL$30-$80.

Best Western Inn (130 Ash St., 57012; 296-3466, 800-528-1234) 28 rooms, children free with parents, a/c, NS rooms, TV, laundry facilities, kitchenettes, wheelchair access, pets OK, meeting facilities, senior rates, CC. SGL/DBL$25-$45.

Canova
Area Code 605

Skoglund Farm (Route 1, 57321; 247-3445) free breakfast, American plan available, TV, a/c, no pets. SGL/DBL$45-$55.

Chamberlain
Area Code 605

Best Western Lee's Motor Inn (220 West King, 57325; 734-5575, 800-528-1234) 60 rooms and 2-room suites, restaurant, lounge, indoor heated pool, exercise center, children free with parents, a/c, NS rooms, TV, laundry facilities, wheelchair access, no pets, meeting facilities, senior rates, CC. SGL/DBL$35-$65.

Cedar Shore Resort (Chamberlain 57325; 734-6376, Fax 734-6854) 95 rooms, restaurant, lounge, indoor heated pool, lighted tennis courts, whirlpools, in-room refrigerators and microwaves, a/c, TV, pets OK, wheelchair access, NS rooms, meeting facilities, senior rates, CC. SGL/DBL$70-$90.

New River View Inn (Chamberlain 57325; 734-6057) 29 rooms, indoor heated pool, sauna, whirlpools, laundry facilities, meeting facilities, senior rates, CC. SGL/DBL$45-$55.

Riverview Ridge (Chamberlain 57325; 734-6084) 29 rooms, free breakfast, TV, a/c, no pets, private baths, water view, CC. SGL/DBL$45-$58.

Custer
Area Code 605

All American Inn (437 Montgomery, 57730; 673-4051) 30 rooms, outdoor pool, a/c, TV, wheelchair access, NS rooms, no pets, senior rates, CC. SGL/DBL$20-$75.

American Presidents Cabins and Resort (Custer 57730; 673-3373) 39 rooms and 2- and 3-bedroom cabins, outdoor heated pool, whirlpools, a/c, TV, children free with parents, pets OK, laundry facilities, wheelchair access, NS rooms, senior rates, CC. SGL/DBL$20-$65.

Deadwood
Area Code 605

The Adams House (22 Van Buren, 57732; 578-3877) free breakfast, TV, 1890s home, NS, no children, private baths, antique furnishings, a/c, no pets, senior rates, CC. SGL/DBL$65-$85.

Best Western Hickock House (137 Charles St., 57732; 578-1611, 578-1855, 800-528-1234) 37 rooms, restaurant, lounge, whirlpools, children free with parents, a/c, NS rooms, TV, laundry facilities, wheelchair access, pets OK, meeting facilities, senior rates, CC. SGL/DBL$50-$93.

Bullock Hotel (633 Main St., 57732; 578-1745, 800-336-1876) 28 rooms, restaurant, lounge, entertainment, whirlpools, a/c, children free with parents, in-room refrigerators and coffee makers, pets OK, gift shop, TV, wheelchair access, NS rooms, senior rates, meeting facilities, CC. SGL/DBL$35-$95.

Days Inn (68 Main St., 57732; 578-3476, 800-325-2525) 38 rooms, restaurant, free breakfast, a/c, TV, wheelchair access, NS rooms, pets OK, laundry facilities, senior rates, CC. SGL/DBL$44-$80.

Deadwood Gulch Resort (Deadwood 57732; 578-1294, 800-695-1876) 97 rooms and suites, restaurant, lounge, outdoor pool, no pets, laundry facilities, children free with parents, a/c, TV, wheelchair access, NS rooms, senior rates, CC. SGL/DBL$50-$80.

First Gold Hotel (270 Main St., 57732; 578-9777, Fax 578-3979, 800-274-1876) 33 rooms and efficiencies, restaurant, lounge, in-room refrigerators, a/c, TV, pets OK, local transportation, wheelchair access, NS rooms, senior rates, CC. SGL/DBL$47-$77.

The Franklin Hotel (700 Main St., 578-2241, 800-688-1876) 74 rooms and apartments, restaurant, a/c, TV, wheelchair access, NS rooms, in-room refrigerators, no pets, senior rates, CC. SGL/DBL$40-$80.

Four U Motel (296 Main St., 57732; 578-3464) 20 rooms and efficiencies, no pets, in-room refrigerators and coffee makers, a/c, TV, wheelchair access, kitchenettes, NS rooms, senior rates, CC. SGL/DBL$30-$65.

Goldiggers Motel (629 Main St., 57732; 578-3213, 800-456-2023) 8 rooms and suites, restaurant, free breakfast, lounge, entertainment, a/c, TV, in-room coffee makers, children free with parents, no pets, wheelchair access, NS rooms, senior rates, CC. SGL/DBL$90-$130.

Mineral Palace Hotel (601 Main St., 57732; 578-2036, 800-84-PALACE) 63 rooms, restaurant, lounge, whirlpools, VCRs, children free with parents, a/c, TV, wheelchair access, NS rooms, no pets, senior rates, CC. SGL/DBL$45-$100.

Super 8 Motel (196 Cliff St., 57732; 578-2535, 800-800-8000) 51 rooms and suites, children under 12 free with parents, free local calls, a/c, TV, in-room refrigerators and microwaves, fax service, NS rooms, no pets, wheelchair access, meeting facilities, senior rates, CC. SGL/DBL$40-$75.

Eureka
Area Code 605

Lakeview Motel (Eureka 57437; 284-2682) 25 rooms, a/c, TV, wheelchair access, NS rooms, pets OK, kitchenettes, senior rates, CC. SGL/DBL$25-$34.

Fort Pierre
Area Code 605

Ben Inn (Hwy. 82, South, 57532; 223-3111) 21 rooms, a/c, TV, no pets, wheelchair access, NS rooms, senior rates, CC. SGL/DBL$20-$32.

Hermosa
Area Code 605

Bunkhouse Inn (14630 Lower Spring Creek Rd., 57744; 342-5462) 3 rooms, free breakfast, a/c, no pets, CC. SGL/DBL$50-$75.

Hill City
Area Code 605

Best Western Inn (Hill City 57745; 574-2577, 800-528-1234) 61 rooms, restaurant, lounge, whirlpools, children free with parents, a/c, NS rooms, TV, laundry facilities, wheelchair access, no pets, meeting facilities, senior rates, CC. SGL/DBL$40-$88.

Lantern Inn Motel (Hill City 57745; 574-2582) 18 rooms, whirlpools, a/c, in-room refrigerators, pets OK, TV, wheelchair access, NS rooms, senior rates, CC. SGL/DBL$35-$70.

Palmer Gulch Ranch (Hill City 57745; 574-2525, 800-233-4331) 28 suites, restaurant, lounge, outdoor pool, laundry facilities, pets OK, a/c, TV, wheelchair access, NS rooms, senior rates, CC. SGL/DBL$50-$80

Peaceful Valley Bed and Breakfast (Hill City 57745; 574-2316) free break-fast, TV, a/c, no pets, CC. SGL/DBL$35-$48.

Robins Roost Cabins (Hill City 57745; 574-2252) 8 rooms, pets OK, TV, CC. SGL/DBL$28-$36.

Spring Creek Inn (Hill City 57745; 574-2591, 800-456-2755) 21 rooms and suites, restaurant, lounge, no pets, a/c, TV, wheelchair access, NS rooms, kitchenettes, senior rates, CC. SGL/DBL$50-$80.

Super 8 Motel (209 Main St., 57745; 574-4141, 800-800-8000) 34 rooms and suites, restaurant, no pets, children under 12 free with parents, free local calls, a/c, TV, in-room refrigerators and microwaves, fax service, NS rooms, wheelchair access, meeting facilities, senior rates, CC. SGL/DBL$56-$70.

Hot Springs
Area Code 605

Battle Mountain Motel (402 Battle Mountain Ave., 57747; 745-3182, 800-888-1304) 26 rooms, a/c, TV, wheelchair access, pets OK, NS rooms, senior rates, CC. SGL/DBL$42-$72.

Best Western Inn (602 West River St., 57747; 745-4292, Fax 745-3584, 800-528-1234) 32 rooms, outdoor heated pool, children free with parents, a/c, NS rooms, TV, laundry facilities, wheelchair access, pets OK, meeting facilities, senior rates, CC. SGL/DBL$34-$80.

Bison Motel (646 South 5th St., 57747; 745-5191, 800-456-5174) 18 rooms and efficiencies, a/c, TV, NS rooms, senior rates, CC. SGL/DBL$28-$36.

Braun Hotel (902 North River St., 57747; 745-3188) 12 rooms and efficiencies, whirlpools, no pets, a/c, TV, wheelchair access, NS rooms, senior rates, CC. SGL/DBL$20-$55.

Comfort Inn (737 South 6th St., 57747; 745-7378, 800-221-2222) 50 rooms, pool, jacuzzi, hot tub, a/c, TV, pets OK, children free with parents, NS rooms, senior rates, CC. SGL/DBL$45-$56.

Dakota Inn (Hot Springs 57747; 745-6447) 20 rooms, restaurant, lounge, no pets, a/c, TV, wheelchair access, NS rooms, senior rates, CC. SGL/DBL$32-$53.

El Rancho Motel (640 South 6th St., 57747; 745-3130, 800-341-8000) 36 rooms, outdoor heated pool, a/c, TV, pets OK, NS rooms, senior rates, CC. SGL/DBL$40-$74.

Hide-Away Cabins (442 South Chicago, 57747; 745-3187) 12 cabins, no pets, a/c, TV, wheelchair access, NS rooms, senior rates, CC. SGL/DBL$42-$100.

The Log Cabin Motel (Hwy. 385 North, 57747; 745-5166) 16 rooms, hot tubs, a/c, TV, wheelchair access, pets OK, NS rooms, senior rates, CC. SGL/DBL$39-$69.

Larive Lake Resort (Hot Springs 57747; 745-3993) 18 rooms, pool, a/c, TV, pets OK, NS rooms, senior rates, CC. SGL/DBL$38-$63.

Skyline Motel (Hwys. 385 and 87 North, 57747; 745-6980) 22 rooms, a/c, TV, laundry facilities, no pets, NS rooms, senior rates, CC. SGL/DBL$22-$60.

Super 8 Motel (800 Mammoth St., 57747; 745-3888, 800-800-8000) 44 rooms and suites, restaurant, lounge, pets OK, children under 12 free with parents, free local calls, a/c, TV, in-room refrigerators and microwaves, fax service, NS rooms, wheelchair access, meeting facilities, senior rates, CC. SGL/DBL$58-$80.

Villa Theresa Guest House (801 Almond St., 57747; 745-4633) 4 rooms, free breakfast, in-room refrigerators and microwaves, TV, a/c, no pets, CC. SGL/DBL$50-$85.

Wayside Motel (510 South 6th St., 57747; 745-3199) 10 rooms, a/c, TV, no pets, NS rooms, senior rates, CC. SGL/DBL$26-$62.

Huron
Area Code 605

Crossroads Motel (Huron 57350; 352-3204) 100 rooms, restaurant, lounge, entertainment, indoor heated pool, sauna, a/c, TV, in-room refrigerators, local transportation, room service, children free with parents, pets OK, wheelchair access, NS rooms, senior rates, meeting facilities, CC. SGL/DBL$50-$130.

Plains Motel (Huron 57350; 352-6755, 800-648-3735) 77 rooms, restaurant, free breakfast, lounge, children free with parents, no pets, meeting facilities, a/c, TV, CC. SGL/DBL$34-$44.

Super 8 Motel (Huron 57350; 352-0740, 800-800-8000) 52 rooms and suites, restaurant, no pets, children under 12 free with parents, free local calls, a/c, TV, fax service, NS rooms, wheelchair access, meeting facilities, senior rates, CC. SGL/DBL$31-$44.

Interior
Area Code 605

Budget Host Badlands (Interior 57750; 433-5335, 800-283-4678) 10 rooms, laundry facilities, NS rooms, in-room coffee makers, wheelchair access, a/c, TV, children free with parents, senior rates, CC. SGL/DBL$35-$43.

Cedar Pass Lodge (Interior 57750; 433-5460) 24 rooms and 2-bedroom cabins, restaurant, a/c, pets OK, gift shop, kitchenettes, CC. SGL/DBL$35-$48.

Prairies Edge (Interior 57750; 433-5441) 3 rooms, free breakfast, a/c, no pets, CC. SGL/DBL$45-$55.

Kadoka

Area Code 605

Best Western H and H El Centro Motel (Kadoka 57543; 837-2287, 800-528-1234) 39 rooms, restaurant, lounge, outdoor heated pool, exercise center, hot tubs, children free with parents, a/c, NS rooms, TV, laundry facilities, wheelchair access, pets OK, meeting facilities, senior rates, CC. SGL/DBL$34-$80.

Cuckleburr Hotel (Kadoka 57543; 837-2151) 34 rooms, outdoor heated pool, pets OK, a/c, TV, wheelchair access, NS rooms, senior rates, CC. SGL/DBL$18-$68.

Ponderosa Motel (Kadoka 57543; 837-2362) 8 rooms, outdoor pool, whirlpools, no pets, a/c, TV, wheelchair access, NS rooms, senior rates, CC. SGL/DBL$25-$55.

Sundowner Motor Inn (Kadoka 57543; 837-2296) 41 rooms, outdoor heated pool, no pets, a/c, TV, CC. SGL/DBL$20-$75.

West Motel (Hwy. 16 West, 57543; 837-2427) 18 rooms, pets OK, a/c, TV, CC. SGL/DBL$20-$40.

Kennebec

Area Code 605

Budget Host Gerry's Motel (South Kennebec 57544; 869-2210, 800-283-4678) 22 rooms and suites, free breakfast, laundry facilities, NS rooms, wheelchair access, a/c, TV, no pets, children free with parents, senior rates, CC. SGL/DBL$35-$48.

Kings Motel (Kennebec 57544; 869-2270) 10 rooms, no pets, TV, CC. SGL/DBL$25-$44.

Keystone

Area Code 605

Bed and Breakfast Inn (208 1st St., 57751; 666-4490) 8 rooms and suites, pets OK, free breakfast, TV, a/c, CC. SGL/DBL$39-$75.

Best Western Four Presidents Motel (Keystone 57751; 666-4472, 800-732-9155, 800-528-1234) 30 rooms, restaurant, children free with parents, a/c, NS rooms, TV, laundry facilities, wheelchair access, pets OK, meeting facilities, senior rates, CC. SGL/DBL$40-$90.

First Lady Inn (Keystone 57751; 666-4990, 800-252-2119) 39 rooms, children free with parents, pets OK, TV, NS rooms, senior rates, CC. SGL/DBL$45-$75.

Friendship Inn Mount Rushmore (Hwy. 40 East, 57751; 666-4417, 800-424-4777) 32 rooms, pool, exercise center, a/c, TV, no pets, NS rooms, children free with parents, wheelchair access, senior rates, CC. SGL/DBL$32-$95.

Holy Smoke Lodge (Hwy. 16A, 57751; 666-4616) 8 rooms, whirlpools, wheelchair access, NS rooms, senior rates, CC. SGL/DBL$45-$65.

Kelly Inn (Keystone 57751; 666-4483) 44 rooms and suites, whirlpools, sauna, exercise center, pets OK, a/c, TV, children free with parents, wheelchair access, NS rooms, laundry facilities, meeting facilities, senior rates, CC. SGL/DBL$30-$65.

Powderhouse Lodge (Keystone 57751; 666-4646) 35 rooms and cabins, restaurant, pets OK, a/c, TV, wheelchair access, NS rooms, senior rates, CC. SGL/DBL$30-$85.

Roosevelt Inn (206 Old Cemetery Rd., 57751; 666-4599) 16 rooms, no pets, a/c, TV, wheelchair access, NS rooms, senior rates, CC. SGL/DBL$37-$80.

Rushmore Manor House (115 Swanzey St., 57751; 666-4443) 64 rooms, outdoor heated pool, no pets, children free with parents, a/c, TV, wheelchair access, NS rooms, senior rates, CC. SGL/DBL$35-$96.

Lead
Area Code 605

Best Western Golden Hills Resort (900 Miners Ave., 57754; 584-1800, Fax 584-3933, 800-528-1234) 105 rooms and suites, restaurant, lounge, indoor heated pool, exercise center, children free with parents, a/c, NS rooms, TV, local transportation, laundry facilities, wheelchair access, pets OK, meeting facilities, senior rates, CC. SGL/DBL$70-$193.

Cheyenne Crossing Bed and Breakfast (Lead 57754; 584-3510) free breakfast, TV, a/c, no pets, CC. SGL/DBL$65-$80.

The White House Inn (395 Glendale Dr., 57754; 584-2000) 70 rooms and suites, a/c, TV, wheelchair access, NS rooms, senior rates, CC. SGL/DBL$45-$55.

Madison
Area Code 605

Lake Park Motel (Madison 57042; 256-3524) 41 rooms, restaurant, outdoor heated pool, pets OK, in-room refrigerators, a/c, TV, wheelchair access, NS rooms, senior rates, CC. SGL/DBL$27-$35.

Super 8 Motel (Madison 57042; 256-6931, 800-800-8000) 34 rooms, restaurant, pets OK, children under 12 free with parents, free local calls, a/c, TV, in-room refrigerators and microwaves, fax service, NS rooms, wheelchair access, meeting facilities, senior rates, CC. SGL/DBL$30-$36.

Millbank

Area Code 605

Lantern Motel (Millbank 57252; 432-4591, 800-627-6075) 30 rooms, restaurant, free breakfast, sauna, no pets, a/c, TV, children free with parents, senior rates, CC. SGL/DBL$26-$38.

Manor Motel (Millbank 57252; 432-4527, 800-341-8000) 30 rooms, restaurant, indoor heated pool, whirlpools, sauna, pets OK, a/c, TV, children free with parents, senior rates, CC. SGL/DBL$27-$44.

Super 8 Motel (Millbank 57252; 432-9288, 800-800-8000) 39 rooms and suites, no pets, children under 12 free with parents, free local calls, a/c, TV, in-room refrigerators and microwaves, fax service, NS rooms, wheelchair access, meeting facilities, senior rates, CC. SGL/DBL$29-$44.

Mitchell

Area Code 605

Anthony Motel (1518 Havens St., West, 57301; 996-7518) 34 rooms and efficiencies, outdoor heated pool, a/c, TV, wheelchair access, NS rooms, no pets, airport transportation, senior rates, CC. SGL/DBL$30-$46.

Best Western Motor Inn (1001 South Burr, 57301; 996-5536, 800-528-1234) 77 rooms, heated pool, exercise center, children free with parents, a/c, NS rooms, TV, laundry facilities, wheelchair access, pets OK, meeting facilities, senior rates, CC. SGL/DBL$30-$60.

Budget Host Inn (1313 South Ohlman, 57301; 996-6647, Fax 996-7339, 800-283-4678) 44 rooms, laundry facilities, NS rooms, wheelchair access, pets OK, a/c, TV, children free with parents, meeting facilities, senior rates, CC. SGL/DBL$30-$45.

Coachlight Motel (100 Havens St., West, 57301; 996-5686) 20 rooms, a/c, TV, pets OK, airport transportation, pets OK, senior rates, CC. SGL/DBL$30-$36.

Comfort Inn (Mitchell 57301; 996-1333, Fax 996-6022, 800-221-2222) 60 rooms, indoor heated whirlpools, no pets, pool, a/c, TV, children free with parents, NS rooms, laundry facilities, wheelchair access, senior rates, CC. SGL/DBL$45-$65.

Days Inn (1506 South Burr, 57301; 996-6208, Fax 996-5220, 800-325-2525) 47 rooms, free breakfast, whirlpools, a/c, TV, wheelchair access, NS rooms, in-room refrigerators, children free with parents, no pets, laundry facilities, senior rates, CC. SGL/DBL$25-$45.

Holiday Inn (1525 West Havens St., 57301; 996-6501, 800-HOLIDAY) 153 rooms, restaurant, lounge, entertainment, indoor and outdoor heated pool, exercise center, game room, children under 19 free with parents, wheelchair access, a/c, TV, NS rooms, fax service, room service, no pets, laundry service, airport transportation, meeting facilities, senior rates, CC. SGL/DBL$50-$80.

Motel 6 (1309 South Ohlman St., 57301; 996-0530, 505-891-6161) 122 rooms, outdoor heated pool, free local calls, children under 17 free with parents, NS rooms, wheelchair access, pets OK, a/c, TV, CC. SGL/DBL$23-$29.

Siesta Motel (1210 Havens St., West, 57301; 996-5544) 22 rooms, children free with parents, a/c, TV, VCRs, pets OK, NS rooms, senior rates, CC. SGL/DBL$30-$45.

Super 8 Motel (Mitchell 57301; 996-9678, 800-800-8000) 83 rooms and suites, restaurant, outdoor heated pool, whirlpools, no pets, children under 12 free with parents, free local calls, a/c, TV, in-room refrigerators and microwaves, fax service, NS rooms, wheelchair access, meeting facilities, senior rates, CC. SGL/DBL$33-$48.

Thunderbird Motel (Mitchell 57301; 996-6645) 48 rooms and efficiencies, restaurant, laundry facilities, airport transportation, whirlpools, sauna, no pets, a/c, TV, wheelchair access, NS rooms, senior rates, CC. SGL/DBL$45-$50.

Murdo

Area Code 605

Anchor Inn (105 South 5th St., 57559; 669-2322) 29 rooms, whirlpools, a/c, TV, wheelchair access, NS rooms, children free with parents, no pets, senior rates, CC. SGL/DBL$26-$52.

Best Western Graham's Inn (301 West 5th St., 57559; 669-2441, 800-528-1234) 45 rooms, restaurant, lounge, outdoor heated pool, children free with parents, a/c, NS rooms, TV, laundry facilities, wheelchair access, pets OK, meeting facilities, senior rates, CC. SGL/DBL$30-$68.

Hospitality Inn (302 West 5th St., 57559; 669-2425) 29 rooms, a/c, pets OK, children free with parents, TV, senior rates, CC. SGL/DBL$25-$70.

Sioux Motel (302 East 5th St., 57559; 669-2422) 23 rooms and 3-bedroom efficiencies, whirlpools, a/c, TV, wheelchair access, NS rooms, senior rates, CC. SGL/DBL$23-$60.

Super 8 Motel (604 East 5th St., 57559; 669-2437, 800-800-8000) 50 rooms, restaurant, whirlpools, no pets, children under 12 free with parents, free local calls, a/c, TV, in-room refrigerators and microwaves, fax service, NS rooms, wheelchair access, meeting facilities, senior rates, CC. SGL/DBL$46-$50.

TeePee Motel (Murdo 57559; 669-2461) 24 rooms, outdoor heated pool, a/c, TV, wheelchair access, NS rooms, no pets, laundry facilities, senior rates, CC. SGL/DBL$25-$60.

Oacoma
Area Code 605

Days Inn (Oacoma 57325; 734-4100, Fax 734-4111, 800-325-2525) 45 rooms, free breakfast, indoor heated pool, jacuzzi, a/c, TV, wheelchair access, NS rooms, no pets, laundry facilities, senior rates, CC. SGL/DBL$35-$80.

Comfort Inn (Oacoma 57325; 734-5593, 800-221-2222) 36 rooms, whirlpools, a/c, TV, children free with parents, NS rooms, pets OK, wheelchair access, senior rates, CC. SGL/DBL$30-$72.

Oasis Inn (Oacoma 57235; 734-6061) 69 rooms, restaurant, lounge, whirlpools, a/c, TV, laundry facilities, local transportation, water view, laundry facilities, children free with parents, wheelchair access, NS rooms, pets OK, senior rates, CC. SGL/DBL$35-$60.

Owanka
Area Code 605

Country Bed and Breakfast (Owanka 57767; 798-5405) free breakfast, TV, private baths, no pets. SGL/DBL$40-$50.

Philip
Area Code 605

Thorson's Homestead (Philip 57567; 859-2120) free breakfast, TV, a/c, no pets, CC. SGL/DBL$35-$50.

Pierre
Area Code 605

Best Western Kings Inn (220 South Pierre St., 57501; 224-5951, Fax 224-5301, 800-232-1112 in South Dakota, 800-528-1234) 104 rooms, restaurant, lounge, sauna, hot tubs, children free with parents, a/c, NS rooms, TV, laundry facilities, wheelchair access, pets OK, meeting facilities for 1,000, senior rates, CC. SGL/DBL$45-$70.

Best Western Ramkota Inn (920 West Sioux St., 57501; 224-6877, Fax 224-1042, 800-528-1234) 151 rooms and suites, restaurant, lounge, indoor heated pool, exercise center, children free with parents, complimentary newspaper, a/c, NS rooms, TV, laundry facilities, airport transportation, wheelchair access, pets OK, meeting facilities for 1,000, senior rates, CC. SGL/DBL$41-$125.

Capitol Inn (815 Wells Ave., 57501; 224-6387, 800-658-3055) 112 rooms and efficiencies, outdoor heated pool, a/c, TV, no pets, wheelchair access, free local calls, fax service, NS rooms, senior rates, CC. SGL/DBL$26-$66.

Dakota Inn (713 West Sioux, 57501; 224-4140, 800-262-0094 in South Dakota) 47 rooms, free breakfast, a/c, TV, no pets, wheelchair access, NS rooms, senior rates, CC. SGL/DBL$27-$41.

Days Inn (520 West Sioux, 57501; 224-0411, 800-325-2525, 800-325-2525) 80 rooms, free breakfast, a/c, TV, wheelchair access, NS rooms, VCRs, free local calls, no pets, laundry facilities, senior rates, CC. SGL/DBL$30-$45.

Fawn Motel (818 North Euclid, 57501; 224-5885) 16 rooms, a/c, kitchenettes, in-room refrigerators, TV, no pets, wheelchair access, NS rooms, senior rates, CC. SGL/DBL$20-$32.

Governors Inn (700 West Sioux, 57501; 224-4200, 800-341-8000) 71 rooms and suites, whirlpools, exercise center, fax service, a/c, TV, no pets, wheelchair access, NS rooms, senior rates, 2 meeting rooms, CC. SGL/DBL$34-$53.

Iron Horse Inn (205 West Pleasant, 57501; 224-5981, 800-742-8612) 90 rooms, a/c, TV, no pets, wheelchair access, NS rooms, senior rates, CC. SGL/DBL$26-$46.

Oahe Lodge (Hwy. 1804, 57501; 224-9340) 10 rooms, a/c, TV, no pets, wheelchair access, NS rooms, senior rates, CC. SGL/DBL$35-$55.

Oahe Marina Resort (Pierre 57501; 223-2627) 7 rooms, a/c, TV, no pets, wheelchair access, NS rooms, senior rates, CC. SGL/DBL$38-$46.

Outpost Lodge (Hwy. 1804, 57501; 264-5450) 12 rooms and cabins, restaurant, lounge, entertainment, kitchenettes, a/c, TV, no pets, wheelchair access, NS rooms, senior rates, CC. SGL/DBL$40-$60.

Pierre Motel (914 North Euclid, 57501; 224-9266) 18 rooms and efficiencies, free local calls, a/c, TV, no pets, wheelchair access, NS rooms, senior rates, CC. SGL/DBL$20-$32.

Spring Creek Resort (Hwy. 1804, 57501; 224-8336) 10 rooms and 2- and 3-bedroom cabins, lounge, kitchenettes, water view, a/c, TV, no pets, wheelchair access, NS rooms, senior rates, CC. SGL/DBL$55.

State Motel (640 North Euclid, 57501; 224-5896, 800-658-3940) 48 rooms, free breakfast, indoor pool, whirlpools, sauna, kitchenettes, in-room refrigerators and coffee makers, pets OK, a/c, TV, wheelchair access, NS rooms, airport transportation, senior rates, CC. SGL/DBL$23-$45.

Sunset Lodge (Pierre 57501; 264-5480) 15 rooms, restaurant, lounge, a/c, TV, no pets, wheelchair access, NS rooms, senior rates, CC. SGL/DBL$40-$50.

Super 8 Motel (320 West Sioux Ave., 57501; 224-1617, 800-800-8000) 79 rooms and suites, free breakfast, free local calls, pets OK, children under 12 free with parents, a/c, TV, in-room refrigerators and microwaves, fax service, NS rooms, wheelchair access, meeting facilities, senior rates, CC. SGL/DBL$30-$47.

Terrace Motel (231 North Euclid Ave., 57501; 224-7797) 46 rooms, a/c, TV, no pets, wheelchair access, NS rooms, kitchenettes, senior rates, CC. SGL/DBL$20-$24.

Platte
Area Code 605

Dakota Country Inn (Platte 57369; 337-2607) 20 rooms, a/c, TV, CC. SGL/DBL$25-$35.

King's Inn (Platte 57369; 337-3385) 18 rooms, pets OK, TV, CC. SGL/DBL$22-$39.

Rapid City
Area Code 605

Alex Johnson Hotel (523 6th St., 57701; 342-1210, 800-888-2539) 120 rooms and suites, restaurant, lounge, indoor heated pool, jacuzzi, sauna, no pets, VCRs, kitchenettes, a/c, TV, wheelchair access, NS rooms, laundry facilities, senior rates, CC. SGL/DBL$80-$112.

Alpine Motel (209 East North, 57701; 348-3701) 16 rooms and suites, restaurant, lounge, outdoor pool, sauna, kitchenettes, a/c, TV, wheelchair access, NS rooms, senior rates, CC. SGL/DBL$50-$80.

Audrie's Cranbury Corner Bed and Breakfast (Rapid City 57702; 342-7788) free breakfast, TV, a/c, no pets, antique furnishings, NS, no children, private baths, CC. SGL/DBL$68-$80.

Avanti Motel (102 North Maple St., 57701; 348-1112, 800-658-5464) 35 rooms and 2-bedroom efficiencies, outdoor heated pool, a/c, TV, wheelchair access, NS rooms, senior rates, CC. SGL/DBL$25-$74.

Best Western Gills Sun Inn (1901 West Main St., 57709; 343-6050, 800-528-1234) 87 rooms, restaurant, lounge, outdoor heated pool, exercise center, children free with parents, a/c, NS rooms, TV, laundry facilities, wheelchair access, no pets, meeting facilities, senior rates, CC. SGL/DBL$35-$100.

Best Western Town n' Country Inn (2505 Mt. Rushmore Rd., 57701; 343-5383, Fax 343-9670, 800-528-1234) 100 rooms, restaurant, indoor and outdoor heated pool, exercise center, children free with parents, a/c, NS rooms, TV, laundry facilities, wheelchair access, no pets, meeting facilities, senior rates, CC. SGL/DBL$35-$95.

Big Sky Motel (4080 Tower Rd., 57701; 348-3200) 31 rooms, a/c, TV, NS rooms, senior rates, CC. SGL/DBL$25-$50.

Black Forest Inn (Hwy. 385, 57702; 574-2000, 800-888-1607) 8 rooms, restaurant, lounge, outdoor pool, jacuzzi, free breakfast, NS rooms, TV, a/c, pets OK, CC. SGL/DBL$50-$80.

Budget Host Bel Air Inn (2101 Mt. Rushmore Rd., 57701; 343-5126, 800-283-4678) 30 rooms and efficiencies, kitchenettes, heated pool, no pets, , restaurant, laundry facilities, NS rooms, wheelchair access, a/c, TV, children free with parents, senior rates, CC. SGL/DBL$27-$70.

Castle Inn (15 East North St., 57701; 348-4120, 800-658-5464) 20 rooms and efficiencies, heated pool, pets OK, a/c, TV, CC. SGL/DBL$25-$82.

Canyon Lake Heights (4110 Fairview Dr., 57701; 348-0141) 1 room, free breakfast, outdoor pool, laundry facilities, wheelchair access, TV, a/c, no pets, CC. SGL/DBL$35-$50.

College Inn (123 Kansas City St., 57701; 394-4978) 38 rooms, restaurant, outdoor pool, a/c, TV, wheelchair access, NS rooms, no pets, senior rates, CC. SGL/DBL$50-$80.

Comfort Inn (1550 North LaCrosse St., 57701; 348-2221, 800-221-2222) 71 rooms, restaurant, indoor heated pool, whirlpools, a/c, TV, children free with parents, NS rooms, no pets, wheelchair access, senior rates, CC. SGL/DBL$57-$100.

Days Inn (125 Main St., 57701; 343-5501, 800-325-2525) 156 rooms, free breakfast, restaurant, lounge, a/c, TV, wheelchair access, NS rooms, in-room refrigerators, no pets, laundry facilities, senior rates, CC. SGL/DBL$32-$95.

Econo Lodge (625 East Disk Dr., 57701; 342-6400, 800-4-CHOICE) 120 rooms, indoor heated pool, whirlpools, game room, children under 12 free with parents, no pets, senior rates, NS rooms, wheelchair access, a/c, TV, senior rates, CC. SGL/DBL$30-$35.

Fair Value Inn (1607 LaCrosse St., 57701; 342-8118) 25 rooms, restaurant, a/c, TV, wheelchair access, no pets, NS rooms, senior rates, CC. SGL/DBL$55-$65.

Family Inn (3737 Sturgis Rd., 57701; 342-2892) 28 rooms and suites, outdoor pool, jacuzzi, a/c, TV, CC. SGL/DBL$30-$50.

Flying B Ranch (Rapid City 57701; 342-5324) 6 rooms and suites, free breakfast, outdoor pool, laundry facilities, TV, a/c, no pets, CC. SGL/DBL$50-$80.

Foothills Inn (1625 LaCrosse St., 57701; 348-5640) 65 rooms, restaurant, outdoor heated pool, a/c, TV, wheelchair access, NS rooms, no pets, senior rates, CC. SGL/DBL$60-$85.

Four Seasons Motel (930 East North, 57701; 343-7822, 800-332-3168) 34 rooms, restaurant, lounge, outdoor pool, a/c, TV, wheelchair access, NS rooms, senior rates, CC. SGL/DBL$50-$80.

Garden Cottages Motel (4030 Jackson Blvd., 57702; 342-6922) 13 rooms and efficiencies, a/c, TV, no pets, CC. SGL/DBL$25-$49.

Happy Holiday Motel (Rapid City 57701; 342-8101) 31 rooms and efficiencies, outdoor heated pool, whirlpools, a/c, TV, wheelchair access, NS rooms, senior rates, CC. SGL/DBL$35-$60.

Hart Ranch Camping Resort (Rapid City 57702; 341-5700) 90 rooms, restaurant, outdoor pool, jacuzzi, pets OK, laundry facilities, a/c, TV, wheelchair access, NS rooms, kitchenettes, senior rates, CC. SGL/DBL$30-$50.

Holiday Inn (1902 LaCrosse St., 57701; 348-9212, Fax 348-1230, 800-HOLIDAY) 211 rooms and suites, restaurant, lounge, indoor heated pool, exercise center, children under 19 free with parents, modified American plan available, wheelchair access, a/c, TV, NS rooms, fax service, airport transportation, room service, no pets, laundry service, meeting facilities for 200, senior rates, CC. SGL/DBL$50-$80.

Holiday Inn Civic Center (505 North 5th St., 348-4000, Fax 348-9777, 800-HOLIDAY) 205 rooms and suites, restaurant, lounge, indoor heated pool, exercise center, children under 19 free with parents, wheelchair access, a/c, airport transportation, TV, NS rooms, fax service, room service, no pets, laundry service, meeting facilities, senior rates, CC. SGL/DBL$80-$110.

Howard Johnson (2211 LaCrosse St., 57709; 343-8550, Fax 343-9107, 800-I-GO-HOJO) 272 rooms and suites, restaurant, lounge, entertainment, indoor and outdoor heated pool, sauna, jacuzzi, exercise center, gift shop, children free with parents, wheelchair access, NS rooms, TV, airport transportation, a/c, no pets, laundry facilities, senior rates, meeting facilities, CC. SGL/DBL$53-$63.

Kings Lodge (525 East Omaha, 57701; 342-2236) 19 rooms, a/c, TV, wheelchair access, no pets, NS rooms, senior rates, CC. SGL/DBL$22-$53.

Lamplighter Inn (27 St. Joe, 57701; 342-3385, 800-775-LAMP) 27 rooms, restaurant, outdoor pool, laundry facilities, a/c, TV, wheelchair access, NS rooms, senior rates, CC. SGL/DBL$45-$78.

Motel 6 (620 East Latrobe St., 57701; 343-3687, 505-891-6161) 150 rooms, pool, free local calls, children under 17 free with parents, NS rooms, wheelchair access, pets OK, a/c, TV, CC. SGL/DBL$24-$30.

Quality Inn (2208 Mt. Rushmore Rd., 57701; 342-3322, 800-221-2222) 110 rooms and suites, restaurant, outdoor heated pool, children free with parents, a/c, TV, wheelchair access, pets OK, in-room refrigerators and coffee makers, room service, laundry service, NS rooms, meeting facilities, senior rates, CC. SGL/DBL$50-$122.

Ramada Inn (1721 North LaCrosse St., 57701; 342-3322, 800-2-RAMADA) 110 rooms and suites, restaurant, lounge, outdoor heated pool, wheelchair access, NS rooms, free parking, a/c, TV, children under 18 free with parents, room service, laundry facilities, pets OK, in-room refrigerators, meeting facilities, senior rates, CC. SGL/DBL$30-$120.

Rockerville Motel (Rapid City 57701; 341-4880) 15 rooms, restaurant, heated pool, a/c, laundry facilities, VCRs, in-room coffee makers, no pets, children free with parents, TV, CC. SGL/DBL$30-$60.

Rushmore Motel (1313 LaCrosse St., 57701; 348-3313, 800-658-3339) 30 rooms, no pets, a/c, in-room coffee makers, children free with parents, TV, CC. SGL/DBL$20-$100.

Sands of the Black Hills Motel (2401 Mt. Rushmore Rd., 57702; 348-1453) 69 rooms and suites, restaurant, lounge, outdoor heated pool, a/c, TV, wheelchair access, NS rooms, no pets, senior rates, CC. SGL/DBL$50-$80.

Stables Motel (518 East Omaha, 57701; 342-9241) 19 rooms, heated pool, laundry facilities, in-room refrigerators, microwaves and coffee makers, a/c, TV, CC. SGL/DBL$40-$58.

Stardust Motel (520 East North St., 57701; 343-8844, Fax 341-0500, 800-456-0084) 37 rooms, outdoor heated pool, kitchenettes, a/c, TV, no pets, children free with parents, NS rooms, senior rates, CC. SGL/DBL$25-$65.

Sunburst Inn (620 Howard Dr., 57701; 343-3313, 800-658-0061) 98 rooms, restaurant, outdoor heated pool, NS rooms, a/c, TV, no pets, children free with parents, senior rates, CC. SGL/DBL$20-$100.

Super 8 Motel (2124 LaCrosse St., 57701; 348-8070, 800-800-8000) 119 rooms and suites, restaurant, no pets, children under 12 free with parents, free local calls, a/c, TV, in-room refrigerators and microwaves, fax service, NS rooms, wheelchair access, meeting facilities, senior rates, CC. SGL/DBL$60-$70.

Thrifty Motor Inn (1303 LaCrosse, 57701; 342-0551) 26 rooms, a/c, TV, wheelchair access, NS rooms, pets OK, senior rates, CC. SGL/DBL$25-$65.

Tip Top Motor Lodge (405 St. Joseph St., 57701; 343-3901) 62 rooms and 2-bedroom efficiencies, outdoor pool, a/c, TV, wheelchair access, NS rooms, pets OK, kitchenettes, senior rates, CC. SGL/DBL$32-$75.

Town House Motel (210 St. Joseph St., 57701; 342-8143, 800-842-1300) 40 rooms, outdoor heated pool, TV, CC. SGL/DBL$25-$68.

Trout Haven Cottages (Hwy. 385, 57701; 342-6009) 5 cabins, restaurant, pets OK, laundry facilities, kitchenettes. SGL/DBL$30-$44.

Silver City
Area Code 605

Whispering Pines Lodging (Silver City 57701; 341-8890) 2 rooms, a/c, TV, CC. SGL/DBL$80-$105.

Sioux Falls
Area Code 605

Albert House Hotel (333 North Phillips Ave., 57104; 336-1680) 26 rooms, a/c, kitchenettes, pets OK, TV, no pets, wheelchair access, NS rooms, senior rates, CC. SGL/DBL$44-$58.

AmericInn (3508 South Gateway, 57106; 361-3538, 800-634-3444) 65 rooms, restaurant, lounge, indoor pool, children under 12 free with parents, a/c, TV, wheelchair access, NS rooms, meeting facilities, CC. SGL/DBL$36-$46.

Arena Motel (2401 West Russell St., 57101; 336-1470) 26 rooms, outdoor pool, a/c, TV, no pets, wheelchair access, NS rooms, airport transportation, senior rates, CC. SGL/DBL$55-$65.

Best Western Empire Towers (4100 West 41st St., 57116; 361-3118, 800-528-1234) 61 rooms, restaurant, free breakfast, indoor heated pool, exercise center, whirlpools, children free with parents, a/c, NS rooms, TV, laundry facilities, wheelchair access, no pets, meeting facilities, senior rates, CC. SGL/DBL$40-$80.

Best Western Ramkota Inn (2400 North Louise Ave., 57107; 336-0650, Fax 336-1687, 800-528-1234) 228 rooms, restaurant, lounge, indoor and outdoor heated pool, exercise center, airport courtesy car, children free with parents, kitchenettes, a/c, NS rooms, TV, laundry facilities, wheelchair access, pets OK, meeting facilities for 3,000, senior rates, CC. SGL/DBL$60-$75.

Best Western Town House Motel (400 South Main St., 57102; 336-2740, Fax 336-7864, 800-528-1234) 66 rooms, restaurant, lounge, outdoor heated pool, exercise center, children free with parents, a/c, NS rooms, TV, local transportation, laundry facilities, wheelchair access, pets OK, meeting facilities, senior rates, CC. SGL/DBL$50-$100.

Brimark Inn (3200 West Russell St., 57104; 332-2000) 109 rooms, outdoor heated pool, airport transportation, a/c, children free with parents, airport transportation, TV, no pets, wheelchair access, NS rooms, senior rates, CC. SGL/DBL$39-$56.

Budget Host Plaza Inn (2620 East 10th St., 57103; 336-1550, Fax 339-0616, 800-283-4678) 38 rooms, restaurant, heated pool, laundry facilities, pets OK, NS rooms, wheelchair access, airport transportation, a/c, TV, children free with parents, senior rates, meeting facilities, CC. SGL/DBL$33-$44.

Budgetel Inn (3200 Meadow Ave., 57106; 362-0835, 800-428-3438) 82 rooms and suites, free breakfast, indoor heated pool, kitchenettes, pets OK, children under 18 free with parents, a/c, wheelchair access, NS rooms, free local calls, in-room computer hookups, fax service, VCRs, TV, meeting facilities, CC. SGL/DBL$34-$38.

Center Inn (900 East 20th St., 57105; 334-9002) 61 rooms, a/c, TV, wheelchair access, NS rooms, pets OK, children free with parents, laundry facilities, in-room refrigerators, airport transportation, senior rates, CC. SGL/DBL$35-$40.

Cloud 9 Motel (4904 North Cliff Ave., 57104; 338-6090) 55 rooms, a/c, TV, no pets, wheelchair access, NS rooms, kitchenettes, senior rates, CC. SGL/DBL$44-$48.

Comfort Inn North (5100 North Cliff Ave., 57104; 331-4490, 800-228-5150) 62 rooms, restaurant, indoor heated pool, whirlpools, in-room refrigerators, children under 18 free with parents, no pets, free local calls, a/c, TV, wheelchair access, senior rates, meeting facilities, CC. SGL/DBL$38-$55.

Comfort Inn South (3216 South Carolyn Ave., 57106; 361-2822, 800-228-5150) 67 rooms, indoor heated pool, whirlpools, children free with parents, pets OK, VCRs, a/c, TV, wheelchair access, meeting facilities, senior rates, CC. SGL/DBL$42-$66.

Comfort Inn Suites (3208 South Carolyn Ave., 57106; 362-9711, 800-228-5150) 61 rooms, indoor heated pool, whirlpools, fax service, children under 16 free with parents, VCRs, in-room refrigerators and microwaves, a/c, TV, wheelchair access, no pets, meeting facilities, senior rates, CC. SGL/DBL$55-$80.

Days Inn South (3401 Gateway Blvd., 57106; 361-9240, 800-325-2525) 80 rooms, free breakfast, a/c, airport transportation, in-room refrigerators and microwaves, children free with parents, TV, wheelchair access, NS rooms, no pets, laundry facilities, senior rates, CC. SGL/DBL$40-$65.

Days Inn North (5001 North Cliff Ave., 57104; 331-5959, 800-325-2525) 87 rooms, free breakfast, a/c, TV, airport transportation, wheelchair access, NS rooms, no pets, laundry facilities, senior rates, CC. SGL/DBL$35-$49.

DeLuxe Motel (1712 West 12th St., 57104; 336-2060) 24 rooms, a/c, TV, no pets, wheelchair access, NS rooms, senior rates, CC. SGL/DBL$40-$50.

El Rancho Motel (428 South Kiwanis Ave., 57106; 336-3380) 20 rooms, outdoor pool, pets OK, a/c, TV, wheelchair access, NS rooms, senior rates, CC. SGL/DBL$36-$42.

Empire Inn (4208 West 41st St., 57116; 361-2345) 84 rooms and suites, indoor heated pool, sauna, whirlpools, a/c, TV, no pets, wheelchair access, children under 16 free with parents, in-room refrigerators, microwaves and coffee makers, NS rooms, senior rates, CC. SGL/DBL$30-$55.

Exel Inn (1300 West Russell St., 57104; 331-5800, 800-356-8013) 63 rooms, indoor heated pool, pets OK, in-room refrigerators and microwaves, children free with parents, laundry facilities, VCRs, a/c, TV, senior rates, meeting facilities, CC. SGL/DBL$30-$45.

Fairfield Inn by Marriott (4501 West Empire Place, 57116; 361-2211, 800-228-2800) 63 rooms, indoor heated pool, children under 18 free with parents, NS rooms, pets OK, kitchenettes, free cable TV, free local calls, laundry service, a/c, wheelchair access, meeting facilities, fax service, senior rates, CC. SGL/DBL$44-$60.

Happy Rest Motel (3307 North Cliff Ave., 57106; 332-0505) 18 rooms, a/c, TV, no pets, wheelchair access, NS rooms, senior rates, CC. SGL/DBL$28-$32.

Harvey Rushmore Motel (2500 East 10th St., 57106; 336-2540) 50 rooms, pool, kitchenettes, a/c, TV, no pets, wheelchair access, NS rooms, senior rates, CC. SGL/DBL$55-$65.

Holiday Inn Airport (1301 West Russell St., 57104; 336-1020, 800-HOLI-DAY) 202 rooms and suites, restaurant, lounge, pool, exercise center, children under 19 free with parents, pets OK, airport transportation, wheelchair access, a/c, TV, NS rooms, fax service, room service, laundry service, meeting facilities, senior rates, CC. SGL/DBL$55-$70.

Holiday Inn City Centre (100 West 8th St., 57102; 339-2000, 800-HOLI-DAY) 306 rooms and suites, restaurant, lounge, pool, exercise center, children under 19 free with parents, airport transportation, wheelchair access, a/c, TV, NS rooms, fax service, room service, no pets, in-room refrigerators, laundry service, meeting facilities, senior rates, CC. SGL/DBL$65-$175.

Howard Johnson Hotel (3300 West Russell St., 57101; 336-9000, 800-I-GO-HOJO) 200 rooms, restaurant, lounge, entertainment, indoor and outdoor pool, sauna, jacuzzi, game room, pool, children free with parents, wheelchair access, NS rooms, TV, a/c, no pets, laundry facilities, senior rates, meeting facilities for 2,000, CC. SGL/DBL$52-$70.

Kelly Inn (3101 West Russell St., 57118; 338-6242, 800-635-3559) 42 rooms, whirlpools, sauna, a/c, airport transportation, TV, no pets, wheelchair access, NS rooms, in-room refrigerators and microwaves, laundry facilities, airport transportation, children free with parents, meeting facilities, senior rates, CC. SGL/DBL$45-$70.

Motel 6 (3009 West Russell St., 57104; 336-7800, 505-891-6161) 87 rooms, outdoor pool, free local calls, children under 17 free with parents, NS rooms, wheelchair access, pets OK, a/c, TV, CC. SGL/DBL$26-$32.

Nites Inn (1223 West 12th St., 57116; 336-1810) 53 rooms, free breakfast, a/c, TV, no pets, wheelchair access, NS rooms, senior rates, CC. SGL/DBL$50-$65.

Pine Crest Motel (4501 West 12th St., 57116; 336-3530, 800-456-5440) 33 rooms and 2-bedroom efficiencies, outdoor heated pool, a/c, TV, no pets, wheelchair access, NS rooms, senior rates, CC. SGL/DBL$32-$42.

Radisson Encore Inn (I-29 and West 41st St., 57116; 361-6684, 800-333-3333) 104 rooms and suites, restaurant, lounge, entertainment, indoor heated pool, exercise center, in-room refrigerators, microwaves and coffee makers, children free with parents, airport transportation, no pets, VCRs, wheelchair access, free parking, NS rooms, TV, a/c, children free with parents, senior rates, CC. SGL/DBL$65-$86.

Ramada Limited (407 South Lyons Ave., 57116; 330-0000, 800-2-RAMADA) 66 rooms and suites, restaurant, lounge, pool, wheelchair access, NS rooms, free parking, pets OK, a/c, airport transportation, kitchenettes, TV, children under 18 free with parents, room service, laundry facilities, meeting facilities, senior rates, CC. SGL/DBL$48-$68.

Residence Inn by Marriott (4509 West Empire Place., 57116; 361-2202, 800-331-3131) 66 rooms and suites, free breakfast, indoor heated pool, in-room refrigerators, coffee makers and microwaves, laundry facilities, TV, a/c, VCRs, pets OK, complimentary newspaper, fireplaces, children free with parents, NS rooms, wheelchair access, kitchenettes, meeting facilities, CC. SGL/DBL$65-$88.

Select Inn (3500 Gateway Blvd., 57104; 361-1864, Fax 361-9287, 800-641-1000) 100 rooms, free breakfast, a/c, TV, NS rooms, free local calls, pets OK, senior rates, laundry facilities, children under age 13 stay free with parents, VCRs, fax service, meeting facilities, senior rates, CC. SGL/DBL$30-$51.

Sleep Inn (1500 North Kiwanis Ave., 57104; 339-3992, 800-221-2222) 100 rooms, free breakfast, exercise center, whirlpools, no pets, wheelchair access, NS rooms, children under 18 free with parents, kitchenettes, a/c, TV, meeting facilities, senior rates, CC. SGL/DBL$38-$63.

Sleep Inn (I-29 and 41st St., 57116; 361-1864, 800-221-2222) 100 rooms, free breakfast, indoor heated pool, wheelchair access, NS rooms, kitchenettes, no pets, children under 18 free with parents, senior rates, a/c, TV, meeting facilities, CC. SGL/DBL$35-$48.

Suburban Motel (3308 East 10th St., 57103; 336-3668) 18 rooms, a/c, TV, no pets, wheelchair access, NS rooms, senior rates, CC. SGL/DBL$25-$35.

Sunset Motel (4213 West 12th St. 57103; 336-3050) 33 rooms, outdoor pool, a/c, TV, no pets, wheelchair access, NS rooms, kitchenettes, senior rates, CC. SGL/DBL$38-$44.

Super 8 Motel (1508 West Russell St., 57104; 339-9330, 800-800-8000) 96 rooms and suites, children under 12 free with parents, free local calls, a/c, TV, in-room refrigerators and microwaves, pets OK, fax service, NS rooms, wheelchair access, meeting facilities, senior rates, CC. SGL/DBL$38-$48.

Super 8 Motel (4100 West 41st St., 57106; 361-9719, 800-800-8000) 92 rooms and suites, no pets, children under 12 free with parents, free local calls, a/c, TV, in-room refrigerators and microwaves, fax service, NS rooms, wheelchair access, meeting facilities, senior rates, CC. SGL/DBL$38-$48.

Super 8 Motel (4808 North Cliff, 57106; 339-9212, 800-800-8000) 57 rooms and suites, no pets, children under 12 free with parents, free local calls, a/c, TV, in-room refrigerators and microwaves, fax service, NS rooms, wheelchair access, meeting facilities, senior rates, CC. SGL/DBL$45-$52.

Thriftlodge (809 West Ave. North, 57104; 336-0230) 55 rooms, outdoor pool, airport transportation, pets OK, a/c, TV, wheelchair access, NS rooms, senior rates, CC. SGL/DBL$40-$44.

Valley Inn Motel (18th and Grange, 57105; 335-2390) 30 rooms, a/c, TV, no pets, wheelchair access, laundry facilities, children under 12 free with parents, NS rooms, senior rates, CC. SGL/DBL$35-$41.

Westwick Motel (5801 West 12th St., 57103; 336-2390) 24 rooms, outdoor pool, kitchenettes, a/c, TV, no pets, wheelchair access, NS rooms, senior rates, CC. SGL/DBL$28-$36.

Spearfish
Area Code 605

Best Western Downtown Spearfish Inn (346 West Kansas, 57783; 642-4676, Fax 642-5314, 800-528-1234) 30 rooms and suites, restaurant, lounge, indoor heated pool, sauna, whirlpools, children free with parents, a/c, NS rooms, TV, laundry facilities, wheelchair access, children under 18 free with parents, pets OK, meeting facilities, senior rates, CC. SGL/DBL$45-$145.

Best Western of Spearfish (Spearfish 57783; 642-8105, 800-528-1234) 64 rooms and suites, restaurant, indoor heated pool, exercise center, whirl-pools, children free with parents, a/c, NS rooms, TV, laundry facilities, wheelchair access, pets OK, meeting facilities, senior rates, CC. SGL/DBL$40-$110, STS$80-$160.

Christensen's Country Home (432 Hillsview, 57783; 642-2859) 4 rooms, free breakfast, TV, a/c, no pets, NS, children over 10 welcome, private baths, CC. SGL/DBL$50-$70.

Days Inn (240 Ryan Rd., 57783; 642-7101, 800-325-2525) 50 rooms, free breakfast, whirlpools, sauna, a/c, TV, wheelchair access, NS rooms, no pets, laundry facilities, senior rates, CC. SGL/DBL$50-$75.

Holiday Inn (Spearfish 57783; 642-4683, 800-HOLIDAY) 160 rooms, restaurant, lounge, indoor heated pool, exercise center, game room, children under 19 free with parents, wheelchair access, a/c, TV, NS rooms, fax service, room service, no pets, laundry service, meeting facilities for 500, senior rates, CC. SGL/DBL$68-$118.

Kelly Inn (540 East Jackson, 57783; 642-7795, 800-635-3559) 50 rooms, restaurant, whirlpools, laundry facilities, children free with parents, a/c, TV, pets OK, wheelchair access, NS rooms, senior rates, CC. SGL/DBL$35-$80.

Queen's Motel (305 Main St., 57783; 642-2631) 12 rooms, TV, NS rooms, children free with parents, CC. SGL/DBL$25-$45.

Royal Rest Motel (444 Main St., 57783; 642-3842) 12 rooms, outdoor heated pool, a/c, TV, wheelchair access, NS rooms, no pets, senior rates, CC. SGL/DBL$25-$45.

Super 8 Motel (Spearfish 57783; 642-4721, 800-800-8000) 61 rooms and suites, no pets, children under 12 free with parents, free local calls, a/c, TV, in-room refrigerators and microwaves, fax service, NS rooms, wheelchair access, meeting facilities, senior rates, CC. SGL/DBL$70-$119.

Sturgis

Area Code 605

Best Western Phil-Town Inn (South Junction St., 57785; 347-3604, Fax 347-2376, 800-528-1234) 56 rooms and suites, restaurant, lounge, indoor heated pool, exercise center, whirlpools, children free with parents, a/c, NS rooms, TV, laundry facilities, in-room refrigerators, wheelchair access, pets OK, meeting facilities, senior rates, CC. SGL/DBL$40-$84.

Junction Inn (1802 South Junction Ave., 57785; 347-5675, Fax 347-5695) 30 rooms, pets OK, kitchenettes, a/c, TV, children free with parents, in-room refrigerators, CC. SGL/DBL$28-$60.

Super 8 Motel (Sturgis 57785; 347-4447, Fax 347-2334, 800-800-8000) 40 rooms and suites, restaurant, whirlpools, sauna, pets OK, children under 12 free with parents, free local calls, a/c, TV, in-room refrigerators and microwaves, fax service, NS rooms, wheelchair access, meeting facilities, senior rates, CC. SGL/DBL$50-$59.

Vermillion

Area Code 605

Budget Host Tomahawk Motel (1313 West Cherry St., 57069; 624-2601, 800-283-4678) 20 rooms, free breakfast, outdoor heated pool, pets OK, airport transportation, laundry facilities, NS rooms, wheelchair access, a/c, TV, children free with parents, senior rates, CC. SGL/DBL$28-$38.

Comfort Inn   (701 West Cherry St., 57069; 624-8333, 800-228-5150) 46 rooms and suites, exercise center, whirlpools, children free with parents, in-room refrigerators and microwaves, a/c, TV, wheelchair access, no pets, CC. SGL/DBL$36-$50.

Super 8 Motel (1208 East Cherry St., 57069; 624-8005, 800-800-8000) 39 rooms and suites, restaurant, pets OK, children under 12 free with parents, free local calls, a/c, TV, in-room refrigerators and microwaves, fax service, NS rooms, wheelchair access, meeting facilities, senior rates, CC. SGL/DBL$29-$50.

Wall

Area Code 605

Best Western Inn (712 Glenn St., 57790; 279-2145, 800-528-1234) 74 rooms, restaurant, outdoor heated pool, exercise center, in-room coffee makers, children free with parents, a/c, NS rooms, TV, laundry facilities, wheelchair access, pets OK, meeting facilities, senior rates, CC. SGL/DBL$30-$80.

Days Inn (Norriss St., 57790; 279-2000, Fax 279-2599, 800-325-2525) 32 rooms, free breakfast, sauna, whirlpools, a/c, TV, wheelchair access, NS rooms, no pets, laundry facilities, children free with parents, senior rates, CC. SGL/DBL$35-$78.

Elk Motel (South Blvd., 57790; 279-2127, Fax 279-2599, 800-782-9402) 47 rooms, outdoor heated pool, a/c, TV, pets OK, NS rooms, senior rates, CC. SGL/DBL$27-$65.

Hitching Post Motel (211 10th Ave., 57790; 279-2133) 30 rooms, outdoor heated pool, a/c, TV, NS rooms, senior rates, CC. SGL/DBL$27-$65.

Kings Inn (Wall 57790; 279-2178) 26 rooms, a/c, TV, wheelchair access, pets OK, children free with parents, NS rooms, senior rates, CC. SGL/DBL$33-$55.

Sands Motel (804 Glenn St., 57790; 279-2121, 800-341-8000) 49 rooms and efficiencies, outdoor heated pool, in-room coffee makers, no pets, a/c, TV, CC. SGL/DBL$30-$65.

Super 8 Motel (711 Glenn St., 57790; 279-2688, 800-800-8000) 29 rooms, no pets, children under 12 free with parents, free local calls, a/c, TV, in-room refrigerators and microwaves, fax service, NS rooms, wheelchair access, meeting facilities, senior rates, CC. SGL/DBL$50-$64.

Watertown

Area Code 605

Best Western Ramkota Inn (1901 9th Ave. Southwest, 57201; 886-8011, Fax 886-3667, 800-528-1234) 101 rooms, restaurant, lounge, indoor heated pool, airport transportation, exercise center, children free with parents, a/c, NS rooms, TV, laundry facilities, wheelchair access, pets OK, meeting facilities, senior rates, CC. SGL/DBL$45-$60.

Comfort Inn (800 35th St. Circle, 57201; 886-3010, 800-228-5150) 60 rooms, indoor heated pool, whirlpool, exercise center, a/c, TV, wheelchair access, no pets, CC. SGL/DBL$42-$88.

Days Inn (2900 9th Ave. Southeast, 57201; 886-3500, 800-325-2525) 57 rooms, free breakfast, indoor heated pool, whirlpools, sauna, in-room refrigerators and microwaves, a/c, TV, wheelchair access, children free with parents, NS rooms, no pets, laundry facilities, senior rates, CC. SGL/DBL$35-$50.

Drake Motor Inn (Watertown 57201; 886-8411) 47 rooms, restaurant, lounge, a/c, TV, airport transportation, children under 12 free with parents, in-room refrigerators and microwaves, wheelchair access, NS rooms, pets OK, meeting facilities, senior rates, CC. SGL/DBL$28-$38.

Guest House Inn (101 North Broadway, 57201; 886-8061, Fax 886-3997) 58 rooms, restaurant, lounge, outdoor heated pool, airport transportation, pets OK, a/c, TV, wheelchair access, NS rooms, in-room refrigerators, senior rates, CC. SGL/DBL$30-$38.

Stones Inn (3900 9th Ave. Southeast, 57201; 882-3630, Fax 886-3022) 34 rooms, a/c, TV, wheelchair access, airport transportation, in-room refrigerators, no pets, NS rooms, senior rates, CC. SGL/DBL$29-$39.

Super 8 Motel (Watertown 57201; 882-1900, 800-800-8000) 58 rooms, indoor heated pool, whirlpools, sauna, no pets, children under 12 free with parents, free local calls, a/c, TV, in-room refrigerators and microwaves, fax service, NS rooms, wheelchair access, meeting facilities, senior rates, CC. SGL/DBL$29-$39.

Travel Host (1714 9th Ave. Southwest, 57201; 886-6120, 800-658-5512) 50 rooms, free breakfast, whirlpools, children free with parents, a/c, no pets, TV, CC. SGL/DBL$26-$44.

Traveler's Inn (920 14th St. Southeast, 57201; 882-2243, 800-351-1477) 50 rooms, free breakfast, no pets, children free with parents, a/c, TV, meeting facilities, senior rates, CC. SGL/DBL$28-$38.

Winner
Area Code 605

Buffalo Trail Motel (Hwys 18 and 44, 57580; 842-2212, Fax 842-1722) 32 rooms, heated pool, a/c, TV, pets OK, NS rooms, airport transportation, CC. SGL/DBL$30-$75.

Warrior Inn Motel (845 East Hwy. 44, 57580; 842-3121) 39 rooms, indoor heated pool, kitchenettes, a/c, pets OK, TV, wheelchair access, NS rooms, senior rates, CC. SGL/DBL$35-$70.

Yankton
Area Code 605

Broadway Motel (1210 Broadway, 57078; 665-7805) 37 rooms, a/c, TV, pets OK, CC. SGL/DBL$25-$35.

Comfort Inn (2118 Broadway, 57078; 665-8053, 800-228-5150) 45 rooms, whirlpools, a/c, children free with parents, in-room refrigerators, TV, wheelchair access, no pets, CC. SGL/DBL$38-$48.

Days Inn (2410 Broadway, 57078; 665-8717, Fax 665-8841, 800-325-2525) 45 rooms, free breakfast, whirlpools, a/c, TV, wheelchair access, NS rooms, no pets, laundry facilities, children under 12 free with parents, senior rates, CC. SGL/DBL$25-$45.

Lewis and Clark Resort (Yankton 57078; 665-2680, Fax 665-6024) 34 rooms and cabins, pets OK, TV, a/c, in-room refrigerators and microwaves, senior rates, CC. SGL/DBL$35-$75.

Super 8 Motel (Yankton 57078; 665-6510, 800-800-8000) 58 rooms, restaurant, lounge, no pets, children under 12 free with parents, free local calls, a/c, TV, in-room refrigerators and microwaves, fax service, NS rooms, wheelchair access, meeting facilities, senior rates, CC. SGL/DBL$45-$55.

The Yankton Inn (Yankton 57078; 665-2906, 800-457-9090) 124 rooms and suites, restaurant, lounge, indoor heated pool, exercise center, whirlpools, sauna, in-room refrigerators, airport courtesy car, in-room computer hookups, children under 12 free with parents, a/c, TV, wheelchair access, NS rooms, meeting facilities, senior rates, CC. SGL/DBL$40-$55, STS$100-$115.

Washington

Washington Bed and Breakfast Guild (2442 Northwest Market St., Seattle 98107; 509-548-6224) bed and breakfast reservations.

Aberdeen

Area Code 206

Nordic Inn (1700 South Boone St. 98520; 533-0100) 66 rooms, restaurant, lounge, children free with parents, VCRs, TV, in-room refrigerators, pets OK, meeting facilities, senior rates, CC. SGL/DBL$35-$60.

The Olympic Inn (616 West Heon, 98520 533-4200) 55 rooms and efficiencies, laundry facilities, TV, in-room refrigerators, kitchenettes, pets OK, children free with parents, CC. SGL/DBL$40-$75.

Red Lion (521 W Wishkah, 98250; 532-5210, Fax 533-8483, 800-547-8010) 67 rooms, TV, wheelchair access, pets OK, children free with parents, NS rooms,free paper, fax, laundry, meeting rooms, senior rates, CC. SGL/DBL$50-$75.

Anacortes

Area Code 206

Albatross Bed and Breakfast (5708 Kingsway West, 98221; 293-0677) 4 rooms, free breakfast, children free with parents, airport transportation, private baths, water view, no pets, CC. SGL/DBL$65-$85.

Anacortes Inn (3006 Commercial Ave. 98221; 293-3153, Fax 293-0209, 800-327-7976) 44 rooms, outdoor heated pool, TV, in-room refrigerators, no pets, NS rooms, senior rates, CC. SGL/DBL$50-$70.

Cap Sante Inn (906 9th St. 98221; 293-0602, 800-852-0846) 34 rooms and efficiencies, no pets, TV, laundry facilities, children free with parents, NS rooms, CC. SGL/DBL$42-$65.

The Campbell House (917 36th, 98221; 293-4910) free breakfast, TV, local transportation, children over 12 welcome, no pets, antique furnishings, no-smoking, CC. SGL/DBL$55-$95.

Channel House (2901 Oakes Ave. 98221; 293-9382) 4 rooms, free breakfast, TV, a/c, no pets, NS, private baths, fireplaces, hot tub, CC. SGL/DBL$65-$100.

Hasty Pudding House (1312 8th St. 98221; 293-5773) free breakfast, TV, a/c, no pets, NS, private baths, antique furnishings, CC. SGL/DBL$65-$90.

Holiday Motel (2903 Commercial Ave. 98221; 293-6511) 10 rooms and suites, restaurant, no pets, TV, CC. SGL/DBL$28-$58.

Island Inn (3401 Commercial Ave. 98221; 293-4644) 36 rooms and 2-bedroom efficiencies, heated pool, whirlpools, in-room refrigerators, pets OK, a/c, TV, in-room coffee makers, water view, CC. SGL/DBL$55-$75.

Marina Inn (3300 Commercial Ave. 98221; 293-1100) 52 rooms and efficiencies, whirlpools, in-room refrigerators and coffee makers, laundry facilities, no pets, senior rates, CC. SGL/DBL$45-$70.

Ship Harbor Motel (5316 Ferry Terminal Rd. 98221; 293-5177, 800-852-8568) 16 rooms and cottages, restaurant, free breakfast, pets OK, laundry facilities, children free with parents, NS rooms, in-room refrigerators, TV, senior rates, CC. SGL/DBL$50-$70.

Sunset Beach Bed and Breakfast (100 Sunset Beach, 98221; 293-5428) free breakfast, TV, NS, private baths, a/c, no pets, CC. SGL/DBL$75-$83.

Anderson Island
Area Code 206

The Inn at Burg's Landing (50324 School Rd. East, 98328; 884-9185) 2 rooms, free breakfast, TV, NS, private baths, jacuzzi, a/c, no pets, CC. SGL/DBL$65-$85.

Arlington
Area Code 206

Arlington Motor Inn (2214 Hwy. 530, 98223; 652-9595) 41 rooms, whirlpools, TV, children free with parents, pets OK, in-room refrigerators, CC. SGL/DBL$35-$55.

Smokey Point Motor Inn (17329 Smokey Point Dr. 98223; 659-8561) 54 rooms and efficiencies, outdoor heated pool, whirlpools, pets OK, TV, VCRs, in-room coffee makers, CC. SGL/DBL$36-$54.

Ashford
Area Code 206

Alexanders Country Inn (Ashford 98304; 569-2300, 800-654-7615) 13 rooms and house, restaurant, lounge, whirlpools, no pets, CC. SGL/DBL$75-$125.

The Cabins at Berry (Ashford 98304; 569-2628) a/c, TV, no pets, CC. SGL/DBL$38-$42.

Gateway Inn (Route 706, 98304; 569-2506) a/c, TV, no pets, CC. SGL/DBL$36-$38.

Growly Bear (37311 Hwy. 706, 98304; 569-2339) free breakfast, TV, 1890 home, NS, private baths, a/c, no pets, CC. SGL/DBL$68-$100.

Jasmer's (300005 Hwy. 706, 98304; 569-2682) free breakfast, TV, a/c, no pets, CC. SGL/DBL$65-$86.

Moore Motel (Hwy. 706, 98304; 569-2504) a/c, TV, no pets, CC. SGL/DBL$40-$48.

Mountain Meadow Inn (28912 Hwy. 796 East, 98304; 569-2788) 5 rooms, free breakfast, no pets, NS, private baths, 1910 home, antique furnishings, CC. SGL/DBL$78-$88.

Nisqually Lodge (Hwy. 706, 89304; 569-8804) 24 rooms, whirlpools, TV, no pets, CC. SGL/DBL$35-$48.

Auburn

Area Code 206

Best Western Pony Soldier Motor Inn (1521 D St. Northwest, 939-5959, Fax 735-4197, 800-634-7669, 800-528-1234) 66 rooms, restaurant, free breakfast, outdoor heated pool, exercise facilities, spa, in-room refrigerators, children free with parents, a/c, NS rooms, TV, laundry facilities, wheelchair access, pets OK, meeting facilities, senior rates, CC. SGL/DBL$65-$88.

Value Inn by Nendels (102 15th St. Northeast, 98002; 833-8007, 800-547-0106, 800-547-0106) 35 rooms, a/c, TV, children under 17 free with parents, in-room refrigerators, laundry facilities, senior rates, CC. SGL/DBL$45-$56.

Val-U-Inn Motel (9 14th Ave. Northwest, 98001; 735-9600) 66 rooms, whirlpools, in-room refrigerators, a/c, TV, laundry facilities, children under 12 free with parents, pets OK, CC. SGL/DBL$56-$69.

Bainbridge Island

Area Code 206

Bainbridge Island Bed and Breakfast (Bainbridge Island 98110; 842-6248) free breakfast, TV, a/c, no pets, CC. SGL/DBL$46-$66.

Bombay House (8490 Beck Rd. Northeast, Bainbridge Island 98110; 842-9260) 5 rooms, bed and breakfast, no pets, a/c, TV, CC. SGL/DBL$69-$89.

Rose Cottage Bed and Breakfast (11744 Olympic Terrace, 98110; 842-6248) 2 rooms, free breakfast, TV, NS, in-room refrigerators and coffee makers, no pets, CC. SGL/DBL$65-$75.

Bellevue

Area Code 206

Bellevue Bed and Breakfast (820 100th Ave. Southeast, 98004; 453-1048) free breakfast, TV, a/c, private baths, NS, no children, no pets, CC. SGL/DBL$65.

Courtyard by Marriott (14615 Northeast 29th Pl. 98007; 869-5300, 800-331-3131) 152 rooms and suites, free breakfast, pool, in-room refrigerators, microwaves and coffee makers, a/c, no pets, complimentary newspaper, children free with parents, kitchenettes, TV, VCRs, NS rooms, wheelchair access, meeting facilities, senior rates, CC. SGL/DBL$80-$95.

Days Inn (3241 156th Ave. Southeast, 98007; 643-6644, Fax 644-7279, 800-325-2525) 108 rooms, free breakfast, pool, spa, children free with parents, fax service, no pets, free local calls, wheelchair access, a/c, TV, NS rooms, CC. 15 miles from the airport and Space Needle, 11 miles from the Kingdome. SGL$44-$54, DBL$49-$59, X$5.

Eastgate Motel (14632 Southeast Eastgate Way, Bellevue 98007; 746-4100) 29 rooms and efficiencies, free local calls, no pets, a/c, TV, in-room refrigerators and microwaves, children free with parents, CC. SGL$35, DBL$45, X$5.

Embassy Suites (3225 158th Ave., Bellevue 98008; 644-2500, Fax 644-2091, 800-EMBASSY) 240 2-room suites, restaurant, lounge, entertainment, free breakfast, indoor heated pool, sauna, whirlpools, exercise center, in-room computer hookups, NS rooms, a/c, airport transportation, TV, gift shop, room service, wheelchair access, meeting facilities, CC. SGL/DBL$110-$225.

Emerald Ridge (3010 118th Ave. Southeast, 98005; 746-5250) a/c, TV, CC. SGL/DBL$60-$75.

Hampton Greens (4747 148th Ave. Northeast, 98007; 800-523-4356) 10 apartments, kitchenettes, a/c, TV, CC. 1BR$95, 2BR$108.

Hilton Bellevue (100 112th Ave. North, 98004; 455-3330, Fax 451-2473, 800-BEL-HILT) 180 rooms and suites, three restaurants, lounge, indoor heated pool, in-room refrigerators, complimentary newspaper, free local calls, local transportation, no pets, wheelchair access, NS rooms, meeting facilities, a/c, TV, CC. SGL$82-$92, DBL$91-$102, STS$150.

Holiday Court Hotel (10 100th Ave. Northeast, 98004; 454-7018) 42 1- and 2-bedroom suites, outdoor pool, a/c, TV, NS rooms, kitchenettes, laundry facilities, pets OK, airport transportation, CC. 1BR$55-$60, 2BR$65-$70.

Hyatt Regency (900 Bellevue Way Northeast, 98004; 462-1234) 382 rooms and suites, restaurant, lounge, indoor pool, exercise center, sauna, laundry service, 24-hour room service, no pets, barber and beauty shop, airport transportation, in-room refrigerators, boutiques, a/c, TV, CC. SGL$145, DBL$165, STS$200-$1,000.

Naco/West Thousand Trails Resort (1000 124th Ave. Northeast, 98009; 646-1350) restaurant, a/c, TV, CC. SGL/DBL$56-$66.

Pacific Guest Suites (915 118th Ave. Southeast, 98005; 454-7888, Fax 454-0123) 84 1-, 2-, and 3-bedroom suites, a/c, TV, wheelchair access, free local calls, CC. 1BR$55-$87, 2BR$66-$97, 3BR$77-$92.

Petersen's Bed and Breakfast (10228 8th Ave. Southeast, 98004; 454-9334) free breakfast, TV, a/c, no pets, CC. SGL/DBL$55-$75.

Red Lion Bellevue (300 112th Ave. Northeast, 98004; 445-1300; 800-547-8010) 335 rooms, restaurant, lounge, entertainment, outdoor heated pool, exercise center, whirlpools, pets OK, children free with parents, gift shop, in-room refrigerators, local transportation, beauty shop, meeting facilities, a/c, TV, CC. SGL/DBL$110-$145, STS$150.

Red Lion Bellevue Center (818 112th Ave. Northeast, 98004; 455-1515, 800-547-8010) 211 rooms and suites, restaurant, lounge, outdoor pool, exercise center, beauty shop, pets OK, NS rooms, laundry facilities, wheelchair access, in-room computer hookups, airport transportation, meeting facilities, a/c, TV, CC. SGL/DBL$90-$118, STS$295-$495.

Residence Inn by Marriott (14455 Northeast 29th Place, 98007; 882-1222, 800-331-3131) 120 suites, free breakfast, outdoor heated pool, whirlpools, in-room refrigerators, coffee makers and microwaves, laundry facilities, TV, a/c, VCRs, pets OK, complimentary newspaper, fireplaces, children free with parents, NS rooms, wheelchair access, meeting facilities, CC. SGL/DBL$135-$195.

The Ridge (10424 Northeast 32nd Place, 98004: 867-9200) a/c, TV, CC. SGL/DBL$40-$50.

Sammamish View (16100 Southeast Eastgate Way, 98008; 800-523-4356) a/c, TV, CC. SGL/DBL$50-$110.

Silver Cloud Inn (10621 Northeast 12th St. 98004; 637-7000) 97 rooms, outdoor heated pool, whirlpools, a/c, TV, laundry facilities, airport transportation, in-room refrigerators and microwaves, no pets, CC. SGL/DBL$60-$66.

TraveLodge (11011 Northeast 8th Ave. 98004; 454-4967, 800-578-7878) 117 rooms, restaurant, lounge, free breakfast, pool, wheelchair access, complimentary newspaper, laundry service, TV, a/c, free local calls, fax service,

NS rooms, in-room refrigerators, microwaves and coffee makers, children under 18 free with parents, no pets, meeting facilities, senior rates, CC. SGL/DBL$65-$110.

Westcoast Hotel (625 116th Ave. Northeast, 98004; 455-9444, Fax 455-2154, 800-426-0670) 176 rooms, restaurant, lounge, entertainment, outdoor heated pool, exercise center, whirlpools, fireplaces, in-room refrigerators, coffee makers, children free with parents, a/c, NS rooms, TV, laundry facilities, wheelchair access, room service, no pets, meeting facilities, senior rates, CC. SGL/DBL$60-$95.

Bellingham
Area Code 206

Anderson Creek Lodge (5602 Mission Rd. 966-2126, Fax 734-9284) 5 rooms, free breakfast, indoor heated pool, exercise center, NS, airport transportation, no pets, CC. SGL/DBL$70-$95.

Bay City Motor Inn (116 North Samish Way, 98225; 676-0332, Fax 676-0899) 52 rooms, whirlpools, exercise center, no pets, children free with parents, TV, a/c, coffee makers, CC. SGL/DBL$45-$55.

Best Western Heritage Inn (151 East McLeod Rd. 98226; 647-1912, Fax 671-3878, 800-528-1234) 92 rooms and suites, restaurant, free breakfast, outdoor pool, whirlpools, children free with parents, a/c, NS rooms, TV, laundry facilities, wheelchair access, no pets, meeting facilities, senior rates, CC. SGL/DBL$48-$65.

Best Western Lakeway Inn (714 Lakeway Dr. 98226; 671-1001, Fax 676-8519, 800-528-1234) 132 rooms, restaurant, lounge, entertainment, indoor heated pool, exercise center, sauna, airport transportation, complimentary newspaper, children free with parents, a/c, NS rooms, TV, laundry facilities, wheelchair access, pets OK, meeting facilities, senior rates, CC. SGL/DBL$50-$135.

Coachman Inn (120 Samish Way, 98225; 671-9000, 800-962-6641) 60 rooms, restaurant, free breakfast outdoor pool, whirlpools, sauna, no pets, in-room refrigerators, children free with parents, a/c, TV, wheelchair access, NS rooms, senior rates, CC. SGL/DBL$55-$64.

Comfort Inn (4282 Meridian St. 98226; 738-1100, 800-228-5150) 80 rooms and suites, free breakfast, indoor heated pool, whirlpools, exercise center, laundry facilities, in-room refrigerators, children free with parents, a/c, TV, wheelchair access, no pets, senior rates, meeting facilities, CC. SGL/DBL$50-$70, STS$85-$100.

Days Inn (125 East Kellogg Ave. 98226; 671-6200, 800-325-2525) 70 rooms and efficiencies, outdoor heated pool, whirlpools, free breakfast, a/c, TV, wheelchair access, NS rooms, no pets, laundry facilities, in-room refrigerators, children free with parents, senior rates, CC. SGL/DBL$45-$65.

Hampton Inn Airport (3985 Bennett Dr. 98225; 676-7700, Fax 671-7557, 800-HAMPTON) 133 rooms, restaurant, free breakfast, pool, exercise facilities, children under 18 free with parents, NS rooms, wheelchair access, in-room computer hookups, fax service, TV, a/c, free local calls, pets OK, airport transportation, meeting facilities, senior rates, CC. SGL/DBL$64-$78.

Holiday Inn (4160 Guide Meridian, 98226; 671-4800, Fax 671-9920, 800-HOLIDAY) 101 rooms, restaurant, lounge, indoor heated pool, exercise facilities, whirlpools, children under 19 free with parents, wheelchair access, a/c, TV, VCRs, NS rooms, airport transportation, in-room refrigerators and microwaves, fax service, room service, no pets, laundry service, meeting facilities, senior rates, CC. SGL/DBL$60-$88.

Key Motel (212 North Samish Way, 98225; 733-4060) 40 rooms, outdoor heated pool, whirlpools, sauna, in-room refrigerators, TV, pets OK, children free with parents, senior rates, CC. SGL/DBL$36-$58.

Lions Inn Motel (2419 Elm St. 98225; 733-2330) 15 rooms and 2-bedroom efficiencies, children free with parents, TV, pets OK, in-room refrigerators, CC. SGL/DBL$42-$46.

Motel 6 (3701 Byron Ave. 98225; 671-4494, 505-891-6161) 60 rooms, pool, free local calls, children under 17 free with parents, NS rooms, wheelchair access, pets OK, a/c, TV, CC. SGL/DBL$30-$36.

North Garden Inn (1014 North Garden, 98225; 671-7828, 800-922-6414) 8 rooms, free breakfast, antique furnishings, NS, private baths, no pets, senior rates, CC. SGL/DBL$58-$75.

Park Motel (101 North Samish Way, 98225; 733-8280, Fax 738-9186) 56 rooms and apartments, whirlpools, a/c, TV, in-room refrigerators, no pets, children free with parents, airport transportation, wheelchair access, NS rooms, senior rates, CC. SGL/DBL$40-$100.

Quality Inn Baron Suites (100 East Kellogg Rd. 98226; 647-8000, 800-221-2222) 86 rooms and suites, outdoor heated pool, exercise center, whirlpools, hot tubs, kitchenettes, no pets, children free with parents, a/c, TV, wheelchair access, in-room refrigerators and microwaves, VCRs, airport transportation, room service, laundry service, NS rooms, meeting facilities, senior rates, CC. SGL/DBL$65-$100.

Queen Regent Inn (125 East Kellogg Rd. 98227; 671-6200, 800-831-0187) 70 rooms and suites, heated pool, sauna, a/c, TV, wheelchair access, NS rooms, in-room refrigerators, laundry facilities, local transportation, meeting facilities, senior rates, CC. SGL/DBL$50-$90.

Ramada Inn (215 Samish Way, 98225; 734-8830, 800-2-RAMADA) 66 rooms and suites, restaurant, lounge, outdoor heated pool, wheelchair access, NS rooms, free parking, no pets, a/c, TV, in-room refrigerators, children under 18 free with parents, room service, laundry facilities, meeting facilities, senior rates, CC. SGL/DBL$60-$90.

The Resort at Sudden Valley (Bellingham 98227; 734-6430) 47 condominiums, lounge, entertainment, outdoor heated pool, exercise center, sauna, lighted tennis courts, game room, a/c, TV, wheelchair access, no pets, children free with parents, gift shop, NS rooms, senior rates, CC. SGL/DBL$95-$180.

Schnauzer Crossing (4421 Lakeway Dr. 98226; 733-0055) 1 suite, free breakfast, TV, a/c, no pets, NS, fireplace, jacuzzi tub, water view, private bath, CC. SGL/DBL$100-$130.

Sunrise Bay (2141 North Shore Rd. 98226; 647-0376) 2 rooms, free breakfast, outdoor heated pool, whirlpools, TV, no pets, CC. SGL/DBL$70-$80.

Travelers Inn (3750 Meridian St. 98225; 671-4600, Fax 671-6487) 124 rooms, outdoor heated pool, whirlpools, children free with parents, in-room refrigerators, no pets, a/c, TV, wheelchair access, NS rooms, senior rates, CC. SGL/DBL$45-$58.

TraveLodge (202 East Holly St. 98225; 734-1900, Fax 647-0709, 800-578-7878) 49 rooms, restaurant, lounge, free breakfast, pool, wheelchair access, complimentary newspaper, laundry service, TV, free local calls, fax service, NS rooms, in-room refrigerators and microwaves, children under 18 free with parents, no pets, meeting facilities, senior rates, CC. SGL/DBL$45-$55.

Val-U-Inn (805 Lakeway Dr. 98226; 671-9600, 800-443-7777) 81 rooms, whirlpools, VCRs, a/c, TV, wheelchair access, NS rooms, laundry facilities, pets OK, children free with parents, senior rates, CC. SGL/DBL$45-$65.

Blaine
Area Code 206

The Inn at Semi-Ah-Moo (9565 Semiahmoo Parkway, 98230; 371-2000, Fax 371-5490) 128 rooms and suites, restaurant, lounge, entertainment, indoor and outdoor heated pools, tennis courts, exercise center, whirlpools, sauna, a/c, TV, wheelchair access, NS rooms, airport courtesy car, no pets, fireplaces, game room, children free with parents, laundry facilities, meeting facilities, senior rates, CC. SGL/DBL$150-$265.

Northwoods Motel (288 D St. 98231; 332-5603) 29 rooms, outdoor heated pool, whirlpools, sauna, a/c, TV, no pets, CC. SGL/DBL$30-$42.

Bothell

Area Code 206

Kenmore Inn Motel (8202 Northeast Bothell Way, 98011; 485-9575) a/c, TV, no pets, CC. SGL/DBL$44-$48.

Residence Inn by Marriott (11920 Northeast 195th St. 98011; 800-331-3131) 124 rooms and 2-bedroom suites, free breakfast, in-room refrigerators, coffee makers and microwaves, laundry facilities, TV, a/c, VCRs, pets OK, complimentary newspaper, fireplaces, children free with parents, NS rooms, wheelchair access, meeting facilities, CC. SGL/DBL$100-$148.

Wagon Wheel Motel (8042 Northeast Bothell Way, 98011; 486-6631) suites, kitchenettes, a/c, TV, in-room refrigerators, no pets OK, CC. SGL/DBL$79-$109.

Wyndham Garden Hotel (19333 Northcreek Parkway, 98011; 485-5557, Fax 486-7314, 800-822-4200) 166 rooms and suites, restaurant, lounge, pool, outdoor heated pool, whirlpools, exercise center, a/c, TV, NS rooms, wheelchair access, room service, airport transportation, in-room refrigerators, meeting facilities, CC. SGL/DBL$50-$80.

Bremerton

Area Code 206

Best Western Bayview Inn (5640 Kitsap Way, 98312; 373-7349, Fax 377-8529, 800-528-1234) 145 rooms, restaurant, lounge, pool, exercise facilities, hot tub, children free with parents, a/c, NS rooms, TV, laundry facilities, wheelchair access, no pets, meeting facilities, senior rates, CC. SGL/DBL$62-$75.

Dunes Motel (3400 11th St. 98312; 377-0093, 800-828-8238) 64 rooms, restaurant, free breakfast, whirlpools, laundry facilities, a/c, TV, wheelchair access, NS rooms, in-room refrigerators and coffee makers, children free with parents, no pets, senior rates, CC. SGL/DBL$30-$55.

Flagship Inn (4320 Kitsap Way, 98312; 479-6566, Fax 479-6745, 800-447-9396) 29 rooms, free breakfast, outdoor heated pool, in-room refrigerators, no pets, a/c, TV, wheelchair access, NS rooms, VCRs, senior rates, CC. SGL/DBL$51-$71.

MidWay Inn (2909 Wheaton Way, 98310; 479-2909, Fax 479-0576, 800-231-0575) 60 rooms and efficiencies, restaurant, a/c, TV, pets OK, children free with parents, in-room refrigerators, wheelchair access, NS rooms, meeting facilities, senior rates, CC. SGL/DBL$42-$52.

Nendels Suites (4303 Kitsap Way, 98312; 377-4402, Fax 377-0597, 800-776-BAY!, 800-547-0106) 103 rooms and suites, free breakfast, outdoor heated pool, laundry facilities, pets OK, in-room refrigerators, kitchenettes, a/c, TV, children under 17 free with parents, senior rates, CC. SGL/DBL$50-$95.

Super 8 Airport (5068 Kitsap Way, Bremerton 98310; 377-8881, Fax 373--8755, 800-800-8000) 77 rooms, free breakfast, children free with parents, NS rooms, wheelchair access, computer hookups, laundry service, fax service, free local calls, a/c, TV, meeting facilities, CC. SGL$50, DBL$55.

Camano Island
Area Code 206

Willcox House Bed and Breakfast (1462 Larkspur Lane, 98292; 629-4746) free breakfast, TV, a/c, no pets, NS, private baths. SGL/DBL$49-$70.

Carnation
Area Code 206

Idyl Inn on the River (4548 Tolt River Rd. 89014; 333-4262) free breakfast, indoor heated pool, spa, antique furnishings, steam room, TV, a/c, no pets, no children, private baths, CC. SGL/DBL$75-$165.

Cashmere
Area Code 509

Village Inn Motel (229 Cottage Ave. 98815; 782-3522) 21 rooms, a/c, TV, NS rooms, in-room refrigerators and microwaves, pets OK, senior rates, CC. SGL/DBL$35-$66.

Wedge Mountain Inn (7335 Hwy. 2, 98815; 548-6694) 28 rooms, outdoor heated pool, laundry facilities, no pets, TV, a/c, CC. SGL/DBL$40-$65.

Castle Rock
Area Code 206

Mount St. Helens Motel (1340 Mt. St. Helens, 98611; 274-7721) 32 rooms, restaurant, a/c, TV, wheelchair access, pets OK, laundry facilities, in-room refrigerators, NS rooms, senior rates, CC. SGL/DBL$30-$49.

Timberline Motor Inn (1271 Mt. St. Helens, 98611; 274-6002, Fax 274-6335) 17 rooms, a/c, TV, in-room refrigerators, laundry facilities, pets OK, CC. SGL/DBL$35-$65.

Centralia
Area Code 206

Ferryman's Inn (1003 Eckerson Rd. 98531; 330-2094) 84 rooms, outdoor heated pool, whirlpools, laundry facilities, pets OK, a/c, TV, wheelchair access, NS rooms, senior rates, CC. SGL/DBL$35-$40.

Huntley Inn (702 West Harrison Ave. 98531; 736-2875, 800-448-5544) 87 rooms and suites, free breakfast, restaurant, outdoor pool, whirlpools, a/c, in-room refrigerators, TV, wheelchair access, NS rooms, airport transportation, no pets, children free with parents, senior rates, CC. SGL/DBL$40-$55.

Motel 6 (1310 Belmont Ave. 98531; 330-2057, 505-891-6161) 123 rooms, pool, free local calls, children under 17 free with parents, NS rooms, wheelchair access, pets OK, a/c, TV, CC. SGL/DBL$25-$32.

Park Motel (1011 Belmont Ave. 98531; 736-9333) 31 rooms, TV, pets OK, in-room refrigerators and coffee makers, kitchenettes, CC. SGL/DBL$30-$38.

Peppertree West Motor Inn (1208 Alder St. 98531; 736-1124) 24 rooms and efficiencies, restaurant, lounge, a/c, TV, wheelchair access, NS rooms, in-room refrigerators, pets OK, laundry facilities, meeting facilities, senior rates, CC. SGL/DBL$32-$40.

Chehalis
Area Code 206

Cascade Motel (550 Southwest Parkland Dr. 98532; 748-8608) 29 rooms, restaurant, lounge, NS, TV, wheelchair access, NS, CC. SGL/DBL$35-$45.

Pony Soldier Motor Inn (122 Interstate Ave. 98532; 748-0101, Fax 748-7591) 69 rooms, restaurant, outdoor heated pool, a/c, TV, wheelchair access, NS rooms, in-room refrigerators, no pets, senior rates, CC. SGL/DBL$42-$58.

Chelan
Area Code 509

The Apple Inn (1002 East Woodin Ave. 98816; 682-4044) 41 rooms, outdoor heated pool, whirlpools, kitchenettes, a/c, TV, wheelchair access, NS rooms, in-room refrigerators, no pets, senior rates, CC. SGL/DBL$30-$60.

Campbell's Resort and Conference Center (104 West Woodin Ave. 98816; 682-2561) 148 rooms and 2-bedroom suites, heated pools, whirlpools, water view, a/c, TV, wheelchair access, NS rooms, no pets, laundry, senior rates, CC. SGL/DBL$50-$125.

Mary Kay's Mansion (415 3rd St. 98816; 682-5735, 800-729-2408) 6 rooms, free breakfast, TV, VCRs, antique furnishings, NS, a/c, no pets, CC. SGL/DBL$100-$125.

The Westview Resort Motel (2312 Woodin Ave. 98816; 682-4396) 25 rooms, outdoor heated pool, whirlpools, a/c, TV, wheelchair access, in-room refrigerators and coffee makers, laundry facilities, no pets, water view, NS rooms, meeting facilities, senior rates, CC. SGL/DBL$40-$95.

Clarkston
Area Code 509

Best Western Rivertree Inn (1257 Bridge St. 99403; 785-9551, 800-528-1234) 47 rooms and efficiencies, restaurant, heated outdoor pool, exercise center, children free with parents, a/c, NS rooms, TV, laundry facilities, no pets, in-room refrigerators, kitchenettes, wheelchair access, pets OK, meeting facilities, senior rates, CC. SGL/DBL$45-$60.

Nendels Valu Inn (222 Bridge St. 99403; 758-1631, 800-547-0106) 83 rooms, restaurant, lounge, outdoor heated pool, pets OK, a/c, TV, children under 17 free with parents, senior rates, meeting facilities, CC. SGL/DBL$37-$45.

Quality Inn (700 Port Dr. 99403; 758-9500, 800-221-2222) 75 rooms and suites, restaurant, outdoor heated pool, exercise facilities, water view, local transportation, no pets, children free with parents, a/c, TV, wheelchair access, room service, laundry service, NS rooms, meeting facilities, senior rates, CC. SGL/DBL$55-$75.

Clinton
Area Code 206

The Beach House (7338 South Maxwelton Rd. 98236; 321-4335) rooms and suites, TV, CC. SGL/DBL$36-$46.

Coulee Dam
Area Code 509

Compass Rose (508 South Main St. 99116; 633-2765) rooms, free breakfast, no pets, CC. SGL/DBL$65-$75.

Coulee House Motel (Hwy. 155, 99116; 633-1101) 61 rooms and suites, restaurant, lounge, heated pool, spa, sauna, whirlpools, kitchenettes, gift shop, laundry facilities, wheelchair access, in-room refrigerators and coffee makers, water view, a/c, TV, pets OK, kitchenettes, NS rooms, CC. SGL/DBL$75-$250.

Four Winds Guest House (301 Lincoln St. 99116; 633-3146) free breakfast, TV, a/c, no pets, CC. SGL/DBL$28-$38.

Ponderosa Motel (10 Lincoln St. 99116; 633-2100) 34 rooms, outdoor pool, in-room coffee makers, children free with parents, a/c, TV, wheelchair access, pets OK, airport transportation, water view, NS rooms, senior rates, CC. SGL/DBL$35-$54.

Coupeville
Area Code 206

The Anchorage Inn (807 North Main St. 98239; 678-5581) free breakfast, TV, a/c, no pets, private baths, CC. SGL/DBL$55-$65.

Captain Whidbey Inn (2072 West Captain Whidbey Inn Rd. 98239; 678-4097, 800-366-4097) TV, no pets, NS rooms, senior rates, CC. SGL/DBL$85-$95.

Colonel Crockett Farm (1012 South Fort Casey Rd. 98239; 678-3711) free breakfast, TV, 1855 home, private baths, a/c, no pets, CC. SGL/DBL$55-$65.

Coupeville Inn (200 Coveland St. 98239; 678-6668) 24 rooms, TV, no pets, senior rates, CC. SGL/DBL$50-$95.

The Inn at Penn Cove (702 North Main St. 98239; 678-8000) 6 rooms and 2 rental homes, exercise center, a/c, no pets, private baths, kitchenettes, CC. SGL/DBL$80-$145.

The Victorian Bed and Breakfast (Coupeville 98239; 678-5305) 2 rooms and 2-bedroom suite, free breakfast, TV, a/c, in-room refrigerators, 1880s home, children free with parents, no pets, private baths, NS, CC. SGL/DBL$75-$100.

Des Moines
Area Code 206

Legend Motel (22204 Pacific Hwy. South, 98198; 878-0366) a/c, TV, no pets, CC. SGL/DBL$55-$65.

Mini-Rate Motel (20620 Pacific Hwy. South, 98198; 824-6930) 30 rooms, a/c, TV, no pets, CC. SGL/DBL$36-$46.

Moongate Inn Motel (22246 Pacific Hwy. South, 98198; 878-5111) a/c, TV, no pets, CC. SGL/DBL$34-$36.

Ramada Limited Inn (22300 7th Ave. South, 98198; 824-9920, 800-2-RAMADA) 42 rooms and suites, restaurant, lounge, whirlpools, sauna, wheelchair access, NS rooms, free parking, pets OK, a/c, in-room computer hookups, airport transportation, TV, children under 18 free with parents, in-room refrigerators and microwaves, VCRs, room service, laundry facilities, meeting facilities, senior rates, CC. SGL/DBL$60-$85.

Three Bears Motel (2727 South 216th, 98198; 824-2331) a/c, TV, no pets, CC. SGL/DBL$55-$63.

Dungeness
Area Code 206

Groveland Cottages (Dungeness 98382; 683-3565) 4 rooms, free breakfast, private baths, children over 12 welcome, no pets, antique furnishings, CC. SGL/DBL$65-$90.

East Wenatchee
Area Code 509

The Four Seasons Inn (11 West Grant Rd. 98802; 884-6611) 101 rooms and efficiencies, outdoor heated pool, whirlpools, sauna, a/c, TV, wheelchair access, NS rooms, in-room refrigerators, children free with parents, pets OK, senior rates, CC. SGL/DBL$45-$66.

Eatonville
Area Code 206

Mill Village Motel (210 Center St. East, 98328; 832-3200) 32 rooms and efficiencies, children free with parents, a/c, TV, no pets, CC. SGL/DBL$50-$60.

Old Mill House (116 Oak St. East, 98328; 832-6506) rooms and suites, free breakfast, TV, a/c, no pets, NS, private baths, CC. SGL/DBL$65-$90.

Edmonds
Area Code 206

Harbor Inn (130 West Dayton St. 98020; 771-5021, Fax 672-2880, 800-441-8033) 61 rooms and efficiencies, free breakfast, exercise center, NS rooms, no pets, in-room refrigerators, children free with parents, CC. SGL/DBL$50-$68.

Homeport Motor Inn (23825 Hwy. 99, 98020; 771-8008) 58 rooms, whirlpools, no pets, a/c, TV, children free with parents, in-room refrigerators, fax service, wheelchair access, NS rooms, meeting facilities, senior rates, CC. SGL/DBL$45-$55.

Pinkhams Pillow Bed and Breakfast (202 3rd Ave. South, 98020; 774-3406) free breakfast, TV, NS, private baths, antique furnishings, a/c, no pets, CC. SGL/DBL$55-$100.

Ellensburg
Area Code 509

Best Western Inn (1700 Canyon Rd. 98926; 925-9801, 800-528-1234) 105 rooms, indoor heated pool, exercise center, whirlpools, in-room refrigerators, pets OK, children free with parents, a/c, NS rooms, TV, laundry facilities, wheelchair access, meeting facilities, senior rates, CC. SGL/DBL$40-$55.

The Regal Lodge (300 West 6th St. 98926; 925-3116) 30 rooms, indoor heated pool, kitchenettes, children free with parents, a/c, TV, pets OK, senior rates, CC. SGL/DBL$40-$155.

Harolds Motel (601 North Water, 98926; 925-4141) 40 rooms and 2-bedroom efficiencies, outdoor heated pool, in-room refrigerators, children free with parents, pets OK, a/c, TV, CC. SGL/DBL$30-$46.

I-90 Motor Inn (1390 Dollar Way Rd. 98926; 925-9844) 72 rooms, a/c, TV, wheelchair access, NS rooms, laundry facilities, no pets, meeting facilities, senior rates, CC. SGL/DBL$30-$45.

Murphys Country Inn (Ellensburg 98926; 925-7986) 2 rooms, free breakfast, children free with parents, no pets, NS, CC. SGL/DBL$55-$60.

Rainbow Motel (1025 Cascade Way, 98926; 925-3544) 13 rooms, TV, no pets, laundry facilities, a/c, CC. SGL/DBL$30-$45.

Enumclaw
Area Code 206

Green River Gorge Resort (29500 Southeast Green River Gorge, 98022; 886-2302) restaurant, a/c, TV, no pets, CC. SGL/DBL$46-$56.

Kings Motel (1334 Roosevelt Way East, 98022; 825-1626) 44 rooms and suites, restaurant, kitchenettes, laundry facilities, a/c, TV, CC. SGL/DBL$55-$65.

Lee's Hotel (1110 Griffin, 98022; 825-3161) a/c, TV, no pets, CC. SGL/DBL$55-$65.

Ridge Motel (448 Griffin, 98022; 825-6352) a/c, TV, no pets, CC. SGL/DBL$27-$38.

Everett
Area Code 206

Comfort Inn (1602 Southeast Everett Mall Way, 98208; 355-1570, 800-221-2222) 75 rooms, heated pool, a/c, TV, in-room refrigerators, no pets, children free with parents, NS rooms, wheelchair access, senior rates, CC. SGL/DBL$45-$65.

Cypress Inn (12619 4th Ave. West, 98208; 347-9099) 70 rooms, outdoor heated pool, whirlpools, a/c, TV, wheelchair access, airport transportation, children free with parents, in-room refrigerators, laundry facilities, no pets, NS rooms, senior rates, CC. SGL/DBL$55-$72.

Days Inn (1122 North Broadway, 98201; 252-8000, 800-325-2525) 51 rooms and 2-room suites, free breakfast, hot tubs, a/c, TV, wheelchair access, NS rooms, no pets, laundry facilities, senior rates, CC. SGL/DBL$45-$55, STS$95-$110.

FarWest Motel (6030 Evergreen Way, 98203; 355-3007) 20 rooms and 2-bedroom efficiencies, no pets, in-room refrigerators, TV, a/c, CC. SGL/DBL$32-$55.

Holiday Inn (101 128th Southeast, 98208; 745-2555, 800-HOLIDAY) 251 rooms, restaurant, lounge, entertainment, indoor heated pool, exercise facilities, airport transportation, children under 19 free with parents, wheelchair access, a/c, TV, NS rooms, fax service, room service, no pets, laundry service, 15,000 square feet of meeting and exhibition space, meeting facilities for 600, senior rates, CC. SGL/DBL$70-$100.

Marine Village Inn (1728 West Marine View Dr. 98201; 259-4040, Fax 252-8419) 27 rooms and suites, restaurant, whirlpools, children free with parents, a/c, TV, wheelchair access, NS rooms, no pets, in-room coffee makers, senior rates, CC. SGL/DBL$75-$100.

Motel 6 North (10006 Evergreen Way, 98204; 347-2060, 505-891-6161) 119 rooms, pool, free local calls, children under 17 free with parents, NS rooms, wheelchair access, pets OK, a/c, TV, CC. SGL/DBL$26-$32.

Motel 6 South (224 128th St. Southwest, 98204; 353-8120, 505-891-6161) 100 rooms, pool, free local calls, children under 17 free with parents, NS rooms, wheelchair access, pets OK, a/c, TV, CC. SGL/DBL$29-$35.

Nendels Inn (2800 Pacific Ave. 98201; 258-4141, 800-547-0106) 134 rooms, restaurant, lounge, outdoor heated pool, exercise center, whirlpools, pets OK, airport transportation, laundry facilities, a/c, TV, children under 17 free with parents, in-room refrigerators and microwaves, meeting facilities, senior rates, CC. SGL/DBL$45-$55.

Ramada Inn (9602 19th Ave. Southeast, 98208; 337-9090, 800-2-RAMADA) 120 rooms and suites, outdoor heated pool, whirlpools, wheelchair access, NS rooms, free parking, pets OK, a/c, TV, children under 18 free with parents, in-room refrigerators, airport transportation, room service, laundry facilities, meeting facilities, senior rates, CC. SGL/DBL$45-$70.

TraveLodge (3030 Broadway, 98201; 259-6141, 800-578-7878) 29 rooms and efficiencies, wheelchair access, complimentary newspaper, laundry service, TV, a/c, free local calls, fax service, NS rooms, in-room refrigerators and microwaves, children under 18 free with parents, no pets, meeting facilities, senior rates, CC. SGL/DBL$40-$65.

Welcome Motor Inn (1205 Broadway, 98201; 252-8828, Fax 252-8880) 42 rooms, restaurant, kitchenettes, a/c, TV, wheelchair access, NS rooms, no pets, in-room refrigerators and microwaves, senior rates, CC. SGL/DBL$35-$56.

West Coast Everett Pacific Hotel and Convention Center (3105 Pine St. 98201; 339-3333, Fax 259-1547, 800-426-0670) 250 rooms and suites, restaurant, lounge, entertainment, indoor heated pool, sauna, jacuzzi, exercise center, children under 16 free with parents, in-room refrigerators and coffee makers, a/c, TV, airport transportation, no pets, meeting facilities, CC. SGL/DBL$70-$325.

Federal Way
Area Code 206

Best Western Federal Way Executel Inn (31611 20th Ave. South 98003; 941-6000, Fax 941-9500, 800-528-1234) 112 rooms, restaurant, lounge, indoor heated pool, exercise center, sauna, whirlpools, airport transportation, in-room refrigerators, children free with parents, a/c, NS rooms, TV, laundry facilities, wheelchair access, pets OK, meeting facilities, senior rates, CC. SGL/DBL$90-$300.

East Wind Motel (33230 Pacific Hwy. South 98063; 952-2622) a/c, TV, no pets, CC. SGL/DBL$28-$32.

Federal Way Motel (29815 Pacific Hwy. South, 98063; 941-6996) a/c, TV, no pets, CC. SGL/DBL$44-$48.

Holiday Inn (34829 Pacific Hwy. South, 98063; 838-3168, 800-HOLIDAY) 54 rooms, restaurant, lounge, children under 19 free with parents, wheelchair access, a/c, TV, NS rooms, fax service, room service, no pets, laundry service, meeting facilities, senior rates, CC. SGL/DBL$55-$63.

New Horizon Motel (33002 Pacific Hwy. South, 98003; 937-2337) a/c, TV, no pets, CC. SGL/DBL$30-$33.

Roadrunners Truckers Motel (1501 South 350th, 98003; 927-6776) a/c, TV, no pets, CC. SGL/DBL$40-$50.

Secoma Motel (35100 Pacific Hwy. South, 98003; 922-7000) a/c, TV, no pets, CC. SGL/DBL$36-$38.

Siesta Motel (35620 Pacific Hwy. South, 98003; 927-2157) a/c, TV, no pets, CC. SGL/DBL$28-$49.

Stevenson Motel (33330 Pacific Hwy. South, 98003; 927-2500) a/c, TV, no pets, CC. SGL/DBL$36-$46

Super 8 Motel (1688 South 348th St. Federal Way 98063; 838-8808, Fax 8746277, 800-848-8888, 800-800-8000) 89 rooms and suites, restaurant, wheelchair access, pets OK, laundry service, NS rooms, fax service, free local calls, a/c, TV, CC. SGL/DBL$48.

Ferndale
Area Code 206

The Anderson House (2140 Main St. 98248; 384-3450) free breakfast, NS, private baths, 1897 home, TV, a/c, no pets, CC. SGL/DBL$55-$90.

Hill Top Bed and Breakfast (5823 Church Rd. 98248; 384-3619) 3 rooms, free breakfast, TV, a/c, no pets, NS, private baths, fireplace, CC. SGL/DBL$45-$60.

The Slater Heritage House (1371 West Axton Rd. 98248; 384-4273) 4 rooms, free breakfast, no pets, NS, CC. SGL/DBL$52-$63.

Fife
Area Code 206

Econo Lodge North (3518 East Pacific Hwy. 98424; 922-0550, 800-4-CHOICE) 81 rooms, children under 12 free with parents, no pets, senior rates, NS rooms, wheelchair access, a/c, TV, senior rates, CC. SGL/DBL$32-$52.

Executive Inn (5700 Pacific Hwy. East, 98424; 922-0080) 140 rooms, restaurant, lounge, entertainment, outdoor heated pool, whirlpools, sauna, in-room refrigerators, microwaves and coffee makers, children free with parents, laundry service, pets OK, a/c, TV, wheelchair access, NS rooms, senior rates, CC. SGL/DBL$70-$80.

Hometel Inn (3520 Pacific Hwy. East, 98424; 922-0555) 102 rooms, laundry facilities, a/c, TV, in-room refrigerators and microwaves, children free with parents, laundry facilities, pets OK, airport transportation, CC. SGL/DBL$30-$40.

Royal Coachman's Inn (Fife 98424; 800-422-3052) 94 rooms, restaurant, lounge, whirlpools, in-room refrigerators, microwaves and coffee makers, VCRs, children free with parents, a/c, TV, no pets, meeting facilities, CC. SGL/DBL$55-$68.

Travelers Inn (3100 Pacific Hwy. East, 98424; 922-9520, Fax 922-2002) 117 rooms and suites, outdoor heated pool, in-room refrigerators, no pets, a/c, TV, children free with parents, CC. SGL/DBL$30-$36.

Forks

Area Code 206

Forks Motel (Forks 98331; 374-6243, 800-544-3416) 73 rooms and efficiencies, outdoor heated pool, a/c, TV, wheelchair access, NS rooms, laundry facilities, no pets, kitchenettes, senior rates, CC. SGL/DBL$45-$65.

Kalaloch Lodge (Forks 98331; 962-2271) 59 rooms and cabins, restaurant, lounge, pets OK, in-room refrigerators, fireplaces, NS rooms, CC. SGL/DBL$73-$100.

Manitou Lodge (Forks 98331; 374-6295) 5 rooms, free breakfast, NS, pets OK, local transportation, senior rates, CC. SGL/DBL$55-$65.

The Miller Tree (Forks 98331; 374-6806) 6 rooms, free breakfast, TV, a/c, pets OK, NS, CC. SGL/DBL$35-$55.

Olympic Suites (Forks 98331; 374-5400, 800-262-3433) 30 rooms and 1- and 2-bedroom efficiencies, no pets, TV, children free with parents, kitchenettes, CC. SGL/DBL$40-$70.

Pacific Inn (Forks 98331; 374-9400, 800-235-7344) 34 rooms, a/c, TV, wheelchair access, NS rooms, laundry facilities, children free with parents, no pets, senior rates, CC. SGL/DBL$40-$50.

Freeland

Area Code 206

Chateau la Mer (4946 South Scurlock Rd. 98249; 221-3753) rooms and suites, hot tub, a/c, TV, CC. SGL/DBL$50-$60.

Cliff House (5440 Windmill Rd. 98249; 321-1566) a/c, TV, CC. SGL/DBL$36-$38.

Harbor Inn (1606 East Main St. 98249; 321-6900) 20 rooms, free breakfast, TV, no pets, children free with parents, CC. SGL/DBL$35-$55.

Mutiny Bay Resort and Motel (5856 South Mutiny Bay, 98249; 321-4500) a/c, TV, no pets, CC. SGL/DBL$65-$105.

Friday Harbor
Area Code 206

Hillside House (365 Carter Ave. 98250; 378-4730) 6 rooms, free breakfast, NS, no children, private baths, water view, TV, a/c, no pets, CC. SGL/DBL$80-$118.

Goldendale
Area Code 509

Ponderosa Motel (775 East Broadway St. 98620; 773-5842) 28 rooms and 2-bedroom efficiencies, a/c, TV, wheelchair access, NS rooms, pets OK, in-room refrigerators, kitchenettes, senior rates, CC. SGL/DBL$32-$44.

Grand Coulee
Area Code 509

Umbrella Motel (404 Spokane Way, 99133; 633-1691) 16 rooms, a/c, TV, CC. SGL/DBL$45-$65.

Greenbank
Area Code 206

Guest House Inn (3366 Hwy. 525 South, 98253; 678-3115) 6 cottages, free breakfast, outdoor heated pool, whirlpools, exercise center, fireplaces, a/c, TV, NS, no pets, senior rates, CC. SGL/DBL$145-$185.

Ilwaco
Area Code 206

The Inn at Ilwaco (120 Williams St. Northeast, 89624; 642-8686) 9 rooms, free breakfast, TV, no pets, NS, CC. SGL/DBL$55-$80.

Issaquah
Area Code 206

Holiday Inn (1801 12th Ave. Northwest, 98027; 392-6421, 800-HOLIDAY) 100 rooms, restaurant, lounge, pool, exercise facilities, children under 19 free with parents, wheelchair access, a/c, TV, NS rooms, fax service, room service, no pets, laundry service, meeting facilities, senior rates, CC. SGL/DBL$60-$75.

Motel 6 (1885 15th Place, Northwest, 98027; 392-8405, 505-891-6161) 103 rooms, pool, free local calls, children under 17 free with parents, NS rooms, wheelchair access, pets OK, a/c, TV, CC. SGL/DBL$30-$36.

Wildflower Inn (25237 Southeast Fall City Rd. 98027; 392-1196) 4 rooms, free breakfast, TV, a/c, no pets, CC. SGL/DBL$45-$90.

Kelso
Area Code 206

Comfort Inn   (440 Three Rivers Dr. 98626; 425-4600, 800-228-5150) 57 rooms, indoor heated pool, whirlpools, sauna, a/c, TV, wheelchair access, no pets, CC. SGL/DBL$44-$78.

Kelso Inn Motel (505 North Pacific, 98626; 636-4610) 51 rooms, pets OK, a/c, TV, children free with parents, CC. SGL/DBL$30-$44.

Motel 6 (106 Minor Rd. 98626; 425-3229, 505-891-6161) 63 rooms, pool, free local calls, children under 17 free with parents, NS rooms, wheelchair access, pets OK, a/c, TV, CC. SGL/DBL$30-$36.

Red Lion Inn (510 Kelso Dr. 98626; 636-4000, Fax 425-3296, 800-547-8010) 163 rooms, restaurant, lounge, entertainment, pool, a/c, TV, wheelchair access, NS rooms, complimentary newspaper, fax service, pets OK, laundry facilities, meeting facilities, senior rates, CC. SGL/DBL$85-$100.

Kennewick
Area Code 509

Cavanaugh's (1101 North Columbia Center Blvd. 99336; 783-0611, Fax 735-3087, 800-843-4667) 162 rooms and suites, restaurant, lounge, entertainment, outdoor pool, whirlpools, a/c, TV, wheelchair access, NS rooms, room service, local transportation, pets OK, meeting facilities, senior rates, CC. SGL/DBL$65-$275.

Nendels Inn (2811 West 2nd, 99336; 800-547-0106) 104 rooms, pool, a/c, TV, children under 17 free with parents, no pets, in-room refrigerators, senior rates, CC. SGL/DBL$43-$55.

Quality Inn (Kennewick 99336; 586-0541, 800-221-2222) 152 rooms and suites, restaurant, outdoor heated pool, whirlpools, exercise facilities, children free with parents, a/c, airport transportation, TV, wheelchair access, room service, laundry service, NS rooms, meeting facilities, senior rates, CC. SGL/DBL$58-$68.

Shaniko Inn (321 North Johnson St. 99336; 735-6385, Fax 736-6631) 47 rooms, outdoor heated pool, laundry facilities, pets OK, children free with parents, a/c, TV, wheelchair access, NS rooms, senior rates, CC. SGL/DBL$45-$55.

Silver Cloud Inn (7901 West Quinault Ave. 99336; 735-6100) 125 rooms and suites, restaurant, free breakfast, indoor and outdoor pools, exercise center, whirlpools, a/c, TV, laundry facilities, local transportation, in-room refrigerators and microwaves, no pets, wheelchair access, NS rooms, senior rates, CC. SGL/DBL$45-$58.

Tapadera Budget Inn (300 North Ely, 99336; 783-6191) 61 rooms, outdoor heated pool, laundry facilities, TV, a/c, in-room refrigerators, VCRs, childen free with parents, pets OK, senior rates, CC. SGL/DBL$35-$60.

Kent
Area Code 206

Best Inn Motel (23408 30th Ave. South, 98032; 870-6280) 27 rooms, laundry service, a/c, in-room refrigerators and microwaves, children free with parents, laundry facilities, pets OK, TV, CC. SGL$35, DBL$45.

Best Western Choice Lodge (24415 Russell Rd. 98032; 854-8767, Fax 850-7667, 800-835-3338) 75 rooms and suites, restaurant, lounge, free breakfast, exercise center, sauna, jacuzzi, local transportation, a/c, laundry facilities, wheelchair access, TV, CC. SGL$60, DBL$70, STS$60-$75.

Best Western Home Court All-Suite Hotel (6329 South 212th, 98031; 395-3800, 800-528-1234) suites, pool, children free with parents, a/c, NS rooms, TV, laundry facilities, wheelchair access, pets OK, meeting facilities, senior rates, CC. SGL/DBL$55-$70.

Best Western Pony Soldier Inn (1233 North Central, 98032; 852-7224, 800-634-7669, 800-528-1234) 86 rooms, outdoor heated pool, whirlpools, in-room computer hookups, children free with parents, a/c, NS rooms, TV, laundry facilities, wheelchair access, in-room refrigerators, pets OK, meeting facilities, senior rates, CC. SGL/DBL$65-$80.

Century Motel (23421 Military Rd. South, 98032; 878-1840) a/c, TV, no pets, CC. SGL/DBL$28-$38.

Cypress Inn (Hwy. 167, Kent 98032; 395-0219, Fax 395117, 800-752-9991) 122 rooms and suites, restaurant, lounge, free breakfast, outdoor heated pool, jacuzzi, spa, airport courtesy car, no pets, in-room coffee makers, laundry service, meeting facilities for 200, a/c, TV, CC. SGL$67-$77, DBL$74-$84.

Days Inn (1711 West Meeker St. 98032; 854-1950, Fax 859-1018; 800-325-2525) 78 rooms, free breakfast, heated outdoor pool, children free with parents, pets OK, laundry service, free local calls, a/c, in-room refrigerators, TV, wheelchair access, NS rooms, airport transportation, CC. SGL$40-$50, DBL$50-$60, STS$65-$75, X$5.

Golden Kent Motel (22203 84th Ave. 98032; 872-8372) a/c, TV, no pets, CC. SGL/DBL$44-$54.

Kent Valley Motel (743 North Central, 98032; 852-1997) a/c, TV, no pets, CC. SGL/DBL$46-$48.

Seaview Motel (25218 Pacific Hwy. South, 98032; 830-5929) a/c, TV, no pets, CC. SGL/DBL$39-$43.

Sunset Motel (25006 Pacific Hwy. South, 98032; 839-6659) a/c, TV, no pets, CC. SGL/DBL$60-$70.

Val-U-Inn (22420 84th St. South, Kent 98032; 872-5525, Fax 872-5458, 800-437-7777) 92 rooms and suites, restaurant, free breakfast, laundry service, wheelchair access, airport transportation, in-room refrigerators, children free with parents, pets OK, NS rooms, meeting facilities, a/c, TV, CC. SGL/DBL$50-$70.

Kennewick

Area Code 509

Comfort Inn (7913 West Quinault Ave. 99336; 800-228-5150) 50 rooms, indoor heated pool, sauna, a/c, TV, wheelchair access, no pets, CC. SGL/DBL$48-$75.

Quality Inn on Clover Island (435 Clover Island, 99336; 586-0541, 800-221-2222) 86 rooms and suites, restaurant, lounge, pool, exercise center, whirlpools, sauna, no pets, children free with parents, a/c, TV, wheelchair access, room service, laundry service, NS rooms, meeting facilities, senior rates, CC. SGL/DBL$56-$69.

Kirkland

Area Code 206

Best Western Arnold's Inn (12223 Northeast 116th, 98034; 822-2300, 800-332-4200, 800-528-1234) 110 rooms, free breakfast, outdoor heated pool, whirlpools, children free with parents, a/c, NS rooms, kitchenettes, airport transportation, TV, laundry facilities, wheelchair access, in-room refrigerators and microwaves, pets OK, meeting facilities for 200, senior rates, CC. SGL/DBL$56-$81.

Clarion Hotel (12233 Northeast Totem Lake Way, 98034; 821-2202, 800-221-2222) 59 rooms and suites, heated pool, whirlpools, sauna, exercise center, no pets, NS rooms, children under 18 free with parents, in-room refrigerators, senior rates, meeting facilities, a/c, TV, CC. SGL/DBL$65-$70.

La Quinta Inn (10530 Northeast Northrup Way, 98033; 828-6585, 800-531-5900) restaurant, free breakfast, lounge, pool, complimentary newspaper, free local calls, fax service, laundry service, NS rooms, wheelchair access, remote control TV, a/c, meeting facilities, senior rates, all CC. SGL/DBL$55-$68.

Motel 6 (12010 120th Place, Northeast, 98033; 821-5618, 505-891-6161) 123 rooms, pool, free local calls, children under 17 free with parents, NS rooms, wheelchair access, pets OK, a/c, TV, CC. SGL/DBL$30-$36.

Shumway Mansion (11410 99th Place, 98033; 823-2303) 7 rooms and suites, free breakfast, TV, children over 12 welcome, antique furnishings, NS, a/c, no pets, CC. SGL/DBL$65-$95.

Silver Cloud Inn (12202 Northeast 124th St. 98034; 821-8300) 99 rooms, outdoor heated pool, whirlpools, exercise center, in-room refrigerators, microwaves and coffee makers, a/c, TV, no pets, children free with parents, CC. SGL/DBL$50-$60.

The Woodmark Hotel at Carillon Point (1200 Carillon Point, 98033; 882-3700, 800-822-3700) 100 rooms and suites, restaurant, lounge, entertainment, exercise center, in-room refrigerators and coffee makers, local transportation, airport transportation, complimentary newspaper, water view, a/c, TV, no pets, children free with parents, meeting facilities, senior rates, CC. SGL/DBL$140-$175, STS$150-$900.

Yarrow Bay Suites (4311 Lake Washington Blvd. Northeast, 98033; 827-4605) suites, pool, sauna, jacuzzi, lighted tennis courts, kitchenettes, fireplaces, a/c, TV, no pets, CC. SGL/DBL$55-$65.

Lacey
Area Code 206

Comfort Inn (4700 Park Center Ave. Northeast, 98503; 456-6300, 800-228-5150) 69 rooms, indoor heated pool, exercise center, whirlpools, a/c, TV, wheelchair access, no pets, CC. SGL/DBL$58-$75.

LaConner
Area Code 206

Country Inn (LaConner 98257; 466-3101, Fax 466-5902) 28 rooms, restaurant, free breakfast, room service, antique furnishings, fireplaces, children free with parents, no pets, TV, wheelchair access, NS rooms, senior rates, CC. SGL/DBL$75-$100.

The Downy House (1880 Chilberg Rd. 98257; 466-3207) 5 rooms, free breakfast, whirlpools, no pets, antique furnishings, NS, CC. SGL/DBL$75-$100.

Heather House (505 Maple St. 98257; 466-4675) 3 rooms, free breakfast, children free with parents, NS, TV, no pets, CC. SGL/DBL$55-$75.

The Heron Inn (117 Maple Ave. 98257; 466-4626) 112 rooms and suites, free breakfast, whirlpools, no pets, fireplaces, NS, TV, CC. SGL/DBL$70-$120.

Katy's Inn (503 South 3rd St. 98257; 466-3366) 4 rooms, free breakfast, TV, 1870s inn, NS, no children, CC. SGL/DBL$60-$90.

LaConner Channel Lodge (205 North 1st St. 98257; 466-1500, Fax 466-1525) 41 rooms, TV, NS rooms, children free with parents, no pets, water view, CC. SGL/DBL$130-$200.

LaConner Country Inn (107 South 2nd St. 98257; 466-3101) 28 rooms and 2-bedroom suites, restaurant, lounge, fireplaces, pets OK, children free with parents, TV, CC. SGL/DBL$80-$122.

Planter Hotel (715 1st St. 98257; 466-4710) 12 rooms, whirlpools, no pets, TV, CC. SGL/DBL$70-$110.

Rainbow Inn (1075 Chilberg Rd. 98257; 466-4587) 8 rooms, free breakfast, NS, a/c, TV, wheelchair access, children over 12 welcome, local transportation, senior rates, CC. SGL/DBL$65-$95.

The Wild Iris (121 Maple Ave. 98257; 466-1400) 20 roms, TV, in-room coffee makers, CC. SGL/DBL$65-$100.

Langley
Area Code 206

Blue House Inn (513 Anthes, 98260; 221-8392) free breakfast, TV, a/c, no pets, CC. SGL/DBL$35-$55.

Christy's Country Inn (2891 East Meinhold Rd. 98260; 321-1815) free breakfast, private baths, TV, a/c, no pets, CC. SGL/DBL$33-$38.

Drake's Landing Lodging (203 Wharf St. 98260; 221-3999) TV, CC. SGL/DBL$60-$75.

Eagles Nest Inn (3236 East Saratoga Rd. 98260; 321-5331) 4 rooms, free breakfast, spa, private baths, no pets, TV, CC. SGL/DBL$85-$115.

Idle Time Motel (2479 Hwy. 525, 98260; 321-5521) rooms and efficiencies, a/c, kitchenettes, TV, CC. SGL/DBL$35-$60.

The Inn at Langley (400 1st St. 98260; 221-3033) 24 rooms, whirlpools, no pets, NS rooms, VCRs, TV, CC. SGL/DBL$160-$185.

Log Castle Bed and Breakfast (3273 East Saratoga Rd. 98260; 321-5483) free breakfast, TV, a/c, no pets, no children, fireplaces, private bath, NS, CC. SGL/DBL$65-$100.

Maple Tree Guest House (2850 Meinhold Rd. 98260; 221-2434) rooms and suites, free breakfast, TV, a/c, no pets, CC. SGL/DBL$65-$80.

Strawbridge Lodge (4667 Strawbridge Lane, 98260; 321-6567) free breakfast, TV, a/c, no pets, CC. SGL/DBL$35-$45.

The Whidby Inn (106 1st St. 98260; 221-7115) rooms, free breakfast, TV, a/c, no pets, private baths, fireplaces, CC. SGL/DBL$60-$80.

Leavenworth
Area Code 509

All Seasons River Inn (8751 Icicle Rd. 98826; 548-1425) 5 rooms, free breakfast, children free with parents, NS, a/c, no pets, CC. SGL/DBL$75-$125.

Alpen Inn (405 West Hwy. 2, 98826; 548-4326) 40 rooms, outdoor heated pool, whirlpools, in-room refrigerators and microwaves, children free with parents, no pets, a/c, TV, wheelchair access, NS rooms, senior rates, CC. SGL/DBL$55-$68.

Bayern on the River (1505 Alpen See Strasse, 98826; 548-5875) 26 rooms, outdoor heated pool, whirlpools, kitchenettes, TV, a/c, pets OK, CC. SGL/DBL$50-$80.

Best Western Icicle Inn (505 Hwy. 2 West, 98826; 548-7000, Fax 548-7050, 800-528-1234) 66 rooms and suites, free breakfast, pool, exercise center, whirlpools, in-room refrigerators, no pets, children free with parents, a/c, NS rooms, TV, laundry facilities, wheelchair access, meeting facilities, senior rates, CC. SGL/DBL$50-$95.

Bosch Garten (9846 Dye Rd. 98826; 548-6900) 3 rooms, free breakfast, whirlpools, NS, children free with parents, TV, a/c, no pets, CC. SGL/DBL$70-$80.

Canyons Inn (185 Hwy. 2, 98826; 548-7992) 32 rooms and 2-bedroom efficiencies, indoor heated pool, whirlpools, children free with parents, pets OK, kitchenettes, CC, TV, a/c, CC. SGL/DBL$55-$70.

Der Ritterhof (190 Hwy. 2, 98826; 548-5854, 800-255-5845) 51 rooms, restaurant, outdoor heated pool, whirlpools, pets OK, a/c, TV, wheelchair access, NS rooms, senior rates, CC. SGL/DBL$65-$70.

Ennzian Motor Inn (590 Hwy. 2, 98826; 548-5269, 800-223-8511) 104 rooms, free breakfast, indoor and outdoor pool, whirlpools, exercise center, no pets, fireplaces, children free with parents, a/c, TV, wheelchair access, NS rooms, senior rates, meeting facilities, CC. SGL/DBL$75-$100.

The Evergreen Inn (1117 Front St. 98826; 548-5515) 41 rooms and 2-bedroom suites, whirlpools, a/c, TV, pets OK, in-room refrigerators and coffee makers, meeting facilities, CC. SGL/DBL$40-$120.

Haus Rohrbach Pension (12882 Ranger Rd. 98826; 548-7024) 15 rooms and suites, free breakfast, pool, whirlpools, a/c, TV, wheelchair access, no pets, local transportation, NS, senior rates, CC. SGL/DBL$65-$160.

Linderhof Motor Inn (690 Hwy. 2, 98826; 548-5283) 26 rooms, outdoor pool, whirlpools, a/c, TV, children free with parents, no pets, kitchenettes, CC. SGL/DBL$59-$75.

Obertal Motor Inn (922 Commercial St. 98826; 548-5204) 25 rooms, whirlpools, in-room refrigerators and coffee makers, children free with parents, pets OK, fireplaces, a/c, TV, wheelchair access, NS rooms, meeting facilities, senior rates, CC. SGL/DBL$60-$99.

Pine River Ranch (19668 Hwy. 207, 98826; 763-3959) 4 rooms, free breakfast, TV, a/c, NS, no pets, CC. SGL/DBL$80-$125.

Rivers Edge Motel (8401 Hwy. 2, 98826; 548-7612) 23 rooms, outdoor heated pool, whirlpools, water view, a/c, NS rooms, TV, pets OK, kitchenettes, CC. SGL/DBL$35-$70.

Run of the River Bed and Breakfast (9308 East Leavenwoth Rd. 98826; 548-7171, 800-288-6491) 5 rooms, free breakfast, TV, NS, no children, no private baths, a/c, no pets, senior rates, CC. SGL/DBL$80-$135.

Tyrolean Ritz Hotel (633 Front St. 98826; 548-5455) 16 rooms, whirlpools, a/c, TV, no pets, in-room refrigerators and coffee makers, children free with parents, CC. SGL/DBL$40-$110.

Long Beach
Area Code 206

Anchorage Motor Court (Long Beach 98361; 642-2351) 9 rooms and efficiencies, TV, kitchenettes, pets OK, water view, CC. SGL/DBL$60-$98.

Breakers Motel (Long Beach 98361; 642-4414, 800-288-8890) 114 rooms, outdoor heated pool, whirlpools, TV, wheelchair access, pets OK, in-room refrigerators, NS rooms, meeting facilities, senior rates, CC. SGL/DBL$55-$155.

Nendels Inn (409 10th St. Southwest, 98361; 642-2311, 800-547-0106) 84 rooms, pets OK, in-room refrigerators, microwaves and coffee makers, TV, children under 17 free with parents, senior rates, CC. SGL/DBL$55-$85.

Our Place at the Beach (1309 South Blvd. 98361; 642-3793, 800-538-5107) 25 rooms, exercise center, sauna, whirlpools, a/c, TV, wheelchair access, NS rooms, in-room coffee makers, kitchenettes, pets OK, in-room refrigerators, senior rates, CC. SGL/DBL$40-$70.

Scandinavian Gardens Inn (1610 California St. 98361; 642-8877) 5 rooms and suites, free breakfast, whirlpools, sauna, TV, NS, no pets, game room, in-room refrigerators, senior rates, CC. SGL/DBL$55-$105.

Shaman Motel (Long Beach 98361; 642-3714, 800-753-3750) 40 rooms and efficiencies, restaurant, outdoor heated pool, TV, NS rooms, pets OK, in-room refrigerators, ktichenettes, senior rates, CC. SGL/DBL$50-$66.

Super 8 Motel (500 Ocean Beach Blvd. 98631; 642-8988, Fax 642-8986, 800-800-8000) 51 rooms and suites, no pets, children under 12 free with parents, free local calls, a/c, TV, in-room refrigerators and microwaves, fax service, NS rooms, wheelchair access, laundry facilities, VCRs, no pets, meeting facilities, senior rates, CC. SGL/DBL$44-$70.

Lopez Island
Area Code 206

The Inn at Swifts Bay (Lopez Island 98261; 5 rooms, free breakfast, whirlpools, shared baths, no children, NS, no pets, local transportation, CC. SGL/DBL$75-$140.

Lynnwood
Area Code 206

Best Western Landmark Inn and Convention Center (4300 100th St. Southwest, 98063; 775-7447, Fax 775-8093, 800-528-1234) 102 rooms, restaurant, lounge, entertainment, indoor heated pool, children free with parents, a/c, NS rooms, TV, laundry facilities, wheelchair access, pets OK, meeting facilities for 1,000, senior rates, CC. SGL/DBL$55-$75.

Embassy Suites (20610 44th Ave. 98036; 775-2500, Fax 774-0485, 800-EM-BASSY) 145 2-room suites, restaurant, lounge, entertainment, free breakfast, pool, sauna, whirlpools, exercise center. SGL/DBL$85-$105.

Holiday Inn (4117 196th St. Southwest, 98036; 775-8030, Fax 774-0344, 800-HOLIDAY) 46 rooms, restaurant, lounge, spa, airport transportation, in-room refrigerators and microwaves, children under 19 free with parents, wheelchair access, a/c, TV, NS rooms, fax service, room service, no pets, laundry service, meeting facilities, senior rates, CC. SGL/DBL$40-$60.

Hotel International (5621 196th St. Southwest, 98036; 771-1777, Fax 776-8520) 51 rooms, restaurant, lounge, entertainment, whirlpools, laundry service, in-room refrigerators and microwaves, children free with parents, pets OK, a/c, TV, wheelchair access, NS rooms, senior rates, meeting facilities, CC. SGL/DBL$45-$57.

Residence Inn North by Marriott (18200 Alderwood Mall Blvd. 98037; 771-1100, Fax 771-6602, 800-331-3131) 120 rooms and 2-bedroom suites, free breakfast, in-room refrigerators, coffee makers and microwaves, laundry facilities, TV, a/c, VCRs, pets OK, complimentary newspaper, fireplaces, children free with parents, NS rooms, wheelchair access, meeting facilities, CC. SGL/DBL$85-$160.

Silver Cloud Inn (19332 36th Ave. West, 98036; 775-7600) 168 rooms, outdoor heated pool, exercise center, laundry service, airport transportation, children free with parents, no pets, in-room refrigerators and microwaves, a/c, TV, wheelchair access, NS rooms, senior rates, CC. SGL/DBL$45-$60.

Manson
Area Code 509

Mountain View Lodge (25 Wapato Point Parkway, 98831; 687-9505) 30 rooms and 2-bedroom efficiencies, outdoor heated pool, whirlpool tubs, in-room refrigerators, no pets, a/c, TV, wheelchair access, NS rooms, senior rates, CC. SGL/DBL$40-$80.

Maple Valley
Area Code 206

Maple Valley Bed and Breakfast (20020 Southeast 228th, 98038; 432-1409) free breakfast, TV, a/c, no pets, CC. SGL/DBL$35-$40.

Marysville
Area Code 201

Best Western Inn (6128 Marine Dr. 98270; 659-4488, Fax 659-5688, 800-528-1234) 69 rooms, restaurant, lounge, indoor heated pool, whirlpools, in-room refrigerators, no pets, children under 18 free with parents, airport transportation, a/c, NS rooms, TV, laundry facilities, wheelchair access, meeting facilities, senior rates, CC. SGL/DBL$60-$75.

Village Motor Inn (235 Beech St. 98270; 659-0005, Fax 658-0866) 45 rooms and suites, free breakfast, restaurant, whirlpools, pets OK, in-room refrigerators, a/c, TV, wheelchair access, NS rooms, children free with parents, meeting facilities, senior rates, CC. SGL/DBL$45-$66.

Mercer Island
Area Code 206

The Deauville Apartments (2760 76th Ave. Southeast, 98040; 236-5911) 1- and 2-bedroom apartments, a/c, TV, kitchenettes, no pets, CC. SGL/DBL$50-$70.

Faye's Bed and Breakfast (Mercer Island, 98040; 236-2828) free breakfast, TV, a/c, no pets, CC. SGL/DBL$65-$85.

Mercer Island Hideaway (Mercer Island 98040; 236-1092) free breakfast, TV, a/c, no pets, CC. SGL/DBL$37-$47.

Mole House Bed and Breakfast (Mercer Island 98040; 232-1611) free breakfast, TV, a/c, no pets, CC. SGL/DBL$26-$30.

TraveLodge (7645 Sunset Hwy. 98040; 232-8000, 800-578-7878) 35 rooms, restaurant, lounge, free breakfast, whirlpools, wheelchair access, complimentary newspaper, laundry service, TV, a/c, free local calls, fax service, NS rooms, in-room refrigerators and microwaves, children under 18 free with parents, no pets, meeting facilities, senior rates, CC. SGL/DBL$45-$60.

Moses Lake
Area Code 509

Best Western Hallmark Inn (3000 Marina Dr. 98837; 765-9211, Fax 766-0493, 800-528-1234) 160 rooms and suites, restaurant, outdoor pool, children free with parents, a/c, NS rooms, TV, laundry facilities, no pets, wheelchair access, room service, meeting facilities, senior rates, CC. SGL/DBL$60-$90, STS$100-$125.

El Ranch Motel (1214 South Pioneer Way, 98837; 765-9173, 800-341-8000) 21 rooms and efficiencies, outdoor heated pool, no pets, in-room refrigerators, a/c, TV, wheelchair access, NS rooms, senior rates, CC. SGL/DBL$28-$45.

Interstate Inn (2801 West Broadway, 98837; 765-1777, Fax 766-9452) 30 rooms, restaurant, indoor heated pool, sauna, whirlpools, pets OK, in-room refrigerators, a/c, TV, wheelchair access, NS rooms, senior rates, CC. SGL/DBL$35-$50.

Motel 6 (2822 Wapato Dr. 98837; 766-0250, 505-891-6161) 111 rooms, pool, free local calls, children under 17 free with parents, NS rooms, wheelchair access, pets OK, a/c, TV, CC. SGL/DBL$25-$32.

Shilo Inn (1819 East Kittleson Rd. 98837; 765-9317, Fax 765-5058, 800-222-2244) 100 rooms and efficiencies, restaurant, lounge, airport courtesy car, in-room refrigerators, a/c, TV, no pets, NS rooms, wheelchair access, children under 12 free with parents, meeting facilities, senior rates, CC. SGL/DBL$65-$85.

TraveLodge (316 South Pioneer Way, 98837; 765-8631, Fax 765-3685, 800-578-7878) 39 rooms, outdoor heated pool, wheelchair access, complimentary newspaper, laundry service, TV, a/c, free local calls, fax service, NS rooms, in-room refrigerators and microwaves, children under 18 free with parents, no pets, meeting facilities, senior rates, CC. SGL/DBL$46-$60.

Mount Vernon

Area Code 206

Best Western Motor Inn (300 West College Way, 98273; 424-4287, Fax 424-6036, 800-528-1234) 66 rooms and suites, restaurant, lounge, outdoor pool, whirlpools, children free with parents, a/c, NS rooms, TV, laundry facilities, wheelchair access, pets OK, meeting facilities, senior rates, CC. SGL/DBL$45-$75.

Best Western Cottontree Inn and Convention Center (2300 Market Place, 98273; 428-5678, 800-528-1234, 800-528-1234) 120 rooms, pool, children free with parents, a/c, NS rooms, TV, laundry facilities, airport transportation, wheelchair access, pets OK, meeting facilities, senior rates, CC. SGL/DBL$60-$69.

Days Inn (2009 Riverside Dr. 98273; 424-4141, Fax 428-8661, 800-325-2525) 86 rooms and suites, restaurant, lounge, outdoor pool, pets OK, room service, a/c, TV, wheelchair access, NS rooms, laundry facilities, senior rates, meeting facilities for 200, CC. SGL/DBL$45-$65, STS$75-$168.

Fulton House (420 Fulton, 98273; 336-2952) 3 rooms, free breakfast, outdoor pool, private baths, no pets, CC. SGL/DBL$70-$85.

Ridgeway Bed and Breakfast (1292 McLean Rd. 98273; 428-8086) 5 rooms, free breakfast, no pets, NS, CC. SGL/DBL$70-$90.

TraveLodge (1910 Freeway Dr. 98273; 428-7020, Fax 428-7838, 800-578-7878) 70 rooms, free breakfast, indoor heated pool, whirlpools, pets OK, wheelchair access, complimentary newspaper, laundry service, TV, a/c, free local calls, fax service, NS rooms, in-room refrigerators and microwaves, children under 18 free with parents, meeting facilities, senior rates, CC. SGL/DBL$44-$75.

Whispering Firs Bed and Breakfast (1957 Kanako Lane, 98273; 428-1990) free breakfast, TV, hot tub, NS, private baths, a/c, no pets, CC. SGL/DBL$70-$90.

The White Swan Guest House (1388 Moore Rd. 98273; 445-6805) 3 rooms and cottages, 1890s inn, free breakfast, TV, a/c, no pets, shared baths, NS, CC. SGL/DBL$70-$165.

North Bend

Area Code 206

Edgewick Inn (14600 468th Ave. Southeast, 98045; 888-9000) a/c, TV, no pets, CC. SGL/DBL$35-$45.

Goldmyer Hotsprings (210 East North Bend Way, 98045; 888-4653) a/c, TV, no pets, CC. SGL/DBL$28-$48.

North Bend Motel (322 East North Bend Way, 98045; 888-1121) a/c, TV, no pets, CC. SGL/DBL$36-$46.

Sunset Motel (227 West North Bend Way, 98045; 888-0381) a/c, TV, no pets, CC. SGL/DBL$55-$58.

Oak Harbor

Area Code 206

Acorn Motor Inn (Hwy. 20, 98277; 675-6646) free breakfast, in-room refrigerators, a/c, TV, CC. SGL/DBL$65-$90.

Auld Holland Inn (5861 Hwy. 20, 98277; 675-2288, 800-228-0148) 34 rooms and suites, restaurant, lounge, free breakfast, outdoor heated pool, spa, exercise center, tennis courts, kitchenettes, a/c, TV, no pets, wheelchair access, in-room refrigerators, laundry facilities, NS rooms, senior rates, CC. SGL/DBL$55-$135.

Best Western Harbor Plaza (5691 Hwy. 20, 98277; 679-4567, Fax 675-2543, 800-528-1234) 80 rooms, restaurant, free breakfast, lounge, heated pool, exercise center, hot tub, children free with parents, a/c, NS rooms, in-room refrigerators and microwaves, room service, TV, laundry facilities, wheelchair access, pets OK, meeting facilities, senior rates, CC. SGL/DBL$65-$100.

Coachman Inn (5563 Hwy. 20, 98277; 675-0727, 800-635-0043) 102 rooms and suites, restaurant, free breakfast, outdoor heated pool, exercise center, whirlpools, a/c, TV, wheelchair access, NS rooms, local transportation, in-room refrigerators, senior rates, CC. SGL/DBL$50-$65.

Harbor Pointe Bed and Breakfast (Oak Harbor 98277; 675-3379) free breakfast, hot tub, exercise center, water view, TV, a/c, no pets, CC. SGL/DBL$50-$55.

Queen Ann Motel (1204 West Pioneer Way, 98277; 675-2209) 21 rooms, restaurant, lounge, indoor heated pool, spa, children free with parents, kitchenettes, a/c, TV, in-room refrigerators, no pets, CC. SGL/DBL$42-$55.

Ocean Shores

Area Code 206

Canterbury Inn (Ocean Shores Blvd. 98569; 289-3317, 800-562-6678) 43 efficiencies, restaurant, indoor heated pool, whirlpools, fireplaces, no pets, TV, NS rooms, senior rates, CC. SGL/DBL$75-$160.

Discovery Inn (1031 Discovery Ave. Southeast, 98569; 289-3371, 800-882-8821) 22 rooms and efficiencies, outdoor pool, whirlpools, children free with parents, kitchenettes, in-room refrigerators, no pets, NS rooms, TV, senior rates, CC. SGL/DBL$52-$80.

Gitche Gumee Motel (648 Ocean Shores Blvd. Northwest, 98569; 289-3323) 80 rooms and efficiencies, indoor and outdoor heated pool, sauna, in-room refrigerators and coffee makers, a/c, TV, wheelchair access, NS rooms, kitchenettes, pets OK, children free with parents, senior rates, CC. SGL/DBL$35-$75.

Grey Gull Inn (Ocean Shores Blvd. 98569; 289-3381, 800-562-9712 in Washington) 36 efficiencies, outdoor heated pool, whirlpools, sauna, NS rooms, TV, in-room refrigerators, senior rates, CC. SGL/DBL$75-$150.

Lighthouse Suites Inn (491 Damon Rd. Northwest 98569; 289-2311) 76 rooms, indoor heated pool, exercise center, whirlpools, in-room refrigerators and microwaves, no pets, laundry facilities, NS rooms, TV, CC. SGL/DBL$85-$158.

Polynesian Motel and Condominiums Resort (Ocean Shores Blvd. 98569; 289-3361, Fax 289-0294, 800-562-4836) 72 rooms and condominiums, restaurant, indoor heated pool, sauna, whirlpool tub, TV, NS rooms, in-room refrigerators, VCRs, laundry facilities, children free with parents, senior rates, CC. SGL/DBL$45-$160.

Olympia
Area Code 206

Best Western Inn (900 Capitol Way, 98501; 352-7200, Fax 352-0846, 800-367-7771, 800-528-1234) 100 rooms, restaurant, lounge, heated pool, children free with parents, a/c, NS rooms, TV, laundry facilities, wheelchair access, pets OK, meeting facilities, senior rates, CC. SGL/DBL$55-$70.

Capital Inn Motel (120 College St. Southeast, 98503; 493-1991) 83 rooms and efficiencies, exercise center, whirlpools, sauna, laundry facilities, in-room refrigerators and microwaves, children free with parents, pets OK, a/c, TV, wheelchair access, NS rooms, senior rates, meeting facilities, CC. SGL/DBL$50-$63.

Carriage Inn (1211 South Quince, 98501; 943-4710) 62 rooms, free breakfast, restaurant, outdoor heated pool, in-room refrigerators, children free with parents, no pets, airport transportation, TV, NS rooms, CC. SGL/DBL$40-$50.

Cinnamon Rabbit Bed and Breakfast (1304 7th Ave. West, 98502; 357-5520) free breakfast, TV, hot tub, NS, private baths, a/c, no pets. SGL/DBL$55-$68.

Golden Gavel Motor Hotel (909 Capitol Way, 98501; 352-8533) 27 rooms and efficiencies, TV, no pets, CC. SGL/DBL$30-$44.

Harbinger Inn (1136 East Bay Dr. 98506; 754-0389) 4 rooms, free breakfast, TV, no pets, NS, CC. SGL/DBL$50-$85.

Quality Inn Westwater (2300 Evergreen Park Dr. 98502; 943-4000, 800-221-2222) 191 rooms and suites, restaurant, pool, exercise center, no pets, children free with parents, a/c, TV, wheelchair access, room service, laundry service, NS rooms, meeting facilities, senior rates, CC. SGL/DBL$65-$125.

Ramada Inn (621 South Capital Way, 98501; 352-7700, 800-2-RAMADA) 121 rooms and suites, restaurant, lounge, outdoor heated pool, wheelchair access, NS rooms, pets OK, a/c, TV, children under 18 free with parents, in-room refrigerators, local transportation, room service, laundry facilities, meeting facilities, senior rates, CC. SGL/DBL$75-$105.

Tyee Hotel (500 Tyee Dr. 98502; 352-0511, Fax 943-6448, 800-648-6440) 146 rooms, restaurant, lounge, entertainment, outdoor heated pool, room service, no pets, a/c, TV, children free with parents, rooms service, in-room refrigerators, wheelchair access, NS rooms, senior rates, CC. SGL/DBL$70-$88.

Nicholas Motel (Omak 98841; 826-4611) 21 rooms and efficiencies, a/c, TV, wheelchair access, NS rooms, in-room refrigerators and coffee makers, senior rates, CC. SGL/DBL$35-$45.

Orcas
Area Code 206

Orcas Hotel (Orcas 98280; 376-4300) 12 rooms, free breakfast, restaurant, lounge, NS, children over 12 welcome and free with parents, no pets, TV, no pets, CC. SGL/DBL$65-$170.

Pasco
Area Code 509

Hallmark Motel (720 West Lewis St. 99301; 547-7766) 54 rooms, outdoor heated pool, kitchenettes, children free with parents, a/c, TV, wheelchair access, pets OK, in-room refrigerators, NS rooms, senior rates, CC. SGL/DBL$28-$38.

Motel 6 (1520 North Oregon St. 99301; 546-2010, 505-891-6161) 106 rooms, pool, free local calls, children under 17 free with parents, NS rooms, wheelchair access, pets OK, a/c, TV, CC. SGL/DBL$30-$36.

Red Lion Inn (2525 North 20th Ave. 99301; 547-0701, 800-547-8010) 279 rooms, restaurant, lounge, entertainment, heated pool, whirlpools, exercise center, a/c, TV, wheelchair access, NS rooms, children free with parents, complimentary newspaper, in-room refrigerators, airport transportation, fax service, laundry facilities, meeting facilities, senior rates, CC. SGL/DBL$77-$97.

Starlite Motel (2634 North 4th Ave. 99301; 547-7531) 19 rooms, kitchenettes, pets OK, a/c, TV, in-room refrigerators, CC. SGL/DBL$26-$36.

Val-U-Inn (1800 West Lewis St. 99301; 547-0791) 165 rooms and suites, indoor heated pool, a/c, TV, VCRs, in-room refrigerators and coffee makers, children free with parents, pets OK, meeting facilities, senior rates, CC. SGL/DBL$40-$55.

Port Angeles

Area Code 206

Aggies Inn (602 East Front St. 98362; 457-0471, Fax 452-1752) 114 rooms, restaurant, lounge, indoor heated pool, sauna, TV, pets OK, local transportation, meeting facilities, senior rates, CC. SGL/DBL$45-$68.

Anniken's Bed and Breakfast (214 Whidbey, 98362; 457-6177) free breakfast, TV, NS, a/c, no pets, CC. SGL/DBL$60.

Bavarian Inn (1126 East 7th St. 98362; 458-4098) 3 rooms, free breakfast, TV, NS, in-room refrigerators, no pets, CC. SGL/DBL$65-$80.

Best Western Olympic Lodge (140 Del Guzzi Dr. 98632; 452-2993, Fax 452-1497, 800-528-1234) 106 rooms, free breakfast, outdoor heated pool, exercise center, children free with parents, a/c, NS rooms, free local calls, fax service, TV, laundry facilities, wheelchair access, pets OK, meeting facilities, senior rates, CC. SGL/DBL$65-$155.

Crescent Bay Inn (3424 Crescent Beach Rd. 98362; 928-3694) 2 rooms, free breakfast, no pets, NS, CC. SGL/DBL$55-$85.

Domaine Madelein (146 Wildflower Lane, 98362; 457-4174) 2 rooms, free breakfast, TV, a/c, no pets, VCRs, water view, NS, senior rates, CC. SGL/DBL$70-$155.

Hill Haus Motel (111 East 2nd St. 98362; 452-9285) 25 rooms and 2-bedroom efficiencies, no pets, TV, water view, NS rooms, CC. SGL/DBL$40-$98.

The Pond Motel (196 Hwy. 101 West, 98362; 452-8422) 10 rooms and efficiencies, TV, no pets, kitchenettes, water view, NS rooms, CC. SGL/DBL$29-$59.

Red Lion Inn (221 North Lincoln St. 98362; 452-9215, Fax 452-4734, 800-547-8010) 187 rooms and efficiencies, restaurant, lounge, entertainment, pool, a/c, TV, wheelchair access, NS rooms, children free with parents, complimentary newspaper, fax service, laundry facilities, meeting facilities, senior rates, CC. SGL/DBL$85-$125.

Royal Victorian Motel (521 East 1st St. 98362; 452-2316, Fax 452-4201) 20 rooms and efficiencies, children free with parents, pets OK, a/c, TV, in-room refrigerators and microwaves, kitchenettes, CC. SGL/DBL$30-$75.

Tudor Inn (1108 South Oak, 98362; 452-3138) 5 rooms, free breakfast, TV, NS, private baths, 1910 home, antique furnishings, fireplaces, a/c, no pets, CC. SGL/DBL$65-$98.

Uptown Motel (101 East 2nd St. 98362; 457-9434, 800-858-3812) 51 rooms, whirlpools, TV, in-room refrigerators, microwaves and coffee makers, CC. SGL/DBL$35-$120.

Port Orchard

Area Code 206

Ogle's Bed and Breakfast (1307 Dogwood Hill, Southwest, 98366) free breakfast, TV, a/c, no pets, water view, NS, no children, shared baths, CC. SGL/DBL$40-$50.

Port Townsend

Area Code 206

Ann Starrett Mansion (744 Clay St. 98368; 385-3205) 10 rooms, free breakfast, NS, no children, private baths, water view, TV, a/c, no pets, CC. SGL/DBL$85-$135.

The Apartment Inn (1208 Franklin St. 98368; 385-6239) 3 rooms and guest house, free breakfast, TV, a/c, no pets, 1870s inn, NS, private baths, water view. SGL/DBL$65-$100.

Bishop Victorian Guest Suites (714 Washington St. 98368; 385-6122, Fax 385-5860) 13 rooms and 2-bedroom efficiencies, kitchenettes, pets OK, NS rooms, children free with parents, CC. SGL/DBL$55-$100.

Harborside Inn (330 Benedict St. 98368; 365-7909) 63 rooms, outdoor heated pool, whirlpools, children free with parents, laundry facilities, in-room refrigerators and microwaves, pets OK, children free with parents, CC. SGL/DBL$45-$95.

Holly Hill House (611 Polk St. 98368; 385-5619, 800-435-1454) 5 rooms and suites, free breakfast, TV, local transportation, antique furnishings, 1870s home, no pets, NS, CC. SGL/DBL$75-$125.

James House (1238 Washington St. 98368; 385-1238) 12 rooms, free breakfast, 1880s home, NS, water view, no pets, CC. SGL/DBL$45-$100.

Lizzie's (731 Pierce St. 98368; 385-4168) 8 rooms, free breakfast, NS, no pets, children over 12 welcome, CC. SGL/DBL$58-$110.

Palace Hotel (1004 Water St. 98368; 385-0773, 800-962-0741) 15 rooms, restaurant, laundry facilities, kitchenettes, no pets, 1880s inn, antique furnishings, CC. SGL/DBL$40-$95.

Ravenscroft (533 Quincy St. 98368; 385-2784, Fax 385-6724) 8 rooms, free breakfast, NS, no pets, CC. SGL/DBL$58-$155.

Rose Cottage (1310 Clay St. 98368; 385-6944) 4 rooms, free breakfast, private baths, no pets, CC. SGL/DBL$70-$95.

Starrett House (744 Clay St. 98368; 385-3205, 800-321-0644) 11 rooms, free breakfast, kitchenettes, local transportation, TV, NS, children over 12 welcome, no pets, antique furnishings, CC. SGL/DBL$70-$185.

Tides Inn (1807 Water St. 98368; 385-0595) 21 rooms, water view, pets OK, in-room refrigerators, TV, VCRs, a/c, CC. SGL/DBL$60-$155.

Trenholm House (2037 Haines, 98368; 385-6059) 5 rooms, free breakfast, TV, a/c, NS, private baths, 1890s home, antique furnishings, water view, no pets, CC. SGL/DBL$70-$110.

Water Street Hotel (635 Water St. 98368; 385-5467) 13 rooms and 2-bedroom efficiencies, children free with parents, kitchenettes, pets OK, TV, NS rooms, CC. SGL/DBL$45-$60.

Pullman

Area Code 509

American Travel Inn (South 515 Grand Ave. 99163; 334-3500) 34 rooms, restaurant, outdoor pool, pets OK, a/c, TV, NS rooms, chidren free with parents, senior rates, CC. SGL/DBL$38-$80.

Holiday Inn (Southeast Bishop Blvd. 99163; 334-4437, Fax 332-6220, 800-HOLIDAY) 84 rooms, restaurant, lounge, indoor heated pool, exercise facilities, sauna, airport transportation, children under 19 free with parents, wheelchair access, a/c, TV, NS rooms, fax service, room service, no pets, laundry service, meeting facilities, senior rates, CC. SGL/DBL$54-$63.

Quality Inn Paradise Creek (1050 Southeast Bishop Blvd. 99163; 332-0500, 800-221-2222) 66 rooms and suites, restaurant, lounge, outdoor heated pool, exercise center, whirlpools, sauna, no pets, children free with parents, a/c, airport transportation, TV, wheelchair access, room service, laundry service, NS rooms, meeting facilities, senior rates, CC. SGL/DBL$60-$150.

Puyallup
Area Code 206

Best Western Inn (9620 South Hill Park Place, 98371; 848-1500, 800-528-1234) 100 rooms, pool, children free with parents, a/c, NS rooms, TV, laundry facilities, wheelchair access, no pets, meeting facilities, senior rates, CC. SGL/DBL$60-$75.

Hart's Tayberry House (7406 80th St. East, 98371; 848-4594) free breakfast, TV, a/c, no pets, NS, private baths, no children, antique furnishings, senior rates. SGL/DBL$50-$70.

Northwest Motor Inn (1409 South Meridian 98371; 841-2600, Fax 841-2600) 51 rooms and efficiencies, whirlpools, in-room refrigerators and microwaves, TV, VCRs, laundry facilities, a/c, children free with parents, pets OK, CC. SGL/DBL$39-$49.

Quinault
Area Code 206

Lake Quinault Lodge (Quinault 98575; 288-2571, Fax 288-2415) 89 rooms and suites, restaurant, lounge, fireplaces, pets OK, in-room refrigerators and coffee makers, water view, children free with parents, NS rooms, CC. SGL/DBL$90-$115.

Redmond
Area Code 206

Bellaire Place (16539 Northeast 39th Court, 98052; 800-523-4356) a/c, TV, CC. SGL/DBL$56-$66.

Best Western Redmond Motor Inn (17601 Redmond Way, 98052; 883-4900, Fax 869-5838, 800-528-1234) 137 rooms, outdoor heated pool, whirlpools, children free with parents, a/c, NS rooms, TV, laundry facilities, wheelchair access, pets OK, meeting facilities, senior rates, CC. SGL/DBL$63-$82.

Cedarym-A-Colonial (1011 240th Ave. Northeast, 98052; 868-4159) free breakfast, TV, a/c, no pets, CC. SGL/DBL$45-$55.

Silver Cloud Inn (15304 Northeast 21st St. 98052; 746-8200) 59 rooms, whirlpools, exercise center, TV, a/c, VCRs, in-room computer hookups, laundry facilities, no pets, CC. SGL/DBL$50-$62.

Renton

Area Code 206

Rental and Reservation Services:

Olympus Properties (2202 Northeast 10th Place, 98056; 226-9042) rental apartments.

Marina Landing (1300 North 20th, 98055; 255-0212, 800-523-4356) rental apartments.

❑❑❑

Don-A-Lisa Motel (111 Meadow Ave. North, 98055; 255-0441) a/c, TV, no pets, CC. SGL/DBL$28-$35.

Foss Shadow Lake Resort (22235 196th Ave. Southeast, 98058; 631-2440) rooms and suites, restaurant, a/c, TV, no pets, CC. SGL/DBL$66-96.

Holiday Inn (800 Ranier Ave. South, 98057; 226-7700, 800-HOLIDAY) restaurant, lounge, pool, exercise facilities, children under 19 free with parents, wheelchair access, a/c, TV, NS rooms, fax service, room service, no pets, laundry service, meeting facilities, senior rates, CC. SGL/DBL$55-$65.

Nendels Valu Inn (3700 East Valley Rd. 98056; 251-9591, 800-547-0106)130 rooms, a/c, TV, children under 17 free with parents, NS rooms, senior rates, CC. SGL/DBL$53-$63.

Renton Silver Cloud Inn (1850 Maple Valley Hwy. 98057; 226-7600, 800-551-7207) 60 rooms, a/c, NS rooms, TV, no pets, CC. SGL/DBL$61-$65.

Travelers Inn (7710 Lake Washington Blvd. Southeast, 98056; 228-2858, 800-633-8300) 119 rooms, outdoor heated pool, wheelchair access, NS rooms, free local calls, children free with parents, no pets, a/c, TV, CC. SGL/DBL$35-$42.

West Wind Motel (110 Ranier South, 98055; 226-5060) a/c, TV, no pets, CC. SGL/DBL$55-$68.

Woodcliffe (1205 Grant Ave. South, 98055; 800-523-4356) a/c, TV, no pets, CC. SGL/DBL$60-$89.

Republic

Area Code 509

Triangle J Ranch (Republic 99166; 775-3933) free breakfast, pool, hot tub, NS, TV, a/c, no pets, CC. SGL/DBL$30-$40.

Richland
Area Code 509

Bali Hi Motel (1201 George Washington Way, 99352; 943-3101, Fax 943-6363) 44 rooms, restaurant, outdoor heated pool, in-room refrigerators and coffee makers, a/c, TV, wheelchair access, NS rooms, senior rates, CC. SGL/DBL$35-$50.

Best Western Towner Inn and Conference Center (1515 George Washington Way, 99352; 946-4121, Fax 946-2222, 800-528-1234) 195 rooms, restaurant, lounge, indoor entertainment, heated pool, children free with parents, a/c, NS rooms, TV, laundry facilities, wheelchair access, pets OK, local transportation, meeting facilities, senior rates, CC. SGL/DBL$62-$90.

Columbia Center Dunes (1751 Fowler Southeast, 99352; 783-8181, Fax 783-2811) 90 rooms, restaurant, outdoor heated pool, sauna, in-room refrigerators and coffee makers, a/c, TV, wheelchair access, NS rooms, no pets, game room, senior rates, CC. SGL/DBL$30-$40.

Econo Lodge Downtown (515 George Washington Way, 99352; 946-6117, 800-4-CHOICE) 40 rooms, outdoor heated pool, children under 12 free with parents, no pets, senior rates, NS rooms, wheelchair access, in-room refrigerators, a/c, TV, senior rates, CC. SGL/DBL$35-$65.

Nendels Inn (615 Jadwin Ave. 99352; 943-4611, 800-547-0106) 98 rooms, free breakfast, outdoor heated pool, kitchenettes, no pets, a/c, TV, children under 17 free with parents, in-room refrigerators, senior rates, CC. SGL/DBL$37-$47.

Red Lion Inn (802 George Washington Way, 99352; 946-7611, Fax 943-8564, 800-547-8010) 150 rooms, restaurant, lounge, entertainment, pool, a/c, TV, wheelchair access, NS rooms, complimentary newspaper, fax service, airport transportation, pets OK, water view, laundry facilities, meeting facilities, senior rates, CC. SGL/DBL$65-$150.

Shilo Inn (50 Comstock St. 99352; 946-4661, Fax 943-6741, 800-222-2244) 150 rooms and suites, restaurant, lounge, outdoor pool, whirlpools, tennis courts, laundry facilities, pets OK, airport courtesy car, in-room refrigerators, a/c, TV, NS rooms, wheelchair access, children under 12 free with parents, meeting facilities, senior rates, CC. SGL/DBL$50-$80.

San Juan Islands
Area Code 206

The Island Lodge (1016 Guard St. 98250; 378-2000, 800-822-4753) 28 rooms, whirlpools, NS rooms, no pets, TV, CC. SGL/DBL$75-$130.

Friday's Inn (35 1st St. 98250; 378-5848, 800-352-2632) 10 rooms, free breakfast, NS, no pets, local transportation, TV, private baths, in-room refrigerators, antique furnishings, CC. SGL/DBL$70-$158.

San Juan Inn (San Juan Islands 98250; 378-2070) 10 rooms, free breakfast, restaurant, NS, no pets, TV, CC. SGL/DBL$75-$100.

Seattle
Area Code 206

Rental and Reservation Services:

Bed and Breakfast Agency (Box 492, Mercer Island, 98040; 206-232-2345) bed and breakfast reservations.

The Hotel Alternative (2453 152nd Ave. Northeast, Redmond, 98052; 800-523-4356) rental 1- , 2- and 3-bedroom condominiums.

Pacific Guest Suites (800-962-6620) rental apartments.

Traveler's Bed and Breakfast Reservation Service (Box 492, Mercer Island 98040; 232-2345).

U.S. Suites (2001 6th Ave. 98121; 800-877-8483) rental suites.

Downtown Seattle

Alexis Hotel (1007 1st Ave. 98104; 624-4844, Fax 621-9009, 800-426-7033) 94 rooms and suites, restaurant, free breakfast, lounge, entertainment, exercise center, tennis courts, no pets, in-room refrigerators, fireplaces, children free with parents, boutiques, complimentary newspaper, 24-hour room service, meeting facilities, a/c, TV, CC. SGL/DBL$150-$190, STS$200-$350.

Aurora Seafair Inn (9100 Aurora Ave. North, 98103; 522-3754, Fax 523-2272) 32 rooms and efficiencies, pets OK, TV, a/c, in-room refrigerators, CC. SGL/DBL$38-$65.

The Baker Guest Apartments (528 15th Ave. East, 98112; 323-5909) 1- and 2-bedroom apartments, a/c, TV, kitchenettes, no pets, senior rates, CC. SGL/DBL$85-$105.

B.D. Williams House Bed and Breakfast (1505 4th Ave. North, 98109; 285-0810) 5 rooms, free breakfast, shared baths, no pets, NS, CC. SGL/DBL$100-$150.

Bed and Breakfast at Mildred's (1202 15th Ave. East, 98112; 325-6072) free breakfast, TV, a/c, no pets, 1890s home, CC. SGL/DBL$50-$70.

Best Western Executive Inn (200 Taylor Ave. North, 98109; 448-9444, Fax 441-7929, 800-528-1234) 123 rooms and suites, restaurant, lounge, entertainment, pool, jacuzzi, airport courtesy car, room service, pets OK, fax service, limousine service, wheelchair access, NS rooms, local transportation, in-room refrigerators, children free with parents, meeting facilities, a/c, TV, senior rates, CC. SGL/DBL$65-$90.

Best Western Inn (2500 North Aurora Ave. 98109; 284-1900, Fax 283-5298, 800-528-1234) 94 rooms and suites, restaurant, free breakfast, lounge, outdoor heated pool, kitchenettes, fax service, children free with parents, in-room refrigerators, NS rooms, a/c, TV, no pets, CC. SGL/DBL$55-$90, X$8.

Best Western Loyal Inn (2310 8th Ave. 98121; 682-0200, Fax 467-8984, 800-528-1234) 91 rooms and suites, restaurant, lounge, whirlpools, sauna, in-room refrigerators and coffee makers, no pets, airport courtesy car, fax service, NSrooms, children free with parents, a/c, TV, CC. SGL/DBL$65-$90.

Black Angus Motor Inn (12245 Aurora North, 98133; 363-3035) a/c, TV, no pets, CC. SGL/DBL$28-$33.

Bush Hotel (621 South Jackson, 98104; 623-8079) 144 rooms, restaurant, lounge, entertainment, gift shop, a/c, TV, CC. SGL$19-$28, DBL$23-$32.

Claremont Hotel (2004 4th Ave. 98121; 448-8600, 800-448-8601) 100 rooms and 1-bedroom suites, restaurant, laundry service, a/c, TV, CC. Near Westlake Center. SGL$49-$59, DBL$69-$79, 1BR$79-$149.

Chambered Nautilus Bed and Breakfast Inn (5005 22nd Ave. Northeast, 98105; 522-2536) 6 rooms, free breakfast, TV, NS, 1915 home, children over 12 welcome, private baths, antique furnishings, a/c, no pets, CC. SGL/DBL$80-$100.

Chelsea Station (4915 Linden Ave. North, 98103; 547-6077) 6 rooms, free breakfast, TV, a/c, private baths, NS, antique furnishings, no children, hot tub, no pets, CC. SGL/DBL$80-$100.

Commodore Motor Hotel (2013 Second Ave. 98121; 448-8868) 102 rooms, laundry service, a/c, TV, CC. SGL/DBL$25-$49.

Days Inn (2205 7th Ave. 98121; 448-3434, Fax 441-6876, 800-225-7169, 800-325-2525) 90 rooms, restaurant, lounge, children free with parents, pets OK, free local calls, wheelchair access, a/c, TV, laundry service, fax service, NS rooms, in-room computer hookups, CC. Near the Convention Center and Space Needle. SGL/DBL$65-$85.

Econo Lodge (325 Aurora Ave. North, 98109; 441-0400, 800-4-CHOICE) 58 rooms, outdoor heated pool, children under 12 free with parents, no pets, senior rates, NS rooms, wheelchair access, a/c, TV, VCRs, airport transportation, laundry facilities, senior rates, CC. SGL/DBL$60-$70.

The Edgewater Inn (2411 Alaskan Way, Pier 67, 98121; 728-7000, Fax 441-4119, 800-624-0670) 237 rooms and suites, restaurant, lounge, entertainment, exercise center, children free with parents, no pets, room service, a/c, local transportation, TV, wheelchair access, meeting facilities, senior rates, CC. SGL/DBL$110-$250.

Emerald Inn (8512 Aurora Ave. North, 98103; 520-5000) 30 rooms and 2-bedroom suites, pets OK, laundry facilities, in-room refrigerators, TV, a/c, senior rates, CC. SGL/DBL$45-$70.

Executive Residence Inn (1312 Minor Ave. 98101; 329-8000, Fax 382-0311) 75 suites, outdoor heated pool, kitchenettes, laundry service, children under 16 free with parents, pets OK, in-room refrigerators and coffee makers, free local calls, a/c, TV, CC. SGL/DBL$70-$89.

Four Seasons Olympic Hotel (411 University St. 98101; 621-1700, 800-223-8772, 800-821-8106 in Washington) 450 rooms, restaurant, lounge, entertainment, indoor pool, jacuzzi, exercise center, pets OK, barber and beauty shop, in-room refrigerators, complimentary newspaper, airport transportation, wheelchair access, boutiques, meeting facilities, a/c, TV, CC. SGL$130-$295, STS$295-$1,150.

Holiday Inn Downtown (1113 6th Ave. 98101; 464-1980, Fax 340-1617, 800-521-2762, 800-HOLIDAY) 415 rooms and suites, restaurant, lounge, whirlpools, children free with parents, wheelchair access, NS rooms, a/c, TV, fax service, room service, no pets, meeting facilities for 460, CC. Near the Convention Center, business district and waterfront, 17 miles from the airport. SGL/DBL$140-$170.

Hilton Seattle (6th and University, 98101; 624-0500, Fax 682-9029, 800-HILTONS) 800-426-0535, 800-542-7700 in Washington) 237 rooms and suites, two restaurants, lounge, entertainment, exercise center, whirlpools, 24hour room service, wheelchair access, NS rooms, gift shop, in-room refrigerators, airport transportation, no pets, a/c, TV, meeting facilities for 1,000, CC. Near the Convention Center, 20 miles from the SeaTac Airport. SGL/DBL$125-$198.

Hotel Vintage Park (1100 Fifth Ave. 98101; 624-8000, Fax 623-0568, 800-624-4433) 129 rooms and suites, restaurant, lounge, entertainment, exercise center, whirlpools, airport transportation, room service, in-room computer hookups, children free with parents, no pets, a/c, TV, wheelchair access, NS rooms, senior rates, CC. SGL/DBL$155-$190.

Inn At The Market (86 Pine St. 98101; 443-3600, Fax 448-0631, 800-464-4484) 65 rooms and suites, restaurant, lounge, exercise center, room service, local transportation, boutiques, no pets, children free with parents, in-room refrigerators, microwaves and coffee makers, water view, a/c, TV, meeting facilities, senior rates, CC. SGL/DBL$100-$160.

Inn At Virginia Mansion (1006 Spring St. 98104; 583-6453, Fax 223-7549, 800-283-6453) 79 rooms and suites, restaurant, antique furnishings, no pets, free local calls, wheelchair access, a/c, TV, NS rooms, in-room refrigerators, microwaves and coffee makers, laundry facilities, CC. Near the Convention Center. SGL/DBL$80-$135, STS$140-$180.

Marriott Residence Inn (800 Fairview Ave. North, 98109; 624-6000, 800--331-3131) 234 rooms and suites, pool, kitchens, in-room refrigerators and microwaves, exercise center, local transportation, laundry service, wheelchair access, NS rooms, pets OK, VCRs, a/c, in-room refrigerators and coffee makers, TV, meeting facilities, CC. Near Lake Union, 1.5 from Seattle Center and the Convention Center, 2 miles from the business district, 12 miles from the airport. SGL/DBL$125-$200.

Mayflower Park Hotel (405 Olive Way, 98101; 623-8700, Fax 382-6997, 800-4-26-5100) 200 rooms, restaurant, lounge, in-room refrigerators, no pets, children free with parents, room service, boutiques, meeting facilities, senior rates, CC. Near the Westlake Center. SGL$110-$120, STS$160-$388.

Meany Tower Hotel (4507 Brooklyn Ave. 98105; 634-2000, Fax 623-2000, 800-648-6440) 155 rooms, restaurant, lounge, exercise center, children free with parents, complimentary newspaper, laundry service, wheelchair access, no pets, water view, NS rooms, meeting facilities, a/c, TV, meeting facilities, senior rates, CC. SGL/DBL$50-$75.

Mildred's Bed and Breakfast (1201 15th Ave. East, 98112; 325-6072) 3 rooms and suites, free breakfast, TV, a/c, no pets, 1890s home, NS, CC. SGL/DBL$55-$70.

The Moore Hotel (1926 Second Ave. 98101; 800-421-8700) 140 rooms and suites, in-room refrigerators, NS rooms, a/c, TV, CC. SGL$34, DBL$39.

O'Brien Haus (2031 Dexter Ave. North, 98109; 285-0144) 2 suites, no-smoking, a/c, TV, CC. SGL/DBL$40-$55.

Pacific Plaza Hotel (400 Spring St. Northeast, 98105; 623-3900, Fax 623-2059. 800-426-1165) 160 rooms, free breakfast, children free with parents, NS rooms, TV, senior rates, no pets, CC. SGL/DBL$75-$85.

Park Inn Club and Breakfast Seattle (225 Aurora Ave. North, 98109; 728-7666, 800-437-PARK) 159 rooms and suites, free breakfast, indoor pool, jacuzzi, exercise center, a/c, TV, NS rooms, complimentary newspaper, meeting facilities for 100, CC. Near the Space Needle and Seattle Center, 5 miles from the Kingdome. SGL$49-$82, DBL$52-$68, STS$92.

Park Plaza Motel (4401 Aurora Ave. North, 98103; 632-2101) 14 rooms and 2-bedroom efficiencies, no pets, TV, in-room refrigerators, CC. SGL/DBL$28-$38.

Pensione Nichols (1923 1st Ave. 98101; 441-7125) 1 room, free breakfast, TV, a/c, no pets, CC. SGL/DBL$55-$90.

Prince of Wales Bed and Breakfast (133 13th Ave. East, 98102; 800-327-9692) 4 rooms, free breakfast, private bath, CC. Near the Convention Center. SGL/DBL$55-$80.

Quality Inn City Center (2224 8th Ave. 98121; 624-6820, Fax 467-6926, 800-437-4867 in Washington, 800-221-2222) 72 rooms and suites, restaurant, lounge, free breakfast, sauna, whirlpools, wheelchair access, children free with parents, NS rooms, a/c, TV, kitchenettes, in-room refrigerators and microwaves, free local calls, complimentary newspaper, meeting facilities, CC. SGL/DBL$80-$92, STS$115-$175.

Ramada Inn (2140 North Northgate Way, 98133; 365-0700, Fax 365-0750, 800-2-RAMADA) 169 rooms and suites, restaurant, lounge, pool, wheelchair access, NS rooms, free parking, pets OK, a/c, TV, children under 18 free with parents, room service, laundry facilities, VCRs, local transportation, meeting facilities, senior rates, CC. SGL/DBL$80-$105.

Ramada Inn Downtown (2200 5th Ave. 98121; 441-9785, 800-2-RAMADA) 120 rooms, restaurant, lounge, children free with parents, NS rooms, wheelchair access, a/c, TV, airport transportation, no pets, two meeting rooms, CC. Near the Kingdome, Coliseum and University of Washington. SGL$100-$125, DBL$110-$135, X$10.

Roberta's Bed and Breakfast Inn (1147 16th Ave. East, 98112; 329-3326) 5 rooms, free breakfast, private bath, CC. Near the Convention Center. SGL/DBL$75-95.

Rocking Horse Inn (2011 10th Ave. East, 98102; 322-0206) 6 rooms, bed and breakfast, in-room refrigerators, CC. Near the Convention Center. SGL/DBL$100.

Salisbury House (750 16th Ave. East, 98112; 328-8682) 4 rooms, bed and breakfast, private bath, no-smoking, a/c, TV, CC. SGL$65-75, DBL$75-$90.

Seattle Hotel (315 Seneca St. 98101; 623-5110) a/c, TV, no pets, CC. SGL/DBL$35-$55.

Seattle International AYH Hostel (84 Union St. 98101; 622-5443) 125 beds, lounge, kitchen, a/c, TV, CC. Near Pike Place Market and the waterfront. SGL$13.

Sheraton Seattle Hotel & Towers (1400 6th Ave. 98101; 621-9000, Fax 621-8441, 800-325-3535) 840 rooms and suites, three restaurants, two lounges, entertainment, 24-hour room service, indoor heated pool, sauna, jacuzzi, exercise center, gift shop, boutiques, wheelchair access, in-room refrigerators and coffee makers, a/c, TV, pets OK, NS rooms, 25 meeting rooms, 42,000 square feet of meeting and exhibition space, meeting facilities for 1,500, CC. Near Pike Place Market and the Space Needle, 7 miles from the airport. SGL/DBL$155-$190, STS$250-$550.

Sixth Avenue Inn (2000 6th Ave. 98121; 441-9300, Fax 441-9903, 800-648-6440) 166 rooms and suites, restaurant, lounge, NS rooms, children free with parents, room service, no pets, a/c, in-room refrigerators, TV, senior rates, meeting facilities, CC. SGL/DBL$48-$85.

Sorrento Hotel (900 Madison St. 98104; 622-6400, 800-426-1266) 76 rooms and suites, restaurant, lounge, entertainment, exercise center, in-room computer hookups, wheelchair access, limousine service, NS rooms, no pets, in-room refrigerators, complimentary newspaper, children free with parents, room service, airport transportation, a/c, TV, meeting facilities for 120, CC. SGL/DBL$130-$200.

St. Regis Hotel (116 Stewart St. 981010; 448-6366) 132 rooms, restaurant, laundry service, a/c, TV, CC. SGL$26-$33, DBL$33-$39.

Stouffer Madison Hotel (515 Madison St. 98104; 583-0300, Fax 624-8125, 800468-3571) 553 rooms and suites, restaurant, lounge, entertainment, indoor heated pool, jacuzzi, exercise center, beauty shop, complimentary newspaper, 24-hour room service, airport transportation, children free with parents, in-room computer hookups, no pets, in-room refrigerators, meeting facilities, a/c, TV, CC. SGL/DBL$155-$215, STS$205-$850.

Tower 801 Apartments (801 Pine St. 98101; 623-1013) 72 rooms, outdoor pool, a/c, TV, CC. SGL/DBL$95-$125.

TraveLodge (2213 8th Ave. 98121; 624-6300, Fax 233-0185) 72 rooms, restaurant, lounge, car rental desk, fax service, a/c, TV, no pets, in-room refrigerators and coffee makers, airport transportation, children under 16 free with parents, laundry service, CC. One mile from the Washington Convention Center, Kingdome and shopping district. SGL/DBL$55-$85.

TraveLodge By The Space Needle (200 6th Ave. North, 98109; 441-7878, Fax 233-0185) 88 rooms, restaurant, lounge, free breakfast, pool, fax service, car rental desk, no pets, a/c, TV, CC. Near the Seattle Center, Monorail and Space Needle. SGL$60-$90, DBL$66-$96, X$6.

Tugboat Challenger (809 Fairview Place, North, 98109; 340-1201) boat accommodations, free breakfast, TV, a/c, no pets, NS, private bath, fireplace, laundry facilities, VCR, water view, CC. SGL/DBL$60-$125.

University Motel (4731 12th Ave. Northeast, 98105; 522-4724) 21 rooms and efficiencies, TV, laundry facilities, airport transportation, pets OK, NS rooms, CC. SGL/DBL$45-$60.

University Plaza Motel (400 Northeast 45th St. 98105; 634-0100, Fax 633-2743, 800-343-7040) 135 rooms, restaurant, lounge, entertainment, outdoor pool, exercise center, room service, beauty shop, no pets, children free with parents, a/c, TV, wheelchair access, NS rooms, senior rates, CC. SGL/DBL$75-$88.

Warwick Hotel (401 Lenora Ave. 98121; 443-4300, Fax 448-1662, 800-426-9280) 230 rooms and 2- and 3-bedroom suites, restaurant, lounge, entertainment, indoor heated pool, whirlpools, sauna, exercise center, local transportation, 24-hour room service, children free with parents, in-room refrigerators, local transportation, pets OK, wheelchair access, NS rooms, meeting facilities, a/c, TV, CC. SGL/DBL$150-$500.

West Coast Camlin (1619 9th Ave. 98101; 682-0100, Fax 682-5415, 800-426-0670) 140 rooms and suites, restaurant, lounge, entertainment, outdoor heated pool, exercise center, in-room refrigerators, wheelchair access, children free with parents, airport transportation, NS rooms, no pets, gift shop, laundry facilities, meeting facilities, a/c, TV, CC. SGL/DBL$80-$175.

West Coast Roosevelt Hotel (1521 7th Ave. 98101; 621-1200) 150 rooms, restaurant, lounge, exercise center, laundry service, wheelchair access, NS rooms, a/c, TV, CC. SGL$85-105, DBL$95-$115.

West Coast Sea-Tac Hotel (182203 Pacific Hwy. South, 98101; 246-5535, Fax 246-5535, 800-426-0670) 146 rooms, restaurant, lounge, outdoor heated pool, whirlpools, room service, sauna, a/c, TV, airport transportation, no pets, senior rates, meeting facilities for 150, CC. SGL/DBL$80-$150.

West Coast Vance Hotel (620 Steward St. 9801; 441-4200, Fax 441-8612) 165 rooms, restaurant, lounge, entertainment, room service, laundry service, a/c, TV, VCRs, no pets, CC. SGL$7191, DBL$81-$101.

Westin Hotel (1900 5th Ave. 98101; 728-1000, Fax 728-2259) 877 rooms and suites, five restaurants, two lounges, entertainment, heated indoor swimming pool, whirlpools, sauna, exercise center, 24-hour room service, boutiques, laundry service, no pets, beauty shop, boutiques, in-room refrigerators, a/c, TV, airline ticket office, airport transportation, wheelchair access/room, NS rooms, 40,000 square feet of meeting and exhibition space, meeting facilities for 2,250, CC. 25 minutes from the airport. SGL/DBL$150-$300, STS$300-$1,100.

Airport Area

Best Western Airport Executel (20717 Pacific Hwy. South, 98198; 878-3300, Fax 824-9000, 800-528-1234) 138 rooms, restaurant, lounge, indoor pool, complimentary newspaper, airport transportation, no pets, fax service, NS rooms, a/c, TV, meeting facilities, CC. 1 mile from the airport, 4 miles from the downtown area. SGL/DBL$55-$90.

Econo Lodge (13910 Pacific Hwy. South, 98168; 244-0810, 800-4-CHOICE) 47 rooms, exercise center, whirlpools, children under 12 free with parents, no pets, senior rates, NS rooms, wheelchair access, a/c, TV, senior rates, CC. SGL/DBL$48-$90.

HoJo Inn (20045 International Blvd. South, 98198; 878-3100, Fax 824-8535, 800-I-GO-HOJO) 58 rooms, free breakfast, airport courtesy car, children free with parents, NS rooms, wheelchair access, CC. Near Angel Lake State Park. SGL/DBL$40-$55.

Holiday Inn Boeing Field (11244 Pacific Hwy. South, 98168; 762-0300, Fax 762-8306, 800-HOLIDAY) 118 rooms, restaurant, lounge, heated outdoor pool, children free with parents, laundry service, wheelchair access, NS rooms, fax service, room service, airport courtesy car, meeting facilities for 250, CC. 3 miles from the airport, 7 miles from the Space Needle and the downtown area. SGL$61, DBL$69.

Kings Arm Motel and Apartments (23226 30th Ave. South, 98198; 824-1300) 41 rooms and apartments, heated outdoor pool, pets OK, a/c, TV, CC. SGL/DBL$29-$50.

Super 8 Airport (3100 South 192nd, 98168; 433-8188, Fax 243-9103, 800-800-8000) 119 rooms and suites, restaurant, wheelchair access, meeting facilities, local transportation, airport parking, NS rooms, fax service, free local calls, a/c, TV, CC. SGL/DBL$40-$68.

TraveLodge Sea-Tac Airport North (14845 Pacific Hwy. South, 98168; 242-7777, Fax 248-2850, 800-255-3050) 72 rooms, restaurant, lounge, exercise center, airport transportation, no pets, fax service, room service, a/c, TV, wheelchair access, NS rooms. 2.4 miles from the airport, a/c, CC. SGL$40-$55, DBL$45-$60, X$5.

North Seattle

Best Western Evergreen Motor Inn (13700 Aurora Ave. North, 98133; 3613700, Fax 361-0338, 800-528-1234) 72 rooms and suites, restaurant, free breakfast, pool, sauna, exercise center, whirlpools, laundry service, children free with parents, VCRs, kitchenettes, no pets, in-room computer hookups, a/c, TV, fax service, NS rooms, wheelchair access, CC. 7 miles from the downtown area. SGL/DBL$60-$75.

Crest Motel (14115 Aurora Ave. North, 98133; 363-0700) 25 rooms, pool, a/c, TV, CC. SGL/DBL$35.

El Dorado Motel (11736 Aurora Ave. North, 98133; 362-9786) a/c, TV, no pets, CC. SGL/DBL$36-$38.

Geisha Inn (9613 Aurora Ave. North, 98103; 524-8880) a/c, TV, no pets, CC. SGL/DBL$26-$48.

Georgia Motel (8801 Aurora Ave. North, 98103; 524-1004) a/c, TV, no pets, CC. SGL/DBL$36-$42.

Green Lake Motel (8900 Aurora Ave. North, 98103; 523-4703) a/c, TV, no pets, CC. SGL/DBL$65.

J.O. Manor (5722 East Greenlake Way, North, 98103; 632-5103) a/c, TV, no pets, wheelchair access, NS rooms, in-room refrigerators and microwaves, CC. SGL/DBL$28-$48.

Kelley's Motel (8816 Aurora Ave. North, 98103; 524-1106) a/c, TV, no pets, CC. SGL/DBL$28-$35.

Klose Inn Motel (9309 Aurora Ave. North, 98103; 527-0330) a/c, TV, no pets, CC. SGL/DBL$33-$36.

Lake Union Motel (3910 Aurora Ave. North, 98103; 632-7063) a/c, TV, no pets, CC. SGL/DBL$28-$48.

Magnolia House (4754 19th Northeast, 98105; 526-9826) a/c, TV, no pets, CC. SGL/DBL$44-$48.

Marco Polo Motel (4114 Aurora Ave. North, 98103; 633-4090) 36 rooms and efficiencies, TV, no pets, children free with parents, TV, CC. SGL/DBL$38-$48.

New Seattle Motel (12059 Aurora Ave. North, 89133; 362-9885) a/c, TV, CC. SGL/DBL$39-$46.

Quest Inn (14817 Aurora Ave. 98133; 367-7880) 29 rooms, whirlpools, in-room refrigerators and microwaves, no pets, a/c, TV, NS rooms, CC. SGL/DBL$45-$53.

Rodeside Lodge (12501 Aurora Ave. North, 98133; 364-7771) 87 rooms and suites, restaurant, lounge, heated outdoor heated pool, exercise center, whirlpools, pets OK, children free with parents, in-room refrigerators and microwaves, wheelchair access, NS rooms, a/c, TV, CC. SGL$39-$60, DBL$40-$65.

University Inn (4140 Roosevelt Way Northeast, 98105; 632-5055, Fax 547-4937, 800-733-3855) 102 rooms, free breakfast, outdoor heated pool, exercise center, whirlpools, in-room refrigerators, kitchenettes, a/c, TV, children free with parents, no pets, CC. SGL$69, DBL$74-$89.

University Plaza (400 Northeast 45th St. 98105; 634-1000) 135 rooms and suites, restaurant, lounge, outdoor pool, exercise center, room service, barber and beauty shop, wheelchair access, a/c, TV, NS rooms, 9,000 square feet of meeting and exhibition space, CC. 5 minutes from the downtown area, .5 miles from the University of Washington. SGL/DBL$75-$90.

South Seattle

Hainesworth House (2657 37th St. Southwest, 98126; 938-1020) free breakfast, TV, a/c, no pets, NS, no children, private baths, CC. SGL/DBL$90-$105.

Inn of West Seattle (3512 Southwest Alaska St. 98126; 937-9920) 49 rooms, laundry service, in-room refrigerators, a/c, TV, CC. SGL/DBL$36-$55.

La Hacienda Motel (5414 First Ave. South, 98108; 762-2460, 800-553-7531) 34 rooms and suites, free breakfast, airport courtesy car, a/c, kitchenettes, TV, CC. SGL/DBL$40-$57.

Sandpiper Villas Apartment and Motel (11000 First Ave. Southwest, 98146; 242-8883) 17 1- and 2-bedroom apartments, outdoor pool, pets OK, a/c, TV, CC. SGL$35-$45, DBL$37-$49.

Other Locations

Bellevue Place (1111 Bellevue Place East, 98102; 325-9253) 2 rooms, bed and breakfast, a/c. SGL/DBL$70-$85.

Broadway Guest House (959 Broadway East, 98102; 329-1864) 3 rooms, bed and breakfast, airport transportation, a/c, TV, CC. SGL$65-$75, DBL$85-$95.

Capital Hill Inn (1713 Belmont Ave. 98122; 323-1955) 5 rooms, bed and breakfast, free local calls, NS rooms, no pets, antique furnishings, CC. SGL/DBL$55-$95.

Continental Court All-Suites Motel (17223 32nd Ave. South, 98188; 241-1500, Fax 243-8951) 50 rooms and 2-bedroom suites, outdoor heated pool, a/c, TV, children free with parents, pets OK, in-room refrigerators and coffee makers, airport transportation, wheelchair access, NS rooms, senior rates, CC. SGL/DBL$40-$60.

Continental Inn Bed and Breakfast (955 10th Ave. East, 98102; 324-9511) 4 rooms, free breakfast, free local calls, private baths, jacuzzi, a/c, TV, CC. SGL$50-$70, DBL$55-$90.

Executive Court Suites (300 10th Ave. 98122; 223-9300) 76 1- and 2-bedroom suites, exercise center, jacuzzi, laundry service, complimentary local transportation, a/c, TV, CC. SGL/DBL$40, 1BR$85, 2BR$110.

The Gaslight Inn (1727 15th Ave. 98122; 325-3654) 9 rooms, bed and breakfast, heated outdoor pool, laundry service, private bath, a/c, TV, CC. SGL/DBL$58-$85.

Georgian Motel (8810 Aurora North, 98103; 524-1004) 18 rooms, a/c, TV, CC. SGL/DBL$28-$32.

Hill House Bed and Breakfast (1113 East John St. 98102; 720-7161) 4 rooms, free breakfast, no pets, a/c, TV, CC. 10 minutes from the downtown area. SGL$55-$65, DBL$60-$70.

Jet Motel Park n' Fly (17300 International Blvd. 98188; 244-6255) 51 rooms, outdoor heated pool, children free with parents, no pets, in-room refrigerators, airport transportation, CC. SGL/DBL$43-$60.

Sea-Tac Crest Motor Inn (18845 Pacific Hwy. South, 98188; 433-0999, 800-554-0300) 46 rooms and suites, free breakfast, no pets, a/c, TV, airport transportation, in-room refrigerators, wheelchair access, NS rooms, meeting facilities, senior rates, CC. SGL/DBL$40-$70.

West Coast Gateway Hotel (18415 Pacific Hwy. South, 98188; 248-8200, Fax 244-1198, 800-426-0670) 150 rooms, restaurant, free breakfast, lounge, a/c, TV, airport transportation, no pets, meeting facilities for 20, CC. SGL/DBL$89-$119.

West Coast Plaza Park Suites (1011 Pike St. 98101; 682-8282, Fax 682-5315, 800-426-0670) 194 rooms and 2-bedroom suites, suites, restaurant, lounge, outdoor pool, exercise center, jacuzzi, a/c, fireplaces, whirlpools, laundry service, TV, children free with parents, in-room refrigerators and coffee makers, airport transportation, no pets, meeting facilities, CC. SGL/DBL$125-$280.

Seaview

Area Code 206

The Shelburne Inn (4415 Pacific Hwy. 98644; 642-2442) 15 rooms, free breakfast, NS, no pets, antique furnishings, 1890s inn, CC. SGL/DBL$80-$165.

Sequim

Area Code 206

Best Western Sequim Bay Lodge (1788 Hwy. 101 East, 98382; 683-0691, Fax 683-3748, 800-528-1234) 54 rooms, restaurant, lounge, outdoor heated pool, hot tubs, jacuzzis, children free with parents, a/c, NS rooms, TV, laundry facilities, wheelchair access, pets OK, meeting facilities, senior rates, CC. SGL/DBL$50-$135.

Best Western Summit Inn (Hwy. 906, 98068; 434-6300, Fax 434-6393, 800-528-1234) 80 rooms, restaurant, outdoor heated pool, sauna, hot tub, fireplaces, children free with parents, a/c, NS rooms, TV, laundry facilities, wheelchair access, no pets, meeting facilities, senior rates, CC. SGL/DBL$60-$90.

Econo Lodge (801 East Washington St. 98382; 683-7113, 800-4-CHOICE) 43 rooms, free breakfast, in-room refrigerators, children free with parents, no pets, NS rooms, wheelchair access, a/c, TV, senior rates, CC. SGL/DBL$52-$68.

The Grey Wolf Inn (395 Keeler Rd. 98382; 683-5889) 6 rooms, free breakfast, whirlpools, no pets, antique furnishings, local transportation, children free with parents, TV, NS, CC. SGL/DBL$52-$110.

Juan de Fuca Cottages (182 Marine Dr. 98382; 683-4433) 6 cottages, TV, kitchenettes, airport transportation, in-room refrigerators and coffee makers, no pets, water view, children free with parents, game room, CC. SGL/DBL$95-$145.

Margie's on the Bay (120 Forrest Rd. 98382; 683-7011) 5 rooms, free breakfast, no pets, NS, CC. SGL/DBL$60-$70.

Sequim West Inn (740 West Washington St. 98382; 683-4144, Fax 683-6452) 21 rooms and 2-bedroom efficiencies, a/c, TV, in-room refrigerators, laundry facilities, microwaves and coffee makers, no pets, senior rates. SGL/DBL$50-$75.

Sundowner Motel (364 West Washington St. 98382; 683-5532) 34 rooms and efficiencies, TV, a/c, NS rooms, in-room refrigerators and microwaves, children free with parents, pets OK, CC. SGL/DBL$45-$70.

Silverdale
Area Code 206

Cimarron Motel (9734 Northwest Silverdale Way, 98383; 692-7777) 63 rooms, laundry facilities, in-room refrigerators and coffee makers, no pets, CC. SGL/DBL$40-$52.

Seabreeze Beach Cottage (16609 Olympic View Rd. Northwest, 98383; 692-4648) free breakfast, TV, a/c, no pets, CC. SGL/DBL$140-$160.

Silverdale on the Bay (3073 Northwest Bucklin Hill Rd. 98383; 698-1000, Fax 692-0932, 800-426-0670) 151 rooms, restaurant, lounge, entertainment, indoor heated pool, sauna, jacuzzi, exercise center, lighted tennis courts, gift shop, a/c, TV, pets OK, in-room refrigerators, laundry facilities, water view, airport transportation, 5,000 square feet of meeting and exhibition space, meeting facilities for 500, CC. SGL/DBL$65-$95.

Snoqualmie Falls
Area Code 206

The Old Honey Farm Country Inn (8910 384th Ave. Southeast, 98065; 888-9399) 10 rooms, NS, no pets, in-room refrigerators, antique furnishings, CC. SGL/DBL$75-$125.

Salish Lodge (Snoqualmie Falls 98065; 888-2556, 800-826-6124) 91 rooms and suites, restaurant, lounge, exercise center, whirlpools, sauna, antique furnishings, pets OK, fireplaces, in-room refrigerators, VCRs, children free with parents, TV, a/c, water view, room service, CC. SGL/DBL$165-$235.

South Cle Elum
Area Code 509

The Moore House (526 Marie St. 98943; 674-5939) 11 rooms and suites, free breakfast, NS, private baths, TV, a/c, airport transportation, shared baths, no pets, CC. SGL/DBL$50-$60.

Spokane
Area Code 509

Apple Tree Inn (9508 North Division St. 99218; 466-3020, Fax 467-4377) 71 rooms and 2-bedroom suites, no pets, a/c, TV, laundry facilities, airport transportation, in-room refrigerators and coffee makers, CC. SGL/DBL$40-$50.

Bel Air Motel (1303 East Sprague Ave. 99202; 535-1677) 17 rooms and efficiencies, a/c, TV, wheelchair access, in-room refrigerators and microwaves, children free with parents, pets OK, NS rooms, senior rates, CC. SGL/DBL$33-$49.

Best Western Thunderbird Inn (120 West 3rd Ave. 99204; 747-2011, Fax 747-9170, 800-528-1234) 90 rooms and suites, restaurant, outdoor heated pool, exercise center, in-room coffee makers, children free with parents, a/c, NS rooms, TV, laundry facilities, wheelchair access, pets OK, meeting facilities, senior rates, CC. SGL/DBL$45-$75.

Best Western Trade Winds Downtown Inn (907 West 3rd Ave. 99204; 838-2091, Fax 838-2094, 800-528-1234) 59 rooms, free breakfast, outdoor pool, whirlpools, hot tubs, free local calls, children free with parents, a/c, NS rooms, TV, laundry facilities, wheelchair access, no pets, meeting facilities, senior rates, CC. SGL/DBL$40-$70.

Best Western Trade Winds North Inn (3033 Division St. North, 99207; 326-5500, Fax 328-1357, 800-621-8593, 800-528-1234) 63 rooms, free breakfast, indoor heated whirlpools, children free with parents, a/c, NS rooms,

TV, free local calls, laundry facilities, wheelchair access, pets OK, meeting facilities, senior rates, CC. SGL/DBL$55-$75.

Cavanaugh's River Inn (700 Division St. 99202; 326-5577, 800-843-4667) 241 rooms and suites, restaurant, lounge, entertainment, indoor and outdoor heated pools, whirlpools, sauna, a/c, no pets, gift shop, airport transportation, in-room refrigerators, pets OK, water view, TV, wheelchair access, NS rooms, meeting facilities, senior rates, CC. SGL/DBL$78-$100, STS$80-$130.

Comfort Inn North (7111 North Division, 99208; 800-221-2222) 96 rooms, pool, whirlpools, sauna, a/c, game room, kitchenettes, TV, senior rates, CC. SGL/DBL$62-$90.

Comfort Inn Broadway (6309 East Broadway Ave. 99212; 535-7185, Fax 535-7185, 800-221-2222) 35 rooms, free breakfast, pool, whirlpools, free local calls, complimentary newspaper, a/c, TV, senior rates, CC. SGL/DBL$50-$80.

Courtyard by Marriott (401 Riverpoint Blvd. 99202; 456-7600, Fax 456-0969, 800-331-3131) 149 rooms and suites, free breakfast, restaurant, indoor heated pool, exercise center, whirlpools, in-room refrigerators, microwaves and coffee makers, a/c, VCRs, no pets, complimentary newspaper, children free with parents, kitchenettes, a/c, TV, NS rooms, wheelchair access, meeting facilities, senior rates, CC. SGL/DBL$80-$115.

Days Inn (1919 Hutchinson Rd. 99212; 926-5399, 800-325-2525) 92 rooms, free breakfast, restaurant, a/c, TV, wheelchair access, NS rooms, pets OK, laundry facilities, meeting facilities, senior rates, CC. SGL/DBL$45-$80.

Friendship Inn Airport (4301 West Sunset Blvd. 99204; 838-1471, 800-424-4777) 89 rooms, restaurant, lounge, entertainment, outdoor, pool, exercise center, whirlpools, sauna, a/c, TV, no pets, NS rooms, children free with parents, wheelchair access, senior rates, CC. SGL/DBL$50-$75.

Hampton Inn (2010 South Assembly Rd. 99204; 747-1100, Fax 747-8722, 800-HAMPTON) 131 rooms, free breakfast, pool, exercise facilities, children under 18 free with parents, airport transportation, NS rooms, wheelchair access, in-room computer hookups, fax service, TV, a/c, free local calls, pets OK, meeting facilities, senior rates, CC. SGL/DBL$65-$75.

Hillside House (18729 East 18th St. 99203; 534-1426) free breakfast, TV, a/c, no pets, NS, CC. SGL/DBL$50-$65.

Holiday Inn (4212 Sunset Blvd. 99204; 747-2021, 800-HOLIDAY) 137 rooms, restaurant, lounge, outdoor heated pool, airport transportation, children under 19 free with parents, wheelchair access, a/c, TV, no pets, NS rooms, fax service, room service, no pets, laundry service, meeting facilities, senior rates, CC. SGL/DBL$50-$70.

Quality Inn (8923 Mission Ave. 99212; 928-5218, 800-221-2222) 92 rooms and suites, restaurant, free breakfast, lounge, indoor heated pool, exercise center, sauna, whirlpools, no pets, beauty shop, gift shop, children free with parents, a/c, TV, wheelchair access, room service, laundry service, NS rooms, meeting facilities, senior rates, CC. SGL/DBL$80-$325.

Quality Inn Oakwood (7919 Division St. 99208; 467-4900, 800-221-2222) 96 rooms and suites, restaurant, lounge, indoor heated pool, exercise center, whirlpools, no pets, children free with parents, a/c, TV, wheelchair access, room service, laundry service, NS rooms, meeting facilities, senior rates, CC. SGL/DBL$60-$85.

Ramada Inn (Spokane 99219; 838-5211, Fax 838-1074, 800-2-RAMADA) 168 rooms and suites, restaurant, lounge, indoor and outdoor heated pool, whirlpools, sauna, wheelchair access, NS rooms, free parking, pets OK, a/c, TV, children under 18 free with parents, room service, laundry facilities, meeting facilities, senior rates, CC. SGL/DBL$60-$175.

Red Lion Inn (1100 Sullivan Rd. 99220; 924-9000, Fax 922-4965, 800-547-8010) 241 rooms and suites, restaurant, lounge, entertainment, pool, a/c, TV, wheelchair access, NS rooms, airport transportation, no pets, in-room refrigerators, complimentary newspaper, fax service, laundry facilities, meeting facilities, senior rates, CC. SGL/DBL$80-$110.

Shangri-La (2922 Government Way, 99204; 747-2066, 800-234-4941) 19 1- to 3-bedroom efficiencies, outdoor heated pool, a/c, TV, wheelchair access, NS rooms, in-room refrigerators, no pets, airport transportation, senior rates, CC. SGL/DBL$40-$65.

Sheraton Hotel (322 Spokane Falls Court, 99201; 455-9600, Fax 455-6285, 800-325-3535) 369 rooms and suites, restaurant, lounge, entertainment, outdoor heated pool, pool, exercise facilities, NS rooms, a/c, room service, TV, children free with parents, beauty shop, water view, wheelchair access, meeting facilities, senior rates, CC. SGL/DBL$90-$450.

Shilo Inn (923 3rd Ave. 99202; 535-9000, Fax 535-5740, 800-222-2244) 105 rooms and suites, restaurant, lounge, indoor heated pool, exercise center, rooms service, airport courtesy car, in-room refrigerators, pets OK, a/c, TV, NS rooms, wheelchair access, children under 12 free with parents, meeting facilities, senior rates, CC. SGL/DBL$55-$69.

Suntree Inn (211 South Division St. 99202; 838-6630) 80 rooms, whirlpools, a/c, VCRs, TV, children free with parents, pets OK, NS rooms, CC. SGL/DBL$40-$55.

Super 8 Motel (11102 West Westbow Blvd. 99204; 838-8800, 800-800-8000) 80 rooms and suites, whirlpools, no pets, children under 12 free with parents, free local calls, a/c, TV, VCRs, in-room refrigerators and microwaves, fax service, NS rooms, wheelchair access, meeting facilities, senior rates, CC. SGL/DBL$44-$58.

Super 8 Motel (2020 Argonne Rd. 99212; 928-4888, 800-800-8000) 164 rooms and suites, no pets, children under 12 free with parents, free local calls, a/c, TV, in-room refrigerators and microwaves, fax service, NS rooms, wheelchair access, meeting facilities, senior rates, CC. SGL/DBL$36-$66.

Town Centre Motor Inn (902 West 1st Ave. 99204; 747-1041) 36 rooms, exercise center, a/c, TV, in-room refrigerators and microwaves, no pets, children free with parents, laundry facilities, meeting facilities, senior rates, CC. SGL/DBL$40-$65.

TraveLodge (827 West 1st Ave. 99204; 456-8040, Fax 747-3574, 800-578-7878) 80 rooms and suites, restaurant, lounge, free breakfast, pool, wheelchair access, complimentary newspaper, laundry service, TV, a/c, free local calls, airport transportation, fax service, NS rooms, in-room refrigerators and microwaves, children under 18 free with parents, no pets, meeting facilities, senior rates, CC. SGL/DBL$40-$85.

West Coast Ridpath Hotel (West 515 Sprague Ave. 99204; 838-2711, Fax 747-6970, 800-426-0670) 350 rooms, restaurant, lounge, entertainment, indoor and outdoor heated pool, whirlpools, a/c, TV, airport transportation, no pets, barber and beauty shop, 20,000 square feet of meeting and exhibition space, meeting facilities for 1,500, CC. SGL/DBL$70-$150.

Stevenson

Area Code 509

Econo Lodge (Frank Johns Rd. 98648; 427-5628, 800-4-CHOICE) 21 rooms, children under 12 free with parents, no pets, senior rates, NS rooms, wheelchair access, a/c, TV, senior rates, CC. SGL/DBL$42-$68.

Home Valley Bed and Breakfast (Stevenson 98648; 427-4773) free breakfast, TV, a/c, no pets, NS, private baths, fireplaces, antique furnishings, senior rates, CC. SGL/DBL$55-$140.

Skamania Lodge (1131 Southwest Skamania Lodge Dr. 98648; 427-7700, Fax 427-2547) 195 rooms, restaurant, lounge, entertainment, indoor heated pool, whirlpools, sauna, tennis courts, exercise center, a/c, TV, wheelchair access, NS rooms, in-room refrigerators and coffee makers, water view, children free with parents, no pets, senior rates, CC. SGL/DBL$85-$145.

Sunnyside
Area Code 509

Friendship Inn (724 Yakima Valley Hwy. 98944; 837-4721, 800-424-4777) 40 rooms, pool, exercise center, a/c, TV, no pets, NS rooms, children free with parents, wheelchair access, senior rates, CC. SGL/DBL$33-$71.

Nendels Inn (408 Yakima Valley Hwy. 98944; 837-7878, 800-547-0106) 73 rooms and efficiencies, outdoor heated pool, a/c, TV, children under 17 free with parents, in-room refrigerators and coffee makers, pets OK, senior rates, CC. SGL/DBL$35-$42.

Sunnyside Inn (800 East Edison, 98944; 839-5557) 8 rooms, free breakfast, TV, private baths, NS, jacuzzis, a/c, no pets, CC. SGL/DBL$50-$70.

Townhouse Motel (509 Yakima Valley Hwy. 98944; 837-5500) 21 rooms, a/c, TV, children free with parents, in-room refrigerators and microwaves, kitchenettes, pets OK, CC. SGL/DBL$35-$48.

Tacoma
Area Code 206

Best Western Tacoma Inn (8726 South Hosmer St. 98444; 535-2880, Fax 537-8379, 800-528-1234) 149 rooms, restaurant, lounge, entertainment, outdoor heated pool, whirlpools, exercise center, in-room coffee makers, children free with parents, a/c, NS rooms, TV, laundry facilities, wheelchair access, pets OK, meeting facilities, senior rates, CC. SGL/DBL$60-$75.

Best Western Lakewood Motor Inn (6125 Motor Ave. Southwest, 98499; 584-2212, Fax 588-5546, 800-528-1234) 78 rooms, restaurant, free breakfast, outdoor heated pool, children free with parents, a/c, NS rooms, TV, laundry facilities, wheelchair access, pets OK, meeting facilities, senior rates, CC. SGL/DBL$50-$61.

Days Inn (6802 Tacoma Mall Blvd. 98409; 475-5900, Fax 475-3540, 800-325-2525) 118 rooms, free breakfast, restaurant, outdoor heated pool, in-room refrigerators, no pets, a/c, TV, wheelchair access, NS rooms, children free with parents, laundry facilities for 250, senior rates, CC. SGL/DBL$65-$85.

Days Inn North (3021 Pacific Hwy. East, 98424; 922-3500, Fax 922-0203, 800-325-2525) 96 rooms, outdoor pool, a/c, TV, wheelchair access, NS rooms, no pets, laundry facilities, senior rates, CC. SGL/DBL$33-$61.

Econo Lodge South (9325 South Tacoma Way, 98499; 582-7500, 800-4-CHOICE) 77 rooms, whirlpools, children under 12 free with parents, no pets, senior rates, NS rooms, wheelchair access, a/c, TV, senior rates, CC. SGL/DBL$33-$68.

Howard Johnson Lodge (8702 South Hosmer, 98444; 535-3100, Fax 537-6497, 800-I-GO-HOJO) 144 rooms, restaurant, lounge, pool, children free with parents, wheelchair access, NS rooms, TV, a/c, no pets, laundry facilities, senior rates, meeting facilities, CC. SGL/DBL$55-$88.

Keenan House Inn (2610 North Warner St. 98407; 752-0702) 6 rooms, free breakfast, NS, TV, no pets, antique furnishings. SGL/DBL$40-$60.

La Quinta Inn (1425 East 27th St. 98421; 383-0146, Fax 627-3280, 800-531-5900) 158 rooms, restaurant, free breakfast, lounge, outdoor pool, complimentary newspaper, free local calls, fax service, laundry service, NS rooms, wheelchair access, remote control TV, a/c, pets OK, room service, water view, meeting facilities, senior rates, CC. SGL/DBL$55-$75.

Royal Coachman Motor Inn (5805 Pacific Hwy. East, 98424; 922-2500, 800-422-3051) 94 rooms and suites, restaurant, whirlpools, in-room coffee makers, children free with parents, pets OK, a/c, TV, wheelchair access, NS rooms, meeting facilities, senior rates, CC. SGL/DBL$55-$140.

Sheraton Hotel (1320 Broadway Plaza, 98402; 572-3200, Fax 591-4105, 800-325-3535) 319 rooms and suites, restaurant, lounge, entertainment, exercise facilities, whirlpools, sauna, NS rooms, a/c, room service, TV, children free with parents, wheelchair access, barber and beauty shop, boutiques, in-room refrigerators, room service, meeting facilities, senior rates, CC. SGL/DBL$95-$525.

Shilo Inn (7414 South Hosmer, 98408; 475-4020, 800-222-2244) 132 rooms and suites, restaurant, free breakfast, lounge, indoor pool, exercise center, whirlpools, sauna, airport courtesy car, in-room refrigerators, a/c, TV, NS rooms, wheelchair access, children under 12 free with parents, laundry facilities, pets OK, meeting facilities, senior rates, CC. SGL/DBL$60-$70.

Tacoma Dome Hotel (2611 East 24th St. 98421; 572-7272, Fax 572-9664) 160 rooms, exercise center, whirlpools, pets OK, children free with parents, in-room refrigerators, NS rooms, a/c, TV, senior rates, CC. SGL/DBL$66-$75.

TraveLodge (8820 South Hosmer, 98444; 539-1153, 800-578-7878) 108 rooms, restaurant, lounge, free breakfast, outdoor heated pool, whirlpools, wheelchair access, complimentary newspaper, laundry service, TV, a/c, free local calls, fax service, NS rooms, in-room refrigerators and microwaves, children under 18 free with parents, no pets, meeting facilities, senior rates, CC. SGL/DBL$50-$65.

Western Inn (9920 South Tacoma Way, 98499; 588-5241) 103 rooms, a/c, TV, pets OK, in-room refrigerators, children free with parents, NS rooms, CC. SGL/DBL$36-$52.

Tukwila
Area Code 206

Airport Plaza Motel (18601 Pacific Hwy. South, 98188; 433-0400, 800-356-1000) 114 rooms and suites, restaurant, lounge, exercise center, whirlpools, airport courtesy car, no pets, laundry facilities, room service, barber and beauty shop, children free with parents, a/c, TV, meeting facilities, senior rates, CC. SGL/DBL$50-$140.

Comfort Inn Sea-Tac (19333 Pacific Hwy. South, 98188; 878-1100, Fax 878-1100, 800-221-2222) 120 rooms and suites, restaurant, free breakfast, jacuzzi, exercise center, sauna, wheelchair access, NS rooms, airport courtesy car, no pets, in-room refrigerators, no pets, a/c, TV, CC. .5 miles from the Seattle-Tacoma International Airport, 15 miles from the Convention Center. SGL/DBL$65-$150.

Courtyard by Marriott (400 Andover Park West, 98188; 575-2500, 800-331-3131) 149 rooms and suites, free breakfast, restaurant, lounge, indoor heated pool, exercise center, in-room refrigerators, microwaves and coffee makers, VCRs, no pets, complimentary newspaper, children free with parents, kitchenettes, airport transportation, a/c, TV, NS rooms, wheelchair access, meeting facilities, senior rates, CC. SGL/DBL$85-$95.

Days Inn Sea-Tac Airport (19015 Pacific Hwy. South, 98188; 244-3600, Fax 244-3600, 800-325-2525) 86 rooms and suites, free breakfast, exercise center, kitchenettes, NS rooms, airport courtesy car, wheelchair access, children under 16 free with parents, no pets, a/c, TV, fax service, meeting facilities, CC. At the airport, 15 minutes from the downtown area. SGL$49-$59, DBL$59-$69, STS$85-$110.

Doubletree Inn At Southcenter (205 Strander Blvd. 98188; 246-8220, Fax 575-4743, 800-528-0444) 198 rooms and suites, restaurant, lounge, indoor and outdoor heated pool, spa, sauna, exercise center, local transportation, a/c, in-room refrigerators, room service, TV, children free with parents, NS rooms, 9 meeting rooms, meeting facilities for 300, CC. 5 minutes from the airport. SGL/DBL$120-$145, STS$160.

Doubletree Suites (16500 Southcenter Parkway, 98188; 575-8220, Fax 575-4743, 800-528-0444) 221 suites, restaurant, free breakfast, lounge, entertainment, heated indoor pool, spa, sauna, exercise center, local transportation, a/c, TV, children free with parents, NS rooms, wheelchair access, pets OK, gift shop, in-room refrigerators, 13 meeting rooms, meeting facilities for 750, CC. 5 minutes from the airport. SGL/DBL$120-$150.

Embassy Suites Airport (15920 West Valley Hwy. 98188; 227-8844, Fax 2279567, 800-EMBASSY) 238 2-room suites, restaurant, lounge, entertainment, free breakfast, pool, sauna, whirlpools, exercise center, a/c, TV, airport transportation, NS rooms, gift shop, room service, wheelchair access, meeting facilities, CC. 3 miles from the airport, 11 miles from the downtown area. STS$79-$129.

Hampton Inn Southcenter (7200 South 156th St. 98188; 228-5800, Fax 228-6812, 800-HAMPTON) 154 rooms, free breakfast, outdoor heated, pool, exercise center, airport transportation, pets OK, children free with parents, NS rooms, wheelchair access, a/c, TV, computer hookups, fax service, free local calls, meeting facilities, CC. 17 miles from the downtown area and the Space Needle, 1 mile from the Southcenter Mall, 4 miles from the airport. SGL/DBL$60-$75.

Hampton Inn Airport (19445 International Blvd. 98188; 878-1700, Fax 8240720, 800-HAMPTON) 131 rooms, free breakfast, pool, exercise center, airport transportation, children free with parents, a/c, TV, NS rooms, wheelchair access, computer hookups, fax service, free local calls, meeting facilities, CC. .3 miles from the airport, 15 miles from the downtown area and Convention Center. SGL/DBL$65-$80.

Heritage Inn (16838 Pacific Hwy. South, 98188; 248-0901, Fax 242-3170, 800-845-2968) 151 rooms and suites, free breakfast, children free with parents, airport courtesy car, laundry service, meeting facilities, a/c, TV, CC. SGL/DBL$75-$95.

Holiday Inn Airport (17338 Pacific Hwy. South, 98188; 248-1000, Fax 2427089, 800-HOLIDAY) 260 rooms, restaurant, lounge, indoor heated pool, exercise center, gift shop, laundry facilities, children free with parents, wheelchair access, NS rooms, fax service, room service, no pets, airport transportation, meeting facilities for 300, CC. 15 miles from the downtown area and the Waterfront. SGL/DBL$90-$105.

Howard Johnson Lodge (17108 Pacific Hwy. South, 98188; 244-1230, Fax 2410893, 800-I-GO-HOJO, 800-654-9122) 74 rooms, free breakfast, children free with parents, NS rooms, wheelchair access, airport courtesy car, CC. 2 miles from Sea-Tac Airport near the Kingdome. SGL/DBL$40-$48.

Homewood Suites (6955 Southcenter Blvd. 98188; 433000, Fax 433-994, 800-ALL-HOME) 106 1- and 2-bedroom suites, kitchens, free breakfast, pool, exercise center, convenience store, complimentary newspaper, in-room computer hookups, laundry service, a/c, TV, fax service, meeting facilities, NS rooms, airport courtesy car, CC. 11 miles from the downtown area, 2.5 miles from the airport. 1BR$79-$119, 2BR$99-$119.

La Quinta Inn Airport (2824 South 188th St. 98188; 241-5211, Fax 246-5596, 800-531-5900) 142 rooms, restaurant, lounge, heated pool, exercise center, complimentary newspaper, airport transportation, free local calls, fax service, laundry service, a/c, TV, pets OK, NS rooms, wheelchair access, meeting facilities, CC. 5 miles from the Longacres Race Course and Sea-Tac Office Center. SGL/DBL$62-$87.

Marriott Residence Inn (16201 West Valley Hwy. 98188; 226-5500, Fax 271-5023, 800-331-3131) 235 suites, kitchens, in-room refrigerators and microwaves, airport transportation, laundry service, wheelchair access, NS rooms, pets OK, VCRs, a/c, TV, meeting facilities for 25, CC. 4 miles from the airport, 12 miles from the downtown area. SGL/DBL$115.

Marriott Sea-Tac Airport Hotel (3201 South 176th St. 98188; 241-2000, Fax 248-0789, 800-228-9290) 459 rooms and suites, Concierge Level, restaurant, lounge, indoor pool, whirlpools, sauna, exercise center, airport courtesy car, a/c, TV, wheelchair access, NS rooms, gift shop, no pets, CC. At the airport, 20 minutes from the downtown area. SGL/DBL$110-$450.

Nendels Inn (15901 West Valley Rd. 98188; 226-1812, Fax 255-7856, 800-547-0106) 146 rooms, restaurant, lounge, outdoor heated pool, whirlpools, a/c, TV, children under 17 free with parents, in-room refrigerators and microwaves, NS rooms, senior rates, CC. SGL/DBL$70-$80.

Red Lion Inn (18740 Pacific Hwy. South, 98188; 246-8600, Fax 242-9727) 850 rooms and suites, 2 restaurants, lounge, entertainment, outdoor heated pool, jacuzzi, exercise center, laundry service, beauty shop, a/c, TV, NS rooms, barber and beauty shop, water view, children free with parents, airport courtesy car, meeting facilities, CC. SGL/DBL$110-$130, STS$275-$450.

Radisson Hotel (17001 Pacific Hwy. South, 98188; 244-6000, Fax 246-6835, 800-333-3333) 300 rooms and suites, restaurant, lounge, outdoor heated pool, sauna, exercise center, gift shop, no pets, room service, children free with parents, boutiques, game room, fax service, a/c, TV, meeting facilities, senior rates, CC. SGL$80-$120, STS$150-$350.

Shadow Motel at Sea-Tac (2930 South 176th St. 98188; 246-9300) 59 rooms, restaurant, airport courtesy car, laundry service, no pets, a/c, TV, CC. SGL$38-$46, DBL$39-$48.

Silver Cloud Inn (13050 48th Ave. South, 98168; 241-2200) 120 rooms, outdoor heated pool, exercise center, whirlpools, a/c, TV, in-room refrigerators, microwaves and coffee makers, laundry facilities, no pets, CC. SGL/DBL$45-$60.

Days Inn Sea-Tac Airport (19015 Pacific Hwy. South, 98188; 244-3600, Fax 244-3600, 800-325-2525) 86 rooms and suites, free breakfast, exercise center, kitchenettes, NS rooms, airport courtesy car, wheelchair access, children under 16 free with parents, no pets, a/c, TV, fax service, meeting facilities, CC. At the airport, 15 minutes from the downtown area. SGL$49-$59, DBL$59$69, STS$85-$110.

Doubletree Suites (16500 Southcenter Parkway, 98188; 575-8220, Fax 575-4743, 800-528-0444) 221 suites, restaurant, lounge, entertainment, heated indoor pool, spa, sauna, exercise center, local transportation, a/c,

TV, children free with parents, NS rooms, wheelchair access, 13 meeting rooms, meeting facilities for 750, CC. 5 minutes from the airport. SGL/DBL$85-$155.

Hilton Airport (17620 Pacific Hwy. South, 98188; 244-4800, Fax 248-4495, 800-HILTONS) 173 rooms and suites, restaurant, lounge, outdoor heated pool, exercise center, jacuzzi, wheelchair access, NS rooms, no pets, a/c, TV, gift shop, airport courtesy car, 14 meeting rooms, meeting facilities for 620, CC. 12 miles from the downtown area, 1 mile from the Sea-Tac International Airport. SGL/DBL$110-$350.

Quality Inn At Sea-Tac (3000 South 176th St. 98188; 246-9110, 800-221-2222) 209 rooms, restaurant, lounge, free breakfast, indoor pool, sauna, whirlpools, a/c, TV, no pets, wheelchair access, NS rooms, meeting facilities, CC. 15 miles from the Space Needle, Convention Center and Pike Place Market. SGL/DBL$65.

Radisson Hotel (1700 Pacific Hwy. South, 98188; 244-6000, Fax 246-6835, 800-333-3333) 300 rooms and suites, restaurant, lounge, pool, sauna, exercise center, gift shop, fax service, meeting facilities, a/c, TV, CC. SGL$80-$120, DBL$86-$109, STS$150-$350.

TraveLodge Airport (2900 South 192nd St. 98188; 241-9292, Fax 242-0681, 800-578-7878) 104 rooms, restaurant, lounge, sauna, VCRs, airport transportation, room service, no pets, fax service, wheelchair access, a/c, TV, meeting facilities for 26, CC. 1 mile from the Seattle-Tacoma International airport, 10 minutes from the downtown area. SGL$40-$55, DBL$45-$60, X$5.

Westcoast Sea-Tac Hotel (18229 Pacific Hwy. South, 98188; 246-5535, Fax 246-5535) 146 rooms, restaurant, lounge, entertainment, outdoor pool, jacuzzi, exercise center, laundry service, airport courtesy car, room service, a/c, TV, CC. SGL/DBL$70-$90, STS$150.

Wyndham Garden Hotel Airport (18118 Pacific Hwy. South, 98188; 244-6666, Fax 244-6679, 800-822-4200) 204 rooms and suites, restaurant, lounge, indoor pool, whirlpools, spa, exercise center, airport courtesy car, a/c, TV, wheelchair access, NS rooms, 4,200 square feet of meeting and exhibition space, meeting facilities for 200, CC. Across from the Seattle-Tacoma International Airport. SGL$109-$119.

Tumwater
Area Code 206

Best Western Inn (5188 Capitol Blvd. 98501; 956-1235, 800-528-1234) 89 rooms, whirlpools, exercise center, children free with parents, a/c, NS rooms, TV, laundry facilities, in-room refrigerators and microwaves, wheelchair access, pets OK, meeting facilities, senior rates, CC. SGL/DBL$55-$75.

Motel 6 (400 West Lee St. 98501; 754-7320, 505-891-6161) 119 rooms, pool, free local calls, children under 17 free with parents, NS rooms, wheelchair access, pets OK, a/c, TV, CC. SGL/DBL$44-$46.

Vancouver

Area Code 206

Best Western Ferryman's Inn (7901 Northeast 6th Ave. 98665; 574-2151, Fax 574-9644, 800-528-1234) 132 rooms, free breakfast, outdoor pool, children free with parents, a/c, NS rooms, TV, laundry facilities, wheelchair access, pets OK, meeting facilities, senior rates, CC. SGL/DBL$40-$70.

Comfort Inn (13207 Northeast 20th Ave. 98686; 574-6000, Fax 573-3746, 800-221-2222) 58 rooms and suites, restaurant, complementary breakfast, indoor heated pool, whirlpools, a/c, TV, children free with parents, NS rooms, wheelchair access, in-room refrigerators, no pets, airport transportation, meeting facilities, senior rates, CC. SGL/DBL$50-$90.

Comfort Suites (4714 Northeast 94th Ave. 98662; 253-3100, 800-221-2222) 68 suites, free breakfast, indoor heated pool, exercise center, whirlpools, a/c, TV, children free with parents, NS rooms, wheelchair access, in-room refrigerators, no pets, senior rates, CC. SGL/DBL$85-$120.

Cape Winds Resort (7400 Ridgewood Ave., 32920; 799-2676, Fax 799-2676, 800-248-1030) 66 1- and 2-bedroom apartments, outdoor heated, pool, lighted tennis courts, sauna, exercise center, beach, TV, a/c, in-room refrigerators, no pets, children free with parents, CC. 1BR$105, 2BR$105-$160.

Holiday Inn (9107 Northeast Vancouver Mall Dr. 98662; 253-5000, 800-HOLIDAY) 57 rooms, indoor heated pool, exercise facilities, VCRs, children under 19 free with parents, wheelchair access, a/c, TV, NS rooms, fax service, room service, no pets, laundry service, meeting facilities, senior rates, CC. SGL/DBL$55-$60.

Mark 205 Motor Inn (221 Northeast Chkalov Dr. 98684; 256-7044, 800-426-5110) 118 rooms and suites, restaurant, indoor pool, pets OK, children free with parents, a/c, TV, wheelchair access, NS rooms, airport transportation, meeting facilities, senior rates, CC. SGL/DBL$40-$100.

Nendels Suites (7001 Northeast Hwy. 99, 98665; 696-0516, Fax 693-8343, 800-547-0106) 72 suites, free breakfast, outdoor heated pool, whirlpools, pets OK, a/c, TV, children under 17 free with parents, laundry facilities, in-room refrigerators, senior rates, CC. SGL/DBL$42-$56.

Red Lion Inn (100 Columbia St. 98660; 694-8341, Fax 694-2023, 800-547-8010) 160 rooms and suites, restaurant, lounge, entertainment, outdoor heated pool, a/c, TV, wheelchair access, NS rooms, complimentary newspaper, airport courtesy car, pets OK, gift shop, room service, fax service, laundry facilities, meeting facilities, senior rates, CC. SGL/DBL$85-$295.

Residence Inn by Marriott (8005 Northeast Parkway Dr. 98662; 253-4800, 800-331-3131) 30 suites, free breakfast, outdoor heated pool, whirlpools, in-room refrigerators, coffee makers and microwaves, laundry facilities, TV, a/c, VCRs, pets OK, complimentary newspaper, fireplaces, children free with parents, NS rooms, wheelchair access, meeting facilities, CC. SGL/DBL$100-$150.

Shilo Inn (13206 Hwy. 99, 98686; 573-0511, Fax 573-4644, 800-222-2244) 66 rooms and efficiencies, restaurant, free breakfast, lounge, indoor heated pool, sauna, whirlpools, airport courtesy car, in-room refrigerators, a/c, pets OK, laundry facilities, TV, NS rooms, wheelchair access, children under 12 free with parents, meeting facilities, senior rates, CC. SGL/DBL$60-$85.

TraveLodge (11506 Northeast 3rd St. 98664; 254-4000, Fax 254-8741, 800-578-7878) 59 rooms, restaurant, lounge, free breakfast, indoor heated pool, whirlpools, wheelchair access, complimentary newspaper, laundry service, TV, a/c, free local calls, fax service, NS rooms, in-room refrigerators and microwaves, children under 18 free with parents, no pets, meeting facilities, senior rates, CC. SGL/DBL$45-$65.

Vashon Island
Area Code 206

Artist's Studio Loft (16529 91st Ave. Southwest, 98070; 463-2583) 1 room, free breakfast, TV, NS, no children, in-room refrigerator and microwave, hot tub, a/c, no pets. SGL/DBL$70.

Veradale
Area Code 509

Comfort Inn Valley (905 North Sullivan Rd. 99037; 924-3838, 800-221-2222) 76 rooms, pool, hot tubs, sauna, kitchenettes, a/c, TV, senior rates, meeting facilities, CC. SGL/DBL$61-$85

Walla Walla
Area Code 509

Best Western Pony Soldier Motor Inn (325 East Main St. 99362; 529-4360, Fax 529-7463, 800-528-1234) 85 rooms, free breakfast, outdoor pool, hot tubs, spa, exercise center, kitchenettes, children free with parents, a/c, NS rooms, TV, laundry facilities, wheelchair access, pets OK, meeting facilities, senior rates, CC. SGL/DBL$65-$73.

Budget Inn (211 North 2nd Ave. 99362; 529-2580, 800-722-8277) 30 rooms, restaurant, children free with parents, no pets, a/c, TV, wheelchair access, NS rooms, senior rates, CC. SGL/DBL$30-$48.

Comfort Inn (520 North 2nd Ave. 99362; 525-2552, 800-221-2222) 49 rooms, pool, whirlpools, sauna, a/c, kitchenettes, free local calls, complimentary newspaper, TV, senior rates, CC. SGL/DBL$55-$82.

Econo Lodge (305 North 2nd Ave. 99362; 529-4410, 800-4-CHOICE) 35 rooms, pool, children under 12 free with parents, no pets, NS rooms, wheelchair access, a/c, TV, senior rates, CC. SGL/DBL$37-$63.

Green Gables Inn (922 Bonsella Ave. 99362; 525-5501) 5 rooms, free breakfast, whirlpools, TV, a/c, no pets, CC. SGL/DBL$65-$100.

Nendels Inn (107 North 2nd Ave. 99362; 525-2200, 800-547-0106) 72 rooms, restaurant, lounge, entertainment, outdoor heated pool, a/c, TV, children under 17 free with parents, airport transportation, in-room refrigerators, senior rates, CC. SGL/DBL$55-$60.

TraveLodge (421 East Main St. 99362; 529-4940, Fax 529-4943, 800-578-7878) 38 rooms, restaurant, lounge, free breakfast, pool, whirlpools, wheelchair access, complimentary newspaper, laundry service, TV, a/c, free local calls, fax service, NS rooms, in-room refrigerators and microwaves, children under 18 free with parents, no pets, meeting facilities, senior rates, CC. SGL/DBL$50-$65.

Washougal
Area Code 206

Econo Lodge (544 6th St. 98671; 835-8591, 800-4-CHOICE) 26 rooms, pool, children under 12 free with parents, no pets, senior rates, NS rooms, wheelchair access, a/c, TV, senior rates, CC. SGL/DBL$40-$68.

Wenatchee
Area Code 509

Avenue Motel (720 North Wenatchee Ave. 98801; 663-8133) 39 rooms and 2-bedroom villas, outdoor heated pool, TV, a/c, VCRs, pets OK, children free with parents, CC. SGL/DBL$33-$53.

Chieftain (Wenatchee 98801; 663-8141, 800-572-4456 in Washington) 105 rooms, restaurant, lounge, entertainment, outdoor heated pool, hot tubs, a/c, TV, wheelchair access, NS rooms, pets OK, senior rates, CC. SGL/DBL$45-$80.

Econo Lodge Downtown (700 North Wenatchee Ave. 98801; 663-8133, 800-4-CHOICE) 41 rooms, pool, children under 12 free with parents, no pets, NS rooms, wheelchair access, a/c, TV, senior rates, CC. SGL/DBL$40-$66.

Holiday Lodge (610 North Wenatchee Ave. 98801; 663-8167, 800-722-0852) 60 rooms, free breakfast, outdoor pool, whirlpools, sauna, no pets, children free with parents, a/c, TV, wheelchair access, NS rooms, senior rates, CC. SGL/DBL$35-$65.

Lyes Motel (924 North Wenatchee Ave. 98801; 663-5155) 22 rooms, outdoor heated pool, whirlpools, children free with parents, pets OK, TV, a/c, CC. SGL/DBL$30-$55.

Orchard Inn (1401 North Miller St. 98801; 662-3443) 103 rooms and 2-bedroom suites, children free with parents, pets OK, in-room refrigerators and microwaves, a/c, TV, CC. SGL/DBL$38-$60.

Red Lion Inn (1225 North Wenatchee Ave. 98801; 663-0711, 800-547-8010) 149 rooms and suites, restaurant, lounge, entertainment, outdoor heated pool, a/c, TV, wheelchair access, airport transportation, pets OK, NS rooms, complimentary newspaper, fax service, laundry facilities, meeting facilities, senior rates, CC. SGL/DBL$68-$85, STS$150.

Rivers Inn (580 Valley Mall Parkway, 98802; 884-1474) 55 rooms, free breakfast, restaurant, lounge, heated pool, whirlpools, no pets, children free with parents, a/c, TV, wheelchair access, NS rooms, senior rates, CC. SGL/DBL$45-$68.

Scotty's Motel (1004 North Wenatchee Ave. 98801; 662-8165) 34 rooms, outdoor heated pool, sauna, whirlpool, no pets, TV, a/c, in-room refrigerators, CC. SGL/DBL$32-$49.

West Coast Wenatchee Center Hotel (201 North Wenatchee Ave. 98801; 662-1234, Fax 662-0782, 800-426-0670) 150 rooms, restaurant, lounge, entertainment, indoor and outdoor pool, exercise center, whirlpools, pets OK, a/c, TV, airport transportation, 40,000 square feet of meeting and exhibition space, meeting facilities for 1,500, CC. SGL/DBL$75-$175.

Whidbey Island
Area Code 206

Guest House Bed and Breakfast (835 East Christerson Rd. 98253; 678-3115) pool, jacuzzi, spa, free breakfast, TV, a/c, no pets, CC. SGL/DBL$36-$46.

White Salmon
Area Code 509

The Inn of the White Salmon (172 West Jewett, 98672; 493-2335) 16 rooms and suites, children free with parents, TV, a/c, pets OK, CC. SGL/DBL$75-$115.

Winthrop

Area Code 509

Best Western Marigot Inn (960 Hwy. 20, 98862; 996-3100, 800-528-1234) 63 rooms, free breakfast, spa, children free with parents, a/c, NS rooms, TV, laundry facilities, wheelchair access, pets OK, meeting facilities, senior rates, CC. SGL/DBL$45-$85.

Hotel Rio Vista (285 Riverside, 98862; 996-3535) 16 rooms, whirlpools, a/c, TV, no pets, CC. SGL/DBL$55-$80.

Piney Woods Inn (Hwy. 20, 98862; 996-2626) 6 rooms, free breakfast, TV, a/c, no pets, NS, hot tubs, CC. SGL/DBL$55-$75.

Rader Road Inn (Rader Rd. 98862; 996-2173) free breakfast, TV, a/c, no pets, pool, hot tub, NS. SGL/DBL$50-$65.

Sun Mountain Lodge (Patterson Lake Rd. 98862; 996-2211, Fax 996-3133, 800-572-0493) 87 rooms and cottages, restaurant, lounge, entertainment, outdoor pool, exercise center, whirlpools, game room, in-room refrigerators, a/c, TV, wheelchair access, NS rooms, no pets, fireplaces, meeting facilities, CC. SGL/DBL$115-$250.

The Virginian Resort (808 North Cascade Hwy. 98862; 996-2535) 40 rooms and cabins, outdoor heated pool, whirlpools, fireplaces, children free with parents, pets OK, TV, a/c, in-room refrigerators and coffee makers, CC. SGL/DBL$40-$150.

Winthrop Inn (Winthrop 98862; 996-2217, 800-444-1972) 30 rooms, outdoor pool, whirlpools, no pets, children free with parents, a/c, TV, wheelchair access, NS rooms, senior rates, CC. SGL/DBL$45-$60.

Yakima

Area Code 509

Bali-Hai Motel (710 North 1st St. 98901; 452-7176) 28 rooms and 2-bedroom efficiencies, outdoor pool, pets OK, TV, CC. SGL/DBL$25-$34.

Best Western Inn (1603 Terrace Heights Dr. 98901; 457-4444, Fax 453-7593, 800-528-1234) 96 rooms and efficiencies, restaurant, lounge, outdoor heated pool, whirlpools, in-room refrigerators, children free with parents, no pets, airport courtesy car, a/c, NS rooms, TV, laundry facilities, wheelchair access, meeting facilities, senior rates, CC. SGL/DBL$55-$65, EFF$65.

Cavanaugh's (607 East Yakima Ave. 98901; 248-5900, Fax 575-8975) 152 rooms, restaurant, lounge, entertainment, outdoor heated pool, VCRs, TV, a/c, in-room refrigerators, pets OK, children free with parents, CC. SGL/DBL$58-$98.

Colonial Motor Inn (1405 North 1st St. 98901; 453-8981, Fax 452-3241) 53 rooms, restaurant, outdoor heated pool, whirlpools, no pets, a/c, TV, wheelchair access, NS rooms, senior rates, CC. SGL/DBL$38-$50.

Comfort Inn (1700 North 1st St. 98901; 248-5650, 800-221-2222) 70 rooms, pool, sauna, no pets, fax service, a/c, TV, senior rates, CC. SGL/DBL$53-$75.

Days Inn (2408 Rudkin Rd. 98903; 248-9700, Fax 248-3607, 800-325-2525) 100 rooms, free breakfast, outdoor pool, a/c, TV, wheelchair access, NS rooms, no pets, laundry facilities, free local calls, meeting facilities, senior rates, CC. SGL/DBL$48-$160.

Econo Lodge (510 North 1st St. 98901; 457-6155, 800-4-CHOICE) 37 rooms, pool, children under 12 free with parents, no pets, senior rates, NS rooms, complimentary newspaper, wheelchair access, a/c, TV, senior rates, CC. SGL/DBL$45-$48.

Holiday Inn (9 North 9th St. 98901; 452-6511, 800-HOLIDAY) 170 rooms, restaurant, lounge, outdoor heated pool, hot tub, airport transportation, children under 19 free with parents, wheelchair access, a/c, TV, NS rooms, fax service, room service, pets OK, laundry service, meeting facilities, senior rates, CC. SGL/DBL$60-$175.

Red Carpet Inn (1608 Fruitvale Blvd. 98902; 457-1131, 800-251-1962) 29 rooms and 2-bedroom suites, outdoor heated pool, sauna, in-room refrigerators, children free with parents, TV, a/c, NS rooms, pets OK, meeting facilities, senior rates, CC. SGL/DBL$30-$44.

Red Lion Inn (1507 North 1st St. 98901; 248-7850, Fax 575-1694, 800-547-8010) 209 rooms and suites, restaurant, lounge, entertainment, heated pool, whirlpools, no pets, airport transportation, in-room refrigerators, a/c, TV, wheelchair access, NS rooms, complimentary newspaper, fax service, laundry facilities, CC. SGL/DBL$75-$95.

Red Lion Inn (818 North 1st St. 98901; 453-0391, 800-547-8010) 58 rooms and 2-bedroom suites, outdoor heated pool, a/c, TV, wheelchair access, NS rooms, children free with parents, in-room refrigerators and microwaves, complimentary newspaper, fax service, laundry facilities, meeting facilities, senior rates, CC. SGL/DBL$50-$79.

The 37th House (4002 Englewood Ave. 98908; 965-5537) 6 rooms, free breakfast, TV, private baths, 1930s home, NS rooms, a/c, no pets, CC. SGL/DBL$65-$120.

TraveLodge (110 Naches Ave. 98901; 453-7151, Fax 575-8394, 800-578-7878) 48 rooms, restaurant, lounge, free breakfast, pool, wheelchair access, complimentary newspaper, laundry service, TV, a/c, free local calls, fax service, NS rooms, in-room refrigerators and microwaves, children under 18 free with parents, no pets, meeting facilities, senior rates, CC. SGL/DBL$45-$56.

Rock Crest Lodge (15 West Mt. Rushmore Rd., 57730; 673-4323) 19 rooms and efficiencies, a/c, TV, no pets, in-room microwaves, wheelchair access, NS rooms, senior rates, CC. SGL/DBL$25-$70.

Rocket Motel (211 Mt. Rushmore Rd., 57730; 673-4401) 27 rooms and 2-bedroom efficiencies, a/c, TV, wheelchair access, NS rooms, senior rates, CC. SGL/DBL$30-$59.

Roost Resort (Custer 57730; 673-2326) 7 rooms and cabins, pets OK, in-room refrigerators and microwaves, a/c, TV, wheelchair access, NS rooms, children free with parents, senior rates, CC. SGL/DBL$35-$60.

State Game Lodge (Custer 57730; 255-4541) 47 rooms and efficiencies, restaurant, a/c, TV, wheelchair access, NS rooms, pets OK, senior rates, CC. SGL/DBL$75-$175.

Sun Mark Inn (342 Mt. Rushmore Rd., 57730; 673-4400, Fax 673-2314) 45 rooms, indoor heated pool, hot tubs, whirlpools, laundry facilities, no pets, a/c, TV, wheelchair access, NS rooms, senior rates, CC. SGL/DBL$39-$70.

Wyoming

Afton
Area Code 307

Best Western Hi Country Inn (Hwy. 89, 83110; 886-3856, 800-528-1234) 30 rooms, outdoor heated pool, children free with parents, a/c, NS rooms, TV, laundry facilities, wheelchair access, pets OK, meeting facilities, senior rates, CC. SGL/DBL$35-$65.

The Corral (161 Washington, 83110; 886-5424) 15 rooms and 2-bedroom efficiencies, pets OK, TV, airport transportation, CC. SGL/DBL$38-$40.

Lazy B Motel (219 Washington, 83110; 886-3187) 25 rooms and efficiencies, TV, pets OK, airport transportation, laundry facilities, senior rates, CC. SGL/DBL$30-$42.

Mountain Inn (Hwy. 89, 83110; 886-3187) 20 rooms, outdoor heated pool, whirlpools, sauna, a/c, pets OK, TV, senior rates, CC. SGL/DBL$42-$56.

Silver Stream Lodge (Hwy. 89, 83110; 883-2440) 12 rooms and efficiencies, restaurant, lounge, a/c, TV, no pets, wheelchair access, NS rooms, senior rates, CC. SGL/DBL$45-$65.

Alpine
Area Code 307

Alpine House Hotel (Alpine 83128; 654-7545, Fax 654-7545, 800-343-6755) 44 rooms, restaurant, lounge, whirlpools, gift shop, in-room refrigerators, children under 12 free with parents, a/c, TV, NS rooms, wheelchair access, meeting facilities, pets OK, CC. SGL/DBL$60-$130.

Best Western Flying Saddle Lodge (Alpine 83128; 654-7561, 800-528-1234) 20 rooms, restaurant, lounge, outdoor heated pool, children free with parents, a/c, NS rooms, TV, laundry facilities, wheelchair access, pets OK, meeting facilities, senior rates, CC. SGL/DBL$65-$155.

Lakeside Motel (Alpine 83128; 654-7507) 11 rooms and efficiencies, restaurant, a/c, TV, wheelchair access, NS rooms, senior rates, pets OK, CC. SGL/DBL$28-$36.

Nordic Inn (Alpine 83128; 654-7556) 8 rooms, restaurant, lounge, a/c, TV, CC. SGL/DBL$44-$54.

Three Rivers Motel (Alpine 83128; 654-7551) 23 rooms and efficiencies, pets OK, a/c, TV, CC. SGL/DBL$48-$52.

Alta

Area Code 307

Grand Targhee Ski and Summer Resort (Alta 83422; 353-2304, Fax 353-8148, 800-443-8146) 96 rooms and 2-bedroom suites, restaurant, lounge, entertainment, heated pool, hot tub, jacuzzi, whirlpools, exercise center, tennis courts, children under 12 free with parents, in-room refrigerators and coffee makers, gift shop, a/c, VCRs, TV, no pets, laundry facilities, meeting facilities, CC. SGL/DBL$67-$145.

High Comforts Lodge (Alta North Rd., 83422; 353-8560, Fax 353-8486) 4 rooms, free breakfast, TV, no pets, children under 12 free with parents, NS, CC. SGL/DBL$60-$90.

Baggs

Area Code 307

Drifters Inn (Hwy. 789, 82321; 383-2015) 31 rooms, restaurant, lounge, pets OK, a/c, TV, wheelchair access, NS rooms, senior rates, CC. SGL/DBL$36-$38.

Banner

Area Code 307

Rafter Y Ranch (Banner 82832; no phone) cabins, dude ranch, private baths, fireplaces, CC. SGL/DBL$65.

Big Horn

Area Code 307

Spahn's Big Horn Mountain Bed and Breakfast (Big Horn 82833; 674-8150) 4 rooms, free breakfast, airport transportation, NS, no pets, CC. SGL/DBL$75-$100.

Big Piney

Area Code 307

C.K. Hunting and Fishing Lodge (Big Piney 83113; 276-3471) cabins, dude ranch, American plan available, CC. SGL/DBL$100-$135.

Bondurant
Area Code 307

Hoback Village Motel (Hwy. 191, 82992; 733-3631) 7 rooms, restaurant, a/c, TV, no pets, wheelchair access, NS rooms, CC. SGL/DBL$50-$60.

Smiling S (Bondurant 82922; 733-3457) 7 rooms, pets OK, TV, CC. SGL/DBL$55-$65.

Spring Creek Ranch (Bondurant 82922; 733-1184) cabins, dude ranch, private baths, American plan available, CC. SGL/DBL$37-$46.

Triangle Lodge (Bondurant 82992; 733-2836) 5 rooms, restaurant, a/c, TV, no pets, CC. SGL/DBL$55-$60.

Boulder
Area Code 307

Big Sandy Lodge (Boulder 82823; 332-6782) 10 cabins, dude ranch, American plan available, CC. SGL/DBL$125-$250.

Buffalo
Area Code 307

Arrowhead Motel (Hwy. 16 West, 82834; 684-9453) 13 rooms and efficiencies, pets OK, a/c, TV, CC. SGL/DBL$28-$33.

Bear Track Lodge (8885 Hwy. 16 West, 82834; 684-2528) 10 rooms, dude ranch, kitchenettes, TV, CC. SGL/DBL$36-$46.

Big Horn Motel (209 North Main St., 82834; 684-7611) 18 rooms, pets OK, kitchenettes, a/c, TV, CC. SGL/DBL$40-$50.

Canyon Motel (Hwy. 16 West, 82834; 684-2957) 18 rooms and efficiencies, pets OK, a/c, TV, CC. SGL/DBL$28-$39.

Crossroads Inn (Buffalo 82834; 684-2256) 60 rooms, restaurant, lounge, pool, laundry facilities, a/c, TV, no pets, wheelchair access, NS rooms, senior rates, CC. SGL/DBL$60-$76.

Frontier Inn (800 North Main St., 82834; 684-7453) 5 rooms, a/c, TV, CC. SGL/DBL$40-$60.

Horseman's Motel (Hwy. 16 East, 82834; 684-2219) 43 rooms, pets OK, a/c, TV, CC. SGL/DBL$28-$38.

Keahey's Motel (350 North Main St., 82834; 684-2225) 39 rooms and efficiencies, pets OK, a/c, TV, CC. SGL/DBL$44-$54.

Mansion House (313 North Main St., 82834; 684-2218) 19 rooms, pets OK, a/c, TV, CC. SGL/DBL$36-$44.

Paradise Guest Ranch (Buffalo 82834; 684-7876) 18 cabins, dude ranch, American plan available, lounge, CC. SGL/DBL$80-$155.

Pines Lodge (Buffalo 82834; no phone) rooms, restaurant, lounge, dude ranch, fireplaces, TV, CC. SGL/DBL$65-$130.

South Fork Inn (Buffalo 82834; 684-9609) 12 cabins, dude ranch, restaurant, CC. SGL/DBL$55-$110.

Super 8 Motel (Clearmont Rd., 82834; 684-2531, 800-800-8000) 48 rooms and suites, no pets, children under 12 free with parents, free local calls, a/c, TV, in-room refrigerators and microwaves, fax service, NS rooms, wheelchair access, meeting facilities, senior rates, CC. SGL/DBL$54-$66.

V Bar F Cattle Ranch (Buffalo 82834; 758-4382) 3 rooms, free breakfast, American plan available, private baths, TV, a/c, no pets, CC. SGL/DBL$80-$160.

Z-Bar Motel (Hwy. 16 West, 82834; 684-5535) 22 rooms, kitchenettes, pets OK, a/c, TV, CC. SGL/DBL$29-$38.

Casper
Area Code 307

Bessemer Bend Bed and Breakfast (6905 Speas Rd., 82604; 265-6819) free breakfast, TV, a/c, no pets, NS, CC. SGL/DBL$40-$50.

Best Western East Inn (2325 East Yellowstone, 82602; 234-3541, 800-528-1234) 40 rooms, restaurant, free breakfast, indoor heated pool, children free with parents, a/c, NS rooms, in-room refrigerators, TV, laundry facilities, wheelchair access, pets OK, meeting facilities, senior rates, CC. SGL/DBL$40-$75.

Commercial Inn (Casper 82604; 235-6688) 42 rooms, restaurant, a/c, TV, no pets, CC. SGL/DBL$25-$35.

First Interstate Inn (Wyoming Blvd., 82601; 234-9125) 60 rooms, a/c, TV, wheelchair access, children free with parents, VCRs, pets OK, in-room refrigerators and microwaves, NS rooms, senior rates, CC. SGL/DBL$27-$37.

Hampton Inn (400 West F St., 82601; 235-6668. 800-HAMPTON) 121 rooms, restaurant, free breakfast, outdoor heated pool, exercise center, sauna, children under 18 free with parents, NS rooms, wheelchair access, in-room computer hookups, fax service, airport transportation, TV, a/c, free local calls, pets OK, meeting facilities, senior rates, CC. SGL/DBL$49-$59.

Hilton Hotel (I-25 and North Poplar, 82602; 266-6000, Fax 473-1010, 800-HILTONS) 225 rooms and suites, restaurant, lounge, entertainment, indoor heated pool, exercise center, whirlpools, children free with parents, NS rooms, wheelchair access, pets OK, beauty shop, airport transportation, room service, laundry facilities, gift shop, a/c, TV, business services, meeting facilities, senior rates, CC. SGL/DBL$60-$70, STS$85-$175.

Holiday Inn (300 West Front St., 82602; 235-2532, Fax 266-0160, 800-HOLIDAY) 197 rooms and suites, restaurant, lounge, entertainment, indoor heated pool, exercise center, sauna, airport transportation, game rooms, children under 19 free with parents, wheelchair access, a/c, TV, NS rooms, fax service, room service, pets OK, laundry service, meeting facilities, senior rates, CC. SGL/DBL$50-$66.

Kelly Inn (821 North Poplar 82601; 266-2400, Fax 266-1146, 800-635-3559) 103 rooms, whirlpools, sauna, pets OK, laundry facilities, children free with parents, airport transportation, a/c, TV, wheelchair access, NS rooms, senior rates, meeting facilities, CC. SGL/DBL$33-$45.

La Quinta Inn (301 East E St., 82601; 234-1159, Fax 265-0829, 800-531-5900) 122 rooms, outdoor heated pool, complimentary newspaper, free local calls, fax service, laundry service, children free with parents, NS rooms, wheelchair access, remote control TV, a/c, pets OK, meeting facilities, senior rates, all CC. SGL/DBL$35-$40.

Motel 6 (1150 Wilkins Circle, 82601; 234-3903, 505-891-6161) 120 rooms, pool, free local calls, children under 17 free with parents, NS rooms, wheelchair access, pets OK, a/c, TV, CC. SGL/DBL$23-$29.

Royal Inn (440 East A St., 82601; 234-3501) 35 rooms and efficiencies, outdoor heated pool, a/c, TV, wheelchair access, NS rooms, in-room refrigerators, kitchenettes, airport transportation, senior rates, CC. SGL/DBL$20-$30.

Sand Lake Lodge (Casper 82605; 234-6064) 26 rooms and cabins, dude ranch, American plan available, CC. SGL/DBL$80-$150.

Showboat Motel (100 West F St., 82601; 235-2711, 800-341-8000) 45 rooms, a/c, TV, in-room refrigerators, VCRs, children free with parents, no pets, no-smoking rooms, meeting facilities, senior rates, CC. SGL/DBL$25-$45.

Super 8 Motel (3838 Cy Ave., 82604; 266-3480, 800-800-8000) 66 rooms and suites, no pets, children under 12 free with parents, free local calls, a/c, TV, in-room refrigerators and microwaves, fax service, NS rooms, wheelchair access, meeting facilities, senior rates, CC. SGL/DBL$30-$50.

Travelier Motel (500 East 1st St., 82601; 237-9343) 14 rooms and 2-bedroom efficiencies, pets OK, a/c, TV, NS rooms, senior rates, CC. SGL/DBL$20-$24.

Westridge Motel (955 Cy Ave., 82601; 234-8911) 28 rooms and 2-bedroom efficiencies, no pets, a/c, TV, wheelchair access, NS rooms, senior rates, CC. SGL/DBL$28-$42.

Centennial
Area Code 307

Friendly Fly Motel (Centennial 82055; 742-6033) 9 rooms, pets OK, kitchenettes, a/c, TV, CC. SGL/DBL$36-$46.

Mountain Meadow Guest Ranch (Centennial 82055; 742-6042) 8 cabins, dude ranch, American plan available, CC. SGL/DBL$75-$150.

Pat's Old Corral Inn (Main St., 82055; 745-5918) 15 rooms, restaurant, lounge, a/c, TV, no pets, wheelchair access, NS rooms, senior rates, CC. SGL/DBL$58-$68.

Cheyenne
Area Code 307

Atlas Motel (1524 West Lincolnway, 82001; 632-9214) 31 rooms and efficiencies, a/c, TV, no pets, wheelchair access, NS rooms, senior rates, CC. SGL/DBL$40-$60.

Best Western Hitching Post Inn (1700 West Lincolnway, 82001; 638-3301, Fax 638-3301, 800-528-1234) 168 rooms, restaurant, lounge, entertainment, indoor and outdoor heated pool, sauna, tennis courts, gift shop, boutiques, children free with parents, a/c, NS rooms, TV, laundry facilities, wheelchair access, airport courtesy car, pets OK, meeting facilities, senior rates, CC. SGL/DBL$55-$160.

Big Horn Motel (2004 East Lincolnway, 82001; 632-3122) 18 rooms and efficiencies, a/c, TV, CC. SGL/DBL$36-$44.

The Bolten Ranch (7000 Valley View Place, 82009; 635-8066) TV, American plan available, CC. SGL/DBL$75-$150.

Capitol Inn (5401 Walker, 82009; 632-8901, 800-876-8901) 104 rooms, restaurant, lounge, entertainment, pool, a/c, TV, pets OK, meeting facilities, CC. SGL/DBL$45-$65.

Cheyenne Motel (1601 East Lincolnway, 82001; 778-7664) 30 rooms, pets OK, kitchenettes, a/c, TV, wheelchair access, NS rooms, senior rates, CC. SGL/DBL$26-$66.

Comfort Inn (2245 Etchepare Dr., 82007; 638-7202, 800-221-2222) 77 rooms, restaurant, free breakfast, outdoor heated pool, pets OK, VCRs, children free with parents, a/c, TV, laundry facilities, meeting facilities, senior rates, CC. SGL/DBL$35-$50.

Days Inn (2360 West Lincolnway, 82001; 778-8877, Fax 778-8697, 800-325-2525) 72 rooms, free breakfast, restaurant, exercise center, jacuzzi, whirlpools, a/c, TV, wheelchair access, NS rooms, children free with parents, pets OK, laundry facilities, senior rates, CC. SGL/DBL$44-$70.

Drummond's Bed and Breakfast (399 Happy Jack Rd., 82007; 634-6042) 3 rooms, free breakfast, hot tub, pets OK, American plan available, NS, TV, children under 12 free with parents, CC. SGL/DBL$66-$80.

Firebird Motel (1905 East Lincolnway, 82001; 632-5505) 49 rooms, pool, pets OK, a/c, TV, wheelchair access, NS rooms, senior rates, CC. SGL/DBL$55-$75.

Fleetwood Motel (3800 East Lincolnway, 82001; 638-8908, 800-634-7763) 22 rooms and efficiencies, outdoor heated pool, a/c, TV, pets OK, wheelchair access, NS rooms, senior rates, CC. SGL/DBL$25-$38.

Frontier Motel (1400 West Lincolnway, 82007; 634-7961) 90 rooms and efficiencies, a/c, TV, pets OK, wheelchair access, NS rooms, senior rates, CC. SGL/DBL$45-$65.

Guest Ranch Motel (1100 West 16th St., 82001; 634-2137) 33 rooms, pool, pets OK, a/c, TV, CC. SGL/DBL$36-$56.

Holding's Little America (2800 West Lincolnway, 82001; 634-2771, Fax 775-8425, 800-445-6945) 189 rooms and suites, restaurant, lounge, entertainment, outdoor pool, no pets, NS rooms, room service, in-room refrigerators, airport courtesy car, children free with parents, a/c, TV, meeting facilities, CC. SGL/DBL$55-$65, STS$65-$70.

Holiday Inn (204 West Fox Farm Rd., 82007; 638-4466, 800-HOLIDAY) 244 rooms, restaurant, lounge, indoor heated pool, exercise center, children under 19 free with parents, wheelchair access, a/c, TV, NS rooms, fax service, room service, pets OK, game room, airport transportation, laundry service, meeting facilities, senior rates, CC. SGL/DBL$65-$125.

Home Ranch Motel (2414 East Lincolnway, 82001; 634-3575) 37 rooms, pets OK, a/c, TV, CC. SGL/DBL$36-$38.

Howard Johnson (1805 Westland Rd., 82001; 638-2550, Fax 778-8113, 800-I-GO-HOJO) 32 rooms, free breakfast, children free with parents, wheelchair access, NS rooms, TV, a/c, no pets, laundry facilities, senior rates, meeting facilities, CC. SGL/DBL$25-$50.

La Quinta Inn (2410 West Lincolnway, 82001; 632-7117, 800-531-5900) 105 rooms and 2-bedroom suites, restaurant, free breakfast, lounge, pool, complimentary newspaper, free local calls, fax service, laundry service, NS rooms, wheelchair access, pets OK, remote control TV, a/c, meeting facilities, senior rates, all CC. SGL/DBL$55-$65.

Lariet Motel (600 Central Ave., 82001; 635-8439) 16 rooms and efficiencies, pets OK, TV, kitchenettes, CC. SGL/DBL$28-$38.

Lincoln Court (1720 West Lincolnway, 82001; 638-3302) 67 rooms, pool, a/c, TV, wheelchair access, airport transportation, laundry facilities, children under 12 free with parents, in-room refrigerators, NS rooms, senior rates, CC. SGL/DBL$40-$160.

Little America (Cheyenne 82003; 634-2771, Fax 632-3344, 800-445-6945) 189 rooms, restaurant, lounge, entertainment, pool, a/c, TV, no pets, meeting facilities, CC. SGL/DBL$45-$65.

Motel 6 (1735 Westland Rd., 82001; 635-6806, 505-891-6161) 108 rooms, pool, free local calls, children under 17 free with parents, NS rooms, wheelchair access, pets OK, a/c, TV, CC. SGL/DBL$26-$32.

Pioneer Motel (209 West 17th St., 82001; 634-3010) 40 rooms, a/c, TV, NS rooms, wheelchair access, pets OK, CC. SGL/DBL$35-$45.

Plaines Motel (1600 Central Ave., 82001; 638-3311) 41 rooms, restaurant, lounge, entertainment, whirlpools, sauna, gift shop, a/c, TV, NS rooms, wheelchair access, no pets, meeting facilities, CC. SGL/DBL$35-$60.

The Porch Swing (712 East 20th St., 82001; 778-7182) 2 rooms, free breakfast, TV, no pets, shared baths, airport transportation, NS, CC. SGL/DBL$42-$54.

Rainsford Inn (219 East 18th St., 82001; 638-2337) 5 rooms, free breakfast, whirlpools, TV, NS, airport transportation, a/c, no pets, meeting facilities, CC. SGL/DBL$50-$95.

Ranger Motel (909 West 16th St., 82001; 634-7995) 22 rooms, pets OK, a/c, TV, CC. SGL/DBL$54-$68.

Rodeway Inn (3839 East Lincolnway, 82001; 634-2171, 800-424-4777) 70 rooms, restaurant, lounge, entertainment, pool, wheelchair access, NS rooms, children free with parents, a/c, TV, pets OK, senior rates, CC. SGL/DBL$35-$56.

Roundup Motel (403 South Greeley Hwy., 82001; 634-7741) 35 rooms and efficiencies, a/c, kitchenettes, TV, CC. SGL/DBL$39-$42.

Sands Motel (1000 West 16th St., 82001; 634-7771) 50 rooms, pool, a/c, TV, NS rooms, wheelchair access, pets OK, CC. SGL/DBL$45-$65.

Sapp Brothers Big C Motel (I-80 and Archer, 82001; 632-6600) 33 rooms, restaurant, a/c, TV, no pets, wheelchair access, NS rooms, senior rates, CC. SGL/DBL$46-$58.

Stagecoach Motel (1515 West Lincolnway, 82001; 634-4495) 23 rooms, no pets, a/c, TV, CC. SGL/DBL$29-$37.

Super 8 Motel (1900 West Lincolnway, 82001; 645-8741, 800-843-1991, 800-800-8000) 61 rooms and suites, children under 12 free with parents, free local calls, a/c, TV, in-room refrigerators and microwaves, fax service, NS rooms, wheelchair access, pets OK, meeting facilities, senior rates, CC. SGL/DBL$34-$41.

Twin Chimneys Motel (2405 East Lincolnway, 82001; 632-8921) 21 rooms and efficiencies, pets OK, TV, a/c, CC. SGL/DBL$28-$36.

Windy Hills Guest House (393 Happy Jack Rd., 82007; 632-6423) 1 room, free breakfast, TV, local transportation, children free with parents, a/c, pets OK, water view, CC. SGL/DBL$65-$75.

Chugwater
Area Code 307

Diamond Guest Ranch (Chugwater 82210; 422-3567) cabins, restaurant, dude ranch, CC. SGL/DBL$100-$225.

Clearmont
Area Code 307

Ucross Guest Ranch (2673 Hwy. 14 East, 82835; 737-2281) 25 rooms, pool, dude ranch, restaurant, lounge, 1912 lodge, TV, CC. SGL/DBL$65-$100.

Cody
Area Code 307

Best Western Sunrise Motor Inn (1407 8th St., 82414; 587-5566, 800-528-1234) 40 rooms, outdoor heated pool, whirlpools, exercise center, children free with parents, a/c, NS rooms, TV, laundry facilities, wheelchair access, pets OK, meeting facilities, senior rates, CC. SGL/DBL$35-$110.

Best Western Sunset Motor Inn (1601 8th St., 82414; 587-4265, Fax 587-9029, 800-528-1234) 100 rooms and suites, restaurant, indoor and outdoor heated pool, children free with parents, a/c, NS rooms, TV, laundry facilities, wheelchair access, pets OK, meeting facilities, senior rates, CC. SGL/DBL$35-$100.

Big Bear Motel (139 Yellowstone Hwy., 82414; 587-3117, 800-325-7163) 42 rooms, outdoor heated pool, a/c, pets OK, TV, senior rates, CC. SGL/DBL$25-$50.

Blackwater Creek Ranch (Cody 82414; 587-5201) 15 cabins, restaurant, lounge, whirlpools, airport courtesy car, American plan available, TV, CC. SGL/DBL$$750W-$1,450W.

Buffalo Bill Village Resort (1701 Sheridan Ave., 82414; 587-5544, Fax 527-7757, 800-527-5544) 83 rooms and 2-bedroom cabins, restaurant, lounge, entertainment, a/c, TV, wheelchair access, NS rooms, airport transportation, children free with parents, no pets, senior rates, CC. SGL/DBL$50-$60.

Carriage House (1816 8th St., 82414; 587-2572, 800-531-2572) 24 rooms and 1- to 3-bedroom cabins, TV, airport transportation, no pets, wheelchair access, NS, senior rates, CC. SGL/DBL$25-$66.

Castle Rock (412 Hwy. 6NS, 82414; 587-2076, 800-356-9965) 9 cabins, restaurant, American plan available, entertainment, heated pool, sauna, airport courtesy car, no pets, TV, CC. SGL/DBL$750W-$1,500W.

Cedar Mountain Motor Lodge (803 Sheridan Ave., 82414; 587-2248) 45 rooms, restaurant, tennis courts, a/c, TV, no pets, wheelchair access, NS rooms, senior rates, meeting facilities, CC. SGL/DBL$45-$75.

Cody Motor Lodge (1455 Sheridan Ave., 82414; 527-6291) 30 rooms, restaurant, a/c, TV, no pets, laundry facilities, children free with parents, CC. SGL/DBL$52-$65.

Cody Ranch Resort (2604 Yellowstone Hwy., 82414; 587-2097) 14 rooms and 2-bedroom suites, restaurant, lounge, whirlpools, no pets, wheelchair access, NS rooms, senior rates, CC. SGL/DBL$100.

Comfort Inn at Buffalo Bill (1601 Sheridan Ave., 82414; 587-5556, 800-221-2222) 49 rooms, outdoor pool, no pets, children free with parents, airport courtesy car, a/c, TV, senior rates, CC. SGL/DBL$25-$95.

Double Diamond X Ranch (3453 Southfork Rd., 82414; 527-6276, Fax 587-2708, 800-833-7262) 10 rooms and cabins, restaurant, lounge, entertainment, indoor heated pool, airport courtesy car, American plan available, gift shop, no pets, CC. SGL/DBL$895W-$1,100W.

Goff Creek Lodge (Cody 82414; 587-3753) 14 cabins, restaurant, lounge, pets OK, TV, CC. SGL/DBL$60-$120.

Holiday Hotel (1807 Sheridan Ave., 82414; 587-4258, 800-341-8000) 20 rooms, a/c, TV, NS rooms, no pets, airport transportation, senior rates, CC. SGL/DBL$26-$48.

The Irma Hotel (1192 Sheridan Ave., 82414; 587-4221) 41 rooms, restaurant, lounge, gift shop, a/c, TV, no pets, wheelchair access, children free with parents, airport courtesy car, antique furnishings, NS rooms, senior rates, meeting facilities, CC. SGL/DBL$50-$85.

Kelly Inn (2513 Greybull Hwy., 82414; 527-5505, 800-635-3559) 50 rooms, whirlpools, airport transportation, laundry facilities, a/c, in-room refrigerators and microwaves, TV, pets OK, CC. SGL/DBL$40-$75.

Lockhart Bed and Breakfast (109 West Yellowstone Hwy., 82414; 587-6074) 14 rooms, free breakfast, TV, a/c, airport transportation, kitchenettes, 1800s home, antique furnishings, no pets, CC. SGL/DBL$45-$95.

Mountaineer Court (1015 Sheridan Ave., 82414; 587-2221) 36 rooms, a/c, TV, wheelchair access, NS rooms, no pets, senior rates, CC. SGL/DBL$28-$78.

Pahaska Tepee Resort (183 Yellowstone Hwy., 82414; 527-7701, 800-628-7791) 55 rooms, restaurant, lounge, whirlpools, a/c, TV, no pets, wheelchair access, NS rooms, senior rates, CC. SGL/DBL$45-$50.

Rainbow Park Motel (1136 17th St., 82414; 587-6251, 800-341-8000) 39 rooms and 2-bedroom efficiencies, a/c, TV, wheelchair access, NS rooms, no pets, laundry facilities, senior rates, CC. SGL/DBL$24-$52.

Rimrock Dude Ranch (2728 Northfork Hwy., 82414; 587-3970) 9 1- and 2-bedroom cabins, restaurant, in-room refrigerators, no pets, fireplaces, airport courtesy cars, CC. SGL/DBL$850W-$1,700W.

Shoshone Lodge (Cody 82414; 587-4044) 16 cabins, restaurant, laundry facilities, fireplaces, kitchenettes, pets OK, CC. SGL/DBL$42-$80.

Skyline Motor Inn (1919 17th St., 82414; 587-4201, 800-843-8809) 46 rooms, restaurant, a/c, TV, no pets, wheelchair access, NS rooms, senior rates, meeting facilities, CC. SGL/DBL$40-$60.

Trout Creek Inn (Cody 82414; 587-6288) 21 rooms, outdoor heated pool, children under 12 free with parents, a/c, TV, pets OK, in-room refrigerators, wheelchair access, NS rooms, senior rates, CC. SGL/DBL$30-$65.

Western Six Gun Motel (423 Yellowstone Ave., 82414; 587-4835) 40 rooms, a/c, TV, no pets, wheelchair access, NS rooms, senior rates, CC. SGL/DBL$40-$70.

Wise Choice Inn (2908 Yellowstone Hwy. 82414; 587-5004) 17 rooms, a/c, TV, wheelchair access, NS rooms, senior rates, CC. SGL/DBL$26-$42.

Yellowstone Valley Inn (3324 Yellowstone Park Hwy., 82414; 587-3961) 34 rooms, restaurant, lounge, laundry facilities, a/c, TV, pets OK, CC. SGL/DBL$30-$60.

Cokeville

Area Code 307

Valley Hi Motel (Cokeville 83114; 279-3251) 22 rooms, a/c, TV, no pets, NS rooms, senior rates, CC. SGL/DBL$28-$34.

Cora

Area Code 307

Box R Ranch (Cora 82925; 367-2291) dude ranch, American plan available, airport transportation, CC. SGL/DBL$100-$185.

Flying U Ranch (Cora 82925; 367-4479) dude ranch, CC. SGL/DBL$65-$85.

Green River Guest Ranch (Cora 82925; 367-2314) dude ranch, American plan available, CC. SGL/DBL$100-$185.

Daniel

Area Code 307

David Ranch (Daniel 83115; 859-8228) rooms and cabins, dude ranch, American plan available, CC. SGL/DBL$90-$140.

Devils Tower

Area Code 307

R-Place (Devils Tower 82714; 467-5938) free breakfast, TV, a/c, no pets, CC. SGL/DBL$45-$55.

Diamondville

Area Code 307

The Energy Inn (Diamondville 83116; 877-6901) 43 rooms, pets OK, NS rooms, a/c, TV, in-room refrigerators, children free with parents, senior rates, CC. SGL/DBL$30-$38.

Dixon

Area Code 307

Umbrella Ranch Vacations (Dixon 82323; no phone) dude ranch, American plan available, CC. SGL/DBL$856W-$1,500W.

Douglas
Area Code 307

Akers Ranch (81 Inez Rd., 82633; 358-3741, Fax 358-3741) 4 rooms and 2- and 3-bedroom cabins, free breakfast, TV, kitchenettes, in-room refrigerators, a/c, no pets, senior rates, CC. SGL/DBL$45-$80.

Alpine Inn (2310 East Richards St., 82633; 358-4780) 40 rooms, a/c, TV, no pets, wheelchair access, NS rooms, senior rates, CC. SGL/DBL$30-$56.

Cheyenne River Ranch (1031 Steinle Rd., 82633; 358-2380) 4 rooms, outdoor pool, a/c, TV, no pets, laundry facilities, wheelchair access, NS rooms, senior rates, CC. SGL/DBL$60-$75.

Chieftain Motel (815 East Richards, 82633; 358-2673) 20 rooms, a/c, TV, children free with parents, airport transportation, in-room refrigerators and coffee makers, pets OK, NS rooms, senior rates, CC. SGL/DBL$30-$44.

Deer Forks Ranch (1200 Poison Lake Rd., 82633; 358-2033) rooms and guest houses, free breakfast, TV, a/c, no pets, NS, private baths, CC. SGL/DBL$40-$80.

Holiday Inn (1450 Riverbend Dr., 82633; 358-9790, Fax 358-6251, 800-HOLIDAY) 114 rooms and suites, restaurant, lounge, indoor heated pool, exercise center, sauna, game room, children under 19 free with parents, wheelchair access, a/c, TV, NS rooms, fax service, room service, pets OK, laundry service, meeting facilities, senior rates, CC. SGL/DBL$45-$65.

I-25 Inn (2349 East Richards St., 82633; 358-2833, 800-462-4667) 43 rooms, restaurant, lounge, a/c, TV, no pets, wheelchair access, NS rooms, senior rates, CC. SGL/DBL$32-$39.

Super 8 Motel (314 Russell Ave., 82633; 358-6800, 800-800-8000) 37 rooms, children under 12 free with parents, free local calls, a/c, TV, in-room refrigerators and microwaves, fax service, NS rooms, wheelchair access, airport transportation, pets OK, meeting facilities, senior rates, CC. SGL/DBL$36-$44.

Dubois
Area Code 307

Absaroka Ranch (Dubois 82513; 455-2275) 4 cabins, restaurant, sauna, pets OK, American plan available. SGL$775W, DBL$1,400W.

Black Bear Inn (505 North Ramshorn, 82513; 455-2344) 16 rooms and 2-bedroom efficiency, pets OK, in-room refrigerators, TV, children under 12 free with parents, CC. SGL/DBL$128-$140.

Branding Iron Motel (401 West Ramshorn, 82513; 455-2893) 22 rooms and cabins, children free with parents, TV, pets OK, CC. SGL/DBL$26-$36.

Chinook Winds Motel (640 South 1st St., 82513; 455-2987) 17 rooms and efficiencies, in-room refrigerators, TV, pets OK, children free with parents, CC. SGL/DBL$25-$55.

Lazy L&B Ranch (Dubois 82513; 455-2839) 19 cabins, restaurant, outdoor heated pool, American plan available, pets OK, TV, CC. SGL/DBL$825W-$1,500W.

Pinnacle Motor Lodge (3577 Hwy. 16, 82513; 455-2506) 10 rooms, restaurant, outdoor heated pool, pets OK, CC. SGL/DBL$30-$47.

Stagecoach Motor Lodge (103 Ramshorn, 82513; 455-2303) 42 rooms, restaurant, outdoor heated pool, in-room refrigerators, TV, pets OK, CC. SGL/DBL$30-$48.

Super 8 Motel (1414 Warm Springs Dr., 82513; 455-3694, 800-800-8000) 32 rooms, pets OK, children under 12 free with parents, free local calls, a/c, TV, in-room refrigerators and microwaves, fax service, NS rooms, wheelchair access, meeting facilities, senior rates, CC. SGL/DBL$25-$50.

Trails End (511 Ramshorn, 82513; 455-2540) 20 rooms and 2-bedroom efficiencies, TV, no pets, CC. SGL/DBL$27-$45.

Twin Pines Lodge (218 West Ramshorn, 82513; 455-2600) 15 rooms and cabins, kitchenettes, pets OK, CC. SGL/DBL$28-$48.

Elk Mountain
Area Code 307

Elk Mountain Motel (Elk Mountain 82324; 348-7774) 12 rooms, restaurant, lounge, a/c, TV, no pets, wheelchair access, NS rooms, senior rates, CC. SGL/DBL$65-$85.

Encampment
Area Code 307

Platt's Rustic Mountain Lodge (Encampment 82325; 327-5539) free breakfast, TV, a/c, no pets, NS. SGL/DBL$45-$80.

Riverside Cabins (Star Route, 82325; 327-5361) 9 rooms and efficiencies, pets OK, a/c, TV, CC. SGL/DBL$36-$46.

Lazy Acres Motel (Encampment 82325; 327-5968) 4 rooms, TV, CC. SGL/DBL$28-$33.

Lorraine's Bed and Breakfast (Encampment 82325; 327-5200) 4 rooms, free breakfast, TV, shared baths, a/c, no pets, CC. SGL/DBL$25-$38.

Platts Bed and Breakfast (Encampment 82325; 327-5539) 3 rooms, free breakfast, fireplaces, TV, a/c, no pets, CC. SGL/DBL$40-$60.

Evanston
Area Code 307

Alexander Motel (Evanston 82930; 789-2346) 14 rooms, kitchenettes, pets OK, a/c, TV, CC. SGL/DBL$37-$44.

Bear River Inn (261 Bear River Dr., 82930; 789-0791) 87 rooms, free breakfast, a/c, TV, no pets, wheelchair access, NS rooms, senior rates, CC. SGL/DBL$35-$48.

Best Western Dunmar Inn (1601 Harrison Dr., 82930; 789-3770, Fax 789-3758, 800-528-1234) 166 rooms, restaurant, lounge, entertainment, outdoor pool, exercise center, free local calls, children free with parents, a/c, NS rooms, TV, laundry facilities, wheelchair access, pets OK, meeting facilities, senior rates, CC. SGL/DBL$55-$95.

Classic Lodge (202 Hwy. 30 East, 82930; 789-6830) 136 rooms and efficiencies, a/c, TV, no pets, kitchenettes, wheelchair access, NS rooms, senior rates, CC. SGL/DBL$65-$105.

Evanston Inn (247 Bear River Dr., 82930; 789-6212, 800-443-1982) 160 rooms, a/c, TV, no pets, kitchenettes, wheelchair access, NS rooms, senior rates, meeting facilities, CC. SGL/DBL$35-$48.

Executive Motor Inn (339 West Lincoln Hwy., 82930; 789-6504) 160 rooms and efficiencies, restaurant, lounge, pool, a/c, TV, no pets, wheelchair access, NS rooms, senior rates, CC. SGL/DBL$50-$78.

Friendship Inn (202 Bear River Dr., 82930; 789-6830, 800-424-4777) 136 rooms, pool, exercise center, a/c, TV, no pets, NS rooms, children free with parents, wheelchair access, senior rates, CC. SGL/DBL$30-$60.

Pine Gables Lodge (1049 Center St., 82930; 789-2069) 4 rooms, free breakfast, antique furnishings, 1883 home, private baths, TV, airport transportation, children free with parents, pets OK, CC. SGL/DBL$30-$50.

Prairie Inn (264 Bear River Dr., 82930; 789-2920) 31 rooms, free breakfast, pets OK, TV, CC. SGL/DBL$35-$45.

Super Budget Inn (1949 Harrison Dr., 82930; 789-2810, Fax 789-5506, 800-333-STAY) 115 rooms, a/c, TV, no pets, wheelchair access, NS rooms, senior rates, CC. SGL/DBL$33-$38.

Super 8 Motel (70 Bear River Dr., 82930; 789-7510, 800-800-8000) 84 rooms and suites, free breakfast, no pets, children under 12 free with parents, free local calls, a/c, TV, in-room refrigerators and microwaves, fax service, NS rooms, wheelchair access, airport courtesy car, meeting facilities, senior rates, CC. SGL/DBL$28-$48.

Western Super Budget (1936 Hwy. 30 East, 82930; 789-2810) 115 rooms, restaurant, lounge, pets OK, a/c, TV, CC. SGL/DBL$40-$54.

Whirl Inn Motel (1724 Hwy. 30 West, 82930; 789-9610) 96 rooms, lounge, a/c, TV, pets OK, wheelchair access, NS rooms, senior rates, CC. SGL/DBL$36-$46.

Westin Lamplighter (1983 Harrison Dr., 82930; 789-0783, Fax 789-7186, 800-333-STAY, 800-228-3000) 100 rooms, restaurant, lounge, entertainment, pool, sauna, exercise center, children under 18 free with parents, wheelchair access, NS rooms, room service, a/c, TV, meeting facilities, senior rates, CC. SGL/DBL$50-$85.

Evansville
Area Code 307

Shilo Inn (I-25 and Curtis Rd., 82636; 237-1335, Fax 577-7429, 800-222-2244) 120 rooms and suites, restaurant, lounge, entertainment, indoor heated pool, whirlpools, sauna, airport courtesy car, in-room refrigerators, a/c, TV, pets OK, VCRs, NS rooms, wheelchair access, children under 12 free with parents, meeting facilities, senior rates, CC. SGL/DBL$45-$55.

Farson
Area Code 307

Sitzman's Motel (Farson 82932; 273-9241) 10 rooms, restaurant, pets OK, TV, a/c, CC. SGL/DBL$30-$36.

Fort Bridger
Area Code 307

Wagon Wheel Motel (270 North Main St., 82933; 782-6361) 54 rooms, restaurant, a/c, TV, no pets, wheelchair access, NS rooms, senior rates, CC. SGL/DBL$28-$46.

Gillette
Area Code 307

Arrowhead Motel (202 Emerson, 82716; 686-0909) 32 rooms and efficiencies, pets OK, a/c, TV, CC. SGL/DBL$30-$44.

Best Western Lodge (109 North Hwy. 14, 82716; 686-2210, Fax 682-5105, 800-528-1234) 190 rooms, restaurant, lounge, entertainment, outdoor heated pool, whirlpools, exercise center, sauna, children free with parents, in-room refrigerators, a/c, NS rooms, TV, laundry facilities, wheelchair access, pets OK, meeting facilities, senior rates, CC. SGL/DBL$47-$60.

Circle L Motel (410 East 2nd St., 82716; 682-9375) 47 rooms and efficiencies, pets OK, a/c, TV, CC. SGL/DBL$28-$30.

Days Inn (910 East Boxelder Rd., 82716; 682-3999, Fax 682-9151, 800-325-2525) 137 rooms, free breakfast, a/c, TV, wheelchair access, NS rooms, pets OK, airport transportation, laundry facilities, meeting facilities, senior rates, CC. SGL/DBL$38-$80.

Holiday Inn (2009 South Douglas Hwy., 82716; 686-3000, Fax 686-4018, 800-HOLIDAY) 158 rooms and suites, restaurant, lounge, entertainment, indoor heated pool, exercise center, children under 19 free with parents, game room, gift shop, wheelchair access, a/c, TV, NS rooms, airport transportation, in-room refrigerators, fax service, room service, pets OK, laundry service, meeting facilities, senior rates, CC. SGL/DBL$66-$78.

Mustang Motel (922 East 3rd St., 82716; 682-4784) 30 rooms and efficiencies, pets OK, a/c, TV, CC. SGL/DBL$30-$35.

The Pettersen Haus (405 Rockpile Blvd., 82716; 686-1030) 1 room, free breakfast, private baths, TV, a/c, no pets, CC. SGL/DBL$45-$70.

Prime Rate Motel (2105 Rodgers Dr., 82716; 686-8600, 800-356-3004) 74 rooms, a/c, TV, no pets, wheelchair access, NS rooms, senior rates, CC. SGL/DBL$28-$60.

Ramada Limited (608 East 2nd St., 82716; 682-9342, 800-2-RAMADA) 76 rooms and suites, heated pool, wheelchair access, NS rooms, free parking, pets OK, a/c, TV, children under 18 free with parents, in-room coffee makers, airport transportation, room service, laundry facilities, meeting facilities, senior rates, CC. SGL/DBL$36-$55.

Rodeway Inn (1020 Hwy. 51 East, 82716; 682-5111, 800-424-4777) 79 rooms, restaurant, lounge, whirlpools, pool, wheelchair access, NS rooms, children free with parents, a/c, TV, senior rates, CC. SGL/DBL$40-$60.

Rolling Hills Motel (409 Butler Spaeth Rd., 82716; 686-4757, Fax 686-6250) 62 rooms, free breakfast, a/c, TV, no pets, wheelchair access, NS rooms, senior rates, CC. SGL/DBL$35-$55.

Sands Motor Lodge (608 East 2nd St., 82716; 682-9341) 76 rooms, restaurant, lounge, pool, a/c, TV, no pets, wheelchair access, NS rooms, senior rates, CC. SGL/DBL$36-$46.

Super 8 Motel (208 South Decker Ct., 82716; 682-8078, 800-848-8888, 800-800-8000) 60 rooms and suites, free breakfast, no pets, children under 12 free with parents, free local calls, a/c, TV, in-room refrigerators and microwaves, fax service, NS rooms, wheelchair access, meeting facilities, senior rates, CC. SGL/DBL$30-$55.

Glendo

Area Code 307

Bellwood Motel (Yellowstone Hwy., 82213; 735-4211) 13 rooms, pets OK, kitchenettes, a/c, TV, CC. SGL/DBL$55-$80.

Glendo Marina Motel (383 Glendo Park Rd., 82213; 735-4216) 7 rooms, restaurant, lounge, pets OK, a/c, TV, CC. SGL/DBL$60-$75.

Lakeview Motel (Glendo 82213; 735-4461) 7 rooms, a/c, TV, CC. SGL/DBL$35-$45.

Glenrock

Area Code 307

All American Inn (500 West Aspen, 82637; 436-2772) 24 rooms and efficiencies, a/c, TV, NS rooms, in-room refrigerators, children under 16 free with parents, pets OK, kitchenettes, senior rates, CC. SGL/DBL$20-$42.

Hotel Higgens (416 West Birch St., 82637; 436-9212, 800-458-0144) 8 rooms and suites, restaurant, lounge, free breakfast, antique furnishings, no pets, a/c, TV, NS rooms, senior rates, CC. SGL/DBL$45-$58, STS$65.

Green River

Area Code 307

Coachman Inn (470 East Flaming Gorge Way, 82935; 875-3681) 81 rooms, a/c, TV, pets OK, wheelchair access, NS rooms, senior rates, CC. SGL/DBL$28-$34.

Desmond Motel (140 North 7th West, 82935; 875-3701) 22 rooms, a/c, pets OK, TV, in-room refrigerators, senior rates, CC. SGL/DBL$22-$34.

Flaming Gorge Motel (316 East Flaming Gorge Way, 82935; 875-3567) a/c, TV, CC. SGL/DBL$44-$56.

Mustang Motel (550 East Flaming Gorge Way, 82935; 875-2468) a/c, TV, CC. SGL/DBL$35-$42.

Walker's Motel (36 North 7th West, 82935; 875-3567) a/c, TV, CC. SGL/DBL$36-$46.

Super 8 Motel (280 West Flaming Gorge Way, 82935; 875-933) 800-800-8000) 38 rooms and suites, no pets, children under 12 free with parents, free local calls, a/c, TV, in-room refrigerators and microwaves, fax service, NS rooms, wheelchair access, meeting facilities, senior rates, CC. SGL/DBL$28-$55.

Western Motel (890 West Flaming Gorge Way, 82935; 875-2840) 32 rooms, a/c, children free with parents, pets OK, TV, in-room refrigerators, CC. SGL/DBL$26-$40.

Guernsey
Area Code 307

Annette's White House (Guernsey 82214; 836-2148) 3 rooms, free breakfast, shared bath, TV, a/c. SGL/DBL$30-$40.

Bunkhouse Hotel (Guernsey 82214; 836-2356, Fax 836-2328) 30 rooms, children free with parents, a/c, TV, pets OK, in-room refrigerators, meeting facilities, CC. SGL/DBL$26-$35.

Hanna
Area Code 307

Golden Rule Motel (305 South Adams, 82327; 325-6525) 21 rooms, pets OK, a/c, TV, CC. SGL/DBL$40-$50.

Hulett
Area Code 302

Hulett Motel (202 Main St., 82720; 467-9900) 19 rooms and efficiencies, restaurant, a/c, TV, CC. SGL/DBL$28-$36.

Motel Pioneer (119 Hunter, 82720; 467-5656) 9 rooms, kitchenettes, pets OK, in-room refrigerators, TV, a/c, CC. SGL/DBL$25-$40.

Jackson
Area Code 307

Rental and Reservation Services:

Accommodations of Jackson Hole (Jackson 83001; 733-3039, 800-422-2927) rental condominiums.

❑❑❑

Best Western Lodge at Jackson Hole (80 Scott Lane, 83002; 739-9703; 733-0844, 800-528-1234) 100 rooms and suites, free breakfast, indoor and outdoor heated pool, hot tubs, kitchenettes, children free with parents, a/c, NS rooms, TV, laundry facilities, wheelchair access, pets OK, meeting facilities, senior rates, CC. SGL/DBL$50-$150.

Best Western Parkway Inn (125 North Jackson St., 83001; 733-3143, Fax 733-0955, 800-528-1234) 50 rooms, indoor heated pool, spa, sauna, children free with parents, a/c, NS rooms, TV, laundry facilities, wheelchair access, no pets, meeting facilities, senior rates, CC. SGL/DBL$68-$135.

Buckrail Lodge (Jackson 83001; 733-2079) 11 rooms, whirlpools, children free with parents, pets OK, NS, CC. SGL/DBL$45-$86.

Budget Host Anvil Motel (215 North Cache, 83001; 733-3668, 800-283-4678) 26 rooms and suites, hot tub, no pets, laundry facilities, NS rooms, wheelchair access, a/c, TV, children free with parents, senior rates, CC. SGL/DBL$42-$98.

Cache Creek Motel (390 North Glenwood, 83001; 733-7781, Fax 733-4652, 800-843-4788) 36 rooms and 2-bedroom efficiencies, whirlpools, hot tubs, no pets, TV, children free with parents, kitchenettes, a/c, wheelchair access, NS rooms, senior rates, CC. SGL/DBL$55-$125.

Cowboy Village Resort (120 South Flat Creek Dr., 83001; 733-3121) 82 rooms, whirlpools, kitchenettes, TV, in-room refrigerators, microwaves and coffee makers, no pets, CC. SGL/DBL$60-$110.

Darwin Ranch (Jackson 83001; 733-5588) 8 rooms, American plan available, sauna, CC. SGL/DBL$105-$200.

Days Inn (1280 West Broadway, 83001; 739-9010, Fax 739-9834, 800-325-2525) 78 rooms, free breakfast, sauna, a/c, TV, wheelchair access, NS rooms, laundry facilities, no pets, in-room refrigerators and microwaves, VCRs, children under 12 free with parents, senior rates, CC. SGL/DBL$60-$165.

Elk Refuge Inn (Jackson 83001; 733-3582) 22 rooms and efficiencies, TV, NS rooms, children free with parents, in-room refrigerators, no pets, CC. SGL/DBL$56-$80.

Flat Creek Motel (Jackson 83001; 733-5276, Fax 733-0374, 800-438-9338) 70 rooms and efficiencies, whirlpools, sauna, TV, laundry facilities, kitchenettes, pets OK, wheelchair access, NS rooms, children free with parents, in-room refrigerators, CC. SGL/DBL$60-$95.

Forty-Niner Inn (330 West Pearl, 83001; 733-7550, Fax 733-2002) 121 rooms, restaurant, lounge, whirlpools, sauna, in-room refrigerators, children free with parents, pets OK, fireplaces, a/c, TV, wheelchair access, NS rooms, senior rates, CC. SGL/DBL$45-$110.

Four Winds Motel (150 North Millward St., 83001; 733-5276, 800-438-9338) 21 rooms, restaurant, laundry facilities, no pets, a/c, TV, CC. SGL/DBL$55-$78.

Friendship Inn Antler (43 West Pearl St., 83001; 733-2535, 800-424-4777) 106 rooms, sauna, a/c, TV, no pets, NS rooms, children free with parents, wheelchair access, senior rates, CC. SGL/DBL$60-$103.

Golden Eagle Motor Inn (325 East Broadway, 83001; 733-2041) 22 rooms, outdoor heated pool, no pets, in-room refrigerators, TV, CC. SGL/DBL$45-$65.

H.C. Richards Bed and Breakfast (Jackson 83002; 733-6704, Fax 733-0930) 3 rooms, free breakfast, hot tubs, game room, NS rooms, TV, a/c, no pets, CC. SGL/DBL$85.

Hitching Post Lodge (460 East Broadway, 83002; 733-2606) 17 rooms and cabins, pool, in-room refrigerators and microwaves, no pets, laundry facilities, TV, CC. SGL/DBL$36-$66.

Jackson Hole Lodge (Jackson 83001; 733-2992) 33 condominiums, pool, sauna, hot tub, kitchenettes, fireplaces, CC. SGL/DBL$125-$250.

MTA Resorts (320 West Broadway, 83001; 531-9011, 800-272-8824) 24 condominiums, pool, sauna, hot tubs, TV, laundry facilities, kitchenettes, fireplaces, game room, no pets, CC. SGL/DBL$135-$250.

Motel 6 (1370 West Broadway, 83001; 733-1620, 505-891-6161) 155 rooms, pool, free local calls, children under 17 free with parents, NS rooms, wheelchair access, pets OK, a/c, TV, CC. SGL/DBL$30-$45.

Nowlin Creek Inn (Jackson 83001; 733-0882, 800-542-2632) 5 rooms and suites, free breakfast, jacuzzi, wheelchair access, NS rooms, TV, a/c, no pets, CC. SGL/DBL$125-$155.

Pioneer Motel (325 North Cache St., 83001; 733-3673) 22 rooms, in-room refrigerators, a/c, TV, CC. SGL/DBL$60-$75.

Pony Express Motel (50 South Millward St., 83001; 733-3835) 42 rooms and efficiencies, heated pool, TV, no pets, CC. SGL/DBL$35-$78.

Prospector Motel (155 North Jackson St., 83001; 733-4858) 19 rooms, whirlpools, NS, a/c, TV, in-room refrigerators and coffee makers, no pets, wheelchair access, NS rooms, senior rates, CC. SGL/DBL$52-$100.

Rancho Elegre Lodge (Jackson 83001; 733-7988, Fax 734-0254) 5 rooms and suites, restaurant, entertainment, sauna, hot tub, laundry facilities, fireplaces, room service, NS rooms, no pets, CC. SGL/DBL$350-$750.

Rawhide Motel (75 South Millward St., 83001; 733-1216) 21 rooms, no pets, TV, children free with parents, CC. SGL/DBL$40-$85.

Rusty Parrot Lodge (175 North Jackson, 83002; 733-2000, Fax 733-5566) 31 rooms, restaurant, free breakfast, whirlpools, a/c, fireplaces, TV, wheelchair access, airport transportation, no pets, antique furnishings, NS, senior rates, CC. SGL/DBL$145-$205.

The Sassy Moose Inn (Jackson 83001; 733-1277, 800-356-1277) 5 rooms, free breakfast, jacuzzi, fireplaces, wheelchair access, NS rooms, TV, a/c, no pets, CC. SGL/DBL$99-$129.

Snow King Resort (Jackson 83001; 733-5200, 800-522-KING) 36 condominiums, restaurant, lounge, entertainment, heated pool, sauna, hot tub, whirlpools, airport courtesy car, room service, barber and beauty shop, laundry facilities, no pets, game room, wheelchair access, NS rooms, CC. SGL/DBL$120-$390.

Split Creek Ranch (Jackson 83001; 733-7522) 9 rooms and cottages, whirlpools, laundry facilities, no pets, senior rates. SGL/DBL$52-$62.

Spotted Horse Ranch (Jackson 83001; 733-2097) 20 rooms, modified American plan available, sauna, CC. SGL/DBL$85-$150.

Spring Creek Resort (Jackson 83001; 733-8833, Fax 733-01524, 800-443-6169) 36 rooms and suites, restaurant, lounge, pool, hot tub, no pets, room service, wheelchair access, NS rooms, airport courtesy car, fireplaces, in-room refrigerators and coffee makers, airport transportation, laundry facilities, gift shop, meeting facilities, CC. SGL/DBL$120-$525.

Teton Inn (165 West Gill, 83001; 733-3883, Fax 739-1551) 14 rooms, TV, children free with parents, CC. SGL/DBL$50-$80.

Teton Pines Resort (3450 Clubhouse Dr., 83001; 733-1005, 800-238-2223) 16 rooms and suites, restaurant, lounge, pool, hot tub, jacuzzi, fireplaces, no pets, room service, wheelchair access, NS rooms, airport courtesy car, CC. SGL/DBL$215-$595.

Trails End Ranch (Jackson 83001; 733-1616, Fax 733-1403) 35 rooms and suites, American plan available, TV, hot tubs, CC. SGL/DBL$112-$117.

Trapper Motel (235 North Cache, 83001; 733-2648, Fax 739-9351, 800-341-8000) 54 rooms, whirlpools, a/c, TV, laundry facilities, in-room refrigerators, microwaves and coffee makers, children free with parents, no pets, CC. SGL/DBL$75-$95.

Twin Mountain River Ranch (Jackson 83001; no phone) 2 rooms, free breakfast, TV, a/c, no pets, CC. SGL/DBL$35-$45.

The Virginian Lodge (Jackson 83001; 733-2792, Fax 733-0281, 800-262-4999) 158 rooms, restaurant, lounge, jacuzzis, heated swimming pool, in-room refrigerators, microwaves and coffee makers, laundry facilities, children free with parents, pets OK, game room, senior rates, CC. SGL/DBL$45-$80.

Wagon Wheel Village (435 North Cache St., 83001; 733-2357, Fax 733-0568, 800-323-9279) 97 rooms and 2-bedroom suites, restaurant, whirlpools, a/c, TV, in-room refrigerators, airport transportation, no pets, wheelchair access, NS rooms, senior rates, CC. SGL/DBL$50-$79, STS$85-$95.

The Wildflower Inn (3725 Teton Village Rd., 83001; 733-4710) 5 rooms, free breakfast, TV, no pets, children under 12 free with parents, jacuzzi, water view, NS, private baths, CC. SGL/DBL$120-$135.

Wort Hotel (50 North Glenwood, 83002; 733-2190, Fax 733-2067, 800-322-2727) 60 rooms and suites, restaurant, whirlpools, exercise center, a/c, TV, children free with parents, airport courtesy car, wheelchair access, no pets, NS rooms, meeting facilities, senior rates, CC. SGL/DBL$110-$145.

Kaycee

Area Code 307

Cassidey Inn Motel (Kaycee 82639; 738-2482) 19 rooms, pets OK, a/c, TV, CC. SGL/DBL$28-$32.

Siesta Motel (Kaycee 82639; 738-2291) 13 rooms, restaurant, pets OK, a/c, TV, CC. SGL/DBL$36-$38.

Kelly

Area Code 307

Budge's Slide Lake Cabins (Kelly 83011; 733-9061) 4 cabins, laundry facilities, kitchenettes, fireplaces, CC. SGL/DBL$190-$1,150W.

Flying Heart Ranch (Kelly 83011; 733-6452) 3 cabins, kitchenettes, fireplaces, wheelchair access, NS, CC. SGL/DBL$55-$125.

Gros Ventre Slide Inn (Kelly 83011; 733-2762) 1 rooms, TV, kitchenettes, CC. SGL/DBL$89.

Red Rock Ranch (Kelly 83001; 733-6288) 30 rooms, American plan available, NS rooms, CC. SGL/DBL$135-$945W.

Kemmerer
Area Code 307

Antler Motel (419 Coral St., 83101; 877-4461) 58 rooms, a/c, TV, pets OK, wheelchair access, NS rooms, senior rates, CC. SGL/DBL$44-$48.

Burnett's New Motel (1326 Central Ave., 83101; 877-4471) 10 rooms, a/c, TV, CC. SGL/DBL$28-$36.

Energy Inn (Kemmerer 83101; 877-6901) 42 rooms, restaurant, no pets, in-room refrigerators, a/c, TV, CC. SGL/DBL$32-$37.

Fairview Motel (Hwy. 30 North, 83101; 877-3938) 51 rooms, a/c, pets OK, TV, CC. SGL/DBL$28-$45.

Lazy U Motel (521 Coral, 83101; 877-4428) 21 rooms, a/c, TV, pets OK, NS rooms, senior rates, CC. SGL/DBL$44-$48.

LaGrange
Area Code 307

Bear Mountain Back Trails (La Grange 82221; 834-2281) 24 rooms, free breakfast, TV, a/c, share bath, pets OK, CC. SGL/DBL$50-$70.

Lander
Area Code 307

Black Mountain Ranch (548 North Ford Rd., 82520; 332-6442) free breakfast, TV, a/c, no pets, NS, private baths, CC. SGL/DBL$65-$70.

Budget Host Pronghorn Lodge (150 East Main St., 82520; 332-3940, Fax 332-2651, 800-283-4678) 42 rooms and suites, restaurant, whirlpools, water view, laundry facilities, kitchenettes, hot tub, airport transportation, pets OK, NS rooms, wheelchair access, a/c, TV, children free with parents, meeting facilities, senior rates, CC. SGL/DBL$30-$50.

Holiday Lodge (210 McFarlane Dr., 82520; 332-2511, Fax 332-2256) 30 rooms and efficiencies, whirlpools, pets OK, in-room refrigerators and microwaves, laundry facilities, TV, NS rooms, senior rates, CC. SGL/DBL$30-$48.

Silver Spur Motel (340 North 10th St., 82520; 332-5189) 25 rooms and efficiencies, heated pool, a/c, TV, wheelchair access, in-room refrigerators and microwaves, pets OK, NS rooms, senior rates, CC. SGL/DBL$25-$36.

Laramie
Area Code 307

Albany Lodge (1148 Hwy. 11, 82070; 745-5782) 7 rooms, restaurant, lounge, a/c, TV, no pets, wheelchair access, NS rooms, senior rates, CC. SGL/DBL$45-$53.

Annie Moore's Guest House (819 University, 82070; 721-4177) 6 rooms, free breakfast, NS, TV, a/c, no pets, CC. SGL/DBL$40-$65.

Best Western Foster's Country Corner Inn (1561 Snowy Range Rd., 82070; 742-8371, Fax 742-0884, 800-528-1234) 112 rooms, restaurant, lounge, indoor heated pool, hot tubs, children free with parents, a/c, NS rooms, TV, laundry facilities, wheelchair access, pets OK, meeting facilities, senior rates, CC. SGL/DBL$40-$58.

Best Western Gas Lite Motel (960 North 3rd St., 82070; 742-6616, 800-942-6610, 800-528-1234) 30 rooms, heated pool, free local calls, children free with parents, a/c, NS rooms, TV, laundry facilities, wheelchair access, pets OK, meeting facilities, senior rates, CC. SGL/DBL$35-$78.

Camelot Motel (I-80 and Snowy Range Exit, 82070; 721-8860, 800-659-7915) 33 rooms, restaurant, laundry facilities, pets OK, a/c, TV, senior rates, CC. SGL/DBL$37-$48.

Circle S Motel (2440 Grand, 82070; 745-4811) 50 rooms and efficiencies, pool, pets OK, a/c, kitchenettes, TV, CC. SGL/DBL$38-$46.

Downtown Motel (Laramie 82070; 742-6671, 800-942-6671) 30 rooms and 2-bedroom efficiencies, a/c, TV, no pets, in-room computer hookups, wheelchair access, NS rooms, senior rates, CC. SGL/DBL$24-$50.

Foster's Country Inn (1561 Jackson, 82070; 742-8371) 112 rooms, restaurant, lounge, a/c, TV, pets OK, wheelchair access, NS rooms, senior rates, CC. SGL/DBL$60-$80.

Holiday Inn (2313 Soldier Springs Rd., 82070; 742-6611, Fax 745-8371, 800-HOLIDAY) 100 rooms and suites, restaurant, lounge, entertainment, indoor heated pool, exercise center, whirlpools, airport transportation, gift shop, children under 19 free with parents, wheelchair access, a/c, TV, NS rooms, fax service, room service, pets OK, laundry service, meeting facilities for 350, senior rates, CC. SGL/DBL$50-$68.

Laramie Inn (421 Boswell, 82070; 742-3721, Fax 742-5473, 800-642-4212) 80 rooms, restaurant, lounge, outdoor heated pool, a/c, TV, wheelchair access, in-room refrigerators and microwaves, children free with parents, airport transportation, pets OK, NS rooms, senior rates, CC. SGL/DBL$28-$68.

Motel 6 (621 Plaza Lane, 82070; 742-2307, 505-891-6161) 122 rooms, pool, free local calls, children under 17 free with parents, NS rooms, wheelchair access, pets OK, a/c, TV, CC. SGL/DBL$23-$29.

Motel 8 (501 Boswell Dr., 82070; 745-4856) 143 rooms and efficiencies, TV, a/c, kitchenettes, pets OK, CC. SGL/DBL$36-$46.

Ranger Motel (453 North 3rd, 82070; 742-6677) 31 rooms, lounge, pets OK, a/c, TV, CC. SGL/DBL$28-$35.

Sunset Inn (1104 South 3rd, 82070; 742-3741) 18 rooms and efficiencies, lounge, outdoor heated pool, in-room refrigerators and microwaves, children under 16 free with parents, a/c, TV, pets OK, CC. SGL/DBL$28-$70.

Super 8 Motel (I-80 and Curtis, 82070; 745-8901, 800-800-8000) 42 rooms and suites, pets OK, children under 12 free with parents, free local calls, a/c, TV, in-room refrigerators and microwaves, fax service, NS rooms, wheelchair access, meeting facilities, senior rates, CC. SGL/DBL$27-$50.

Thunderbird Lodge (1369 North 3rd, 82070; 745-4871) 10 rooms and efficiencies, a/c, TV, wheelchair access, NS rooms, pets OK, senior rates, CC. SGL/DBL$55-$100.

Travel Inn (262 North 3rd St., 82070; 745-4853, Fax 721-4943) 28 rooms, outdoor heated pool, a/c, TV, wheelchair access, NS rooms, in-room refrigerators, children free with parents, no pets, senior rates, CC. SGL/DBL$31-$50.

U Bar Lodge and Ranch (Laramie 82070; 745-7036) 14 rooms and cabins, TV, free breakfast, dude ranch, CC. SGL/DBL$55-$65.

Vee Bar Guest Ranch (2019 Hwy. 130, 82070; 745-7036, Fax 745-7433) 9 rooms and 2-bedroom suites, free breakfast, TV, no pets, private baths, 1890s home, antique furnishings, CC. SGL/DBL$75-$150.

Waystation Bed and Breakfast (111 Grand Ave., 82070; 742-0619) complimentary breakfast, TV, 1893 home, antique furnishings, a/c, no pets, CC. SGL/DBL$25-$32.

Wyo Motel (1720 Grand Ave., 82070; 742-6633) 37 rooms, pets OK, a/c, kitchenettes, TV, CC. SGL/DBL$30-$40.

Little America

Area Code 307

Holding's Little America (Little America 82929; 875-2400, 800-634-2401) 129 rooms, restaurant, lounge, heated pool, gift shop, a/c, children under

12 free with parents, in-room refrigerators, laundry facilities, TV, no pets, wheelchair access, NS rooms, senior rates, CC. SGL/DBL$44-$65.

Lovell

Area Code 307

Cattlemen Motel (470 Montana Ave., 82431; 548-2296) 15 rooms and efficiencies, TV, kitchenettes, no pets, NS rooms, CC. SGL/DBL$30-$37.

Horsehoe Bend Motel (375 East Main St., 82431; 548-2221) 22 rooms, outdoor pool, in-room refrigerators and microwaves, pets OK, TV, NS rooms, CC. SGL/DBL$35-$40.

Lusk

Area Code 307

Best Western Pioneer Court Inn (731 South Main St., 82225; 334-2640, 800-528-1234) 30 rooms and suites, outdoor heated pool, children free with parents, a/c, NS rooms, TV, laundry facilities, wheelchair access, no pets, local transportation, meeting facilities, senior rates, CC. SGL/DBL$28-$60.

Covered Wagon Motel (730 South Main St., 82225; 334-2836, 800-341-8000) 48 rooms, indoor heated pool, whirlpools, sauna, a/c, airport transportation, VCRs, TV, no pets, CC. SGL/DBL$38-$54.

Town House (Lusk 82225; 334-2376) 20 rooms, a/c, pets OK, TV, CC. SGL/DBL$30-$45.

Trail Motel (305 West 8th St., 82225; 334-2530, 800-333-LUSK) 22 rooms and efficiencies, heated pool, a/c, TV, airport transportation, children under 12 free with parents, pets OK, in-room refrigerators, wheelchair access, NS rooms, senior rates, CC. SGL/DBL$33-$54.

Medicine Bow

Area Code 307

Trampus Lodge (Medicine Bow 82329; 379-2280) 20 rooms, pets OK, a/c, TV, CC. SGL/DBL$34-$38.

Virginian Hotel and Motel (404 Lincoln Hwy., 82329; 379-2377) 31 rooms, restaurant, a/c, TV, no pets, wheelchair access, NS rooms, senior rates, CC. SGL/DBL$40-$58.

Moorcroft

Area Code 307

Cozy Motel (219 Converse, 82721; 756-3486) 23 rooms, a/c, TV, CC. SGL/DBL$36-$56.

Keyhole Motel Marina (213 McKean Rd., 82721; 756-9529) 11 rooms, a/c, pets OK, TV, CC. SGL/DBL$28-$34.

Moorecourt Motel (Hwy. 14 and Devils Tower Rd., 82721; 756-3411) 30 rooms and efficiencies, a/c, pets OK, kitchenettes, TV, CC. SGL/DBL$35-$65.

Moose
Area Code 307

Gros Ventre River Ranch (Moose 83012; 733-4138, Fax 733-4272) 18 rooms and suites, restaurant, lounge, gift shop, pets OK, NS rooms, airport courtesy car, American plan available, CC. SGL/DBL$1,680W-$2,670W.

Lost Creek Ranch (Moose 83012; 733-3435, Fax 733-1954) 30 rooms and suites, restaurant, entertainment, heated pool, no pets, game room, fireplaces, TV, airport courtesy car, meeting facilities, American plan available, CC. SGL/DBL$3,595W-$8,150W.

Moose Head Ranch (Moose 83012; 733-3141) 40 rooms and 1- and 2-bedroom suites, restaurant, NS rooms, no pets, fireplaces, airport courtesy car, American plan available, CC. SGL/DBL$260-$320.

Triangle X Ranch (Moose 83012; 733-2183, Fax 733-8685) 40 rooms, American plan available, CC. SGL/DBL$100-$200.

Moran
Area Code 307

Rental and Reservation Services:

Grand Teton Lodge Company (Moran 83013; 543-2855) rental rooms and condominiums.

❑❑❑

Atkinson Motel (Moran 83013; 543-2442) 5 rooms, kitchenettes, pets OK, TV, wheelchair access, CC. SGL/DBL$65-$75.

Colter Bay Village (Moran 83013; 543-2811) 209 rooms and cabins, restaurant, lounge, water view, laundry facilities, children free with parents, pets OK, CC. SGL/DBL$50-$98.

Flagg Ranch Village (Moran 83013; 733-8761, Fax 543-2356, 800-443-2311) 60 rooms, restaurant, lounge, a/c, TV, pets OK, in-room refrigerators and microwaves, children under 12 free with parents, water view, wheelchair access, NS rooms, senior rates, meeting facilities, CC. SGL/DBL$65-$85.

Hatchet Motel (Moran 83013; 543-2413) 23 rooms, restaurant, no pets, CC. SGL/DBL$50-$63.

Heart Six Ranch (Moran 83013; 543-2477) 25 rooms and suites, restaurant, heated pool, laundry facilities, no pets, airport transportation, American plan available, TV, meeting facilities, CC. SGL/DBL$950W-$1,650W.

Jackson Lake Lodge (Moran 83013; 543-2811) 385 rooms and suites, restaurant, lounge, entertainment, heated pool, whirlpools, children under 12 free with parents, pets OK, laundry service, boutiques, barber and beauty shop, fireplaces, wheelchair access, NS rooms, in-room refrigerators, senior rates, meeting facilities, CC. SGL/DBL$85-$155.

Jenny Lake Lodge (Moran 83013; 733-4647, Fax 543-2869) 37 rooms and cottages, restaurant, lounge, entertainment, whirlpools, fireplaces, room service, in-room refrigerators, wheelchair access, no pets, NS rooms, CC. SGL/DBL$308-$450.

Signal Mountain Lodge (Moran 83013; 543-2831) 79 rooms and 2-bedroom suites, restaurant, lounge, water view, pets OK, TV, gift shop, in-room refrigerators and microwaves, children under 12 free with parents, wheelchair access, water view, NS rooms, meeting facilities, senior rates, CC. SGL/DBL$65-$155.

Togwotee Mountain Lodge (Moran 83013; 543-2847, 800-543-2847) 34 rooms and suites, restaurant, lounge, sauna, jacuzzi, whirlpools, gift shop, laundry facilities, in-room refrigerators and microwaves, children free with parents, pets OK, NS rooms, laundry facilities, airport courtesy car, meeting facilities, CC. SGL/DBL$65-$95.

Turpin Meadow Ranch (Moran 83013; 543-2496, 800-743-2496) 20 rooms, American plan available, TV, airport courtesy car, CC. SGL/DBL$100-$200.

Newcastle
Area Code 307

Fountain Mountain Inn (Hwys. 16 and 85, 82701; 746-4426, 800-882-8858) 60 rooms and efficiencies, restaurant, lounge, outdoor heated pool, a/c, kitchenettes, VCRs, children under 12 free with parents, TV, pets OK, wheelchair access, NS rooms, senior rates, CC. SGL/DBL$45-$65.

Hill Top Motel (1121 South Summit Ave., 82701; 746-4494) 15 rooms and efficiencies, pets OK, a/c, TV, CC. SGL/DBL$44-$48.

Morgan Motel (205 South Spokane, 82701; 746-2715) 10 rooms, pets OK, a/c, TV, CC. SGL/DBL$36-$40.

Pines Motel (248 East Wentworth, 82701; 746-4334) 10 rooms and efficiencies, a/c, TV, CC. SGL/DBL$40-$50.

Roadside Motel (1605 West Main St., 82701; 746-9640) 13 rooms, pets OK, a/c, TV, CC. SGL/DBL$35-$46.

Sage Motel (1227 South Summit, 82701; 746-2724) 13 rooms, pets OK, a/c, TV, in-room coffee makers, CC. SGL/DBL$30-$35.

Starburst Motel (815 South Summit, 82701; 746-4719) 16 rooms, pets OK, a/c, TV, CC. SGL/DBL$44-$48.

Sundowner Inn (451 West Main St., 82701; 746-2796) 28 rooms, restaurant, lounge, kitchenettes, pets OK, a/c, TV, wheelchair access, NS rooms, senior rates, CC. SGL/DBL$50-$60.

Supreme Motel (2503 West Main St., 82701; 746-2734) 20 rooms, pool, pets OK, a/c, TV, CC. SGL/DBL$36-$56.

Pine Bluffs
Area Code 307

Sunset Motel (316 West 3rd., 82082; 245-9905) 14 rooms, pets OK, a/c, TV, CC. SGL/DBL$28-$32.

Travelyn Motel (Pine Bluffs 82082; 31 rooms, pets OK, a/c, TV, wheelchair access, NS rooms, senior rates, CC. SGL/DBL$35-$45.

Pinedale
Area Code 307

Camp O'Pines Motel (38 North Fremont, 82941; 367-4536) 14 rooms, pets OK, a/c, TV, CC. SGL/DBL$30-$40.

Elk Ridge Lodge (Pinedale 82941; 367-2553) dude ranch, American plan available, CC. SGL/DBL$26-$44.

Flying A Ranch (Pinedale 82941; 367-2385, 800-678-6543) 6 cabins, dude ranch, no pets, private baths, fireplaces, American plan available, CC. SGL$1,050W-$1,575W.

Half Moon Lodge Motel (46 North Sublett Ave., 82941; 367-2851) 19 rooms and efficiencies, a/c, TV, pets OK, CC. SGL/DBL$40-$48.

Lakeside Lodge (Pinedale 82941; 367-2221) 13 rooms and efficiencies, restaurant, kitchenettes, pets OK, a/c, TV, CC. SGL/DBL$65-$78.

Log Cabin Motel (Pinedale 82941; 367-4579) 11 rooms and efficiencies, a/c, TV, CC. SGL/DBL$40.

Ponderosa Lodge (Pinedale 82941; 367-2516) 5 cabins, dude ranch, lounge, American plan available, private baths, CC. SGL/DBL$36-$46.

Rivera Lodge (442 West Marilyn, 82941; 367-2424) 8 rooms, kitchenettes, a/c, TV, no pets, wheelchair access, NS rooms, senior rates, CC. SGL/DBL$50-$65.

Sundance Motel (148 East Pine St., 82941; 367-4336) 18 rooms and efficiencies, a/c, TV, in-room refrigerators, no pets, wheelchair access, NS rooms, senior rates, CC. SGL/DBL$35-$55.

Teton Court Motel (123 East Magnolia St., 82941; 367-4317) 17 rooms, kitchenettes, pets OK, a/c, TV, CC. SGL/DBL$45-$55.

Wagon Wheel Motel (407 South Hwy. 191, 82941; 376-2871) 15 rooms, TV, no pets, wheelchair access, NS rooms, airport transportation, senior rates, CC. SGL/DBL$45-$80.

Window on the Winds (10151 Hwy. 191, 82941; 367-2600) 4 rooms, whirlpools, free breakfast, pets OK, NS, CC. SGL/DBL$45-$60.

The ZZZZ Inn (327 South Hwy. 191, 82941; 367-2121) 34 rooms, pets OK, TV, CC. SGL/DBL$50-$75.

Powell
Area Code 307

Best Western Kings Inn (777 East 2nd St., 82345; 754-5117, 800-528-1234) 48 rooms, restaurant, lounge, outdoor heated pool, children free with parents, a/c, NS rooms, in-room coffee makers, TV, laundry facilities, wheelchair access, pets OK, meeting facilities, senior rates, CC. SGL/DBL$38-$75.

Rawlins
Area Code 307

Bel Air Inn (23rd St. and Spruce, 82301; 324-2737) 122 rooms, restaurant, lounge, pool, pets OK, a/c, TV, room service, kitchenettes, in-room refrigerators, wheelchair access, NS rooms, senior rates, CC. SGL/DBL$45-$80.

Best Western Inn (Rawlins 82301; 324-2737, 800-528-1234) 122 rooms, restaurant, lounge, indoor heated pool, children free with parents, gift shop, a/c, NS rooms, TV, laundry facilities, wheelchair access, pets OK, meeting facilities, senior rates, CC. SGL/DBL$49-$79.

Bridger Inn (1904 East Cedar, 82301; 328-1401) 50 rooms, a/c, TV, children under 12 free with parents, pets OK, CC. SGL/DBL$37-$35.

Buckaroo Lodge (803 West Spruce, 82301; 324-9936) 6 rooms, TV, CC. SGL/DBL$38-$44.

Bucking Horse Motel (1720 West Spruce, 82301; 324-3471) 49 rooms, restaurant, pool, kitchenettes, pets OK, a/c, TV, CC. SGL/DBL$28-$56.

Cliff Motor Lodge (1500 West Spruce, 82301; 324-3493) 38 rooms, a/c, TV, pets OK, CC. SGL/DBL$48-$55.

Days Inn (2222 East Cedar, 82301; 324-6615, 800-325-2525) 118 rooms, restaurant, lounge, indoor pool, free breakfast, a/c, TV, wheelchair access, NS rooms, pets OK, laundry facilities, meeting facilities, senior rates, CC. SGL/DBL$44-$65.

Ferris Mansion Bed and Breakfast (607 West Maple, 82301; 324-3961) 4 rooms, free breakfast, TV, private baths, 1903 home, NS, a/c, no pets, CC. SGL/DBL$55-$60.

Golden Spike Motel (1617 West Sprice, 82301; 324-2271) 62 rooms, restaurant, lounge, pool, a/c, TV, no pets, wheelchair access, NS rooms, senior rates, CC. SGL/DBL$44-$55.

Hi Top Motel (713 West Sprice, 82301; 324-4561) 14 rooms, pets OK, a/c, TV, CC. SGL/DBL$29-$38.

Jade Lodge (5th St., and Spruce, 82301; 324-2791) 26 rooms, pets OK, a/c, TV. SGL/DBL$26-$30.

Key Motel (1806 East Cedar, 82301; 324-2728) 32 rooms, pets OK, TV, a/c, CC. SGL/DBL$26-$38.

Rawlins Ideal Motel (905 West Spruce St., 82301; 324-3456) 26 rooms and 2-room efficiencies, airport transportation, a/c, children free with parents, pets OK, TV, CC. SGL/DBL$28-$44.

Rawlins Inn (1801 East Cedar, 82301; 324-2783) 132 rooms, restaurant, lounge, pool, pets OK, a/c, TV, room service, senior rates, CC. SGL/DBL$40-$65.

Sleep Inn (1400 Higley Blvd., 82301; 328-1732, 800-221-2222) 81 rooms, restaurant, free breakfast, sauna, wheelchair access, NS rooms, pets OK, children under 18 free with parents, a/c, TV, laundry facilities, VCRs, meeting facilities, CC. SGL/DBL$40-$46.

Sunset Motel (1302 Spruce St., 82301; 324-3448, 800-336-6752) 18 rooms and efficiencies, a/c, in-room refrigerators and coffee makers, airport transportation, TV, pets OK, CC. SGL/DBL$22-$35.

Super 8 Motel (2338 Wagon Circle Rd., 82301; 328-0630, Fax 328-1814, 800-800-8000) 47 rooms and suites, restaurant, exercise center, no pets, children under 12 free with parents, free local calls, a/c, TV, in-room refrigerators and microwaves, fax service, NS rooms, wheelchair access, meeting facilities, senior rates, CC. SGL/DBL$46-$52.

Riverton
Area Code 307

Days Inn (909 West Main St., 82501; 856-9677, Fax 856-9677, 800-325-2525) 28 rooms, free breakfast, a/c, TV, in-room refrigerators and microwaves, wheelchair access, NS rooms, pets OK, laundry facilities, senior rates, CC. SGL/DBL$30-$45.

Holiday Inn Convention Center (900 East Sunset Dr., 82501; 856-8100, Fax 856-0266, 800-HOLIDAY) 121 rooms, restaurant, lounge, indoor heated pool, exercise center, sauna, airport transportation, game room, beauty shop, children under 19 free with parents, wheelchair access, a/c, TV, NS rooms, fax service, room service, no pets, laundry service, meeting facilities for 500, senior rates, CC. SGL/DBL$42-$54.

Paintbrush Motel (1550 North Federal, 82501; 856-9238) 23 rooms, a/c, TV, wheelchair access, NS rooms, VCRs in-room refrigerators, no pets, airport transportation, senior rates, CC. SGL/DBL$35-$42.

Sundowner Station (1616 North Federal, 82501; 856-6503) 60 rooms and suites, restaurant, outdoor heated pool, whirlpools, sauna, in-room refrigerators, children under 12 free with parents, pets OK, a/c, TV, wheelchair access, NS rooms, senior rates, CC. SGL/DBL$42-$49.

Super 8 Motel (1040 North Federal Blvd., 82501; 857-2400, 800-800-8000) 32 rooms and suites, no pets, children under 12 free with parents, free local calls, a/c, TV, in-room refrigerators and microwaves, pets OK, fax service, NS rooms, wheelchair access, meeting facilities, senior rates, CC. SGL/DBL$31-$48.

Thunderbird Motel (302 East Fremont, 82501; 856-9201) 50 rooms, pets OK, a/c, TV, wheelchair access, NS rooms, in-room refrigerators, senior rates, CC. SGL/DBL$30-$40.

Tomahawk Motor Lodge (208 East Main St., 82501; 856-9205, Fax 856-2879, 800-341-8000) 32 rooms and 2-bedroom suites, a/c, TV, wheelchair access, children free with parents, no pets, in-room refrigerators and coffee makers, airport transportation, NS rooms, senior rates, CC. SGL/DBL$30-$44.

Rock River
Area Code 307

Dodge Creek Ranch (402 Tunnel Rd., 82083; 322-2345) dude ranch, American plan available, CC. SGL/DBL$100.

Trails End (Rock River 82083; 742-8131) 3 rooms, kitchenettes, pets OK, TV, CC. SGL/DBL$39-$44.

Rock Springs
Area Code 307

American Family Inn (1635 North Elk St., 82901; 382-4212, 800-548-6621) 97 rooms, restaurant, lounge, outdoor heated pool, a/c, room service, TV, children under 16 free with parents, laundry facilities, pets OK, wheelchair access, NS rooms, senior rates, CC. SGL/DBL$25-$45.

Best Western Outlaw Inn (1630 Elk St., 82901; 362-6623, Fax 362-2633, 800-528-1234) 100 rooms, restaurant, lounge, entertainment, indoor heated pool, children free with parents, airport transportation, a/c, NS rooms, TV, laundry facilities, wheelchair access, pets OK, meeting facilities, senior rates, CC. SGL/DBL$48-$70.

Cody's Motel (75 North Center St., 82901; 362-6675) 39 rooms and efficiencies, a/c, TV, no pets, wheelchair access, NS rooms, senior rates, CC. SGL/DBL$36-$45.

Comfort Inn (1670 Sunset Dr., 82901; 382-9490, 800-221-2222) 103 rooms, restaurant, free breakfast, heated pool, exercise center, whirlpools, laundry facilities, a/c, children under 18 free with parents, pets OK, TV, senior rates, CC. SGL/DBL$45-$60.

Days Inn (545 Elk St., 82901; 362-5646, Fax 382-9440, 800-325-2525) 107 rooms, free breakfast, a/c, TV, wheelchair access, NS rooms, pets OK, airport transportation, in-room refrigerators and microwaves, free local calls, laundry facilities, senior rates, CC. SGL/DBL$39-$66.

Elk Street Motel (1100 Elk St., 82901; 362-3705) 18 rooms, a/c, TV, CC. SGL/DBL$36-$46.

Friendship Inn (1004 Dewar Dr., 82901; 362-6673, 800-424-4777) 32 rooms and efficiencies, a/c, TV, no pets, NS rooms, airport transportation, children free with parents, wheelchair access, senior rates, CC. SGL/DBL$30-$60.

Holiday Inn (1675 Sunset Dr., 82901; 382-9200, 800-HOLIDAY) 114 rooms and suites, restaurant, lounge, indoor heated pool, exercise center, hot tubs, airport transportation, children under 19 free with parents, wheelchair access, a/c, TV, NS rooms, fax service, room service, no pets, laundry service, meeting facilities, senior rates, CC. SGL/DBL$55-$68.

The Inn at Rock Springs (2518 Foothill Blvd., 82901; 362-9600, Fax 362-8846, 800-442-9692) 150 rooms, restaurant, lounge, indoor heated pool, whirlpools, a/c, TV, wheelchair access, room service, fax service, local transportation, pets OK, game room, NS rooms, senior rates, CC. SGL/DBL$50-$73.

Irwin Hotel (138 Elk St., 82901; 382-9817) 15 rooms, TV, a/c, pets OK, CC. SGL/DBL$29-$44.

La Quinta Inn (2717 Dewar Dr., 82901; 362-1770, 800-531-5900) 130 rooms, restaurant, free breakfast, lounge, outdoor heated pool, complimentary newspaper, free local calls, fax service, laundry service, NS rooms, children free with parents, wheelchair access, remote control TV, a/c, meeting facilities, pets OK, senior rates, all CC. SGL/DBL$41-$50.

Motel 6 (2615 Commercial Way, 82901; 362-1850, 505-891-6161) 130 rooms, pool, free local calls, children under 17 free with parents, NS rooms, wheelchair access, pets OK, a/c, TV, CC. SGL/DBL$25-$31.

Motel 8 (108 Gateway Blvd., 82901; 362-8200) 91 rooms, pets OK, TV, a/c, CC. SGL/DBL$28-$45.

Springs Motel (1525 9th St., 82901; 362-6683) 23 rooms and efficiencies, TV, no pets, NS rooms, CC. SGL/DBL$30-$40.

Sweetwater Gap Ranch (Rock Springs 82901; 362-2798) 10 rooms and cabins, dude ranch, American plan available, CC. SGL/DBL$40-$60.

Saratoga

Area Code 307

Hacienda Motel (Saratoga 82331; 326-5751) 31 rooms and efficiencies, a/c, TV, pets OK, children free with parents, in-room refrigerators, wheelchair access, NS rooms, senior rates, CC. SGL/DBL$32-$55.

Hood House Bed and Breakfast (214 North 3rd St., 82331) complimentary breakfast, TV, a/c, no pets, CC. SGL/DBL$30-$40.

Medicine Bow Guest Ranch and Lodge (Saratoga 82331; 326-5439) cabins, free breakfast, private baths, American plan available, TV, a/c, no pets, CC. SGL/DBL$80-$145.

Sage and Sand Motel (311 South 1st St., 82331; 326-8339) 18 rooms and efficiencies, pets OK, kitchenettes, a/c, TV, CC. SGL/DBL$36-$46.

Saratoga Inn (Saratoga 82331; 326-5261) 60 rooms, restaurant, lounge, a/c, TV, no pets, wheelchair access, NS rooms, senior rates, CC. SGL/DBL$28-$80.

Saratoga Safaris Bed and Breakfast (Saratoga 82331; no phone) 3 rooms, free breakfast, TV, shared baths, a/c, no pets, CC. SGL/DBL$27-$38.

Silver Moon Motel (Saratoga 82331; 326-5974) 14 rooms and efficiencies, a/c, TV, kitchenettes, pets OK, CC. SGL/DBL$33-$48.

Wolf Motel (101 East Bridge St., 82331; 326-5525) 17 rooms, restaurant, lounge, no pets, a/c, TV, wheelchair access, CC. SGL/DBL$36-$46.

Riviera Lodge (Saratoga 82331; 326-5651) 10 rooms, pets OK, a/c, TV, CC. SGL/DBL$28-$32.

Savery
Area Code 307

Savery Creek Thorobred Ranch (Savery 82332; 383-7840) cabins, dude ranch, fireplace, American plan available, tennis courts, CC. SGL/DBL$100-$300.

Sheridan
Area Code 307

Alamo Motel (1326 North Main St., 82801; 672-2455) 19 rooms, a/c, no pets, CC. SGL/DBL$35-$40.

American Inn (1744 North Main St., 82801; 672-9064) 24 rooms, pool, kitchenettes, TV, laundry facilities, no pets, CC. SGL/DBL$40-$56.

Best Western Sheridan Center Motor Inn (612 North Main St., 82801; 674-7421, Fax 672-3018, 800-528-1234) 138 rooms, restaurant, free breakfast, lounge, indoor heated pool, whirlpools, airport transportation, in-room refrigerators and coffee makers, children free with parents, a/c, NS rooms, TV, laundry facilities, wheelchair access, pets OK, meeting facilities, senior rates, CC. SGL/DBL$35-$76.

Days Inn (Hwy. 14, 82801; 82801, 800-325-2525) 45 rooms, free breakfast, indoor pool, jacuzzi, a/c, TV, free local calls, wheelchair access, NS rooms, no pets, laundry facilities, meeting facilities, senior rates, CC. SGL/DBL$38-$86.

Guest House Motel (2007 North Main St., 82801; 674-7496) 45 rooms and efficiencies, pool, laundry facilities, in-room refrigerators and microwaves, TV, VCRs, pets OK, CC. SGL/DBL$26-$36.

Holiday Inn (1809 Sugarland Dr., 82801; 672-8931, Fax 672-6388, 800-HOLIDAY) 212 rooms, restaurant, lounge, indoor heated pool, exercise center, children under 19 free with parents, wheelchair access, a/c, TV, NS rooms, fax service, room service, pets OK, airport transportation, beauty shop, gift shop, laundry service, meeting facilities, senior rates, CC. SGL/DBL$48-$125.

Holiday Lodge (625 Coffeen Ave., 82801; 672-2407) 23 rooms and efficiencies, pool, a/c, TV, no pets, wheelchair access, NS rooms, senior rates, CC. SGL/DBL$45-$67.

K-B Motel (2366 North Main St., 82801; 674-4902) 16 rooms, pets OK, a/c, TV, CC. SGL/DBL$35-$40.

Killbourne Kastle Bed and Breakfast (320 South Main St., 82801; 674-8716) 2 rooms, free breakfast, TV, a/c, no pets, CC. SGL/DBL$25-$40.

Mill Inn (2161 Coffeen Ave., 82801; 672-6401) 42 rooms and efficiencies, whirlpools, exercise center, pets OK, a/c, TV, fax service, CC. SGL/DBL$42-$52.

Rancher Motel (1552 Coffeen Ave., 82801; 672-2428) 23 rooms, a/c, TV, CC. SGL/DBL$28-$36.

Rock Trim Motel (449 Coffen Ave., 82801; 672-2464) 18 rooms and efficiencies, pets OK, in-room refrigerators and microwaves, laundry facilities, a/c, TV, CC. SGL/DBL$26-$38.

Sheriden Center Motor Inn (612 North Main St., 82801; 674-7421) 140 rooms, restaurant, lounge, pool, laundry facilities, a/c, TV, no pets, wheelchair access, NS rooms, senior rates, CC. SGL/DBL$44-$56.

Stage Stop Motel (2167 North Main St., 82801; 672-3459) 21 rooms, a/c, TV, CC. SGL/DBL$40-$50.

Super 8 Motel (2435 North Main St., 82801; 672-9725, 800-800-8000) 40 rooms and suites, no pets, children under 12 free with parents, free local calls, a/c, TV, in-room refrigerators and microwaves, fax service, NS rooms, wheelchair access, meeting facilities, senior rates, CC. SGL/DBL$45-$56.

Super Saver Inn (1789 Main St., 82801; 672-0471) 44 rooms, a/c, TV, CC. SGL/DBL$40.

Sundance
Area Code 307

Apache of the Black Hills (121 South 6th St., 82729; 283-2073) 40 rooms, pool, pets OK, a/c, TV, CC. SGL/DBL$43-$58.

Arrowhead Motel (Sundance 82729; 283-3307) 12 rooms, a/c, no pets, TV, CC. SGL/DBL$30-$55.

Bear Lodge Motel (Sundance 82729; 283-1611, 800-341-8000) 31 rooms and 2-bedroom efficiencies, whirlpools, a/c, TV, CC. SGL/DBL$30-$56.

Best Western Inn at Sundance (121 6th St., 82729; 283-2800, Fax 283-2727, 800-528-1234) 40 rooms, indoor heated pool, spa, whirlpools, children free with parents, a/c, NS rooms, TV, laundry facilities, wheelchair access, pets OK, meeting facilities, senior rates, CC. SGL/DBL$35-$78.

Budget Host Arrowhead Motel (214 Cleveland, 82729; 283-3307, 800-283-4678) 12 rooms, restaurant, laundry facilities, NS rooms, airport transportation, wheelchair access, a/c, TV, children free with parents, senior rates, CC. SGL/DBL$30-$55.

Hawken Guest Ranch (Sundance 82729; 756-9319) 3 rooms, dude ranch, American plan available, shared baths, CC. SGL/DBL$200-$375.

Pineview Motel (Sundance 82729; 283-2262) 19 rooms and efficiencies, a/c, TV, pets OK, CC. SGL/DBL$30-$40.

Teton Village
Area Code 307

Alpenhof Lodge (Teton Village 83025; 73303242, Fax 739-1516, 800-732-3244) 42 rooms and suites, restaurant, lounge, pool, hot tub, sauna, laundry facilities, fireplaces, game room, no pets, room service, wheelchair access, NS rooms, meeting facilities, CC. SGL/DBL$65-$225.

Best Western Inn at Jackson Hole (3345 McCollister, 83025; 733-2311, Fax 733-0844, 800-528-1234) 83 rooms, restaurant, lounge, outdoor pool, children free with parents, fireplaces, kitchenettes, a/c, NS rooms, TV, laundry facilities, wheelchair access, no pets, meeting facilities, senior rates, CC. SGL/DBL$50-$150.

Crystal Springs Inn (Teton Village 83025; 733-4423, Fax 733-3183) 15 rooms, TV, children free with parents, in-room refrigerators, laundry facilities, pets OK, CC. SGL/DBL$45-$85.

The Hostel (Teton Village 83025; 733-3425) 54 rooms, laundry facilities, game room, CC. SGL/DBL$35-$70.

The Inn at Jackson Hole (Teton Village 83025; 732-2311, Fax 733-0844) 83 rooms, restaurant, lounge, outdoor heated pool, whirlpools, sauna, kitchenettes, laundry facilities, no pets, NS rooms, TV, CC. SGL/DBL$90-$250.

R Lazy S Ranch (Teton Village 83025; 733-2655) 45 rooms, restaurant, entertainment, American plan available, laundry facilities, airport courtesy car, CC. SGL/DBL$840W-$2,240W.

Sojourner Inn (Teton Village 83025; 733-3657, Fax 733-9543, 800-445-4655) 100 rooms and suites, restaurant, lounge, indoor heated pool, sauna, hot tub, laundry facilities, in-room refrigerators and microwaves, no pets, children under 14 free with parents, kitchenettes, NS rooms, wheelchair access, meeting rooms, CC. SGL/DBL$59-$145.

Village Center Inn (Teton Village 83025; 733-3155, Fax 733-3183, 800-735-8342) 16 rooms and efficiencies, TV, children free with parents, kitchenettes, no pets, CC. SGL/DBL$45-$120.

Thermopolis
Area Code 307

Bah-Gue Wana Motel (401 Park, 82443; 864-2303) 20 rooms and efficiencies, pets OK, a/c, TV, CC. SGL/DBL$43-$56.

Best Western Moonlight Motel (600 Broadway, 82443; 864-2321, 800-528-1234) 26 rooms, outdoor pool, children free with parents, a/c, NS rooms, TV, laundry facilities, wheelchair access, pets OK, meeting facilities, senior rates, CC. SGL/DBL$37-$65.

The Cactus Motel (605 South 6th, 82443; 864-3155) 14 rooms and efficiencies, pets OK, in-room refrigerators, a/c, TV, CC. SGL/DBL$30-$40.

Coachman Inn (112 Hwy. 20 South, 82443; 864-3141) 10 rooms, a/c, pets OK, TV, CC. SGL/DBL$29-$48.

El Rancho Motel (924 Shoshoni, 82443; 864-2341) 13 rooms and 2-bedroom efficiencies, pets OK, a/c, TV, CC. SGL/DBL$22-$40.

Holiday Inn (115 Park St., 82443; 864-3131, Fax 864-3131, 800-HOLIDAY) 80 rooms, restaurant, lounge, indoor heated pool, exercise center, whirlpools, children under 19 free with parents, wheelchair access, a/c, TV, NS rooms, fax service, room service, pets OK, laundry service, meeting facilities, senior rates, CC. SGL/DBL$50-$89.

Plaza Inn The Park (Hot Springs State Park, 82443; 864-2252) 25 rooms and efficiencies, TV, a/c, spa, pets OK, CC. SGL/DBL$45-$55.

Rainbow Court Motel (408 Park, 82443; 864-2129, 800-554-8815) 21 rooms and efficiencies, a/c, TV, wheelchair access, NS rooms, senior rates, CC. SGL/DBL$65-$85.

Roundtop Mountain Motel (412 North 6th, 82443; 864-3126, 800-584-9126) 17 cabins, a/c, TV, CC. SGL/DBL$44-$68.

Wind River Motel (501 6th, 82443; 864-2326) 16 rooms, a/c, TV, in-room refrigerators, pets OK, CC. SGL/DBL$38-$45.

Tie Siding
Area Code 307

Two Bar Seven Ranch (Tie Siding 82084; 742-6072) 13 rooms, American plan available, TV, dude ranch, CC. SGL/DBL$58-$100.

Torrington
Area Code 307

Blue Lantern Motel (1402 South Main St., 82240; 532-9986) 14 rooms, a/c, pets OK, TV, CC. SGL/DBL$36-$44.

Kings Inn (1555 South Main St., 82240; 532-4011, 800-528-1234) 54 rooms, restaurant, lounge, indoor heated pool, pets OK, a/c, TV, room service, wheelchair access, NS rooms, senior rates, CC. SGL/DBL$42-$48.

Maverick Motel (Hwys. 26 and 85, 82240; 532-4064) 11 rooms and efficiencies, pets OK, a/c, TV, CC. SGL/DBL$27-$32.

Super 8 Motel (1548 South Main St., 82240; 532-7118, 800-800-8000) 32 rooms and suites, no pets, children under 12 free with parents, free local calls, a/c, TV, in-room refrigerators and microwaves, fax service, NS rooms, wheelchair access, meeting facilities, senior rates, CC. SGL/DBL$45-$55.

Western Motel (Torrington 82240; 532-2104) 20 rooms, a/c, TV, CC. SGL/DBL$60.

Wamsutter
Area Code 307

Sagebrush Motel (Wamsutter 82336; 328-1584) 8 rooms, kitchenettes, pets OK, TV, CC. SGL/DBL$35-$38.

Wapiti
Area Code 307

Absaroka Mountain Lodge (1231 East Yellowstone Hwy., 82450; 587-3963) 16 cabins, restaurant, lounge, airport transportation, kitchenettes, American plan available, pets OK, children free with parents, TV, CC. SGL/DBL$50-$70.

Elephant Head Lodge (Wapiti 82450; 587-3980) 11 cabins, restaurant, lounge, entertainment, American plan available, pets OK, kitchenettes, NS rooms, CC. SGL/DBL$45-$55.

Goff Creek Lodge Resort (Wapiti 82450; 587-3753) 14 rooms and cabins, restaurant, lounge, pets OK, CC. SGL/DBL$60-$82.

Wheatland
Area Code 307

Best Western Torchlite Motor Inn (1809 North 16th St., 82201; 322-4070, 800-528-1234) 50 rooms, free breakfast, outdoor heated pool, in-room refrigerators, children free with parents, a/c, NS rooms, TV, laundry facilities, wheelchair access, pets OK, meeting facilities, senior rates, CC. SGL/DBL$37-$57.

Blackbird Inn (1101 11th St., 82201; 322-4540) 4 rooms, free breakfast, TV, a/c, no pets, shared baths, CC. SGL/DBL$45-$90.

Flying X Ranch (799 Halleck Canyon Rd., 82201; 322-9626) American plan available, TV, dude ranch, CC. SGL/DBL$75-$150.

Kamp Dakota Guest Ranch (Wheatland 82201; 322-2772) dude ranch, CC. SGL/DBL$65-$100.

Mill Iron Spear Ranch (Wheatland 82201; no phone) dude ranch, American plan available, CC. SGL/DBL$80-$150.

Plains Motel (208 16th St., 82201; 322-3416) 11 rooms, pets OK, a/c, TV, CC. SGL/DBL$45-$55.

Western Motel (1450 South, 82201; 322-9952) 8 rooms and efficiencies, a/c, TV, no pets, wheelchair access, NS rooms, senior rates, CC. SGL/DBL$36-$46.

West Winds Motel (1756 South Rd., 82201; 322-2705) 30 rooms, a/c, pets OK, TV, CC. SGL/DBL$27-$52.

Vimbos Motel (203 16th St., 82201; 322-3942) 37 rooms, restaurant, a/c, TV, CC. SGL/DBL$35-$44.

Wilson
Area Code 307

Crescent H Ranch (Wilson 83014; 733-3674, Fax 733-8475) 25 rooms, American plan available, TV, tennis courts, airport courtesy car, CC. SGL/DBL$180-$200.

Fish Creek Ranch (Wilson 83014; 733-3166) 10 cabins, TV, kitchenettes, fireplaces, CC. SGL/DBL$325W.

Teton Tree House (Wilson 83014; 733-3233) 5 rooms, free breakfast, TV, a/c, no pets, NS, private baths, CC. SGL/DBL$90-$125.

Teton View Bed and Breakfast (2136 Coyote Loop, 83014; 733-7954) complimentary breakfast, TV, a/c, no pets, NS, private baths, CC. SGL/DBL$63-$90.

Trail Creek Ranch (Wilson 83014; 733-2610) 15 rooms, American plan available, CC. SGL/DBL$80-$120.

Worland
Area Code 307

Best Western Settlers Inn (2200 Big Horn Ave., 82401; 347-8201, Fax 347-9323, 800-528-1234) 43 rooms, free breakfast, in-room coffee makers, children free with parents, a/c, NS rooms, TV, laundry facilities, wheelchair access, pets OK, meeting facilities, senior rates, CC. SGL/DBL$40-$55.

Sun Valley Motel (500 North 10th St., 82401; 347-4251) 32 rooms, laundry facilities, a/c, TV, wheelchair access, airport transportation, in-room coffee makers, pets OK, senior rates, CC. SGL/DBL$25-$48.

Super 8 Motel (2500 Big Horn Ave., 82401; 347-9236, 800-800-8000) 36 rooms and suites, children under 12 free with parents, in-room refrigerators, pets OK, free local calls, a/c, TV, in-room refrigerators and microwaves, fax service, NS rooms, wheelchair access, meeting facilities, senior rates, CC. SGL/DBL$31-$50.

Yellowstone National Park
Area Code 307

Grant Village (Yellowstone National Park 82190; 344-7311) 299 rooms, restaurant, lounge, wheelchair access, no pets, NS rooms, laundry facilities, children free with parents, water view, meeting facilities, CC. SGL/DBL$56-$62.

Canyon Lodge (Yellowstone National Park 82190; 242-3900) 609 rooms and suites, restaurant, lounge, laundry facilities, NS rooms, children under 11 free with parents, pets OK, CC. SGL/DBL$45-$80.

Lake Lodge (Yellowstone National Park 82190; 344-7311) 186 cabins, restaurant, lounge, laundry facilities, pets OK, wheelchair access, children free with parents, gift shop, NS rooms, CC. SGL/DBL$39-$72.

Lake Yellowstone Hotel (Yellowstone National Park 82190; 344-7322) 194 rooms and suites, restaurant, lounge, entertainment, NS rooms, wheelchair access, no pets, CC. SGL/DBL$70-$125, STS$250-$300.

Mammoth Hot Springs Hotel (Yellowstone National Park 82190; 344-7311) 205 rooms and cabins, restaurant, lounge, hot tubs, no pets, children free with parents, gift shop, a/c, TV, meeting facilities, CC. SGL/DBL$25-$175.

The Old Faithful Inn (Yellowstone National Park 82190; 344-7311) 194 rooms and suites, restaurant, lounge, entertainment, wheelchair access, NS rooms, no pets, CC. SGL/DBL$68-$108, STS$225.

Old Faithful Snow Lodge (Yellowstone National Park 82190; 344-7311) 32 rooms, restaurant, lounge, laundry facilities, wheelchair access, no pets, CC. SGL/DBL$35-$40.

Additional Reading

from Hunter Publishing

INSIDER'S GUIDE TO WESTERN CANADA
$15.95, ISBN 1-55650-580-9, 205pp

".... The lively, sometimes whimsical text makes reading a pleasure... major sites and attractions are intelligently discussed; there's an emphasis on fine arts and performing arts, and culture...." *Travel Books Worldwide.*

INSIDER'S GUIDE TO EASTERN CANADA
$15.95, ISBN 1-55650-581-7, 256pp

"... text and abundant photographs [are] so outstanding.... This would make a fine addition to most libraries." *Library Journal.*

Filled with history, tour information, local museums and galleries, where to shop, where to eat, these are the most complete guides to Canada in the bookstores. Superb color photos and maps complement the text. Complete accommodation information. As with all the books in this series, a free pull-out color map makes planning your days easy.

Among other guides in this series:

FLORIDA $15.95, ISBN 1-55650-452-7, 256pp
HAWAII $15.95, ISBN 1-55650-495-0, 230pp
NEW ENGLAND $17.95, ISBN 1-55650-455-1, 256pp
MEXICO $18.95, ISBN 1-55650-454-3, 320pp
RUSSIA $17.95, ISBN 1-55650-558-2, 224pp
CALIFORNIA $14.95, ISBN 1-55650-163-3, 192pp
INDONESIA $15.95, ISBN 1-55650-453-5, 224pp
TURKEY $17.95, ISBN 1-55650-283-4, 209pp
INDIA $16.95, ISBN 1-55650-164-1, 360pp
NEW ZEALAND $15.95, ISBN 1-55650-624-4, 224pp

ADVENTURE GUIDE TO THE HIGH SOUTHWEST
$14.94, ISBN 1-55650-633-3, 384pp

"... a conscientious and beautifully written guide...."

Hiking, mountaineering, trail riding, cycling, camping, river running, ski touring, wilderness trips – a guide to enjoying the natural attractions of the Four Corners area of Northwest New Mexico, Southwest Colorado, Southern Utah, Northern Arizona, and the Navajo Nation and Hopiland. Includes all practical details on transportation, services, where to eat, where to stay and travel tips on how to cope with the harsh terrain and climate. The most adventurous guide to this region on the market. Maps.

Among other guides in the Adventure Guide series:

COSTA RICA 2nd Ed. $15.95, ISBN 1-55650-598-1, 470pp
PUERTO RICO 2nd Ed. $14.95, ISBN 1-55650-628-7, 304pp
CANADA $15.95, ISBN 1-55650-315-6, 320pp
VIRGIN ISLANDS 3rd Ed. $14.95, ISBN 1-55650-597-3, 280pp
EVERGLADES & THE FLORIDA KEYS $14.95,
    ISBN 1-55650-494-2, 192pp
BAJA CALIFORNIA $11.95, ISBN 1-55650-590-6, 280pp

**ADVENTURE GUIDE TO COASTAL ALASKA
& THE INSIDE PASSAGE**
$15.95, ISBN 1-55650-630-9, 228pp

How to travel the Alaska Marine Highway by ferry up to Ketchikan, Sitka, Skagway, Juneau, Homer, and Seward, then on to the Aleutian Islands and Kodiak. Maps and color photos.

ADVENTURE GUIDE TO THE ALASKA HIGHWAY
$15.95, ISBN 1-55650-457-8

Everything you will find along the Highway, plus all worthwhile side-traps and approaches, such as the Alaska Marine Highway, Klondike Highway, Top-of-the-World Highway. Maps and color photos.

**CRUISING ALASKA: A TRAVELLER'S GUIDE TO CRUISING
ALASKAN WATERS & DISCOVERING THE INTERIOR**
$11.95, ISBN 1-55650-650-3

All you need to know about the cruise ships and their routes, from Glacier Bay and the Gulf of Alaska to the Inside Passage. Filled with concise profiles of all the ships, such as stateroom size, passenger/crew ratio, dining arrangements, prices, amenities, cruise itineraries. All of the ports of call are described, with walking tours, plus land excursions to Denali and other parks.

THE NORTHERN ROCKIES: A TOURING GUIDE
$12.95. ISBN 1-55650-684-8, 184pp

The natural spledors, historic sites and cities of the Northern Rockies in Idaho, Montana, and Wyoming, plus the Black Hills and Badlands of South Dakota. Suggested touring plans with detailed itineraries, travel times, accommodations, what you must see, and what you can safely skip. Maps show walking tours of the major cities.

THE GREAT AMERICAN WILDERNESS: TOURING AMERICA'S NATIONAL PARKS
$11.95, ISBN 1-55650-567-1, 320pp

The 41 most scenic parks throughout the US including Acadia, the Great Smokey Mountains, Yellowstone, Hawaii Volcanoes, the Grand Canyon, Big Bend, the Everglades and many more. This tells you where to stay, where to eat, which roads are most crowded or most beautiful, how much time to allow, what you can safely skip and what you must not miss. Detailed maps of each park show all the surrounding access routes and special sections tell you how to make the most of your time if you only have a couple of hours.

CANADIAN ROCKIES ACCESS GUIDE 3rd Ed.
15.95, ISBN 0-91943-392-8, 369pp

The ultimate guide to outdoor adventure from Banff to Lake Louise to Jasper National Park. This book covers walking and canoeing routes, climbs, cycling and hiking in one of the most spectacular regions on earth. Maps, photos and contact numbers.

WHERE TO STAY IN NEW ENGLAND
$11.95, ISBN 1-55650-602-3, 512pp

"... isn't just your usual B&B or hotel listing, but a selection of almost all hotels, motels, country houses, condos and cottages for rent in the region.... Highly recommended: much more comprehensive in scope than competitors." *Reviewer's Bookwatch.*

Over 5,000 places are listed in this all-inclusive guide. Brief descriptions are supplemented by address, phone number (toll-free when available) and prices. Special sections are dedicated to chain hotels and deals they offer to business travellers, school groups, government workers and senior citizens.

Among other guides in the *Where to Stay* series:

AMERICA'S EASTERN CITIES $11.95, ISBN 1-55650-600-7, 416pp
AMERICA'S WESTERN CITIES $11.95, ISBN 1-55650-420-9, 416pp
MID-ATLANTIC STATES $12.95, ISBN 1-55650-631-7, 446pp
AMERICA'S HEARTLAND $13.93, ISBN 1-55650-632-5, 572pp
THE AMERICAN SOUTHEAST $12.95, ISBN 1-55650-651-1, 512 pp
THE AMERICAN SOUTHWEST $12.95, ISBN 1-55650-652-X, 450 pp
FLORIDA 2nd Edition $12.95, ISBN 1-55650-682-1, 400 pp
SOUTHERN CALIFORNIA $12.95, ISBN 1-55650-573-6, 394pp
NORTHERN CALIFORNIA $12.95, ISBN 1-55650-572-8, 280pp

ARIZONA, COLORADO & UTAH: A TOURING GUIDE
$11.95, ISBN 1-55650-656-2, 160pp

A compact guide written for those eager to see the unforgettable attractions of these three states. Driving tours begin in the state capital and cover the museums, parks, zoos and historical buildings in each city. They then lead the reader out into the fascinating land of giant arches, pinnacles, natural bridges, canyons and deserts for which the region is so well known. All the sights are described, along with the best routes to reach them whether on a daytrip or as part of a month-long tour. Accommodations and attractions are listed with opening times and fees. State and city maps make planning easy.

HAWAII: A CAMPING GUIDE
$11.95, ISBN 1-55650641-4, 160pp

A unique look at campsites and park cabins on each island – the public campgrounds as well as the little-known private places where you can pitch a tent or stay in a rustic lodge. Facilities, prices, ambience, things to do nearby are described. Candid evaluations tell you which spots are the magical hideaways and which will give you nightmares!

STATE PARKS OF THE SOUTH
$13.95, ISBN 1-55650-655-4, 224pp

This book takes you to 250 state parks in the states of Georgia, Alabama, Tennessee, Kentucky and Florida. From small ones that are largely undiscovered by the public, to others whose names you will recognize – each offers something unique. History, background on the ecosystem, lodges, camping facilities, local attractions, activities, maps and photos put this guide way above any other for practical tips and usability.

All of these titles plus thousands more are available from Hunter Publishing. To receive our free color catalog or to find out more about our books and maps, contact Hunter Publishing, 300 Raritan Center Parkway, Edison NJ 08818, or call (908) 225 1900.